## AN INFORMATION THEORETIC APPROACH TO ECONOMETRICS

This book is intended to provide the reader with a firm conceptual and empirical understanding of basic information theoretic econometric models and methods. Because most data are observational, practitioners work with indirect noisy observations and ill-posed econometric models in the form of stochastic inverse problems. Consequently, traditional econometric methods in many cases are not applicable for answering many of the quantitative questions that analysts wish to ask. After initial chapters deal with parametric and semiparametric linear probability models, the focus turns to solving nonparametric stochastic inverse problems. In succeeding chapters, a family of power divergence measure–likelihood functions is introduced for a range of traditional and nontraditional econometric-model problems. Finally, within either an empirical maximum likelihood or loss context, George G. Judge and Ron C. Mittelhammer suggest a basis for choosing a member of the divergence family.

George G. Judge is a Professor at the University of California, Berkeley. Professor Judge has also served on the faculty of the University of Illinois, University of Connecticut, and Oklahoma State University and has been a visiting professor at several U.S. and European universities. He is the coauthor or editor of 15 books in econometrics and related fields and author or coauthor of more than 150 articles in refereed journals. His research explores specification and evaluation of statistical decision rules, improved inference methods, and parametric and semiparametric estimation and information recovery in the case of ill-posed inverse problems with noise. Judge is a Fellow of the Econometric Society, the *Journal of Econometrics*, and the American Agricultural Economics Association.

Ron C. Mittelhammer is Regents Professor of Economic Sciences and Statistics at Washington State University. He is the author of *Mathematical Statistics for Economics and Business* (1996); lead coauthor with George G. Judge and Douglas J. Miller of *Econometric Foundations* (Cambridge University Press, 2000); and the author of numerous book chapters and articles in refereed economics, statistics, and econometrics journals. Professor Mittelhammer's current research focuses on econometric theory for applications in a range of economics fields. With more than two decades of graduate-level teaching experience, his skill as a teacher of statistics and econometrics is documented by teaching evaluations and awards. He served as president of the Agricultural and Applied Economics Association in 2009–10.

# An Information Theoretic Approach to Econometrics


GEORGE G. JUDGE

University of California, Berkeley

RON C. MITTELHAMMER

Washington State University



CAMBRIDGE
UNIVERSITY PRESS

CAMBRIDGE
UNIVERSITY PRESS

Shaftesbury Road, Cambridge CB2 8EA, United Kingdom

One Liberty Plaza, 20th Floor, New York, NY 10006, USA

477 Williamstown Road, Port Melbourne, VIC 3207, Australia

314–321, 3rd Floor, Plot 3, Splendor Forum, Jasola District Centre, New Delhi – 110025, India

103 Penang Road, #05–06/07, Visioncrest Commercial, Singapore 238467

Cambridge University Press is part of Cambridge University Press & Assessment, a department of the University of Cambridge.

We share the University's mission to contribute to society through the pursuit of education, learning and research at the highest international levels of excellence.

www.cambridge.org
Information on this title: www.cambridge.org/9780521689731



First published 2012

*A catalogue record for this publication is available from the British Library*

*Library of Congress Cataloging-in-Publication data*
Judge, George G.
An information theoretic approach to econometrics / George G. Judge, Ron C. Mittelhammer.
p. cm.
Includes bibliographical references and index.
ISBN 978-0-521-86959-1 (hardback) – ISBN 978-0-521-68973-1 (paperback)
1. Econometrics. I. Mittelhammer, Ron. II. Title.
HB139.J795 2011
330.01′5195–dc23 2011018358

ISBN 978-0-521-86959-1 Hardback
ISBN 978-0-521-68973-1 Paperback

*To Heather Judge-Price*

*To Linda, and to my good friends and colleagues*

# Contents

# Preface

In one sense, the idea for this book started 15 years ago with a six-hour meeting of the two authors between planes at the O'Hare Hilton. At this meeting, maximum entropy and empirical likelihood principles were the major areas of discussion. Since that time the two of us have worked together and have only looked forward. As a result, *Econometric Foundations* appeared in 2000, and a range of related information theoretic articles emerged in the last decade. Pieces of some of these articles appear in this book.

This book was a pleasure to write. We hope the reader will feel our enthusiasm in entering the information theoretic world and leaving behind many conventional econometric methods that we spent a good part of our lives learning.

To write this book, we had the help of many colleagues. Several years of work with Amos Golan provided a base for dealing with pure and noisy inverse problems and the maximum entropy principle. Douglas Miller was involved in this early work and also worked with us on the *Econometric Foundations* book. Marian Grendar, a longtime colleague of one of the authors, worked with us concerning the theoretical underpinning of information theoretic methods and read and commented on many of the chapters in this book. Art Owen was always available to discuss issues relating to the empirical likelihood approach to estimation and inference. Wendy Tam Cho was a creative partner in solving a range of important pure inverse applied problems. To a large group of colleagues, too numerous to mention, we express our warm thanks and appreciation and hope they have been appropriately acknowledged in references throughout the book.

For a book to reach the publication stage, two persons are necessary in addition to the author. One involves a person that takes incoherent words and other symbols and converts them to a working copy. In this context, Danielle Engelhardt, with intelligence, good humor, and word-processing skills, worked with us to get each chapter just right and to turn it into a beautiful copy. A second person is an editor who understands the subject matter and shares your goals. In Scott Parris, we found such a person and a full partner every step of the way. For the two authors, this has been a joint venture; the order of the names has only alphabetical significance.

George G. Judge
Ron C. Mittelhammer

# ONE

# Econometric Information Recovery

## 1.1 Book Objectives and Problem Format

The objectives of this book are to

i) develop a plausible basis for reasoning in situations involving incomplete-partial econometric model information,
ii) develop principles and procedures for learning or recovering information from a sample of indirect noisy data, and
iii) provide the reader with a firm conceptual and empirical understanding of basic information theoretic econometrics models and methods.

What makes the econometric information recovery process interesting is that

- economic-behavioral systems, such as physical and biological systems, are statistical in nature;
- the conceptual econometric model contains parameters and noise components that are unknown and unobserved and, indeed, not subject to direct observation or measurement;
- the recovery of information on the unknown parameters or components requires, for analysis purposes, the use of indirect noisy measurements based on observable data and the solution of an inverse problem that maps the indirect noisy observations, into information on the unknown model and its unobservable components;
- the models may be ill-posed or, in the context of traditional procedures, may be undetermined and the solution not amenable to conventional rules of logic or to being written in closed form.

These problems, taken either individually or in some combination, represent the intellectual challenge of modern econometric analysis and research.

Building on the productive efforts of our precursors in the areas of theoretical economics and inferential statistics, we hope, in this book, to provide an operational understanding of a rich set of information theoretic methods that may be used in theoretical and applied econometrics.

Econometrics is a work in progress. Anyone who doubts this should review a sampling of econometric books starting in the mid-1930s and map the development of econometrics over time. Advances in econometric methodology have been substantial in both content and number, and they continue at a geometric rate.

Information theoretic methods, which have a base in statistical mechanics in physics, have developed in econometrics over the last two decades. In this book we provide a conceptual and empirical understanding of information theoretic methods in some of the major areas of econometrics. Because in econometrics, and in other subject-matter areas, we must work with indirect noisy observations and ill-posed econometric models, traditional econometric methods may not be applicable in answering many of the quantitative questions we wish to ask.

To be a bit more specific, as noted previously, in econometric analyses the unknown and uncontrolled components of the econometric model cannot generally be observed directly. Thus, the analyst must use indirect noisy observations based on observable data to recover information relative to these unknown and unobservable components. This situation is associated with a concept in systems and information theory called the *inverse problem*, which is the problem of recovering information about unknown and uncontrolled components of a model from indirect noisy observations. The adjective *indirect* refers to the fact that although the observed data are considered to be directly influenced by the values of model components, the observations are not themselves the direct values of these components but only indirectly reflect the influence of the components. Thus, the relationship characterizing the effect of unobservable components on the observed data must be somehow inverted to recover information about the unobservable model components from the data-observations. Because econometric relations generally contain a systematic and a noise component, the problem of recovering information about unknowns and unobservables $(\boldsymbol{\theta}, \boldsymbol{\varepsilon})$ from sample observations $(\mathbf{y}, \mathbf{x})$ within the context of an econometric model $\mathbf{Y} = \eta(\mathbf{X}, \boldsymbol{\theta}, \boldsymbol{\varepsilon})$ is referred to as an *inverse problem with noise* or as a *stochastic inverse problem.* A solution to this inverse problem is of the general form $(\mathbf{y}, \mathbf{x}) \Rightarrow (\boldsymbol{\theta}, \boldsymbol{\varepsilon})$. Because most econometric analyses are of this form, it would seem natural that solution methods should be used that are consistent with the underlying information recovery problem.

## 1.2 Organization of the Book

To establish notation and connect with reader knowledge, the book starts with the specification and analysis of the simplest parametric and semiparametric probability models. The book is organized in five parts.

Part I is concerned with estimation and inference procedures for parametric and semiparametric linear probability models. In Chapter 2, a notational basis for the econometric models ahead is specified. Estimation and inference is considered for both parametric and semiparametric models and the idea of extremum estimation is introduced. In Chapter 3, estimation and inference methods are introduced for obtaining information on parameters that are functionally related to moments of the data sampling distribution. The focus is on just and overdetermined cases and the chapter starts with an examination of both the method of moments and the generalized method of moments. Finally, the concept of estimating equations, which subsumes the moment equation approaches, is introduced. With an eye to the chapters ahead, we note how extremum estimation relates to the aforementioned methods.

In Part II, we leave the traditional econometric world and focus on econometric models in the form of ill-posed stochastic inverse problems, where information recovery is based on indirect noisy observations and asymptotic considerations come into play. In Chapter 4, a nonparametric stochastic linear inverse problem (econometric model) is defined and a solution (estimation method) is proposed. In Chapter 5, we consider the problem of inference as it is related to the evolving stochastic empirical likelihood inverse problem. In Chapter 6, we introduce the Kullback-Leibler information criterion and the Shannon-Jaynes maximum entropy principle, and provide an estimation and inference basis for the evolving maximum empirical exponential likelihood estimator.

In Part III, we introduce the Cressie-Read family goodness of fit-power divergence measures and provide, in Chapter 7, a framework for estimation and inference. In Chapter 8, sampling experiments are used to illustrate the finite sampling properties of this family of estimators. Recognizing there may be uncertainty regarding the specification of the estimating equations, a choice rule under quadratic loss is proposed.

In Part IV, we consider an information theoretic approach to the binary-discrete choice stochastic inverse problem. In Chapter 9, a minimum power divergence (MPD) family of distribution functions for the binary response discrete choice model is proposed, an estimation framework is specified, and the corresponding statistical properties are identified. In Chapter 10, an estimation and inference basis for the binary MPD family is demonstrated and sampling experiments are used to illustrate finite sample results.

In Part V, we recognize that a basic limitation of traditional likelihood-divergence approaches is the impossibility of describing or identifying estimators-distributions of an arbitrary form. In Chapter 11, we address this estimation and inference problem by suggesting a loss-function-based way of choosing an optimum member from the Cressie-Read family.

Finally, in Chapter 12, we look back over the preceding chapters with a critical eye and make predictions about the econometric information theoretic road ahead.

## 1.3 Selected References

Cavalier, L., 2008. "Nonparametric Statistic Inverse Problems," *Inverse Problems*, **24**:1–19.

Mittelhammer, R., M. Judge, and D. Miller, 2000. *Econometric Foundations*, Cambridge University Press, New York.

# PART I

# TRADITIONAL PARAMETRIC AND SEMIPARAMETRIC ECONOMETRIC MODELS: ESTIMATION AND INFERENCE

In Part I, we use a familiar data sampling process to focus on parametric and semiparametric econometric models. This grouping nicely reflects the information, real or imagined, that the analyst uses in terms of the economic and data sampling process that is being modeled. In contrast to fully defined parametric models, semiparametric models cannot be fully defined in terms of the values of a finite number of parameters. In particular, there is no assertion made that a particular parametric family of probability distribution is known that fully defines the probability distribution underlying the data sampling process. Building on this base, in Part I we move in the direction of extremum formulations for analyzing models of this type. For a more complete discussion of the material and relevant proofs in Chapters 2 and 3, see Mittelhammer, Judge, and Miller (2000) and Mittelhammer (1996).

TWO

# Formulation and Analysis of Parametric and Semiparametric Linear Models

Consider a data sampling process (DSP) that results in an $(n \times 1)$ vector $\mathbf{y} = (y_1, y_2, \ldots, y_n)'$ of observable numbers whose range is contained in $\mathbb{R}^n$. Clearly, without any further assumptions or constraints regarding the process by which such numbers came about, there are no explicit unknowns to speak of other than the entire DSP. Effectively, at this point little can be said about the modeling process.

## 2.1 Data Sampling Processes (DSPs) and Notation

Given the DSP noted previously, the early chapters of this book are devoted to presenting base formulations of some rather well-established estimation and inference methods, as well as some introductory information-theoretic approaches to estimation and inference. The simplest formulations of these methods involve DSPs characterized by independent and identically distributed (*iid*) outcomes of a random variable (which can be a *vector*), with a generally unknown joint probability distribution. Assembling together $n$ *iid* outcomes of this random variable constitute the random sample of data used to calculate estimates and conduct inference about the unknown elements of the econometric models being analyzed. More complicated, and often more realistic, formulations of these methods involve *independent* outcomes of random variables that are *not iid*, or else outcomes of a set of *dependent* random variables that represent the data used in an econometric analysis. To facilitate and clarify discussion of the statistical basis for the econometric models and analysis methods we present, we identify some basic notation here together with general representations of DSPs.

First of all, with few exceptions, we use uppercase letters to denote random variables and lowercase letters to denote numerical outcomes of random variables or fixed numerical values of other variables. Thus, Y denotes a random variable, and $y$ denotes an outcome of the random variable. Exceptions are cases in the literature in which using a particular notation has become so pervasive that we choose to remain consistent with the convention. For example, it is commonplace to use $\varepsilon$ to denote a random noise variable, so we adopt that practice, and we use $e$ to denote an outcome of that random variable. We use bold notation to indicate vectors or matrices and nonbold to indicate scalars. Thus, $\mathbf{Y}$ denotes a vector or matrix random variable, and $\mathbf{y}$ denotes the corresponding numerical outcome of the random vector or matrix. Parameters are denoted by Greek letters, again with bold letters denoting vectors or matrices and nonbold letters denoting scalars. We reserve the notation $\mathbf{I}_n$ to indicate the identity matrix of dimension $n$, $\mathbf{0}_n$ to denote a vector of $n$ zeros, and $\mathbf{1}_n$ to denote a vector of $n$ ones.

We use the notation $\mathcal{D}$ as a generic representation of the collective of information that defines the DSP[1] and whose outcomes represent $n$ sample data observations on $r$ variables. Generating information on the unknowns in $\mathcal{D}$ is the objective of econometric estimation and inference, and the nature of the information contained in $\mathcal{D}$ determines which econometric methods are appropriate for recovering information on the unknowns. Information in $\mathcal{D}$ includes a specification of the random variables involved in the process as well as nonrandom (fixed) variables that may affect or condition the sampled outcomes of the random variables. The information also includes the specification of any functional relationships between the variables involved in the DSP, as well as information relating to the probability distribution of the random variables involved, in which one or both may depend on parameters $\boldsymbol{\Theta}$.

In general, the content of $\mathcal{D}$ includes information relating to four basic components of the DSP. Not all of the components need to be explicitly specified and, if specified, a given component may be defined in varying degrees of detail. Notation wise, this situation is summarized by $\mathcal{D} = \{\mathcal{V}, \boldsymbol{n}, \boldsymbol{g}(\mathcal{V}, \boldsymbol{n}, \boldsymbol{\Theta}) = \mathbf{0}, \mathcal{F}_{\mathcal{U}}(\boldsymbol{u}|\boldsymbol{n}, \boldsymbol{\Theta})\}$, where $\mathcal{V}$ denotes the random variables involved in the DSP, $\boldsymbol{u}$ denotes an outcome of $\mathcal{V}$, $\boldsymbol{n}$ represents given nonrandom variables having fixed numerical values, $\boldsymbol{g}(\mathcal{V}, \boldsymbol{n}, \boldsymbol{\Theta}) = \mathbf{0}$ denotes functional relationships that exist between the variables and parameters $\boldsymbol{\Theta}$, and $\mathcal{F}_{\mathcal{U}}(\boldsymbol{u}|\boldsymbol{n}, \theta)$ denotes information relating to the probability distribution of $\mathcal{V}$, which may be affected or conditioned by values of $\boldsymbol{n}$ and $\boldsymbol{\Theta}$.

[1] Some authors refer to this concept as the *data generating process*. The process defines how the data being used in an analysis comes about, that is, how these data are sampled or observed.

In the most straightforward case of an *iid* random sample of *scalar* outcomes from some population distribution $\mathcal{F}(\bullet|\Theta)$, the DSP can be represented as $\mathcal{D} = \{\mathcal{V}, \{\mathcal{F}_{\boldsymbol{\upsilon}}(\boldsymbol{\upsilon}|\Theta), \mathcal{V}_i's \sim iid\, \mathcal{F}(\bullet|\Theta)\}\}$, indicating that an observed $n \times 1$ random sample of data $\mathcal{V}$ from $\mathcal{D}$ is simply the result of $n$ repeated independent outcomes of *iid* scalar random variables $\mathcal{V}_i$, $i = 1, \ldots, n$ with some univariate probability distribution $\mathcal{F}(\bullet|\Theta)$. The information in $\mathcal{D}$ implies that the joint probability distribution of the sample outcome $\boldsymbol{\upsilon}$ of $\mathcal{V}$ is given by $\mathcal{F}_{\boldsymbol{\upsilon}}(\boldsymbol{\upsilon}|\Theta) = \prod_{i=1}^{n} \mathcal{F}(\upsilon_i|\Theta)$. More generally, it could be the case that the sample consists of *iid* outcomes of a random $1 \times r$ vector, in which case the observed $n \times r$ sample of data from $\mathcal{D}$ is the result of $n$ repeated independent outcomes of an $r$-variate random *vector* with some *multivariate* probability distribution $\mathcal{F}(\bullet\,|\Theta)$. In this multivariate case, we would still have $\mathcal{D} = \{\mathcal{V}, \{\mathcal{F}_{\boldsymbol{\upsilon}}(\boldsymbol{\upsilon}|\Theta), \mathcal{V}_i's\ iid\, \mathcal{F}(\bullet\,|\Theta)\}\}$, but $\mathcal{V}$ would be a random matrix, the $\mathcal{V}_i's$ would be random $1 \times r$ vectors, and $\mathcal{F}(\bullet\,|\Theta)$ would be the common multivariate distribution of the $\mathcal{V}_i$s.

There can be many reasons why the sample data cannot be represented as outcomes of independent and/or identically distributed random variables. One of the most prevalent cases is where the sampling is independent but not identically distributed, so that in effect, one is sampling from independent *conditional* distributions that depend on given fixed values of explanatory variables in various ways. Such is the case, for example, in the *parametric* general linear model, where one can specify $\mathcal{D}$ as

$$\mathcal{D} = \{(\mathbf{Y}, \boldsymbol{\varepsilon}), \mathbf{x}, \mathbf{Y} = \mathbf{x}\boldsymbol{\beta} + \boldsymbol{\varepsilon}, N_{\varepsilon}(\mathbf{0}_n, \sigma^2\mathbf{I}_n)\} \quad (2.1.1)$$

indicating that the DSP involves the random variables $\mathbf{Y}$ and $\boldsymbol{\varepsilon}$ and is affected or conditioned by the fixed values in $\mathbf{x}$, there is a functional relationship between the variables and parameters given by $\mathbf{Y} = \mathbf{x}\boldsymbol{\beta} + \boldsymbol{\varepsilon}$, and the probability distribution of the random vector e is $N_{\varepsilon}(\mathbf{0}_n, \sigma^2\mathbf{I}_n)$, which then implies that $\mathbf{Y} \sim N_{\mathbf{Y}}(\mathbf{x}\boldsymbol{\beta}, \sigma^2\mathbf{I}_n)$ because of the linear functional relationship between the variables and parameters. Sampling, although independent across sample observations, is clearly not *iid* because the means of the elements of the $\mathbf{Y}$ vector vary with the values of the corresponding elements of $\mathbf{x}\boldsymbol{\beta}$. The unknowns of the DSP are $\boldsymbol{\beta}$, $\sigma^2$, and $\boldsymbol{\varepsilon}$, which are the objects of econometric estimation and inference.

Another example is the *semiparametric* general linear model, where only moment information is specified about the probability distribution of $\boldsymbol{\varepsilon}$ without any assumption of a specific parametric family of probability distributions, in which case we could specify the DSP as

$$\mathcal{D} = \{(\mathbf{Y}, \boldsymbol{\varepsilon}), \mathbf{x}, \mathbf{Y} = \mathbf{x}\boldsymbol{\beta} + \boldsymbol{\varepsilon}, \{E(\boldsymbol{\varepsilon}) = \mathbf{0}_n, Cov(\boldsymbol{\varepsilon}) = \sigma^2\mathbf{I}_n\}\}. \quad (2.1.2)$$

Comparing (2.1.2) to (2.1.1), it is apparent that the essential difference is that knowledge of the parametric functional form of the probability distribution of $\boldsymbol{\varepsilon}$ has been replaced by only moment information about that probability distribution, specifying the means, variances, and covariances of the elements of $\boldsymbol{\varepsilon}$. Note that the moments $E(\mathbf{Y}) = \mathbf{x}\boldsymbol{\beta}$ and $Cov(\mathbf{Y}) = \sigma^2\mathbf{I}_n$ are implied through the linear functional relationship between the variables and parameters. The unknowns in the DSP (2.1.2) include $\boldsymbol{\beta}$, $\sigma^2$, and $\boldsymbol{\varepsilon}$ as before and now also include the functional form as well as other characteristics than the moments specified, of the probability distribution of $\boldsymbol{\varepsilon}$ and $\mathbf{Y}$.

A third alternative would be a general *nonparametric* version of the regression model, where even the conditional means of the random variables $\mathbf{Y}$ are not specified as known parametric functions of $\mathbf{x}$, in which case the representation of the DSP could take the form

$$\mathcal{D} = \{(\mathbf{Y}, \boldsymbol{\varepsilon}), \mathbf{x}, \mathbf{Y} = \mathbf{g}(\mathbf{x}) + \boldsymbol{\varepsilon}, \{E(\boldsymbol{\varepsilon}) = \mathbf{0}_n, Cov(\boldsymbol{\varepsilon}) = \sigma^2\mathbf{I}_n\}\} \quad (2.1.3)$$

Comparing (2.1.3) to (2.1.2), it is apparent that the essential difference is that knowledge of the parametric functional form of the relationship between $\mathbf{x}$ and $\mathbf{Y}$ is now not assumed, so that $E(\mathbf{Y}) = \mathbf{g}(\mathbf{x})$ for an *unspecified* function $\mathbf{g}(\bullet)$. Note that $Cov(\mathbf{Y}) = \sigma^2\mathbf{I}_n$ is still implied by this general functional relationship between the variables and parameters. The unknowns in the DSP (2.1.3) are now $\sigma^2$, $\boldsymbol{\varepsilon}$, and the functional form and other characteristics of the probability distribution of $\boldsymbol{\varepsilon}$ and $\mathbf{Y}$, as well as the function of $\mathbf{x}$ that determines the mean of $\mathbf{Y}$.

Various specifications of $\mathcal{D}$ are possible, and each has its corresponding implications for econometric estimation and inference. For example, in all of the aforementioned specifications of $\mathcal{D}$, the nature of the covariance matrix of $\boldsymbol{\varepsilon}$ may be more uncertain than the highly specific $Cov(\boldsymbol{\varepsilon}) = \sigma^2\mathbf{I}_n$, reflecting issues of heteroskedasticity and/or autocorrelation of the noise terms, and this uncertainty could be reflected by a more general representation of $Cov(\boldsymbol{\varepsilon})$. At the outset of any econometric analysis, it is imperative that $\mathcal{D}$ be specified carefully and as fully as possible within the limits of the information available about the DSP, to frame the types of econometric methods that are appropriate for providing information about the unknowns of the DSP.

## 2.2 A Parametric General Linear Model

To start, we examine the problem of estimation and inference in the normal distribution-based general linear model, with the data sampling process for this model represented by the $\mathcal{D}$ in (2.1.1). We begin climbing the assumption mountain, with the fundamental assumption that the observed data arose as outcomes of random variables having some statistical distribution, so that the data are of the *stochastic*, as opposed to deterministic, variety. This assumption is formalized by stating that

$$\mathbf{Y} = \mathbf{x}\boldsymbol{\beta} + \boldsymbol{\varepsilon}, \tag{2.2.1}$$

where $\mathbf{Y}$ is an $(n \times 1)$ vector of observable random variables whose range is contained in $R^n$ and whose outcomes produce the $\mathbf{y}$-vectors referred to earlier, $\mathbf{x}$ is an $(n \times k)$ matrix representing the $n$ fixed numerical values taken on by $k$ explanatory variables, $\boldsymbol{\beta}$ is a $k$-dimensional fixed vector of unknown and unobservable parameters representing coefficients multiplying the explanatory variables, and $\boldsymbol{\varepsilon}$ is an $(n \times 1)$ noise vector of unobserved and unobservable random variables. The linear specification (2.2.1), in the absence of any other assumptions, frames a problem in which the outcomes of the observable random variables $\mathbf{Y}$ can be considered *indirect noisy observations* on the unknown and unobservable $\boldsymbol{\beta}$ and $\boldsymbol{\varepsilon}$, given the fixed and known values of $\mathbf{x}$.

For the problem to possess only a finite number of unknowns of interest, one needs to go beyond simply specifying the linear relationship (2.2.1) and be more specific regarding sampling characteristics of the random components of the model. We proceed by constraining the first- and second-order moments of the elements in $\boldsymbol{\varepsilon}$, which is tantamount to constraining the first- and second-order moments of $\mathbf{Y}$ given the linear functional relationship assumed in (2.2.1). The assumption that $\mathbf{x}$ is fixed and known implies that repeated observations on $(\mathbf{Y}, \mathbf{x})$ consist of varying values for the sample outcome of the random vector $\mathbf{Y}$ paired with the same known value of the matrix of explanatory variable values, $\mathbf{x}$. In the context of the linear relationship $\mathbf{Y} = \mathbf{x}\boldsymbol{\beta} + \boldsymbol{\varepsilon}$, only the outcomes of $\mathbf{Y}$ and $\boldsymbol{\varepsilon}$ change in repeated sampling, with the value of $\mathbf{x}\boldsymbol{\beta}$ remaining exactly the same from sample to sample. Because $\mathbf{x}$ is fixed, conditioning on $\mathbf{x}$ is effectively redundant, and so moment assumptions relating to $\boldsymbol{\varepsilon}$ and $\mathbf{Y}$ can be stated unconditionally, and the first-order moment assumptions that we make are $E(\boldsymbol{\varepsilon}) = \mathbf{0}$, which implies and is implied by $E(\mathbf{Y}) = \mathbf{x}\boldsymbol{\beta}$.

We next assume that the outcomes of the $n$ elements in $\boldsymbol{\varepsilon}$ are independent and identically distributed, in which case it follows immediately that the value of all of the covariances between pairs of elements in $\boldsymbol{\varepsilon}$ are zero. Assuming further that the elements of $\boldsymbol{\varepsilon}$ all share the same variance value, $\sigma^2$, that is, they are homoskedastic, leads to the conclusion that the covariance matrix of the noise vector is given by $\mathbf{cov}(\boldsymbol{\varepsilon}) = \sigma^2\mathbf{I}_n$. This assumption implies and is implied by $\mathbf{cov}(\mathbf{Y}) = \sigma^2\mathbf{I}_n$ given the fixed nature of $\mathbf{x}\boldsymbol{\beta}$ in the linear relationship $\mathbf{Y} = \mathbf{x}\boldsymbol{\beta} + \boldsymbol{\varepsilon}$. A final implication of the preceding assumptions is that the elements of $\mathbf{Y}$ are independent random variables, although they are generally not identically distributed because the mean vector $E(\mathbf{Y}) = \mathbf{x}\boldsymbol{\beta}$ will generally not be a vector of identical values.

If the parametric family of probability distributions for $\boldsymbol{\varepsilon}$ is left unspecified, then literally any probability distribution $F$ that does not violate the stated specific *iid* and moment conditions can be considered a potential probability distribution for $\boldsymbol{\varepsilon}$. Any corresponding distribution for $\mathbf{Y}$ given by the distribution of $\mathbf{x}\boldsymbol{\beta} + \boldsymbol{\varepsilon}$ is then admissible as the probability distribution of $\mathbf{Y}$. In this eventuality, the model would be semiparametric in nature.[2] In the next subsection, we consider the transition to a parametric model that is induced by the additional assumption of a normal probability distribution for the noise component, and we examine general issues relating to the problem of estimating the unknown parameters of the model.

### 2.2.1 The Parametric Model and Maximum Likelihood (ML) Estimation of $\boldsymbol{\beta}$ and $\sigma^2$

In developing a basis for recovering information about the unknowns of the linear model (2.2.1), we focus here on the maximum likelihood (ML) concept and assume a multivariate normal specification for the probability component of the model. Given this parametric model specification, the question naturally arises as to how one can make use of all of the stated model information when solving the associated inverse problem.

In this parametric version of the linear regression model, we make use of the likelihood function and the ML principle introduced by R. A. Fisher. The basic idea in the ML approach is to find the value of the parameter vector, say $\boldsymbol{\theta}$, that maximizes the likelihood[3] associated with the sample outcomes, $\mathbf{y}$, that are actually observed. As a result of Fisher's idea, likelihood methods for parametric estimation and hypothesis testing have emerged that have good statistical properties in a wide range of applications and, in particular, an elegant asymptotic theory underpins its use. The likelihood function, $L(\boldsymbol{\theta}; \mathbf{y})$, provides a window to the data that is a fundamental component of many classical and Bayesian inference procedures.

[2] A model is *semiparametric* if after assigning values to all of the model parameters, the probability distributions of $\mathbf{Y}$ and $\boldsymbol{\varepsilon}$ are nevertheless still not determined. A model is *parametric* if after specifying all model parameters, one also then specifies the probability distributions of $\mathbf{Y}$ and $\boldsymbol{\varepsilon}$.

[3] The maximized likelihood function is simply proportional to, and is generally set equal to, the joint probability density function of the random sample of data, evaluated at the observed sample outcome and treated as a function of the model parameters. In practice, the proportionality factor is generally taken to be 1.

Based on the foregoing assumptions and Fisher's idea, we have the following parametric general linear model

$$\mathbf{Y} = \mathbf{x}\boldsymbol{\beta} + \boldsymbol{\varepsilon}, \text{ with } \boldsymbol{\varepsilon} \sim N(\mathbf{0}_n, \sigma^2\mathbf{I}_n) \quad \text{and} \quad \mathbf{Y} \sim N(\mathbf{x}\boldsymbol{\beta}, \sigma^2\mathbf{I}_n), \tag{2.2.2}$$

where $\mathbf{Y}$ is an $(n \times 1)$ random dependent variable vector, $\mathbf{x}$ is an $(n \times k)$ nonstochastic explanatory variable matrix, $\boldsymbol{\beta}$ is a $(k \times 1)$ vector of unknown parameters, and $\sigma^2$ is a scalar unknown parameter. This model is equivalent to the DSP $\mathcal{D}$ in (2.1.1). The information-recovery problem is one of using observations on sample data outcomes, $\mathbf{y}$, given the associated fixed and known values of $\mathbf{x}$, to generate information on (estimates of) the $k+1$ unknowns $\boldsymbol{\theta} = \{\boldsymbol{\beta}, \sigma^2\}$. In the process of obtaining information on $\boldsymbol{\theta}$, one clearly also gains information on the specific normal distributions defined in (2.1.2) that are applicable to the DSP.

Given the normality assumption, we can define the joint probability density function (PDF) for a sample of observations, $\mathbf{y}$, and the likelihood function of the parameters of the inverse problem, as

$$\begin{aligned} L(\boldsymbol{\beta}, \sigma^2; \mathbf{y}, \mathbf{x}) &= f(\mathbf{y}; \mathbf{x}, \boldsymbol{\beta}, \sigma^2) \\ &= (2\pi\sigma^2)^{-n/2} \exp\left[\frac{-(\mathbf{y} - \mathbf{x}\boldsymbol{\beta})'(\mathbf{y} - \mathbf{x}\boldsymbol{\beta})}{2\sigma^2}\right] \end{aligned} \tag{2.2.3}$$

The functional form for both functions is precisely the same, where the PDF has the argument $\mathbf{y}$, for given values of the parameters $\boldsymbol{\beta}$ *and* $\sigma$ and values of $\mathbf{x}$, and the likelihood function has the arguments $\boldsymbol{\beta}$ *and* $\sigma$, for given values of the sample outcome $\mathbf{y}$ and values of $\mathbf{x}$. In this fully parametric model formulation, a large amount of information about the sampling process is specified but the parameters $\boldsymbol{\beta}$ and $\sigma^2$ nonetheless remain unknown and unobserved and are, indeed, unobservable.

To determine an ML estimator for $\boldsymbol{\beta}$ and $\sigma^2$, assume a sample of observations $\mathbf{y}$ has been obtained from $\mathcal{D}$ in (2.1.1), and rewrite the likelihood function (2.2.3) in the following logarithmic form:

$$\ln L(\boldsymbol{\beta}, \sigma^2; \mathbf{y}, \mathbf{x}) = -\frac{n}{2}\ln(2\pi) - \frac{n}{2}\ln(\sigma^2) - \frac{(\mathbf{y} - \mathbf{x}\boldsymbol{\beta})'(\mathbf{y} - \mathbf{x}\boldsymbol{\beta})}{2\sigma^2} \tag{2.2.4}$$

The ML estimates for $\boldsymbol{\beta}$ and $\sigma^2$ are obtained by solving the following optimality (first-order) conditions:

$$\frac{\partial \ln L(\boldsymbol{\beta}, \sigma^2; \mathbf{y}, \mathbf{x})}{\partial \boldsymbol{\beta}} = \frac{\mathbf{x}'\mathbf{y} - \mathbf{x}'\mathbf{x}\boldsymbol{\beta}}{\sigma^2} = \mathbf{0} \tag{2.2.5}$$

and

$$\frac{\partial \ln L(\boldsymbol{\beta}, \sigma^2; \mathbf{y}, \mathbf{x})}{\partial \sigma^2} = \frac{-n}{2\sigma^2} + \frac{1}{2\sigma^4}(\mathbf{y} - \mathbf{x}\boldsymbol{\beta})'(\mathbf{y} - \mathbf{x}\boldsymbol{\beta}) = 0 \quad (2.2.6)$$

The ML estimate of $\boldsymbol{\beta}$ is then given by

$$\hat{\mathbf{b}}_{\mathrm{ML}} = (\mathbf{x}'\mathbf{x})^{-1}\mathbf{x}'\mathbf{y} \quad (2.2.7)$$

and the ML estimate of $\sigma^2$ is given by

$$s^2_{\mathrm{ML}} = n^{-1}(\mathbf{y} - \mathbf{x}\,\hat{\mathbf{b}}_{\mathrm{ML}})'(\mathbf{y} - \mathbf{x}\,\hat{\mathbf{b}}_{\mathrm{ML}}) \quad (2.2.8)$$

The corresponding ML *estimators* are given by

$$\hat{\boldsymbol{\beta}}_{\mathrm{ML}} = (\mathbf{x}'\mathbf{x})^{-1}\mathbf{x}'\mathbf{Y} \quad (2.2.9)$$

and

$$\mathrm{S}^2_{\mathrm{ML}} = n^{-1}(\mathbf{Y} - \mathbf{x}\hat{\boldsymbol{\beta}}_{\mathrm{ML}})'(\mathbf{Y} - \mathbf{x}\hat{\boldsymbol{\beta}}_{\mathrm{ML}}) \quad (2.2.10)$$

Because the ML estimator for $\boldsymbol{\beta}$ is a linear combination of the multivariate normally distributed vector $\mathbf{Y}$, it follows that the ML estimator has a normal distribution $N(\boldsymbol{\beta}, \sigma^2(\mathbf{x}'\mathbf{x})^{-1})$. It can also be shown that the ML estimator of $\sigma^2$ can be bias-adjusted to define the unbiased estimator $\mathrm{S}^2 = (\frac{n}{n-k})\mathrm{S}^2_{\mathrm{ML}} \sim$ *Gamma* $(\frac{n-k}{2}, \frac{2\sigma^2}{n-k})$. Moreover, given that $\boldsymbol{\varepsilon}$ and $\mathbf{Y}$ are each multivariate normally distributed, $\hat{\boldsymbol{\beta}}$ and $\mathrm{S}^2$ are functions of complete sufficient statistics and are therefore minimum variance unbiased estimators (MVUE) of $(\boldsymbol{\beta}, \sigma^2)$. This result implies that the MLE $\hat{\boldsymbol{\beta}}$ is the best linear unbiased estimator (BLUE) for $\boldsymbol{\beta}$ because the linear (in $\mathbf{Y}$) estimator $\hat{\boldsymbol{\beta}}$ is best in the class of *all* unbiased estimators. Furthermore, as the number of sample observations increases, all of the hypothetical outcomes of the ML estimator eventually cluster in an arbitrarily small neighborhood around the appropriate value of the unknown and unobservable $\boldsymbol{\beta}$, whatever its value, with probability converging to 1.

In summary, under the current statistical model assumptions, the ML estimator $\hat{\boldsymbol{\beta}}$ of $\boldsymbol{\beta}$ is unbiased, BLUE, MVUE and efficient, normally distributed in finite samples, consistent, asymptotically normally distributed, and asymptotically efficient. Regarding sampling properties of the bias-adjusted ML estimator $\mathrm{S}^2$ of $\sigma^2$, the estimator is unbiased, MVUE and efficient, gamma-distributed in finite samples, consistent, asymptotically normally distributed, and asymptotically efficient.

### 2.2.2 The Parametric Model and Inference

Knowledge of the multivariate normal probability model and of the finite and asymptotic sampling properties of the corresponding ML point estimators delineated previously can be used to define procedures for conducting statistical inference based on the information contained in a given sample of observations. In particular, using the ideas of Neyman-Pearson, one can define hypothesis tests and confidence regions that provide additional information relating to the solution of the normal linear inverse problem.

A hypothesis testing procedure with generally good properties is the generalized likelihood ratio (GLR) test procedure associated with the null hypothesis $H_0$ and alternative hypothesis $H_a$ and based on the GLR statistic

$$\Lambda = \lambda(\mathbf{Y}) = \frac{\max_{\theta \in H_0} L(\boldsymbol{\theta}; \mathbf{Y})}{\max_{\theta \in H_0 \cup H_a} L(\boldsymbol{\theta}; \mathbf{Y})}, \tag{2.2.11}$$

where again $\boldsymbol{\theta} = \{\boldsymbol{\beta}, \sigma^2\}$ in this model. The associated level $\alpha$ GLR test of $H_0$ versus $H_a$ is defined as follows:

$$\textit{If}\ \lambda(\mathbf{Y}) \begin{Bmatrix} \leq \\ > \end{Bmatrix} \tau(\alpha), \quad \textit{then} \begin{Bmatrix} \textit{do not reject} \\ \textit{reject} \end{Bmatrix} H_0, \tag{2.2.12}$$

where $\tau(\alpha)$ is chosen such that $\max_{\boldsymbol{\theta} \in H_0} \pi(\boldsymbol{\theta}) = \max_{\boldsymbol{\theta} \in H_0} P_{\boldsymbol{\theta}}(\lambda(\mathbf{y}) \leq \tau(\alpha)) = \alpha$. Note in the definition that $\pi(\boldsymbol{\theta}) = P_{\boldsymbol{\theta}}(\lambda(\mathbf{y}) > \tau(\alpha))$ represents the power function of the test (i.e., the probability of rejecting the null hypothesis expressed as a function of $\boldsymbol{\theta}$). The GLR statistic has an asymptotic Chi-square distribution under generally applicable regularity conditions with degrees of freedom equal to the number of functionally independent restrictions on the parameter vector implied by the null hypothesis $\boldsymbol{\theta} \in H_0$. An advantage of the GLR test is that the test is invariant (i.e., unaffected) by any 1-to-1 functional transformations of the parameter space.

Other popular tests in econometric practice, including the Lagrange multiplier and *W* tests (discussed in Section 2), do not necessarily possess the invariance property. The GLR approach leads to many of the *t*, Chi-square, and F tests used in econometric practice that are, in certain cases, uniformly most powerful unbiased (UMPU), uniformly most powerful invariant (UMPI), and sometimes even uniformly most powerful (UMP).

One can also define confidence intervals or regions for parameters of interest using the GLR statistic. Using the duality between hypothesis tests and confidence regions, the latter is effectively the collection of all possible nonrejected null hypotheses for the value of the parameter or parameter vector of interest. For example, if one were seeking a confidence region for the entire parameter vector $\boldsymbol{\theta}$, then the definition of a confidence region having confidence level $(1-\alpha)$ would be based on the $\alpha$ level GLR test and would be given by

$$\mathrm{CR}_{\boldsymbol{\theta}}(1-\alpha) = \left\{ \boldsymbol{\theta} : \frac{L(\boldsymbol{\theta};\mathbf{Y})}{\max_{\boldsymbol{\theta}\in\Theta} \mathrm{L}(\boldsymbol{\theta};\mathbf{Y})} \leq \tau(\alpha) \right\}, \qquad (2.2.13)$$

where $\Theta$ denotes all admissible values of the parameter $\boldsymbol{\theta}$. Such confidence regions are asymptotically unbiased, uniformly most accurate, and consistent.

To summarize the econometric implications of the likelihood principle, statistical evidence is presented by likelihood functions and the strength of the statistical evidence is measured by likelihood ratios. We now move on to a model specification that does not require as much information in the specification of the data sampling process.

## 2.3 A Semiparametric General Linear Model

In this section, we analyze a semiparametric variant of the linear stochastic inverse problem where no apparent parametric family of probability distributions is assumed. The primary focus is again on a basis for recovering information about the unknown coefficient vector $\boldsymbol{\beta}$ and the variance $\sigma^2$. However, because the parameters are not associated with any assumed parametric family of distribution, no information about the functional form of the probability distribution underlying the observed sample data is forthcoming. For completeness, note again that our focus is on a linear model of the data sampling process:

$$\mathbf{Y} = \mathbf{x}\boldsymbol{\beta} + \boldsymbol{\varepsilon}, \qquad (2.3.1)$$

where $\mathbf{Y} = (\mathrm{Y}_1, \mathrm{Y}_2, \ldots, \mathrm{Y}_\mathrm{n})'$ is a $(n \times 1)$ vector of observable random dependent variables whose range is contained in $\mathbb{R}^n$, $\mathbf{x}$ is a $(n \times k)$ matrix with $\operatorname{rank}(\mathbf{x}) = k$ reflecting the numerical values taken on by $n$ fixed explanatory variables, $\boldsymbol{\beta}$ is a $k$-dimensional fixed vector of unknown and unobservable parameters, and $\boldsymbol{\varepsilon}$ is a $(n \times 1)$ noise component vector of unobserved and unobservable random variables. We continue to assume that the mean of the noise component vector is the zero vector so that the value of $\mathbf{x}\boldsymbol{\beta}$ represents the mean of the dependent variable vector. Also we assume that the covariance matrix of both the noise component and the dependent variable vector are identical and proportional to the identity matrix, the proportionality factor being represented by the common variance $\sigma^2$. Finally, the elements within the noise component and dependent variable vectors are assumed to be independent random variables across observations.

This linear model specification (2.3.1) suggests a specification where again the outcomes of the observable random variables $\mathbf{Y}$ can be considered indirect noisy observations on the unknown and unobservable $\boldsymbol{\beta}$ and $\boldsymbol{\varepsilon}$, given the fixed value of $\mathbf{x}$. Our objective is to use these observations in some manner to recover information about $\boldsymbol{\beta}$ and $\boldsymbol{\varepsilon}$. Note again that the observed value of $\mathbf{y}$ is not a direct observation on the values of $\boldsymbol{\beta}$ and $\boldsymbol{\varepsilon}$. Rather, $\mathbf{y}$ conveys information about $\boldsymbol{\beta}$ and $\boldsymbol{\varepsilon}$ through the relation $\mathbf{e} = \mathbf{y} - \mathbf{x}\boldsymbol{\beta}$ that is implied directly by (2.3.1). The data sampling process in this instance is representable in the form of $\mathcal{D}$ in (2.1.2).

### 2.3.1 The Squared Error Metric and the Least Squares (LS) Principle

The least squares (LS) principle for providing a solution to the semiparametric general linear model dates back to Gauss, Laplace, and Legendre in the early nineteenth century. Using this principle, the LS estimator is defined through minimizing the sum of squared errors metric

$$s(\boldsymbol{\beta}, \mathbf{Y}, \mathbf{x}) = \frac{1}{n}(\mathbf{Y} - \mathbf{x}\boldsymbol{\beta})'(\mathbf{Y} - \mathbf{x}\boldsymbol{\beta}) \tag{2.3.2}$$

with respect to the choice of $\boldsymbol{\beta}$. One supporting argument for use of the metric is based on the following simple reasoning. Letting $\boldsymbol{\beta}_0$ denote the true value of the parameter vector, the linear semiparametric model characteristics imply that

$$\begin{aligned} E[s(\boldsymbol{\beta}, \mathbf{Y}, \mathbf{x})] &= n^{-1}E[(\mathbf{Y} - \mathbf{x}\boldsymbol{\beta}_0 + \mathbf{x}\boldsymbol{\beta}_0 - \mathbf{x}\boldsymbol{\beta})'(\mathbf{Y} - \mathbf{x}\boldsymbol{\beta}_0 + \mathbf{x}\boldsymbol{\beta}_0 - \mathbf{x}\boldsymbol{\beta})] \\ &= \sigma^2 + (\boldsymbol{\beta}_0 - \boldsymbol{\beta})'(n^{-1}\mathbf{x}'\mathbf{x})(\boldsymbol{\beta}_0 - \boldsymbol{\beta}). \end{aligned} \tag{2.3.3}$$

Because $(\mathbf{x}'\mathbf{x})$ is positive definite, the minimum of (2.3.3) is attained uniquely at the value $\boldsymbol{\beta} = \boldsymbol{\beta}_0$. If the analyst could actually choose $\boldsymbol{\beta}$ so as to minimize $E[s(\boldsymbol{\beta}, \mathbf{Y}, \mathbf{x})]$, then the value of $\boldsymbol{\beta}_0$ would be recovered exactly.

In practice, the distribution of $\mathbf{Y}$ is unknown and the expectation in (2.3.3) cannot be calculated, and so minimizing $E[s(\boldsymbol{\beta}, \mathbf{Y}, \mathbf{x})]$ is not an operational objective. But a sample analog of (2.3.3) can be defined by eliminating the expectation operator, resulting in (2.3.2). Under an appropriate law of large numbers for independent random variables, (2.3.2) converges to (2.3.3). Thus, one would expect that minimizing (2.3.2) through choice of $\boldsymbol{\beta}$ should result in an estimate close to $\boldsymbol{\beta}_0$ for large enough $n$.

The concept of *minimizing a random variable*, $s(\boldsymbol{\beta}, \mathbf{Y}, \mathbf{x})$, through the choice of $\boldsymbol{\beta}$, is not a standard minimization problem. However, we can minimize the *outcome* $s(\boldsymbol{\beta}, \mathbf{y}, \mathbf{x})$ for every possible contingency for the outcome $\mathbf{y}$ of $\mathbf{Y}$, which *is* a standard minimization problem. In particular, given an *outcome* of $\mathbf{Y}$, the so-called LS criterion for choosing the LS *outcome*, $\hat{\mathbf{b}}$, is based on the solution to the standard unconstrained optimization problem

$$\hat{\mathbf{b}} = \operatorname{argmin}_{\beta}[s(\boldsymbol{\beta}, \mathbf{y}, \mathbf{x})] = \operatorname{argmin}_{\beta}[n^{-1}(\mathbf{y} - \mathbf{x}\boldsymbol{\beta})'(\mathbf{y} - \mathbf{x}\boldsymbol{\beta})] \quad (2.3.4)$$

because $\hat{\mathbf{b}}$ minimizes the sum of squared errors for each possible outcome $\mathbf{y}$,

$$s(\hat{\mathbf{b}}, \mathbf{y}, \mathbf{x}) \leq s(\tilde{\mathbf{b}}, \mathbf{y}, \mathbf{x}) \, \forall y \Rightarrow P_Y(s(\hat{\mathbf{b}}, \mathbf{y}, \mathbf{x}) \leq s(\tilde{\mathbf{b}}, \mathbf{y}, \mathbf{x})) = 1, \quad (2.3.5)$$

where $\tilde{\mathbf{b}}$ is any other choice of estimates. Thus, we can state that choosing such an *estimator*, $\hat{\boldsymbol{\beta}}$, *minimizes* the *random* LS objective function, $s(\boldsymbol{\beta}, \hat{\mathbf{Y}}, \mathbf{x})$, and thus minimizes the sum of squared prediction errors, *with probability 1.*

### 2.3.2 The LS Estimator

Adopting the squared error metric as the estimation objective function on which to base the estimator of $\boldsymbol{\beta}$ in the linear semiparametric regression model, the LS *estimator* is defined by

$$\hat{\boldsymbol{\beta}} = \operatorname{argmin}_{\beta}\left(\frac{1}{n}(\mathbf{Y} - \mathbf{x}\boldsymbol{\beta})'(\mathbf{Y} - \mathbf{x}\boldsymbol{\beta})\right). \quad (2.3.6)$$

Point estimates are given by

$$\hat{\mathbf{b}} = \operatorname{argmin}_{\beta}\left(\frac{1}{n}(\mathbf{y} - \mathbf{x}\boldsymbol{\beta})'(\mathbf{y} - \mathbf{x}\boldsymbol{\beta})\right). \quad (2.3.7)$$

and the first-order conditions

$$2n^{-1}(\mathbf{x}'\mathbf{x}\boldsymbol{\beta} - \mathbf{x}'\mathbf{y}) = \mathbf{0} \quad (2.3.8)$$

lead to the *estimate*

$$\hat{\mathbf{b}} = (\mathbf{x}'\mathbf{x})^{-1}\mathbf{x}'\mathbf{y}. \quad (2.3.9)$$

Consequently, $\hat{\boldsymbol{\beta}} = (\mathbf{x}'\mathbf{x})^{-1}\mathbf{x}'\mathbf{Y}$ is a random vector and raises interesting questions concerning its sampling characteristics.

### 2.3.3 Finite Sample Statistical Properties of the LS Estimator

In terms of sampling properties, by basing our choice and evaluation of an estimator for $\boldsymbol{\beta}$ on the sampling distribution of $\mathbf{Y}$, the information obtained about $\boldsymbol{\beta}$ from point estimation depends not only on the observed data being analyzed but also on whatever data sets one might have observed but did not.[4]

One important question concerns whether or not the LS estimator is unbiased. The following straightforward result demonstrates that it is:

$$\begin{aligned} E[\hat{\boldsymbol{\beta}}] &= E[(\mathbf{x}'\mathbf{x})^{-1}\mathbf{x}'\mathbf{Y}] = E[(\mathbf{x}'\mathbf{x})^{-1}\mathbf{x}'(\mathbf{x}\boldsymbol{\beta} + \boldsymbol{\varepsilon})] \\ &= \boldsymbol{\beta} + (\mathbf{x}'\mathbf{x})^{-1}\mathbf{x}'E(\boldsymbol{\varepsilon}) = \boldsymbol{\beta}, \end{aligned} \tag{2.3.10}$$

because $E(\boldsymbol{\varepsilon}) = \mathbf{0}$. Furthermore, the covariance matrix of the random vector $\hat{\boldsymbol{\beta}}$ is:

$$\begin{aligned} Cov(\hat{\boldsymbol{\beta}}) &= E[(\hat{\boldsymbol{\beta}} - E[\hat{\boldsymbol{\beta}}])(\hat{\boldsymbol{\beta}} - E[\hat{\boldsymbol{\beta}}])'] \\ &= E[(\hat{\boldsymbol{\beta}} - \boldsymbol{\beta})(\hat{\boldsymbol{\beta}} - \boldsymbol{\beta})'] \end{aligned} \tag{2.3.11}$$

Moreover, the Gauss-Markov Theorem demonstrates that the LS estimator is best linear unbiased where *best* refers to the estimator with the minimum covariance matrix among all of the estimators in the linear unbiased class. Note that we cannot claim that the LS estimator is the MVUE estimator of $\boldsymbol{\beta}$. In fact, in the absence of a parametric family of densities assumption, and concomitantly in the semiparametric model with the absence of the availability of such concepts as the Cramer-Rao Lower Bound, the information matrix, and (complete) sufficient statistics, the investigation of the MVUE property is essentially intractable.

### 2.3.4 Consistency and Asymptotic Normality of the LS Estimator

Consistency of the LS estimator can be demonstrated if additional probability model assumptions are made relating to the limiting behavior of the $\mathbf{x}$ matrix. A straightforward and generally applicable sufficient condition for consistency is $\sigma^2(\mathbf{x}'\mathbf{x})^{-1} \to [\mathbf{0}]$ as $n \to \infty$, in which case the estimator clearly converges in mean square, $\hat{\boldsymbol{\beta}} \xrightarrow{m} \boldsymbol{\beta}$, and this implies that the estimator also converges in probability, $\hat{\boldsymbol{\beta}} \xrightarrow{p} \boldsymbol{\beta}$. Thus, as the number of sample observations increases, all of the hypothetical outcomes of the LS estimator

[4] This, of course, assumes that we are investigating sampling properties within the classical frequentist paradigm of repeated sampling, as opposed to a Bayesian approach, for example.

eventually cluster in a small neighborhood around the appropriate value of the unknown and unobservable $\boldsymbol{\beta}$, whatever its value, with probability converging to 1.

An analysis of whether the LS estimator is asymptotically normally distributed is somewhat more involved than the issue of consistency. However, the basic rationale for the asymptotic normality of $\hat{\boldsymbol{\beta}}$ is that in the limit as $n \to \infty$, the LS estimator is a linear combination of multivariate normally distributed random variables, and so it is normally distributed. Note the following scaled deviation between the estimator and the unknown parameter vector $\boldsymbol{\beta}$, as

$$n^{1/2}(\hat{\boldsymbol{\beta}} - \boldsymbol{\beta}) = n^{1/2}(\mathbf{x}'\mathbf{x})^{-1}\mathbf{x}'\boldsymbol{\varepsilon} = (n^{-1}\mathbf{x}'\mathbf{x})^{-1}n^{-1/2}\mathbf{x}'\boldsymbol{\varepsilon}. \quad (2.3.12)$$

The asymptotic normality of the LS estimator follows if $n^{-1}\ \mathbf{x}'\mathbf{x} \to \Xi$, where $\Xi$ is a finite positive definite symmetric matrix, the elements in x are bounded in absolute value, and $\mathrm{E}[|\varepsilon_i|^{2+\delta}\ ] \leq \xi$, for some choice of positive finite constants $\delta$ and $\xi$. It follows via central limit theory that $n^{-1/2}\mathbf{x}'\boldsymbol{\varepsilon} = n^{-1/2}\sum_{i=1}^{n}\mathbf{x}_i'\varepsilon_i \xrightarrow{d} N(\mathbf{0}, \Xi)$, where $\mathbf{x}_i'$ denotes the *i*th row of $\mathbf{x}$ written as a column vector, in which case it follows that $n^{1/2}(\hat{\boldsymbol{\beta}} - \boldsymbol{\beta}) \xrightarrow{d} N(\mathbf{0}, \sigma^2\Xi^{-1})$.

Now that we have defined an estimation rule, and we have a well-defined approach for evaluating its sampling properties and answering questions regarding such properties as unbiasedness, consistency, and asymptotic normality.

### 2.3.5 Linear Semiparametric Model Inference

In this section, we broaden the scope of hypothesis testing and confidence region estimation procedures to encompass the case of the semiparametric general linear model. Unlike inference procedures for the case of a normal parametric probability model discussed in Section 2.2, the semiparametric nature of the current model means that normal distribution theory is not available for use in characterizing the finite-sample probability distributions of test statistics and confidence interval-region estimators. As such, inference in the semiparametric linear probability model relies much more heavily on asymptotic results, which enables normal distribution theory to be used as a large sample approximation in establishing the sampling distributions of hypothesis testing and confidence region estimation procedures.

As noted in the preceding subsection, $\hat{\boldsymbol{\beta}} \xrightarrow{p} \boldsymbol{\beta}$ and $n^{1/2}(\hat{\boldsymbol{\beta}} - \boldsymbol{\beta}) \xrightarrow{d} N(\boldsymbol{\beta}, \sigma^2\Xi^{-1})$ as $n \to \infty$, indicating the consistency and asymptotic normality properties of $\hat{\boldsymbol{\beta}}$. Regarding the estimator of the noise variance parameter, the estimator

$$S^2 = (\mathbf{Y} - \mathbf{X}\hat{\boldsymbol{\beta}})'(\mathbf{Y} - \mathbf{X}\hat{\boldsymbol{\beta}})/(n-k), \tag{2.3.13}$$

is an unbiased estimator of $\sigma^2$ and assuming that the noise terms are *iid*, $S^2 \xrightarrow{p} \sigma^2$, so that $S^2$ is a consistent estimator. Under higher order moment assumptions relating to the $\varepsilon_i s$, $S^2$ is asymptotically normally distributed with mean $\sigma^2$ and asymptotic variance $(\mu_4' - \sigma^4)/n$, where $\mu_4'$ is the fourth moment of the $\varepsilon_i$s.

### 2.3.6 Inferential Asymptotics

Because we make *no* specific distributional assumptions relating to $\boldsymbol{\varepsilon}$ or $\mathbf{Y}$ in the current semiparametric probability model, it should come as no surprise that hypothesis testing and confidence region estimation procedures must be based on approximate or asymptotic distributions of statistics. Nonetheless, it is often the case that a large sample approximate (i.e., asymptotic) distributions can be established on the basis of moment assumptions and assumptions that limit the degree to which the elements of $\mathbf{Y}$ can exhibit interdependence. Such is the realm of Central Limit Theorems, which when applicable can result in well-known and tractable PDF families of distributions being available for characterizing the approximate distribution of test and confidence region statistics. Many of the following results are useful in the chapters ahead as we consider other semi- and nonparametric formulations.

All of the tests we consider rely, in one way or another, on the asymptotic normality of the LS estimator $\hat{\boldsymbol{\beta}}$ of $\boldsymbol{\beta}$, where again $n^{1/2}(\hat{\boldsymbol{\beta}} - \boldsymbol{\beta}) \xrightarrow{d} N(\mathbf{0}, \sigma^2 \boldsymbol{\Xi}^{-1})$, $\hat{\boldsymbol{\beta}} \overset{a}{\sim} N(\boldsymbol{\beta}, \sigma^2(\mathbf{x}'\mathbf{x})^{-1})$, and $(n^{-1}\mathbf{x}'\mathbf{x}) \to \boldsymbol{\Xi}$. The Wald (W) and the Lagrange multiplier (LM) tests emerge as a basis for testing hypotheses about the values of linear combinations of the elements in $\boldsymbol{\beta}$, as $H_0$: $\mathbf{c}\boldsymbol{\beta} = \mathbf{r}$ versus $H_a$: $\mathbf{c}\boldsymbol{\beta} \neq \mathbf{r}$. The $W$ and LM statistics have asymptotic Chi-square distributions derived from the asymptotic normality of $\hat{\boldsymbol{\beta}}$. The tests are asymptotically equivalent, meaning that their asymptotic distributions are identical; thus, a choice between them cannot be made on the basis of their asymptotic behavior. The $W$ test is based on the *unrestricted* (by $H_0$) LS estimator, whereas the LM test is based on the *restricted* (by $H_0$) LS estimator. Based on the duality between hypothesis tests and confidence region estimation, $W$ and LM-based confidence regions can be defined that have predefined asymptotic levels of confidence for covering the true value of $\mathbf{c}\boldsymbol{\beta}$.

The asymptotic coverage levels are derived from the asymptotic Chi-square distributions of the $W$ and LM statistics, which in turn are derived from the asymptotic normality of $\hat{\boldsymbol{\beta}}$, as indicated previously.

The central limit theory used to establish the asymptotic normality of the LS estimator of $\boldsymbol{\beta}$ is extended next to establish the asymptotic distributions and other asymptotic properties of the W, LM test, and confidence region procedures relating to linear combinations of the elements in $\boldsymbol{\beta}$. Finally, we note that the size, power, and other properties of hypothesis tests, as well as the confidence level and other properties of confidence sets based on asymptotic distribution theory, are all approximate because they are only valid asymptotically.

### 2.3.7 Hypothesis Testing: Linear Equality Restrictions on β

In this section, we examine solutions to the problem of recovering information relating to the validity of hypotheses about linear combinations of the unknown and unobservable parameter vector $\boldsymbol{\beta}$. The hypotheses corresponding to linear restrictions on the elements of the $\boldsymbol{\beta}$ vector can be represented in the generic form $\mathbf{c}\boldsymbol{\beta} = \mathbf{r}$. Here, $\mathbf{c}$ is a $(j \times k)$ matrix of fixed constants representing the coefficients that define the $j$ linear combinations of the $k$ entries in $\boldsymbol{\beta}$ that are of interest, and $\mathbf{r}$ is a $(j \times 1)$ vector representing the corresponding hypothesized values of the individual linear combinations. Adopting the asymptotic normal approximation for $\hat{\boldsymbol{\beta}}$, it follows that *if the null hypothesis* $H_0 : \mathbf{c}\boldsymbol{\beta} = \mathbf{r}$ *is true*, then $\mathbf{c}\hat{\boldsymbol{\beta}} - \mathbf{r} \overset{a}{\sim} N(\mathbf{0}, \sigma^2\mathbf{c}(\mathbf{x}'\mathbf{x})^{-1}\mathbf{c}')$. Also, because the sum of the squares of $j$ independent standard normal random variables has a central Chi-square distribution with $j$ degrees of freedom,

$$\begin{aligned}&(\mathbf{c}\hat{\boldsymbol{\beta}} - \mathbf{r})'(\sigma^2\mathbf{c}(\mathbf{x}'\mathbf{x})^{-1}\mathbf{c}')^{-1}\\ &\times(\mathbf{c}\hat{\boldsymbol{\beta}} - \mathbf{r}) \overset{a}{\sim} \text{Chi-square}(j, 0) \text{ under } \mathrm{H}_0. \end{aligned} \tag{2.3.14}$$

Based on the consistency of the estimator $S^2$, an application of Slutsky's theorem yields

$$\begin{aligned}W = {} & (\mathbf{c}\hat{\boldsymbol{\beta}} - \mathbf{r})'(S^2\mathbf{c}(\mathbf{x}'\mathbf{x})^{-1}\mathbf{c}')^{-1}\\ &\times(\mathbf{c}\hat{\boldsymbol{\beta}} - \mathbf{r}) \overset{a}{\sim} \text{Chi-square}(j, 0) \text{ under } \mathrm{H}_0. \end{aligned} \tag{2.3.15}$$

The statistic $W$ is referred to in the literature as the Wald statistic, named after Abraham Wald, who first derived its general form in 1943. The intuition underlying this test is that the more distant the outcomes of $\mathbf{c}\hat{\boldsymbol{\beta}}$ are from the hypothesized value of $\mathbf{c}\boldsymbol{\beta}$ represented by $\mathbf{r}$, the less plausible is $\mathrm{H}_0$. The operational version of the *W* test used in practice, (2.3.15), is a consistent test of $\mathbf{H}_0 : \mathbf{c}\hat{\boldsymbol{\beta}} = \mathbf{r}$.

The LM test is based on the statistical behavior of the LMs in the Lagrangian form of the *constrained* (by $\text{H}_0$) LS problem defining the *restricted* LS estimate

$$\hat{\mathbf{b}}_r = \text{argmin}_{\boldsymbol{\beta}} [(\mathbf{y} - \mathbf{x}\boldsymbol{\beta})'(\mathbf{y} - \mathbf{x}\boldsymbol{\beta}) \text{ subject to } \mathbf{c}\boldsymbol{\beta} = \mathbf{r}]. \quad (2.3.16)$$

The Lagrange expression for the constrained LS minimization problem is

$$L(\boldsymbol{\beta}, \gamma) = (\mathbf{y} - \mathbf{x}\boldsymbol{\beta})'(\mathbf{y} - \mathbf{x}\boldsymbol{\beta}) - \boldsymbol{\gamma}'(\mathbf{c}\boldsymbol{\beta} - \mathbf{r}), \quad (2.3.17)$$

where $\boldsymbol{\gamma}$ is a $(j \times 1)$ vector of LMs corresponding to the $j$ constraints $\mathbf{c}\boldsymbol{\beta} = \mathbf{r}$.

The first-order conditions for the stationary point of (2.3.17) are given by

$$\begin{aligned} \frac{\partial L}{\partial \boldsymbol{\beta}} &= -2\mathbf{x}'\mathbf{y} + 2\mathbf{x}'\mathbf{x}\boldsymbol{\beta} - \mathbf{c}'\boldsymbol{\gamma} = \mathbf{0} \\ \frac{\partial L}{\partial \gamma} &= \mathbf{r} - \mathbf{c}\boldsymbol{\beta} = \mathbf{0}, \end{aligned} \quad (2.3.18)$$

which have solutions for $\boldsymbol{\beta}$ and $\gamma$ given by

$$\begin{aligned} \hat{\mathbf{b}}_r &= \hat{\mathbf{b}} + (\mathbf{x}'\mathbf{x})^{-1}\mathbf{c}'[\mathbf{c}(\mathbf{x}'\mathbf{x})^{-1}\mathbf{c}']^{-1}(\mathbf{r} - \mathbf{c}\hat{\mathbf{b}}) \\ \boldsymbol{\gamma}_r &= 2[\mathbf{c}(\mathbf{x}'\mathbf{x})^{-1}\mathbf{c}']^{-1}(\mathbf{r} - \mathbf{c}\hat{\mathbf{b}}). \end{aligned} \quad (2.3.19)$$

Substituting the random (unrestricted) LS estimator $\hat{\boldsymbol{\beta}} = (\mathbf{x}'\mathbf{x})^{-1}\mathbf{x}'\mathbf{Y}$ for $\hat{\boldsymbol{\beta}}$ in (2.3.19), the LM

$$\Gamma_r = 2[\mathbf{c}(\mathbf{x}'\mathbf{x})^{-1}\mathbf{c}']^{-1}(\mathbf{r} - \mathbf{c}\hat{\boldsymbol{\beta}}) \quad (2.3.20)$$

is a random vector representing all of the hypothetically possible outcomes of the optimal LM relating to all of the hypothetically possible $\hat{\boldsymbol{\beta}}$ outcomes in a classical predata frequentist context.

Based on the asymptotic normal approximation to the probability distribution of $\hat{\boldsymbol{\beta}}$, and under the null hypothesis $\text{H}_0 : \mathbf{c}\boldsymbol{\beta} = \mathbf{r}$, it follows that $\mathbf{r} - \mathbf{c}\hat{\boldsymbol{\beta}} \overset{\alpha}{\sim} N(\mathbf{0}, \sigma^2\mathbf{c}(\mathbf{x}'\mathbf{x})^{-1}\mathbf{c}')$, and because the sum of squares of $j$ standard normal random variables has a central Chi-square distribution with $j$ degrees of freedom, and we have that

$$\frac{\Gamma_r'[\mathbf{c}(\mathbf{x}'\mathbf{x})^{-1}\mathbf{c}']\Gamma_r}{4\sigma^2} \overset{\text{a}}{\sim} \text{Chi-square}(j, 0) \text{ under } \text{H}_0. \quad (2.3.21)$$

To define an observable version of the random variable in (2.3.21), we let $S_r^2$ represent the *restricted* estimator of $\sigma^2$,

$$S_r^2 = \frac{(\mathbf{Y} - \mathbf{x}\hat{\boldsymbol{\beta}}_r)'(\mathbf{Y} - \mathbf{x}\hat{\boldsymbol{\beta}}_r)}{n - k + j} \tag{2.3.22}$$

where $\hat{\boldsymbol{\beta}}_r$ denotes the restricted LS *estimator* whose outcomes are $\hat{\boldsymbol{\beta}}_r$ and

$$\mathrm{LM} = \frac{\Gamma_r'[\mathbf{c}(\mathbf{x}'\mathbf{x})^{-1}\mathbf{c}']\Gamma_r}{4\,\mathrm{S}_\mathrm{r}^2} \overset{a}{\sim} \text{Chi-square}(j, 0) \text{ under } \mathrm{H}_0 \tag{2.3.23}$$

We note that there is an alternative form of the LM statistic called the *score form of the LM statistic*, suggested by C. R. Rao (1948), that is algebraically equivalent to (2.3.23). An advantage of the score form of the LM test is that calculation of the LM is not needed to generate a value of the test statistic. All one needs for calculating the value of (2.3.23) is the restricted LS estimate. The LM test is asymptotically equivalent to the *W* test and so shares all of the *W* test's asymptotic properties. The operational version of the LM test used in practice, (2.3.23), or the *W* test (2.3.24) ahead, are consistent tests of $H_0 : \mathbf{c}\boldsymbol{\beta} = \mathbf{r}$. If one were to add the assumption of normality, then if the assumption were true, it allows one to claim that under $\mathrm{H}_0$,

$$W = (\mathbf{c}\hat{\boldsymbol{\beta}} - \mathbf{r}')(S^2\mathbf{c}(\mathbf{x}'\mathbf{x})^{-1}\mathbf{c}')^{-1}(\mathbf{c}\hat{\boldsymbol{\beta}} - \mathbf{r}) \sim jF, \tag{2.3.24}$$

where the *F*-statistic has the *F*-distribution with *j* and (*n*-*k*) degrees of freedom, and the same noncentrality parameter $\lambda$ as the *F*-statistic. In this case, the distribution is the exact finite sample distribution, as opposed to only an asymptotically valid one. All of the properties claimed for the *F-test* and GLR tests then apply to the *W* test as well, and all three tests are in fact identical. We emphasize that whereas asymptotically, the *W* and LM tests are equivalent, they are generally not identical in finite samples in the absence of the normality assumption. In terms of confidence region estimation, for example, we can define a confidence region for any linear combination of the entries in $\boldsymbol{\beta}$, that is, $\mathbf{c}\boldsymbol{\beta}$, by exploiting the duality between confidence regions and the *W* and LM hypothesis testing procedures.

Given this estimation and inference base, we have made a large step toward more general probability models that are discussed in Chapter 3.

## 2.4 General Linear Model with Stochastic X

In previous sections, we analyzed methods of estimation and inference for the linear model

$$\mathbf{Y} = \mathbf{x}\boldsymbol{\beta} + \boldsymbol{\varepsilon} \tag{2.4.1}$$

where the matrix of right-hand-side (RHS) explanatory variables is fixed or nonstochastic. In this section, we generalize the model to include the case

$$\mathbf{Y} = \mathbf{X}\boldsymbol{\beta} + \boldsymbol{\varepsilon} \tag{2.4.2}$$

where the matrix of RHS explanatory variables is random or a combination of fixed and random variables. Fixed or nonstochastic explanatory variables can, of course, be viewed as a special or limiting case in which the regressors are degenerate random variables. For present purposes, we consider **X** to be stochastic if any elements of **X** are nondegenerate random variables, and we use **X** rather than **x** to denote the explanatory variable matrix.

In many cases, the economist must work with observational-indirect noisy data where outcomes of some of the explanatory variables are generated by some stochastic process and exhibit random behavior in repeated samples. Consequently, in this section, we extend the probability model to accommodate a data sampling process where a sample of size $n$ is drawn from a multivariate population distribution that encompasses not only the dependent variable but also one or more of the explanatory variables.

### 2.4.1 Linear Model Assumptions

When **X** is stochastic, we begin with the case where **X** and $\boldsymbol{\varepsilon}$ are statistically independent random variables. If $E[\mathbf{X}]$ exists and $E[\boldsymbol{\varepsilon}] = \mathbf{0}$, then

$$E[\mathbf{Y}] = E[\mathbf{X}]\boldsymbol{\beta} + E[\boldsymbol{\varepsilon}] = E[\mathbf{X}]\beta, \tag{2.4.3}$$

and the *expectation* of random variable $\mathbf{X}\beta$ equals the mean of **Y**.

When **X** and $\boldsymbol{\varepsilon}$ are contemporaneously uncorrelated and not necessarily independent, the zero contemporaneous correlation condition may be represented as $E[\mathbf{X}'\boldsymbol{\varepsilon}] = \mathbf{0}$, where the expectation is computed using the joint distribution of **X** and $\boldsymbol{\varepsilon}$.

Regarding second-order moments, it is possible to state the classical assumption about the conditional variance of $\boldsymbol{\varepsilon}$ as

$$Cov(\boldsymbol{\varepsilon}\,|\mathbf{X}) = E[\boldsymbol{\varepsilon}\boldsymbol{\varepsilon}'|\mathbf{X}] = \sigma^2\mathbf{I}_n, \tag{2.4.4}$$

which is equivalent to $\text{var}[\varepsilon_i\,|\mathbf{X}] = \sigma^2$ for all $i$ and $\text{cov}(\varepsilon_i, \varepsilon_j\,|\mathbf{X}) = 0$ for all $i \neq j$. The conditional moments for model (2.4.2) imply that

$$E[\mathbf{Y}\,|\mathbf{x}] \equiv \mathbf{x}\boldsymbol{\beta} \quad \textit{and} \quad Cov(\mathbf{Y}\,|\,\mathbf{x}) \equiv \sigma^2\mathbf{I}_n. \tag{2.4.5}$$

The data sampling process for this model can then be represented by

$$\begin{aligned} \mathcal{D} = \{(\mathbf{Y}, \mathbf{X}), \mathbf{Y} = \mathbf{X}\boldsymbol{\beta} + \boldsymbol{\varepsilon}, \{E(\boldsymbol{\varepsilon}\,|\,\mathbf{X}) = \mathbf{0}_n, \\ Cov(\boldsymbol{\varepsilon}\,|\,\mathbf{X}) = \sigma^2\mathbf{I}_n,\ E(\mathbf{X}'(\mathbf{Y} - \mathbf{X}\boldsymbol{\beta})) = \mathbf{0}_k\}\}. \end{aligned} \tag{2.4.6}$$

The main practical consequence of stochastic explanatory variables, in either the stochastically independent or contemporaneously uncorrelated case, is the need to condition on outcomes of **X** to establish information linkages between the outcomes and expectation of **Y** and the observable values of **X**.

When the $(n \times k)$ matrix **X** is random, the rank assumption $\text{rank}(\mathbf{x}) = k$ used earlier can no longer be interpreted as a deterministic condition. To ensure that the LS estimator exists in the case at hand, the assumption is redefined to be $P(rank(\mathbf{x}) = k) = 1$, or equivalently $\text{P}((\mathbf{x}'\mathbf{x})^{-1} \text{ exists}) = 1$.

### 2.4.2 LS Estimator Properties: Finite Samples

Adopting the assumptions stated in the previous section, the LS estimator

$$\hat{\boldsymbol{\beta}} = (\mathbf{X}'\mathbf{X})^{-1}\mathbf{X}'\mathbf{Y} = \boldsymbol{\beta} + (\mathbf{X}'\mathbf{X})^{-1}\mathbf{X}'\boldsymbol{\varepsilon} \tag{2.4.7}$$

exists with probability 1 and is also unbiased. The unbiasedness property follows from the condition $E[\boldsymbol{\varepsilon}\,|\text{X}] = 0$, and

$$E[\hat{\boldsymbol{\beta}}] = E_{\mathbf{x}}[E[\hat{\boldsymbol{\beta}}|\mathbf{X}]] = E_{\mathbf{x}}[\boldsymbol{\beta} + (\mathbf{X}'\mathbf{X})^{-1}\mathbf{X}'E[\boldsymbol{\varepsilon}|\mathbf{X}]] = \boldsymbol{\beta}. \tag{2.4.8}$$

In either the independent or contemporaneously uncorrelated cases, the conditional covariance matrix of the estimator is from (2.4.7),

$$\begin{aligned} Cov(\hat{\boldsymbol{\beta}}|\mathbf{X}) &= E[(\mathbf{X}'\mathbf{X})^{-1}\mathbf{X}'\boldsymbol{\varepsilon}\boldsymbol{\varepsilon}'\mathbf{X}(\mathbf{X}'\mathbf{X})^{-1}|\mathbf{X}] \\ &= (\mathbf{X}'\mathbf{X})^{-1}\mathbf{X}'E[\boldsymbol{\varepsilon}\boldsymbol{\varepsilon}'|\mathbf{X}]\mathbf{X}(\mathbf{X}'\mathbf{X})^{-1} = \sigma^2(\mathbf{X}'\mathbf{X})^{-1} \end{aligned} \tag{2.4.9}$$

and

$$Cov(\hat{\boldsymbol{\beta}}) = E_{\mathbf{x}}[Cov(\hat{\boldsymbol{\beta}}\,|\,\mathbf{X})] = \sigma^2 E[(\mathbf{X}'\mathbf{X})^{-1}] \tag{2.4.10}$$

given that $E[(\mathbf{X}'\mathbf{X})^{-1}]$ exists.

Finally, the usual variance estimator, $S^2 = (\mathbf{Y} - \mathbf{X}\hat{\boldsymbol{\beta}})'(\mathbf{Y} - \mathbf{X}\hat{\boldsymbol{\beta}})/(n-k)$, has an expectation that may be expressed as

$$E[S^2] = \text{E}_{\mathbf{x}}[E[S^2\,|\mathbf{X}]] = E_{\mathbf{x}}[\sigma^2] = \sigma^2 \tag{2.4.11}$$

and, therefore, the estimator $S^2$ is a conditionally and unconditionally unbiased estimator of $\sigma^2$.

### 2.4.3 LS Estimator Properties: Asymptotics

The asymptotic properties of the LS estimator when **X** is stochastic parallel those established in the case where **x** is fixed. Regarding consistency of the LS estimator, if $n^{-1}\mathbf{X}'\boldsymbol{\varepsilon} \xrightarrow{p} \mathbf{0}$ and $n^{-1}\mathbf{X}'\mathbf{X} \xrightarrow{p} \boldsymbol{\Xi}$, then $\hat{\boldsymbol{\beta}}$ exists with probability converging to 1 and $\hat{\boldsymbol{\beta}} \xrightarrow{p} \boldsymbol{\beta}$ when $n \to \infty$.

Regarding conditions for the consistency of $\mathbf{S}^2$ for stochastic $\mathbf{X}$, we also assume that either the $\varepsilon_i$s are independent or else $n^{-1}\boldsymbol{\varepsilon}'\boldsymbol{\varepsilon} \xrightarrow{p} \sigma^2$, and then $S^2 \xrightarrow{p} \sigma^2$.

Asymptotic normality of $\hat{\boldsymbol{\beta}}$ is analogous to the case where $\mathbf{X}$ is fixed. The result relies on the application of central limit theory to a properly scaled and centered $\hat{\boldsymbol{\beta}}$. The asymptotic normality of $\hat{\boldsymbol{\beta}}$ follows if $n^{-1/2}\mathbf{X}'\boldsymbol{\varepsilon} \xrightarrow{d} N(\mathbf{0}, \sigma^2\boldsymbol{\Xi})$. Then, $n^{1/2}(\hat{\boldsymbol{\beta}} - \boldsymbol{\beta}) \xrightarrow{d} N(\mathbf{0}, \sigma^2\boldsymbol{\Xi}^{-1})$.

### 2.4.4 ML Estimation of $\boldsymbol{\beta}$ and $\sigma^2$ under Conditional Normality

When $\mathbf{X}$ is stochastic, it is clear that the PDF of $\mathbf{Y} = \mathbf{X}\boldsymbol{\beta} + \boldsymbol{\varepsilon}$ might no longer be determined by a simple mean-shifting of the distribution of $\boldsymbol{\varepsilon}$ because the probability distribution of $\mathbf{X}$ must now be accounted for as well. Furthermore, even the conditional distribution of $\mathbf{Y}|\mathbf{x}$ can be complicated because it is determined through mean-shifting (by $\mathbf{x}\boldsymbol{\beta}$) of the *conditional* distribution of $\boldsymbol{\varepsilon}$ given $\mathbf{x}$; that is, $(\mathbf{Y}|\mathbf{x}) \sim \mathbf{x}\boldsymbol{\beta} + (\boldsymbol{\varepsilon}\,|\mathbf{x})$.

One situation in which the familiar ML approach is directly applicable is the case where $\boldsymbol{\varepsilon}$ and $\mathbf{X}$ are independent and the distribution of $\mathbf{X}$ does not depend on $\boldsymbol{\beta}$ or $\sigma^2$. In this case, the distribution of $\mathbf{Y}|\mathbf{x}$ is in fact determined by a mean-shifting of the distribution of $\boldsymbol{\varepsilon}$; that is, $(\mathbf{Y}|\mathbf{x}) \sim \mathbf{x}\boldsymbol{\beta} + \boldsymbol{\varepsilon}$. Thus, once the distribution of $\boldsymbol{\varepsilon}$ is specified, the distribution of $\mathbf{Y}|\mathbf{x}$ is defined directly via mean translation of the distribution of $\boldsymbol{\varepsilon}$. It follows in this case that the ML procedure for determining estimates of $\boldsymbol{\beta}$ and $\sigma^2$ and conducting testing and confidence region generation can proceed as in Section 2.1 if $\boldsymbol{\varepsilon} \sim N(\mathbf{0}, \sigma^2\mathbf{I})$, because then $(\mathbf{Y}|\mathbf{x}) \sim N(\mathbf{x}\boldsymbol{\beta}, \sigma^2\mathbf{I})$.

More generally, consider the following universal representation of the joint probability distribution of $(\mathbf{Y}, \mathbf{X})$:

$$(\mathbf{Y}, \mathbf{X}) \sim f(\mathbf{y}, \mathbf{x}; \boldsymbol{\beta}, \sigma^2, \boldsymbol{\xi}) = \mathrm{h}(\mathbf{y}; \boldsymbol{\beta}, \sigma^2|\mathbf{x})g(\mathbf{x}; \boldsymbol{\xi}) \qquad (2.4.12)$$

where $\boldsymbol{\xi}$ denotes the parameters of the marginal probability distribution of $\mathbf{X}$, $g(\mathbf{x}; \boldsymbol{\xi})$. The distributional characteristics in (2.4.12) characterize the situation where $\mathbf{X}$ is *weakly exogenous* to the DSP generating the outcomes of $\mathbf{Y}$. The log likelihood function for the parameters of the problem is then given by

$$\ln(L(\boldsymbol{\beta}, \sigma^2, \boldsymbol{\xi}; \mathbf{y}, \mathbf{x})) = \ln(h(\mathbf{y}; \boldsymbol{\beta}, \sigma^2|\mathbf{x})) + \ln(g(\mathbf{x}; \boldsymbol{\xi})). \quad (2.4.13)$$

If the parameter vector $\boldsymbol{\xi}$ is unrelated to the parameters $(\boldsymbol{\beta}, \sigma^2)$, then the problem of finding the ML estimator of $(\boldsymbol{\beta}, \sigma^2)$ depends only on maximizing

$\ln(h(\mathbf{y}; \boldsymbol{\beta}, \sigma^2|\mathbf{x}))$, which is separable from the problem of finding the ML estimator of $\xi$ via maximizing $\ln(g(\mathbf{x}; \boldsymbol{\xi}))$.

Again, consider the important special case $(\mathbf{Y}|\mathbf{x}) \sim N(\mathbf{x}\boldsymbol{\beta}, \sigma^2\mathbf{I})$. Then, the joint distribution of $\mathbf{Y}$ and $\mathbf{X}$ (recall (2.4.12)) can be represented as

$$(\mathbf{Y}, \mathbf{X}) \sim \frac{1}{(2\pi)^{n/2}\sigma^n} \exp\left(-\frac{1}{2\sigma^2}(\mathbf{y} - \mathbf{x}\boldsymbol{\beta})'(\mathbf{y} - \mathbf{x}\boldsymbol{\beta})\right) g(\mathbf{x}; \boldsymbol{\xi}). \quad (2.4.14)$$

It follows that the ML estimators of symbol $\boldsymbol{\beta}$ and $\sigma^2$ are given by the familiar equations $\hat{\boldsymbol{\beta}} = (\mathbf{X}'\mathbf{X})^{-1}\mathbf{X}'\mathbf{Y}$ and $S^2_{ML} = (\mathbf{Y} - \mathbf{X}\hat{\boldsymbol{\beta}})'(\mathbf{Y} - \mathbf{X}\hat{\boldsymbol{\beta}})/n$. Thus, given our earlier results in this section, the ML estimator of $\boldsymbol{\beta}$ is unbiased, whereas the ML estimator of $\boldsymbol{\sigma}^2$ is biased, with a bias of $(-k/n)\sigma^2$. This result is precisely the same as the case of nonstochastic $\mathbf{x}$. The typical MLE asymptotics of consistency, asymptotic normality, and asymptotic efficiency also apply to these estimators. Furthermore, $\hat{\boldsymbol{\beta}}$ is conditionally normally distributed in finite samples, and $S^2 = (\frac{n}{n-k})S^2_{ML}$ is conditionally Chi-square($n$-$k$, 0) distributed.

## 2.4.5 Hypothesis Testing and Confidence Region Estimation

### 2.4.5a Semiparametric Case

Given the asymptotic normality of $\hat{\boldsymbol{\beta}}$, hypothesis tests in the semiparametric framework can be based on precisely the same W/LM/pseudo-likelihood/Z-statistic procedures that were discussed in Section 2.3. The asymptotic distributions of the test statistics are again Chi-square (W, LM, and pseudo-likelihood ratio [PLR]statistics) and normal (Z-statistic). The key assumptions in making the transition from the nonstochastic to the stochastic $\mathbf{X}$ case are those listed in Section 2.4.3. These assumptions are sufficient conditions. Weaker conditions leading to the validity of the standard testing procedures can be found in White (1984). Confidence regions can then be based on duality with the hypothesis testing procedures, again precisely as they were defined previously.

### 2.4.5b Parametric Case

It is also true that the testing and confidence region procedures discussed in Section 2.1 relating to the parametric framework apply as well to the case where $\mathbf{X}$ is stochastic. However, the rationale for the transition from fixed to stochastic $\mathbf{X}$ is conceptually more involved in the parametric case when considering *finite* sample properties of test and confidence region procedures, and so we examine more of the details for this case here.

Consider the linear statistical model in the parametric case where $(\mathbf{Y}|\mathbf{x}) \sim N(\mathbf{x}\boldsymbol{\beta}, \sigma^2\mathbf{I})$ and $(\boldsymbol{\varepsilon}|\mathbf{x}) \sim N(\mathbf{0}, \sigma^2\mathbf{I})$. It follows immediately from the results in Section 2.1, operating *conditionally* on $\mathbf{x}$, that

$$(T|\mathbf{x}) = \frac{\mathbf{c}\hat{\boldsymbol{\beta}} - r}{[S^2\mathbf{c}(\mathbf{x}'\mathbf{x})^{-1}\mathbf{c}']^{1/2}} \sim Tdist(n-k, \delta), \tag{2.4.15}$$

and

$$(F|\mathbf{x}) = \frac{(\mathbf{c}\hat{\boldsymbol{\beta}} - \mathbf{r})'[\mathbf{c}(\mathbf{x}'\mathbf{x})^{-1}\mathbf{c}']^{-1}(\mathbf{c}\hat{\boldsymbol{\beta}} - \mathbf{r})}{jS^2} \sim Fdist(j, n-k, \delta). \tag{2.4.16}$$

Therefore, all of the finite sample properties relating to the T, F, W, LM, and GLR tests discussed in Section 2.1 apply, *conditionally* on $\mathbf{x}$. Thus, *conditionally* on $\mathbf{x}$, all of the properties of confidence regions that are dual to these tests are identical to those described in Section 2.1.

We now note that nothing changes to the distributions of $T$ and $F$ if we *do not condition* an $\mathbf{x}$, so that all of the finite sample test and confidence region procedures described in Sections 2.1 apply directly and *unconditionally*. The marginal probability distribution of $F$ can be obtained in the usual way by integrating out $\mathbf{x}$ from the joint distribution of $F$ and $\mathbf{X}$. The distribution of $F|\mathbf{x}$, which is the noncentral $F$-distribution, *does not depend on* $\mathbf{x}$; that is, it is the same regardless of $\mathbf{x}$. Consequently,

$$\begin{aligned} h_F(f;j,n-k,\delta) &= \int_{\mathbf{x}\in R^K} h_{F|\mathbf{x}}(f;j,n-k,\delta|\mathbf{x})g(\mathbf{x};\boldsymbol{\xi})d\mathbf{x} \\ &= h_{F|\mathbf{x}}(f;j,n-k,\delta)\underbrace{\int_{\mathbf{x}\in R^K} g(\mathbf{x};\boldsymbol{\xi})d\mathbf{x}}_{=1} \\ &= Fdist(f;j,n-k,\delta). \end{aligned} \tag{2.4.17}$$

An analogous argument can be applied to the $T$-statistic to demonstrate that the conditional-on-$\mathbf{x}$ and unconditional distributions of T are the same noncentral $T$-distribution $Tdist(t; n-k, \delta)$. Thus, the testing and confidence region procedures identified in Section 2.1 apply to the stochastic $\mathbf{X}$ case as well.

### 2.4.6 Summary: Statistical Implications of Stochastic X

Because this section is especially important relative to the chapters ahead, we summarize the principal implications of **X** being stochastic as follows:

1. One needs to condition on the outcomes of **X** to establish information linkages between the outcomes and expectation of **Y** and the observable values of **X**.
2. Under both independent and contemporaneously uncorrelated **X** and $\boldsymbol{\varepsilon}$, with $E[\boldsymbol{\varepsilon}\,|\mathbf{X}] = \mathbf{0}$, the LS estimator is unconditionally unbiased, its unconditional covariance matrix is $\sigma^2 E[(\mathbf{X}'\mathbf{X})^{-1}]$, and $S^2 = (\mathbf{Y} - \mathbf{X}\hat{\boldsymbol{\beta}})'(\mathbf{Y} - \mathbf{X}\hat{\boldsymbol{\beta}})/(n-k)$ is an unconditionally unbiased estimator of the noise component variance.
3. If $\boldsymbol{\varepsilon}$ is multivariate normally distributed and the distribution of **X** does not depend on $\boldsymbol{\beta}$ or $\sigma^2$, then $\hat{\boldsymbol{\beta}} = (\mathbf{X}'\mathbf{X})^{-1}\mathbf{X}'\mathbf{Y}$ and $S^2_{ML} = (\mathbf{Y} - \mathbf{X}\hat{\boldsymbol{\beta}})'(\mathbf{Y} - \mathbf{X}\hat{\boldsymbol{\beta}})/n$ are the ML estimators of $\boldsymbol{\beta}$ and $\sigma^2$.
4. The asymptotic properties of the LS estimators when **X** is stochastic, as well as properties for the ML estimator under conditional normality of $(\mathbf{Y}|\mathbf{x})$ and weak exogeneity of **X**, follow those established for the case when the **x**'s are fixed.
5. Given the asymptotic normality of the LS estimator, asymptotically valid hypothesis tests can be based on the W, LM, PLR, and Z-statistic procedures developed in Section 2.1.
6. Given the conditional normality of $(\mathbf{Y}|\mathbf{x})$ and the weak exogeneity of **X**, standard $T$ and $F$ tests can be used to conduct hypothesis testing and confidence region estimation analogous to their use in Section 2.1.

## 2.5 Extremum (E) Estimation and Inference

For the chapters ahead, note that ML and LS estimators are members of a large class of estimators called "extremum (E) estimators." In fact, the $E$ estimators represent a class of estimators that encompass most of the estimators used in econometric practice. In addition, the concept of $E$ estimation provides a basis for a unified asymptotic theory applicable to a wide range of econometric estimators. To introduce the class of $E$ estimators, consider the stochastic inverse problems associated with the general linear models in which the observations $(\mathbf{Y}, \mathbf{x})$ are used to recover information on the values or functions of the unknown and unobservable $\boldsymbol{\beta}$, $\sigma^2$, and $\boldsymbol{\varepsilon}$.

The ML and LS estimators introduced in Sections 2 and 3, which provide point and interval estimation solutions, are special cases in which the estimator can be written in explicit closed form and the solution for $\hat{\boldsymbol{\beta}}$

outcomes is easily obtained. More generally, E estimators encompass any estimator that can be defined by optimizing an estimation metric or estimation objective function depending on parameters $\boldsymbol{\theta}$ and random $\mathbf{D}$ obtained from some data sampling process $\mathcal{D}$. Specifically, these estimators may be defined as

$$\hat{\boldsymbol{\Theta}} = \arg\max_{\boldsymbol{\theta}\in\Omega}[m(\boldsymbol{\theta}, \mathbf{D})], \tag{2.5.1}$$

where we explicitly assume maximization is the objective. Of course, this is completely general because we can minimize an objective function by maximizing the negative of the same objective function.

The properties of an *E* estimator depend on the properties of the estimation metric or estimation objective function being optimized. For the metrics commonly used in econometric practice, the properties of consistency and asymptotic normality are achieved under general regularity conditions relating to $\mathcal{D}$. Given the wide variety of different choices that are possible for the estimation objective function component of the *E* estimation problem, there are no broad finite sample property generalizations that can be made for *E* estimators, and so our focus vis-à-vis general sampling properties is restricted to asymptotic properties.

When an *E* estimator can be defined as an *explicit* function of the data, it is often possible, and often more straightforward, to analyze the estimator function directly to establish statistical properties of the estimator. Such was the case for the ML estimator of $\boldsymbol{\beta}$ and $\sigma^2$ in the context of the multivariate normal linear regression model as well as the LS estimator of $\boldsymbol{\beta}$ in the context of the semiparametric linear regression model. However, an E estimator might, as in chapters ahead, be defined only as an *implicit* function of the data that cannot be written in closed form, or else the estimator function may be too complicated to analyze directly. For example, this is often the case in applications of nonlinear LS, as well as the case of ML procedures applied to nonlinear models or nonnormal probability distributions. In these latter cases, general theorems on asymptotic properties of E estimators can be helpful in providing at least large sample results when small sample properties cannot be established.

### 2.5.1 ML and LS Estimators Expressed in *E* Estimator Form

Using the concept of *E* estimation, the general ML estimator can be formulated as the E estimator:

$$\hat{\boldsymbol{\Theta}} = \arg\max_{\boldsymbol{\theta}\in\Omega}[m(\boldsymbol{\theta}, \mathbf{D})], \tag{2.5.2}$$

where the estimation objective function is defined as

$$m(\boldsymbol{\theta}, \mathbf{D}) \equiv L(\boldsymbol{\theta}, \mathbf{D}). \tag{2.5.3}$$

Specific estimators are defined when $L(\boldsymbol{\theta}; \mathbf{D})$ is given a specific functional form, such as the case in this chapter where $L(\boldsymbol{\theta}; \mathbf{D})$ was based on the normal distribution.

In similar fashion, the LS estimator in the general linear model context with $\mathbf{D} = [\mathbf{Y}, \mathbf{X}]$ can be characterized in standard $E$ estimator form as the value of the parameter vector $\boldsymbol{\beta}$ that *maximizes* the metric or objective function

$$m(\boldsymbol{\beta}, \mathbf{Y}, \mathbf{x}) = -\frac{1}{n}(\mathbf{Y} - \mathbf{x}\boldsymbol{\beta})'(\mathbf{Y} - \mathbf{X}\boldsymbol{\beta}). \tag{2.5.4}$$

For this objective function, we have already seen that the LS estimator

$$\hat{\boldsymbol{\beta}} = \arg\max_{\boldsymbol{\beta}}\{m(\boldsymbol{\beta}, \mathbf{Y}, \mathbf{X})\} = \arg\max_{\boldsymbol{\beta}}\left\{-\frac{1}{n}(\mathbf{Y} - \mathbf{X}\boldsymbol{\beta})'(\mathbf{Y} - \mathbf{X}\boldsymbol{\beta})\right\} \tag{2.5.5}$$

is characterized by the explicit estimator function $\hat{\boldsymbol{\beta}} = (\mathbf{x}'\mathbf{x})^{-1}\mathbf{x}'\mathbf{Y}$. Recognizing that the LS and ML estimators are in the class of E estimators permits us to use these cases for illustrating the general asymptotic results developed in the next section.

### 2.5.2 Asymptotic Properties of *E* Estimators

*E* estimators are both consistent and asymptotically normally distributed under general regularity conditions. We provide some brief intuition here for why it is reasonable to expect that these properties are achieved quite generally for *E* estimators when the estimation objective function is chosen appropriately. We also note that in general, *E* estimators can be cast in terms of estimating equations; thus, properties relating to the latter estimator, which are discussed in Chapter 3, apply as well to *E* estimators.

The intuitive rationale underlying consistency is to have the criterion function being optimized, converge to a nonstochastic function of $\boldsymbol{\theta}$, say $m_0(\boldsymbol{\theta})$, that is maximized uniquely at the true value of $\theta$. If the limit of the maximum of $m(\boldsymbol{\theta}, \mathbf{Y}, \mathbf{X})$ is equal to maximum of the limit of $m(\boldsymbol{\theta}, \mathbf{Y}, \mathbf{X})$, then the optimized argument, $\hat{\boldsymbol{\Theta}}$, of the estimation objective function converges to the maximum of $m_0(\boldsymbol{\theta})$, the true value $\boldsymbol{\theta}_0$.

General theorems relating to the consistency of $E$ estimators and a theorem relating to asymptotic normality, that cover a large number of applications are given by Newey and McFadden (1994, pp. 2121–34). These consistency theorems rely on the compactness of the parameter space, $\Omega$, and on the concept of *uniform convergence in probability* of random variables. In some cases, it is possible to relax the requirements of compactness of the parameter space and of uniform convergence in probability of the estimation metric. In this case, the conditions are replaced by the requirements that the estimation metric $m(\boldsymbol{\theta}, \mathbf{Y}, \mathbf{X})$ be concave in $\boldsymbol{\theta}$ and exhibit ordinary convergence in probability, and the parameter space be convex. The intuitive underlying rationale is the same.

It may be useful at this point to consider the problem of estimating $\boldsymbol{\beta}$ and $\sigma^2$ in the multivariate normal linear regression model and see how we can investigate the asymptotic properties of ML estimator within the context of $E$ estimation. We noted earlier that the ML criterion for estimating $\boldsymbol{\theta}$ is subsumed under the $E$ estimation concept. We also noted that the ML estimator can be represented in $E$ estimator form as

$$\hat{\boldsymbol{\Theta}} = \arg \max_{\boldsymbol{\theta} \in \Omega} [m(\boldsymbol{\theta}, \mathbf{Y}, \mathbf{x})], \tag{2.5.6}$$

where the estimation objective function is defined specifically as

$$m(\boldsymbol{\theta}, \mathbf{Y}, \mathbf{x}) \equiv L(\boldsymbol{\theta}; \mathbf{Y}, \mathbf{x}). \tag{2.5.7}$$

Recognizing that the ML estimator is in the class of $E$ estimators allows us to transfer the general asymptotic results for $E$ estimation to the case of ML estimation. We settled in Section 2.2 the issue of the consistency and asymptotic normality of the ML or bias-adjusted ML estimator of $\boldsymbol{\beta}$ and $\sigma^2$ in the context of the multivariate normal linear model. In the context of $E$ estimation, one can establish and motivate more general results that can be applied to ML estimation problems in other parametric probability models. Various types of regularity conditions can be invoked for the MLE to exhibit asymptotic normality, and the possibilities are broad enough that the property of asymptotic normality can be assumed to hold quite generally in practice. Thus, a basis for asymptotic inference regarding $E$ estimation is established.

### 2.5.3 Inference Based on $E$ Estimation

Asymptotically valid hypotheses testing and confidence region procedures for the entire class of $E$ estimators can be based on the asymptotic properties of the estimators in the class. This provides at least an approximate method of testing hypotheses and generating confidence regions about linear combinations of the elements in the parameter vector when finite sample distributions of test and confidence region procedures cannot be established. Utilizing the consistency and asymptotic normality of *E* estimators, asymptotically valid W, LM, and PLR ratio tests (the latter are also called quasi-likelihood, distance metric, or likelihood ratio [in the parametric case] tests) for the general hypothesis $\mathrm{H}_0 : \mathbf{c}\boldsymbol{\theta} = \mathbf{r}$ can be readily defined. Asymptotically valid tests of inequality hypotheses can be based on an asymptotically normally distributed *Z*-statistic. Confidence region estimators can be defined in the usual way based on duality with hypothesis testing procedures (see Mittelhammer, Judge, and Miller [2000, pp. 144–153]).

### 2.5.4 Summary and Forward: *E* Estimators

As the reader likely has already surmised, once the available information about the data sampling process is specified, the next question in the use of *E* estimation concerns the estimation criterion-objective to use in recovering the unknown parameters from the sample data. This suggests that a general method of defining estimators is through the definition of estimation metrics or estimation objective functions. This idea leads to a general class of *E* estimators that, for a wide range of data sampling processes, serves as a basis for developing estimation rules and deriving sampling properties. In particular, once the estimation metric is chosen and the regularity conditions are specified, the extremum concept provides a well-defined basis for deriving the corresponding estimator and answering questions regarding consistency and asymptotic normality. In addition, an asymptotic basis for inference is provided and the trinity of W, LM, and pseudo or generalized likelihood ratio test statistics from ML and LS estimation extends readily to this more general setting. Consequently, a unified framework for large sample theory of hypothesis testing and confidence region estimation emerges in the context of ML and LS methods, as well as other traditional probability model formulations and stochastic inverse problem solutions.

We note that in many cases in practice, we are not able to solve the *E* estimation problem analytically, or even explicitly, for the value of the parameter vector that optimizes the estimation objective function. This is typical of cases in which the first-order conditions for the *E* estimation problem are highly nonlinear functions of the parameters. In these cases, one must resort to the computer and numerical procedures when solving for the *E* estimate of the parameter vector.

To place the concepts developed in this section in their proper context relative to the literature, it is important to note that what we call *E* estimators, Huber (1981) calls M-estimators (where the M denotes *ML-like*). In the chapters ahead, we apply the *E* estimation concept to a variety of data sampling processes of substantial importance to econometricians.

## 2.6 Selected References

Amemiya, T. (1985), *Advanced Econometrics*. Cambridge, MA: Harvard University Press, chapter 4.

Bunke, H. and O. Bunke (1986), *Statistical Inference in Linear Models*. New York: Wiley.

Huber, P. J. (1981), *Robust Statistics*. New York: John Wiley and Sons.

Lehmann, E. and G. Casella (1998), *Theory of Point Estimation*. New York: Springer-Verlag.

McCullagh, P. and J. A. Nelder (1989), *Generalized Linear Models*, 2nd ed. London: Chapman and Hall.

Mittelhammer, R. C. (1996), *Mathematical Statistics for Economics and Business*. New York: Springer-Verlag.

Mittelhammer, R., G. Judge, and D. Miller (2000), *Econometric Foundations*. New York: Cambridge University Press.

Newey, W. K. and D. McFadden (1994), "Large Sample Estimation and Hypothesis Testing," in *Handbook of Econometrics*, edited by Robert F. Engle and Daniel L. McFadden, Volume **4**, pp. 2111–2245.

Van Der Vaart, A. W. (1998), *Asymptotic Statistics*, Cambridge: Cambridge University Press.

White, H. (1984), *Asymptotic Theory for Econometricians*. Orlando, FL: Academic Press.

THREE

# Method of Moments, Generalized Method of Moments, and Estimating Equations

## 3.1 Introduction

In the previous chapter, we generalized the linear model to include stochastic regressors and examined the corresponding statistical implications. In this chapter, we examine estimation and inference methods for obtaining information on parameters that are functionally related to moments of the sampling distribution underlying a sample of data. The approach can be categorized on the basis of the number of functionally independent moment equations relative to the number of parameters being analyzed and the extent to which the set of moment equations can be solved simultaneously to yield values of the parameters. One possible outcome is the case that the parameters are *underdetermined* by the system of moment equations, meaning that there is insufficient information in the system to solve for the parameters uniquely. Another possible outcome is that the parameters can be *just-determined* by the system of moment equations, in which case there is just enough information in the system for there to be a unique solution for the parameters. Finally, the parameters may be *overdetermined*, in which case there is an overabundance of information in the system of moment equations such that there is no value of the parameters that can solve all of the moment equations in the system simultaneously. The case in which a unique solution exists subsumes the classical Pearson's method of moments (MOM), also referred to as the *ordinary* method of moments, and the overdetermined case relates to the generalized method of moments (GMM). We focus on the just-determined and overdetermined cases in this chapter and examine both the MOM and the GMM approaches to estimation and inference. The case in which the set of moments underdetermines the parameters is a major focus of this book and is addressed in later chapters.

We also introduce the concept of *estimating equations* (EEs), which subsumes the moment equation approaches, and also subsumes the least squares (LS), maximum likelihood (ML), and extremum (E) estimation methods of estimation and inference when estimates are characterized by first-order conditions. In this context, the EE approach is a unifying estimation and inference paradigm for defining estimators and estimates for unknowns in an econometric model. We also note how the E estimation approach for obtaining information on the unknowns of an econometric model, introduced in Section 2.5, relates to the methods examined in this chapter.

The method of moments approaches, E estimation, and the EEs approach are discussed in the context of *semiparametric* methods of estimation and inference. These methods do not require an explicit functional specification of the parametric family of probability distributions underlying the data sampling process (DSP) to be used in practice. Indeed, knowing the values of all of the parameters in the model does not imply a specific probability distribution for the underlying DSP and, in general, a range of distributions may be consistent with the information used in these approaches. As such, this context mitigates the problem of misspecifying the functional form of the probability distribution underlying the DSP (or, equivalently, the likelihood function underlying ML estimation and inference applications).

The DSP underlying the models we examine in this chapter focuses on the case of *linear* functions of the data in the specification of moments, regression (or conditional expectation) functions, and EEs. In addition, the DSPs that are examined are characterized by *stochastic independence* across sample observations. All of the methods we review subsequently can be extended to nonlinear functions of the data, as well as data that are stochastically dependent in various ways. These issues are pursued later in this volume when ill-posed inverse sampling models are examined in the context of information theoretic approaches to estimation and inference.

### 3.1.1 A Just-Determined Moment System with Random Sampling of Scalars

For expository purposes, we first consider the simplest form of DSP in which we have $n$ *iid* observations on outcomes of a scalar random variable $\mathcal{Y}$ having some *unknown* probability distribution with mean $\beta$ and variance $\sigma^2$ (hence, a semiparametric model). The DSP underlying the $n \times 1$ sample outcome $\mathbf{y}$ is then

$$\mathcal{D} = \{\mathrm{Y}, \{E(\mathrm{Y}_i) = \beta, \mathrm{var}(\mathrm{Y}_i) = \sigma^2, \mathrm{Y}_i s \sim iid\,\mathcal{Y}\}\}. \qquad (3.1.1)$$

Placing this in the context of the general probability linear model, this is a special case in which the $n$ *iid* random variables in $\mathbf{Y}$ are represented by $\mathbf{Y} = \mathbf{x}\boldsymbol{\beta} + \boldsymbol{\varepsilon}$, with the $\varepsilon_i$'s being *iid*, and $\mathbf{x} = \mathbf{1}_n$ with $\mathbf{1}_n$ being an $n \times 1$ vector of 1's.

The first and second moments of $\mathcal{Y}$ about the origin (i.e., around the point zero) are defined by

$$\begin{bmatrix} \mu_1' \\ \mu_2' \end{bmatrix} = \begin{bmatrix} E(\mathcal{Y}) \\ E(\mathcal{Y}^2) \end{bmatrix} = \begin{bmatrix} \beta \\ \sigma^2 + \beta^2 \end{bmatrix}, \tag{3.1.2}$$

which can be viewed as a two-equation system defining two population distribution moments $(\mu_1', \mu_2')$ in terms of two unknown parameters $(\beta, \boldsymbol{\sigma}^2)$. In this particular application, the moment equations just-determine the two parameters, and (3.1.2) can be solved uniquely for the parameters in terms of the moments as

$$\begin{bmatrix} \beta \\ \sigma^2 \end{bmatrix} = \begin{bmatrix} \mu_1' \\ \mu_2' - (\mu_1')^2 \end{bmatrix}. \tag{3.1.3}$$

Unless we know the values of the population moments $(\mu_1', \mu_2')$, we cannot directly recover the values of the unknown parameters, $\beta$ and $\boldsymbol{\sigma}^2$. However, we can use the sample data $\mathbf{y}$ and define sample moments $m_1' = n^{-1} \sum_i y_i = \bar{y}_n$ and $m_2' = n^{-1} \sum_i y_i^2$ as *estimates* of the respective population moments $(\mu_1', \mu_2')$, and obtain estimates of the parameters via substitution as

$$\begin{bmatrix} \hat{\beta} \\ \hat{\sigma}^2 \end{bmatrix} = \begin{bmatrix} m_1' \\ m_2' - (m_1')^2 \end{bmatrix} = \begin{bmatrix} \bar{y}_n \\ n^{-1} \sum_{i=1}^{n} (y_i - \bar{y}_n)^2 \end{bmatrix}. \tag{3.1.4}$$

This is an example of an MOM estimation approach in which a just-determined system of sample moment equations is solved uniquely for estimates of the unknown parameters in $\mathfrak{D}$. It can be shown that the estimator of the parameters in (3.1.4) is a consistent estimator and is also asymptotically normally distributed. The properties actually derive from the fact that the sample moments $(m_1', m_2')$ are consistent for estimating their population counterparts and are jointly asymptotically normally distributed. The estimator for $\beta$ is also unbiased and, whereas the estimator $\boldsymbol{\sigma}^2$ is biased, its bias can be corrected by simply changing the premultiplier $n^{-1}$ to $(n-1)^{-1}$ in the definition of the estimator in (3.1.4).

We emphasize that the aforementioned approach to estimating the parameters is a semiparametric approach. No parametric functional form for the population distribution of $\mathbf{Y}$ was assumed and, moreover, given numerical values of the parameters $\beta$ and $\sigma^2$, no particular probability distribution is identified thereby. *In fact, an infinite number of possible probability distributions will generally be consistent with given values of these two moments of the distribution.* The preceding approach has the advantage of being immune to the problem of misspecifying the functional form of the underlying population distribution because no specification is ever attempted.

## 3.2 Just-Determined Moment Systems, Random Sampling, and Method of Moments (MOM)

We now generalize beyond the case of simple random sampling of scalars and the use of simple moments about the mean or about the origin. Suppose we have a $k \times 1$ vector of model parameters $\boldsymbol{\theta} \in \boldsymbol{\Theta}$ that is to be estimated, and suppose further that we define an $\ell \times 1$ vector of moment conditions

$$E[\mathbf{h}_*(\mathcal{Y}, \boldsymbol{\theta})] = \mathbf{0}_\ell \tag{3.2.1}$$

that relate expectations of $\ell$ functions of the scalar or multivariate random variable $\mathcal{Y}$, with the parameter vector $\boldsymbol{\theta}$. The $\mathbf{0}_\ell$ in (3.2.1) denotes an $\ell \times 1$ vector of zeros. Note that this is a canonical representation general enough for any type of moment equation system that relates expectations of functions of random sample data outcomes from $\mathcal{Y}$ to the parameters of interest. The DSP underlying the analysis is of the general form

$$\mathcal{D} = \{\mathbf{Y}, \{E[\mathbf{h}_*(\mathcal{Y}, \boldsymbol{\theta})] = \mathbf{0}_\ell, \quad \mathbf{Y}_i\text{'s} \sim iid\,\mathcal{Y}\}\}, \tag{3.2.2}$$

where we allow for the possibility that sample observations are now vector outcomes of $\mathbf{Y}_i$, $i = 1, \ldots, n$.

For example, in our previous two-moment example where $\ell = 2$, $\mathbf{h}_*(\mathcal{Y}, \boldsymbol{\theta})$ in (3.2.1) would be the special case of a two-dimensional vector function of a scalar $\mathcal{Y}$ defined explicitly as

$$\mathbf{h}_*(\mathcal{Y}, \boldsymbol{\theta}) = \begin{bmatrix} h_{*1}(\mathcal{Y}, \beta, \sigma) \\ h_{*2}(\mathcal{Y}, \beta, \sigma) \end{bmatrix} = \begin{bmatrix} \mathcal{Y} - \beta \\ \mathcal{Y}^2 - \beta^2 - \sigma^2 \end{bmatrix}, \tag{3.2.3}$$

where $\boldsymbol{\theta} = (\beta, \sigma^2)$. The MOM estimate $\hat{\boldsymbol{\theta}}$, in this application, would be obtained by choosing the unique value of $\boldsymbol{\theta}$ that satisfies the sample moment counterpart to (3.2.1) given by

$$n^{-1} \sum_{i=1}^{n} \mathbf{h}_*(y_i, \boldsymbol{\theta}) = \mathbf{0}, \tag{3.2.4}$$

where $\mathbf{y} = [y_1, y_2, \ldots y_n]'$ is a sample outcome from a size $n$ *iid* random sample from the population distribution of $\mathcal{Y}$. The two equations represented by (3.2.4) are algebraically equivalent to (3.1.4); thus, the solution to (3.2.4) is precisely the same as the solution to (3.1.4).

In practice, if there are $\ell$ moment equations, then generally $\ell = k$ is required; that is, there are an equal number of independent linear equations and parameters,[1] and we henceforth assume this is the case when applying the MOM approach. The true value of the parameter vector, $\boldsymbol{\theta}_0$, would be determined if one could actually solve uniquely the system of *population* moment equations

$$\boldsymbol{\theta}_0 = arg_{\boldsymbol{\theta}}\{E[\mathbf{h}_*(\mathcal{Y}, \boldsymbol{\theta})] = \mathbf{0}_\ell\}. \tag{3.2.5}$$

A MOM estimate of the parameters exists if one can solve uniquely the system of *sample* moment equations

$$\hat{\boldsymbol{\theta}}_{MOM} = arg_{\boldsymbol{\theta}}\left\{n^{-1}\sum_{i=1}^{n}\mathbf{h}_*(y_i,\ \boldsymbol{\theta}) = \mathbf{0}_l\right\}, \tag{3.2.6}$$

where $\mathbf{y}$ denotes an outcome of $\mathbf{Y}$.

### 3.2.1 General Asymptotic Properties

There is some compelling intuition underlying the use of (3.2.5) or (3.2.6) to solve for $\boldsymbol{\theta}$ and thereby obtain information about the value of $\boldsymbol{\theta}$. First of all, if we could calculate the actual value of the expectation indicated in (3.2.5) for any given $\boldsymbol{\theta}$, and then solve for the unique value of $\boldsymbol{\theta}$ that satisfies (3.2.5), we will have derived the *true* value, $\boldsymbol{\theta}_0$, of the unknown $\boldsymbol{\theta}$ and our estimate of the value of the parameter vector would be perfect. We emphasize that "true value" here means the value of $\boldsymbol{\theta}$ that indexes the probability distribution for which the outcomes from $\mathcal{D}$ are actually sampled.

Because the distribution underlying the expectation operation in (3.2.5) is generally unknown, we approximate the expectation with a sample estimate of this expectation as in (3.2.6). If the $\mathcal{Y}_i'$s are *iid*, then the $\mathbf{h}(\mathcal{Y}_i, \boldsymbol{\theta})$'s are also *iid* and one could invoke Khinchin's weak law of large numbers to claim that the sample estimate converges to the true value of the moment equations, as $n^{-1}\sum_{i=1}^{n}\mathbf{h}_*(\mathcal{Y}_i,\ \boldsymbol{\theta}) \xrightarrow{p} E[\mathbf{h}_*(\mathcal{Y},\ \boldsymbol{\theta})]$. Then, we would anticipate that the value of $\boldsymbol{\theta}$ that solves $n^{-1}\sum_{i=1}^{n}\mathbf{h}_*(\mathcal{Y}_i, \boldsymbol{\theta}) = \mathbf{0}$ should generally

[1] This assumes that the equations in the system are linearly independent, so no equations are redundant, and also that there are no functional constraints on the parameters.

converge in probability to the value of $\boldsymbol{\Theta}$ that solves $E[\mathbf{h}(\mathcal{Y}, \boldsymbol{\Theta})] = \mathbf{0}$. This implies that the MOM estimator should converge in probability to the true value, $\boldsymbol{\Theta}_0$, of $\boldsymbol{\Theta}$ and be a consistent estimator. In fact, it can be shown that the preceding intuition can be made rigorous and, under generally applicable regularity, the convergence does apply, and the estimator is a consistent estimator of the parameters. It can also be shown that the estimator is generally asymptotically normally distributed as well.

### 3.2.2 Linear Model Semiparametric Estimation through Moment Equations

In this section, we apply the MOM concept to the case of a general linear model using the moment-based condition that the noise component elements and the explanatory variable values are orthogonal (or, equivalently, contemporaneously uncorrelated). The linear model with stochastic $\mathbf{X}$ is specified as $\mathbf{Y} = \mathbf{X}\boldsymbol{\beta} + \boldsymbol{\varepsilon}$, with $E(\boldsymbol{\varepsilon} \mid \mathbf{X}) = \mathbf{0}_n$ and $Cov(\boldsymbol{\varepsilon} \mid \mathbf{X}) = \sigma^2\mathbf{I}_n$. The sample data observations $\mathbf{z}_i = (\mathbf{y}_i, \mathbf{x}_{i.})'$ are an outcome from the DSP

$$\mathcal{D} = \{(\mathbf{Y}, \mathbf{X}),\ \mathbf{Y} = \mathbf{X}\boldsymbol{\beta} + \boldsymbol{\varepsilon},\ \{E(\boldsymbol{\varepsilon} \mid \mathbf{X}) = \mathbf{0}_n,\ Cov(\boldsymbol{\varepsilon} \mid \mathbf{X}) = \sigma^2\mathbf{I}_n,\ E(\mathbf{X}'(\mathbf{Y} - \mathbf{X}\boldsymbol{\beta})) = \mathbf{0}_k\}\}, \tag{3.2.7}$$

where the orthogonality condition is represented by $E[\mathbf{X}'\boldsymbol{\varepsilon}] = E(\mathbf{X}'(\mathbf{Y} - \mathbf{X}\boldsymbol{\beta})) = \mathbf{0}_k$.

We follow the MOM format and use sample moments, based on the sample data $[\mathbf{y}, \mathbf{x}]$, to represent the orthogonality condition in $\mathcal{D}$, as

$$n^{-1}\sum_{i=1}^{n} \mathbf{x}'_{i.}(\mathrm{y}_i - \mathbf{x}_{i.}\boldsymbol{\beta}) = n^{-1}[\mathbf{x}'(\mathbf{y} - \mathbf{x}\boldsymbol{\beta})] = \mathbf{0} \tag{3.2.8}$$

and obtain the MOM estimate by choosing a value for $\boldsymbol{\beta}$ that satisfies (3.2.8), as

$$\hat{\mathbf{b}}_{MOM} = \arg_{\boldsymbol{\beta}}\{n^{-1}[\mathbf{x}'(\mathbf{y} - \mathbf{x}\boldsymbol{\beta})] = \mathbf{0}\} = (\mathbf{x}'\mathbf{x})^{-1}\mathbf{x}'\mathbf{y}. \tag{3.2.9}$$

Note that (3.2.8) is simply a scalar multiple of the first-order conditions for the LS problem

$$\hat{\mathbf{b}}_{LS} = \arg\min_{\mathbf{b}}\{(\mathbf{y} - \mathbf{x}\mathbf{b})'(\mathbf{y} - \mathbf{x}\mathbf{b})\} = (\mathbf{x}'\mathbf{x})^{-1}\mathbf{x}'\mathbf{y}. \tag{3.2.10}$$

The resulting MOM estimate is therefore identical to the LS estimate, which is an E estimator for the unknown parameters. As is generally the case in MOM estimation problems, the MOM estimator $\hat{\boldsymbol{\beta}}_{\mathrm{MOM}}$ is a consistent and asymptotically normally distributed estimator of $\boldsymbol{\beta}$, under generally applicable regularity conditions. We underscore that the MOM estimator was made possible by the information that was contained in the specification of $\mathfrak{D}$ and, in contrast, there is insufficient information in $\mathfrak{D}$ to enable a parametric approach to estimation, such as the classical ML approach, which would be an alternative E estimator for the parameters.

The MOM is a precursor to the modern *estimating equations approach* that we introduce in Section 3.4. Later in the book, we revisit the practice of aggregating the data into sample moments as a basis for defining EEs and seek alternative weighting of the observations that lead to good or optimal estimates of parameters. For now, we emphasize that MOM estimators are quite generally consistent and asymptotically normal estimators of the model parameters and that these estimators are based on only a few characteristics of the DSP and do not rely on strong assumptions about the underlying functional form of the probability distribution governing the DSP. At this point, one can begin to understand some of the underlying rationale for the heated discussions between Pearson and Fisher regarding the benefits (e.g., distributional robustness) and costs (e.g., *possible* nonoptimality) of choosing between the MOM and ML approaches to estimation.

### 3.2.3 MOM Conclusions

In this section, we have enlarged the set of estimation and inference procedures to include moment estimators that do not rely on strong distributional assumptions. In this context, we examined estimators for which population moments of the form (3.2.5) hold that have sample analogs of the form (3.2.6). In each case, the estimators solved from the sample moment equations had the desirable properties of consistency and asymptotic normality under generally applicable conditions. *Hypothesis testing and confidence region estimation follow the usual asymptotic approach based on asymptotic normality of the estimators.*

From a historical standpoint, Godambe and Heyde (1987) note that Gauss (in 1821–1823) developed the Gauss–Markov Theorem using only the "first two moments" of the underlying distribution. *Thus, it is important to note that the optimality, in finite samples of LS estimators, depends on assumptions concerning only the first two population moments* but is otherwise independent of the functional form of the population probability distribution underlying the DSP. *On the other hand, ML estimators of parameters generally depend critically on the functional form of the population probability distribution.* Thus, as Godambe and Heyde note, the observation that the methods of ML and LS give identical results if the distribution is normal contains the germ of the modern theory of EEs and is consistent with the MOM approach, which subsumes the LS procedure under appropriate moment conditions.

## 3.3 Generalized Method of Moments (GMM)

In this section, we analyze an extension of the ordinary MOM approach to cases in which the number of moment conditions, $\ell$, exceeds the number of unknown parameters, $k$, that we seek to estimate. When $\ell > k$ and the (inverse) problem is overdetermined, it is not possible to find a value of the parameter vector that simultaneously sets all of the sample moment conditions exactly equal to zero. In effect, there are more equations than unknown parameters, and the system of moment condition equations is overdetermined. The solution proposed by Hansen (1982) is to choose model parameters that set the moment functions as close to zero as possible, where closeness is measured in terms of weighted Euclidean distance. Although each weighting scheme may provide a different consistent estimator, the weights may be selected to achieve a consistent estimator that is asymptotically normally distributed within a broad class of alternative estimators.

### 3.3.1 GMM Framework

The GMM framework begins by considering a $(\ell \times 1)$ random vector function of the form $\mathbf{h}_*(\mathcal{Y}, \boldsymbol{\theta})$ that has moments

$$E[\mathbf{h}_*(\mathcal{Y}, \boldsymbol{\theta})] = \mathbf{0} \tag{3.3.1}$$

where the scalar or multivariate random variable $\mathcal{Y}$ has some population probability distribution on which the expectation in (3.3.1) is based. We initially assume a DSP that produces data via *iid* outcomes of $\mathcal{Y}$, as in (3.2.2).

Given that $\ell > k$ and assuming no functional redundancies in the equation system (3.3.1), there does not exist a unique parameter vector $\boldsymbol{\beta}$ that solves the sample moment conditions via the ordinary MOM approach, which would attempt to find the unique value of $\boldsymbol{\beta}$ that satisfies the sample moment counterpart to the equation system given by

$$\hat{E}[\mathbf{h}_*(\mathcal{Y}, \boldsymbol{\theta})] = n^{-1} \sum_{i=1}^{n} \mathbf{h}_*(y_i, \boldsymbol{\theta}) = \mathbf{0}. \tag{3.3.2}$$

Under the GMM approach, the parameter vector chosen is the one for which the sample moment conditions are as close to the zero vector as possible.

In pursuit of this objective, to define our estimate, we solve the following minimum weighted Euclidean distance problem:

$$\hat{\beta}_{GMM} = \arg\min_{\theta}\left\{\left(n^{-1}\sum_{i=1}^{n}\mathbf{h}_*(y_i,\theta)\right)'\mathbf{W}\left(n^{-1}\sum_{i=1}^{n}\mathbf{h}_*(y_i,\theta)\right)\right\}, \quad (3.3.3)$$

where $\mathbf{W}$ is some $(m \times m)$ positive definite symmetric weight matrix. The GMM estimator defined by (3.3.3) is clearly an E estimator for the unknown parameters of the model.

Note that the form of the estimation objective is similar to the LS estimator, where instead of minimizing the squared distance between $[\mathbf{y} - \mathbf{xb})]$ and $\mathbf{0}$, the estimator seeks to minimize the weighted squared distance between $\hat{E}[\mathbf{h}_*(\mathcal{Y}, \theta)]$ and $\mathbf{0}$. Note further that the fundamental rationale for choosing $\theta$ to satisfy the sample moment conditions (3.3.2) as closely as possible is analogous to the (ordinary) MOM. Namely, we are assuming that an appropriate uniform law of large numbers applies so that $n^{-1}\sum_{i=1}^{n}\mathbf{h}_*(\mathcal{Y}_i, \theta) \xrightarrow{p} \mathbf{0}$ uniquely when $\theta$ is set equal to the true value, $\theta_0$, of the parameter vector. Then, solving the sample moment conditions for $\theta$ leads to a sequence of solutions, $\{\hat{\Theta}_n\}$, for which $\hat{\Theta}_n \xrightarrow{p} \theta_0$ as $n \to \infty$ so that the estimator is consistent. We discuss sampling properties of GMM estimators in more detail ahead.

A major issue in implementing the GMM estimator is the choice of the weighting matrix, $\mathbf{W}$, which has an effect on the relative efficiency of the estimator. In fact, for any given set of EEs-moment conditions, (3.3.3) identifies an entire infinite class of estimators as a function of $\mathbf{W}$, and the efficient choice of $\mathbf{W}$, though theoretically defined, is almost always unknown in practice. We address the choice of $\mathbf{W}$ in sections ahead.

### 3.3.2 GMM Linear Model Estimation

Referring to the overdetermined linear model context, GMM moment conditions in the case of the linear model are based on the $(1 + k + \ell) \times 1$ random vector $\mathcal{Y} = vec[\mathrm{Y}, \mathcal{X}', \mathcal{Z}']$, where Y is a scalar, $\mathcal{X}$ is $k \times 1$, $\mathcal{Z}$ is $\ell \times 1$, and $vec(\bullet)$ is the standard vectorization operator. The $\ell$ population moments are represented by

$$E[\mathbf{h}_*(\mathcal{Y}, \theta)] = E[\mathcal{Z}(\mathrm{Y} - \mathcal{X}'\beta)] = \mathbf{0}. \quad (3.3.4)$$

Given that the DSP generating the sample data is characterized by

$$\mathcal{D} = \{(\mathbf{Y}, \mathbf{X}, \mathbf{Z}),\ \{\mathbf{E}(\mathbf{Z}'(\mathbf{Y} - \mathbf{X}\beta)) = \mathbf{0}_{\ell},\ (\mathrm{Y}_i, \mathbf{X}_i, \mathbf{Z}_i)'\mathrm{s} \sim iid\,\mathcal{Y}\}\}, \quad (3.3.5)$$

the sample moment counterpart is

$$\hat{E}[\mathbf{h}_*(\mathcal{Y}, \boldsymbol{\theta})] = n^{-1}\sum_{i=1}^{n}\mathbf{h}_*(y_i, \boldsymbol{\beta}) = n^{-1}\mathbf{z}'(\mathbf{y} - \mathbf{x}\boldsymbol{\beta}) = \mathbf{0}], \quad (3.3.6)$$

where $\mathbf{x}$ is $n \times k$ and $\mathbf{z}$ is $n \times \ell$.

The GMM approach is implemented by defining a weighted Euclidean distance-based estimation objective function and defines a GMM estimator as

$$\hat{\boldsymbol{\beta}}_{GMM} = \arg\min_{\boldsymbol{\beta}}\{[\mathbf{Z}'(\mathbf{Y} - \mathbf{X}\boldsymbol{\beta})]'\mathbf{W}[\mathbf{Z}'(\mathbf{Y} - \mathbf{X}\boldsymbol{\beta})]\}. \quad (3.3.7)$$

Differentiating the estimation objective function in (3.3.7) with respect to $\boldsymbol{\beta}$ yields the first-order conditions

$$-2\mathbf{X}'\mathbf{Z}\mathbf{W}\mathbf{Z}'(\mathbf{Y} - \mathbf{X}\boldsymbol{\beta}) = \mathbf{0}, \quad (3.3.8)$$

which provides a closed-form solution for the GMM estimator

$$\hat{\boldsymbol{\beta}}(\mathbf{W}) = [\mathbf{X}'\mathbf{Z}\mathbf{W}\mathbf{Z}'\mathbf{X}]^{-1}\mathbf{X}'\mathbf{Z}\mathbf{W}\mathbf{Z}'\mathbf{Y}. \quad (3.3.9)$$

Note that in (3.3.8), a $(k \times m)$ matrix $\mathbf{X}'\mathbf{Z}\mathbf{W}$ is used to project the $\ell$ moment conditions (3.3.6) to a set of $k$ equations in $k$ unknowns. This transformation leads to a just-determined problem that can be solved uniquely for $\boldsymbol{\beta}$, assuming that the inverse matrix exists in (3.3.9). This is generally the case when the data obtained from $\mathcal{D}$ in (3.3.5) is such that $E[\mathcal{Z}\mathcal{X}']$ has full column rank.

### 3.3.2a Optimal GMM Weight Matrix

To make the GMM estimator operational, one needs to choose a weight matrix $\mathbf{W}$, and an optimal choice of $\mathbf{W}$ is preferable if such a choice is available. Hansen (1982) indicates that the choice of $\mathbf{W}$ that defines the most efficient estimator of the form (3.3.9) is to set $\mathbf{W}$ equal to the *inverse* of the covariance matrix $Cov(n^{-1/2}\mathbf{Z}'\boldsymbol{\varepsilon})$. Assuming that $\mathbf{a}^n_{\mathbf{zz}} = E[n^{-1}\mathbf{Z}'\mathbf{Z}]$ exists as a finite positive definite matrix, we can apply the iterated expectation theorem to express the optimal $\mathbf{W}^{-1}$ as

$$\begin{aligned}\mathbf{w}_*^{-1} &= Cov(n^{-1/2}\mathbf{Z}'\boldsymbol{\varepsilon}) = n^{-1}E_{\mathbf{Z}}[E[\mathbf{Z}'\boldsymbol{\varepsilon}\boldsymbol{\varepsilon}'\mathbf{Z}|\mathbf{Z}]] \\ &= n^{-1}E_{\mathbf{Z}}[\mathbf{Z}'(\sigma^2\mathbf{I})\mathbf{Z}] = n^{-1}\sigma^2E(\mathbf{Z}'\mathbf{Z}) = \sigma^2\mathbf{a}^n_{\mathbf{ZZ}}, \quad (3.3.10)\end{aligned}$$

where we have used the assumption that $E(\boldsymbol{\varepsilon}\boldsymbol{\varepsilon}'|\mathbf{Z}) = \sigma^2\mathbf{I}$.

In practice, both $\sigma^2$ and $\mathbf{a}^n_{\mathbf{ZZ}}$ are unknown, and so we have an operational dilemma. To define an estimated optimal GMM (EOGMM) estimator, we can insert consistent estimators in place of $\sigma^2$ and $E(n^{-1}\mathbf{Z}'\mathbf{Z})$ in the definition of $\mathbf{w}_*$. Furthermore, $\sigma^2$ can actually be eliminated from the definition of the weight matrix because the optimal $\hat{\boldsymbol\beta}(\mathbf{W})$ obtained from (3.3.9) is completely unaffected if the weight matrix is multiplied by any positive scalar; that is, $\hat{\boldsymbol\beta}(\mathbf{W}) = \hat{\boldsymbol\beta}(c\mathbf{W})$ for any $c > 0$.

If the $\mathbf{Z}_i$'s are *iid*, a simple consistent estimator of $\mathbf{a}_{ZZ}$ is given by

$$\hat{\mathbf{a}}^n_{ZZ} = n^{-1}\sum_{i=1}^{n} \mathbf{Z}'_{i.}\mathbf{Z}_{i.} = n^{-1}\mathbf{Z}'\mathbf{Z}. \tag{3.3.11}$$

Even if the $\mathbf{Z}_i$'s were not *iid*, so long as $n^{-1}\mathbf{Z}'\mathbf{Z} - \mathbf{a}^n_{ZZ} \xrightarrow{p} \mathbf{0}$ as $n \to \infty$, $\hat{\mathbf{a}}^n_{ZZ}$ can still be used to define the EOGMM estimator.

Substituting the sample estimator of the optimal weighting matrix, $\hat{\mathbf{W}} \propto [n^{-1}\mathbf{Z}'\mathbf{Z}]^{-1}$, into (3.3.9) yields the EOGMM estimator,

$$\hat{\boldsymbol\beta}_{GMM} = (\mathbf{X}'\mathbf{Z}(\mathbf{Z}'\mathbf{Z})^{-1}\mathbf{Z}'\mathbf{X})^{-1}\mathbf{X}'\mathbf{Z}(\mathbf{Z}'\mathbf{Z})^{-1}\mathbf{Z}'\mathbf{Y}. \tag{3.3.12}$$

We indicate ahead that this GMM estimator is asymptotically efficient relative to the class of all estimators formed by alternative choices of the weighting matrix $\mathbf{W}$ in (3.3.9).

#### 3.3.2b Sampling Properties of Estimated Optimal GMM (EOGMM) Estimator

To establish consistency of the EOGMM estimator, note that we can rewrite the estimator as

$$\hat{\boldsymbol\beta}(\hat{\mathbf{W}}_n) = \boldsymbol\beta + [\mathbf{X}'\mathbf{Z}\hat{\mathbf{W}}_n\mathbf{Z}'\mathbf{X}]^{-1}\mathbf{X}'\mathbf{Z}\hat{\mathbf{W}}_n\mathbf{Z}'\boldsymbol\varepsilon. \tag{3.3.13}$$

Given that $\hat{\mathbf{W}}_n - \mathbf{w} \xrightarrow{p} \mathbf{0}$, where $\mathbf{w}$ is a finite positive definite symmetric matrix, it follows that

$$\begin{aligned} \mathrm{p}\lim \hat{\boldsymbol\beta}(\hat{\mathbf{W}}_n) &= \boldsymbol\beta + \mathrm{p}\lim\left(\left[\left(\frac{\mathbf{X}'\mathbf{Z}}{n}\right)\hat{\mathbf{W}}_n\left(\frac{\mathbf{Z}'\mathbf{X}}{n}\right)\right]^{-1}\left(\frac{\mathbf{X}'\mathbf{Z}}{n}\right)\hat{\mathbf{W}}_n\left(\frac{\mathbf{Z}'\boldsymbol\varepsilon}{n}\right)\right), \\ &= \boldsymbol\beta + [\mathbf{a}_{XZ}\mathbf{w}\mathbf{a}_{ZX}]^{-1}\mathbf{a}_{XZ}\mathbf{w}\,\mathbf{0} = \boldsymbol\beta, \end{aligned} \tag{3.3.14}$$

under the prevailing assumptions. It is important to note that if the weight matrix must be consistently estimated, even if a nonoptimal weight matrix is used, the GMM estimator is a consistent estimator of $\boldsymbol\beta$.

The asymptotic normality of the GMM estimator can be established under the assumption

$$n^{-1/2}\mathbf{Z}'\boldsymbol\varepsilon \xrightarrow{d} N[\mathbf{0}, \Delta], \tag{3.3.15}$$

which may be justified by the use of an appropriate central limit theorem (e.g., Lindeberg-Levy if $\mathbf{Z}'_{i.}\varepsilon_i$, $i = 1, \ldots, n$ were *iid*). Accordingly, we may utilize the expression in (3.3.13) to define

$$n^{1/2}(\hat{\boldsymbol{\beta}}(\hat{\mathbf{W}}_{\mathrm{n}}) - \boldsymbol{\beta}) = \left[\left(\frac{\mathbf{X}'\mathbf{Z}}{n}\right)\hat{\mathbf{W}}_{\mathrm{n}}\left(\frac{\mathbf{Z}'\mathbf{X}}{n}\right)\right]^{-1}\left(\frac{\mathbf{X}'\mathbf{Z}}{n}\right)\hat{\mathbf{W}}_{\mathrm{n}}\left(n^{-1/2}\mathbf{Z}'\boldsymbol{\varepsilon}\right). \quad (3.3.16)$$

It follows that

$$n^{1/2}(\hat{\boldsymbol{\beta}}(\hat{\mathbf{W}}_n) - \boldsymbol{\beta}) \xrightarrow{d} (\mathbf{a}_{\mathrm{xz}}\mathbf{w}\mathbf{a}_{\mathrm{zx}})^{-1}\mathbf{a}_{\mathrm{xz}}\mathbf{w}\mathbf{V}, \quad (3.3.17)$$

where $\mathrm{V} = n^{-1/2}\mathbf{Z}'\boldsymbol{\varepsilon} \sim \mathrm{N}(\mathbf{0}, \Delta)$, so that using results on linear combinations of multivariate normally distributed random vectors,

$$n^{1/2}(\hat{\boldsymbol{\beta}}(\hat{\mathbf{W}}_n) - \hat{\boldsymbol{\beta}}) \xrightarrow{d} N(\mathbf{0}, (\mathbf{a}_{\mathrm{xz}}\mathbf{w}\mathbf{a}_{\mathrm{zx}})^{-1}\mathbf{a}_{\mathrm{xz}}\mathbf{w}\Delta\mathbf{w}\mathbf{a}_{\mathrm{zx}}(\mathbf{a}_{\mathrm{xz}}\mathbf{w}\mathbf{a}_{\mathrm{zx}})^{-1}). \quad (3.3.18)$$

Finally, if one is using the EOGMM estimator, so that $Cov(n^{-1/2}\mathbf{Z}'\boldsymbol{\varepsilon}) \to \mathbf{w}^{-1} = \Delta = p\lim(n^{-1}\mathbf{Z}'\Phi\mathbf{Z})$ under the current assumptions, the asymptotic distribution of the EOGMM estimator implied by (3.3.18) simplifies to

$$\hat{\boldsymbol{\beta}}(\hat{\mathbf{W}}_n) \overset{a}{\sim} N(\boldsymbol{\beta}, n^{-1}(\mathbf{a}_{\mathrm{xz}}\Delta^{-1}\mathbf{a}_{\mathrm{zx}})^{-1}). \quad (3.3.19)$$

The asymptotic covariance matrix of the EOGMM estimator in (3.4.19) can be estimated by the matrix

$$\hat{Cov}(\hat{\boldsymbol{\beta}}(\hat{\mathbf{W}}_n)) = n^{-1}[(n^{-1}\mathbf{x}'\mathbf{z})\hat{\mathbf{w}}_n(n^{-1}\mathbf{z}'\mathbf{x})]^{-1} \quad (3.3.20)$$

where $\hat{\mathbf{w}}_n^{-1}$ is the outcome of a consistent estimator of $Cov(n^{-1/2}\mathbf{Z}'\boldsymbol{\varepsilon})$. Asymptotic normality can be established using other weaker conditions, and the reader is referred to Hansen (1982) and Newey and McFadden (1994) for results and references along these lines.

#### 3.3.2c Hypothesis Testing and Confidence Regions

Testing hypotheses regarding values of functions of the parameter vector, $\boldsymbol{\beta}$, can be accomplished using Wald (W), Lagrange multiplier, pseudo-likelihood ratio, or *Z*-statistics. The statistics have asymptotic Chi-square or normal distributions based on the asymptotic normality of the estimator $\hat{\boldsymbol{\beta}}(\hat{\mathbf{W}}_{\mathrm{n}})$. Confidence region estimates can be generated via duality with hypothesis tests. These are, in fact, all special cases of the EE method, discussed in Section 3.4.

### 3.3.2d Additional Properties of the GMM Approach

One important aspect of the GMM estimation procedure is that it can be applied to a myriad of other estimation contexts in addition to the linear regression model context. We sketch here some of the general properties that can be attributed to the GMM estimator. For additional information, see section 8.4 in Mittelhammer (1996), chapter 3 of Gallant (1987), sections 2.5 and 3.3 in Newey and McFadden (1994), Bates and White (1985, 1988), and Gallant and White (1988).

Recall that, in general, the GMM estimator is found by minimizing the quadratic form (3.3.3) with respect to the choice of $\boldsymbol{\theta}$. For purposes of defining consistent and asymptotically normal estimators, the weight matrix $\mathbf{W}$ can be set equal to any positive definite symmetric matrix, and the moment conditions can be based on a variety of moment conditions of the form $E[\mathbf{h}_*(\mathcal{Y}, \boldsymbol{\theta})] = \mathbf{0}$ believed to hold for the DSP under investigation. In practice, when the number of moment conditions exceeds the number of parameters, one will generally seek to utilize an estimate of the optimal weight matrix. The choice of $\mathbf{W}$ that results in the asymptotically most efficient estimator, within the class of GMM estimators based on a given set of EEs-moment conditions, is the inverse of the covariance matrix $Cov(n^{1/2}\mathbf{h}_*(\mathcal{Y}, \boldsymbol{\theta})) \equiv Cov(n^{-1/2}\sum_{i=1}^{n} \mathbf{h}_*(\mathcal{Y}_i, \boldsymbol{\theta}))$. Optimality in the current context refers to choosing a $\mathbf{W}$ matrix in the definition of the GMM estimator

$$\hat{\boldsymbol{\Theta}}_{GMM} = \arg\min_{\boldsymbol{\theta}} \left\{ \left( n^{-1} \sum_{i=1}^{n} \mathbf{h}_*(\mathcal{Y}_i, \boldsymbol{\theta}) \right)' \mathbf{W} \left( n^{-1} \sum_{i=1}^{n} \mathbf{h}_*(\mathcal{Y}_i, \boldsymbol{\theta}) \right) \right\}, \tag{3.3.21}$$

such that $\hat{\boldsymbol{\Theta}}_{GMM}(\mathbf{W})$ has the smallest asymptotic covariance matrix. Because the optimal weight matrix implied by $\mathbf{w}_*^{-1} = Cov(n^{1/2}\mathbf{h}_*(\mathcal{Y}, \boldsymbol{\theta}))$ is generally unknown and thus $\hat{\boldsymbol{\Theta}}_{GMM}(\mathbf{W}_*)$ is not operational, a consistent estimator, $\hat{\mathbf{W}}_n$ of $\mathbf{w}_*$ is used, and then the EOGMM estimator is defined by $\hat{\boldsymbol{\Theta}}_{GMM}(\mathbf{W}_n)$.

The EOGMM estimator is consistent under general conditions, the principal condition being that the objective function (3.3.21) of the GMM procedure converges appropriately to a continuous nonstochastic function $(\bar{\mathbf{h}}(\boldsymbol{\theta}))'\mathbf{w}(\bar{\mathbf{h}}(\boldsymbol{\theta}))$ that has a unique minimum at the true value of the parameter vector, $\boldsymbol{\theta}_0$. Appropriate regularity conditions ensure that the minimum of the limit function, $(\bar{\mathbf{h}}(\boldsymbol{\theta}))'\mathbf{w}(\bar{\mathbf{h}}(\boldsymbol{\theta}))$, is equal to the limit of the sequence of minimums of $(n^{-1}\sum_{i=1}^{n} \mathbf{h}_*(\mathcal{Y}_i, \boldsymbol{\theta}))'\mathbf{W}(n^{-1}\sum_{i=1}^{n} \mathbf{h}_*(\mathcal{Y}_i, \boldsymbol{\theta}))$ in probability, so that $\hat{\boldsymbol{\Theta}}_{GMM} \xrightarrow{p} \boldsymbol{\theta}_0$. We emphasize that it is not necessary for $\hat{\mathbf{W}}_n$ to be estimating the optimal weighting matrix for consistency to be obtained. All that is required in the preceding argument is that $\hat{\mathbf{W}}_n$ converge to some positive definite symmetric matrix. Thus, there generally exist many choices of consistent GMM estimators.

Under general conditions in addition to those leading to consistency, including differentiability of $\bar{\mathbf{h}}(\boldsymbol{\theta})$, the GMM estimator is asymptotically normally distributed. For a given weight matrix $\mathbf{w}$, the limiting distribution result is

$$n^{1/2}(\hat{\boldsymbol{\Theta}} - \boldsymbol{\theta}_0) \xrightarrow{d} N\left(\mathbf{0}, \left[\frac{\partial \bar{\mathbf{h}}(\boldsymbol{\theta}_0)}{\partial \boldsymbol{\theta}} \mathbf{w} \frac{\partial \bar{\mathbf{h}}(\boldsymbol{\theta}_0)}{\partial \boldsymbol{\theta}'}\right]^{-1} \right.$$
$$\left. \times \frac{\partial \bar{\mathbf{h}}(\boldsymbol{\theta}_0)}{\partial \boldsymbol{\theta}} \mathbf{w}\,\mathbf{v}\,\mathbf{w} \frac{\partial \bar{\mathbf{h}}(\boldsymbol{\theta}_0)}{\partial \boldsymbol{\theta}'} \left[\frac{\partial \bar{\mathbf{h}}(\boldsymbol{\theta}_0)}{\partial \boldsymbol{\theta}} \mathbf{w} \frac{\partial \bar{\mathbf{h}}(\boldsymbol{\theta}_0)}{\partial \boldsymbol{\theta}'}\right]^{-1}\right), \qquad (3.3.22)$$

assuming that the inverse matrices exist, which they will if $\frac{\partial \bar{\mathbf{h}}(\boldsymbol{\theta}_0)}{\partial \boldsymbol{\theta}}$ has full row rank. If the EOGMM estimator, say $\hat{\boldsymbol{\Theta}}_*$, is being used, so that $\hat{\mathbf{W}} \xrightarrow{p} \mathbf{w} = \mathbf{v}^{-1}$, then the covariance matrix of the limiting distribution in (A.1.2) simplifies substantially to

$$n^{1/2}(\hat{\boldsymbol{\Theta}}^*_{GMM} - \boldsymbol{\theta}) \xrightarrow{d} N\left(\mathbf{0}, \left[\frac{\partial \bar{\mathbf{h}}(\boldsymbol{\theta}_0)}{\partial \boldsymbol{\theta}} \mathbf{v}^{-1} \frac{\partial \bar{\mathbf{h}}(\boldsymbol{\theta}_0)}{\partial \boldsymbol{\theta}'}\right]^{-1}\right). \qquad (3.3.23)$$

The asymptotic efficiency of $\hat{\boldsymbol{\Theta}}^*_{GMM}$ can be motivated by the fact that the covariance matrix in (3.3.23) exceeds the covariance matrix in (3.3.22) by a positive semidefinite matrix. In practice, the EOGMM is calculated by first obtaining a consistent estimator of $\boldsymbol{\theta}$, usually by setting $\mathbf{W} = \mathbf{I}$ and calculating $\hat{\boldsymbol{\Theta}}^*_{GMM}(\mathbf{I})$. Then, assuming sample observations are independent, $\mathbf{v}$ is estimated by an outcome of $\hat{\mathbf{V}} = n^{-1}\sum_{i=1}^{n} \mathbf{h}_*(\mathcal{Y}_i, \hat{\boldsymbol{\theta}}(\mathbf{I}))\mathbf{h}_*(\mathcal{Y}_i, \hat{\boldsymbol{\theta}}(\mathbf{I}))'$, and $\hat{\mathbf{W}}$ is defined as $\hat{\mathbf{W}} = \hat{\mathbf{V}}^{-1}$. Finally, the EOGMM estimator is defined as $\hat{\boldsymbol{\Theta}}^*_{GMM}(\hat{\mathbf{W}})$. An estimate of the covariance matrix in (3.3.23) can be obtained by calculating $[\frac{\partial n^{-1}\sum_{i=1}^{n} \mathbf{h}_*(\mathcal{Y}_i, \boldsymbol{\theta})}{\partial \boldsymbol{\theta}} \hat{\mathbf{W}} \frac{\partial n^{-1}\sum_{i=1}^{n} \mathbf{h}_*(\mathcal{Y}_i, \boldsymbol{\theta})}{\partial \boldsymbol{\theta}'}]^{-1}$, where the calculation of $\hat{\mathbf{W}}$ can be updated using the outcome of the EOGMM estimator.

### 3.3.2e Summary and Forward: The GMM Approach

The GMM approach provides a way of extending the ordinary MOM approach to the case in which there are more moment conditions than unknown $\boldsymbol{\theta}$ elements. It is fundamentally also an E type estimator. For a given set of moment conditions, the GMM procedure defines a family of consistent and asymptotically normally distributed estimators as a function of the weight matrix, $\mathbf{W}$. A theoretically optimal choice for the weight matrix exists, but it is generally unknown in practice and must be consistently estimated from the data. Whereas asymptotically optimal, the resulting EOGMM estimator, defined as a two-step estimator in which the first step involves the construction of some consistent estimator of the optimal weight matrix, is not necessarily optimal in finite samples. Moreover, the finite sample properties of the EOGMM estimator depend on the choice of weight matrix estimator, for which there are many possibilities. Thus, there is still reason to consider alternative estimation procedures in the overdetermined linear model case, and we do so ahead.

Our principal focus in the preceding discussion of GMM was on the overdetermined nature of the moment equation system. We note at this point that in our discussion of applications within the linear model context, we were not explicit about the status of the orthogonality condition between the explanatory variable matrix $\mathbf{X}$ and the noise component $\varepsilon$. In fact, the preceding discussion of the GMM method follows through whether or not orthogonality holds. However, we see ahead that it is actually only in the case where $\mathbf{X}$ and $\varepsilon$ are nonorthogonal that the notion of using an overdetermined set of moment conditions such as $n^{-1}\mathbf{Z}'(\mathbf{Y} - \mathbf{X}\boldsymbol{\beta})$ will be of benefit because, in the orthogonal case, $\mathbf{Z} = \mathbf{X}$ turns out to be the asymptotically optimal choice of $\mathbf{Z}$, resulting in a just-determined system being the optimal choice of EEs. Thus, it follows that using any other choice of $\mathbf{Z}$ in the preceding GMM estimator definitions produces an inferior estimator in the orthogonal case. In the next section, we develop EEs that we then link to a minimum divergence family of estimators in the chapters ahead.

## 3.4 Estimating Equations

In statistics, EEs provide a way for the parameters of a statistical econometric model to be estimated and may be thought of as a generalization of the methods discussed in Chapter 2 and in the previous sections of this chapter. In particular, upon reviewing the LS-ML-E–Moments-GMM estimation approaches presented heretofore, it is apparent that the estimators we have examined can all be recast in one way or another in terms of solving a vector of *estimating equations* (EEs)

$$\mathbf{h}(\mathbf{D}, \boldsymbol{\theta}) = \mathbf{0}_\ell, \tag{3.4.1}$$

for solutions in terms of the $k \times 1$ parameter vector $\boldsymbol{\theta}$, where $\mathbf{D}$ is an $n \times r$ random matrix of data. *Note that a fundamental difference between this specification and the systems of moment equations* $\mathbf{E}(\mathbf{h}_*(\mathcal{Y}, \boldsymbol{\theta})) = \mathbf{0}_\ell$ *is that* $\mathbf{D}$ *is the full random matrix of data, and there is no expectation operator applied* *to* $\mathbf{h}(\mathbf{D},\boldsymbol{\theta})$. The function $\mathbf{h}(\mathbf{D},\boldsymbol{\theta})$ in (3.4.1) is referred to as an *estimating function* (EF). In fact, R. A. Fisher (1935) noted long ago that *any* procedure for defining an estimate of a parameter $\boldsymbol{\theta}$, in terms of sample data outcomes d, can be regarded as a solution to an equation of the form $\mathbf{h}(\mathbf{d},\boldsymbol{\theta}) = \mathbf{0}_\ell$.

Estimators defined via solving EEs for the unknown parameters are represented by

$$\hat{\boldsymbol{\Theta}}_{\mathrm{EE}} = arg_{\boldsymbol{\theta}}\{\mathbf{h}(\mathbf{D},\boldsymbol{\theta}) = \mathbf{0}_\ell\}, \tag{3.4.2}$$

where both $\boldsymbol{\theta}$ and $\mathbf{h}(\mathbf{D},\boldsymbol{\theta})$ are $k \times 1$. Regarding the specific choice of (3.4.1) for defining LS, ML, and general E estimators, note that $\mathbf{h}(\mathbf{D},\boldsymbol{\theta}) = \mathbf{0}_\ell$ can be specified as the first-order conditions for the respective extremum problems. This choice, which occurs often in practice, is appropriate for all cases in which the first-order conditions characterize the global solution to the optimization problem. We emphasize that even in cases in which first-order conditions do not characterize solutions for estimators, equations (3.4.1)–(3.4.2) still apply as implicit representations of estimators defined by vector functions of the data. For example, in the case in which the estimator is represented in terms of a system of sample moment equations, the EEs can be specified in the general form $\mathbf{h}(\mathbf{d}, \boldsymbol{\theta}) = n^{-1}\sum_{i=1}^{n} \mathbf{h}_*(\mathbf{d}_i, \boldsymbol{\theta}) = \mathbf{0}_\ell$ (recall 3.2.5).

The EE approach represents a unifying representation of estimators and suggests that there may be another level of specification that can serve as the primary focal point for defining estimators of unknown parameters contained in probability models. Indeed, this is the focus of the developing EEs approach to estimation and inference in the statistical literature. In this approach, it is recognized that the sampling properties of estimators $\hat{\boldsymbol{\Theta}}_{\mathrm{EE}}$ defined via (3.4.2) are in fact derivable from the sampling properties of the EFs themselves; therefore, attention is directed toward the notion of specifying good or, if possible, optimal (in some sense) EFs.

### 3.4.1 Duality between Estimating Equations (EEs) and E Estimators

We note that when specifying EEs $\mathbf{h}(\mathbf{D}, \boldsymbol{\theta}) = \mathbf{0}$ *directly* to define estimators of parameters (as opposed to being derived indirectly as first-order conditions to an extremum problem), it is possible that an E estimation approach is nevertheless implied. This is the case when the system of partial differential equations

$$\frac{\partial m(\boldsymbol{\theta};\mathbf{D})}{\partial \boldsymbol{\theta}} = \mathbf{h}(\mathbf{D}, \boldsymbol{\theta}) \tag{3.4.3}$$

has a solution for a function $m(\boldsymbol{\Theta}; \mathbf{D})$ that can be interpreted as an estimation objective function. *In this case, the use of the estimating equation approach is equivalent to an extremum estimation approach in which the extremum estimator is the solution of first-order conditions.* The point is that an estimator *initially* characterized as the solution to a set of EEs may have some equivalent general E estimator characterization, just as the estimators initially characterized as a general E estimator can have an EE characterization.

It is useful to recognize that a necessary condition for there to exist an E estimator interpretation of a differentiable EE characterization is that the matrix of continuous derivatives $\frac{\partial \mathbf{h}(\mathbf{D}, \boldsymbol{\Theta})}{\partial \boldsymbol{\Theta}}$ be *symmetric.* This follows directly from a theorem regarding the symmetry of second-order partial derivatives of a twice-continuously differentiable scalar function on open sets. A sufficient condition for the unique solution $\hat{\boldsymbol{\Theta}}_{EE} = \arg_{\boldsymbol{\Theta}}[\mathbf{h}(\mathbf{D}, \boldsymbol{\Theta}) = \mathbf{0}]$ to represent the solution to the extremum problem, $\hat{\boldsymbol{\Theta}}_{Ext} = \arg\max_{\boldsymbol{\Theta}}[m(\mathbf{D}, \boldsymbol{\Theta})]$, is that $\frac{\partial \mathbf{h}(\mathbf{D}, \boldsymbol{\Theta})}{\partial \boldsymbol{\Theta}}$ be continuous in $\boldsymbol{\Theta}$, symmetric, and negative definite.

The EE literature is large and growing, and we do not enter into an extensive discussion of all of the issues involved in this estimation approach. Instead, we focus on some basic principles here and then continue to develop the EE idea in a number of specific estimation contexts throughout the remaining chapters. Interested readers wishing to delve more deeply into the use of EEs as a primary means of defining point estimators are advised to consult the works of Godambe and Kale (1991), Godambe (1991, 1997), Heyde (1989, 1994, 1997), Vinod (1997), Desmond (1997), and Mittelhammer et al. (2000) to begin additional readings and to obtain additional references on the subject.

### 3.4.2 Linear Estimating Functions (EFs)

To review some fundamental concepts relating to the use of EEs as a primary method of defining estimators of parameters, we focus on the linear functional form for EFs. We also focus on the pervasive case in which the data is in the form $\mathbf{D} = [\mathbf{Y}, \mathbf{X}]$, with $\mathbf{Y}$ being the dependent variable in a regression type of relationship. The DSP is specified in the form

$$\mathcal{D} = \{(\mathbf{Y}, \mathbf{X}), \mathbf{Y} = \mathbf{g}(\mathbf{X}, \boldsymbol{\Theta}) + \boldsymbol{\varepsilon}, \{E(\boldsymbol{\varepsilon} \,|\mathbf{X}) = \mathbf{0}_n, \quad Cov(\boldsymbol{\varepsilon} \,|\mathbf{X}) = \sigma^2 \mathbf{I}_n, (\mathbf{Y}_i, \mathbf{X}_i) \sim iid\, \mathcal{Y}\}\}. \tag{3.4.4}$$

Linear in the context of EFs refers to the fact that $\mathbf{h}(\mathbf{Y}, \mathbf{X}, \boldsymbol{\Theta})$ is linear in $\mathbf{Y}$, given values of $\mathbf{X}$ and $\boldsymbol{\Theta}$. Linear EFs can be represented in the basic form

$$\mathbf{h}(\mathbf{y}, \mathbf{x}, \boldsymbol{\Theta}) = \eta(\mathbf{x}, \boldsymbol{\Theta})(\mathbf{y} - \mathbf{g}(\mathbf{x}, \boldsymbol{\Theta})), \tag{3.4.5}$$

where $\eta(\mathbf{x}, \boldsymbol{\theta})$ is a $k \times n$ matrix that may or may not depend on $\mathbf{x}$ and/or the $k \times 1$ parameter vector $\boldsymbol{\theta}$, but the matrix does *not* depend on $\mathbf{y}$. The linear EFs case is the most straightforward case in which to establish asymptotic distribution properties of the EF. In particular, if $\mathbf{g}(\mathbf{x}, \boldsymbol{\theta})$ represents the means of the $Y_i's$ conditioned on the $\mathbf{x}'_{i.}s$, there is good reason to expect that a properly scaled EF will be asymptotically normally distributed for suitably chosen specifications of $\eta(\mathbf{x}, \boldsymbol{\theta})$. In particular, when the $(Y_i, \mathbf{X}_i)$'s are independent, $\mathbf{h}(\mathbf{Y}, \mathbf{X}, \boldsymbol{\theta})$ can then be viewed as a weighted sum of independent random vectors, as

$$\mathbf{h}(\mathbf{Y}, \mathbf{X}, \boldsymbol{\theta}) = \sum_{i=1}^{n} \varepsilon_i \eta_{.i}(\mathbf{X}, \boldsymbol{\theta}), \tag{3.4.6}$$

where $\varepsilon_i = Y_i - g(\mathbf{X}_i, \boldsymbol{\theta})$, $i = 1, \ldots, n$ are independent random variables, $\eta_{.i}(\mathbf{X}, \boldsymbol{\theta})$ is the $i^{th}$ column of $\eta(\mathbf{x}, \boldsymbol{\theta})$, and $\eta_{.i}(\mathbf{X}, \boldsymbol{\theta})$ is a function of only $\mathbf{x}_{i.}$, for $i = 1, \ldots, n$, so that a standard central limit theorem for independent random vectors can be applied to establish asymptotic normality of the sum of independent random variables in (3.4.6).

A prominent example of an estimator that can be defined within the linear EE framework using the combination of (3.4.2) and (3.4.5) is the LS estimator of $\boldsymbol{\beta}$ in the linear semiparametric regression model. In the linear probability model case, we define the components of (3.4.5) as $\boldsymbol{\theta} = \boldsymbol{\beta}$ and

$$\eta(\mathbf{x}, \boldsymbol{\beta}) = \mathbf{x}' \quad \textit{and} \quad \mathbf{g}(\mathbf{x}, \boldsymbol{\beta}) = \mathbf{x}\boldsymbol{\beta}, \tag{3.4.7}$$

in which case it is clear that the solution to the EEs is $\hat{\mathbf{b}}_{EE} = (\mathbf{x}'\mathbf{x})^{-1}\mathbf{x}'\mathbf{y}$, which is recognized as the LS estimator.

Regarding the asymptotic distribution of the EF based on (3.4.7), note that under general regularity conditions, it follows in the linear regression case that

$$\begin{aligned} n^{1/2}\mathbf{h}(\mathbf{Y}, \mathbf{X}, \boldsymbol{\beta}) &= 2n^{-1/2}(\mathbf{X}'\mathbf{X}\boldsymbol{\beta} - \mathbf{X}'\mathbf{Y}) \\ &= -2n^{-1/2}\mathbf{X}'\boldsymbol{\varepsilon} \xrightarrow{d} N(\mathbf{0}, 4\sigma^2\boldsymbol{\Xi}), \end{aligned} \tag{3.4.8}$$

where $n^{-1}\mathbf{X}'\mathbf{X} \xrightarrow{p} \boldsymbol{\Xi}$. As we noted before, it is generally the case that the scaled (most often by $n^{1/2}$) EF is asymptotically normally distributed for linear EFs used in practice.

The preceding examples of linear EFs illustrate a number of properties in addition to asymptotic normality that is important in our discussion ahead. First of all, note that the expectation and probability limit of each of the EFs equals the zero vector; that is, $E_{\boldsymbol{\theta}}[\mathbf{h}(\mathbf{Y}, \mathbf{X}, \boldsymbol{\theta})] = \mathbf{0}$

and $p\,lim_{\Theta}[\mathbf{h}(\mathbf{Y}, \mathbf{X}, \Theta)] = \mathbf{0}$, where $E_{\Theta}[\,]$ and $p\,\text{lim}_{\Theta}[\,]$ denote an expectation and a probability limit taken when the value of $\Theta$ is the true value of the parameter vector. Furthermore, assuming that the parameters are just-determined, both the expectation and probability limit are unequal to zero when $\Theta$ is not the true value; that is, $E_{\Theta_0}[\mathbf{h}(\mathbf{Y}, \mathbf{X}, \Theta)] \neq \mathbf{0}$ and $p\,\text{lim}_{\Theta_0}[\mathbf{h}(\mathbf{Y}, \mathbf{X}, \Theta)] \neq \mathbf{0}$ when $\Theta \neq \Theta_0$. We see ahead that these properties figure prominently in the evaluation of the efficacy of a set of EEs for parameter estimation and inference purposes.

Also note that EEs are not unique. Any scaling or one-to-one transformation of a set of EEs results in the same estimator being defined by the equations. This allows for some flexibility in the specification of EFs but also suggests that some type of normalization of the EFs is necessary if variances of competing sets of EFs are to be compared in a meaningful way.

### 3.4.3 Optimal Unbiased EFs

Much of the statistical literature relating to the evaluation of statistical properties in the EE estimation context is concerned with sampling properties of the EFs themselves rather than sampling properties of the estimators that the procedure produces. As one author remarked, "This is like admiring the pram rather than the baby." Whereas this may seem like an indirect way of evaluating the EE procedure, especially if the primary objective is to estimate the parameters of an econometric model and not the EF per se, it turns out that choosing appropriate properties of the EF has important implications for the sampling properties of $\hat{\Theta}_{EE}$. At least at a general conceptual level, it is clear that there is a fundamental interrelationship between the sampling properties of $\mathbf{h}(\mathbf{Y}, \mathbf{X}, \Theta)$ and the sampling properties of $\hat{\Theta}_{EE}$ because from (3.4.2), we have that $\hat{\Theta}_{EE} = \mathbf{h}^{-1}(\mathbf{Y}, \mathbf{X}, \mathbf{0})$, where $\mathbf{h}^{-1}(\cdot)$ denotes the inverse function (or relation) of the EF evaluated at $\text{h} = 0$. In effect, the EE estimator $\hat{\Theta}_{EE}$ inherits its sampling properties from the sampling properties of the EF via an inverse transformation, so the sampling properties of $\mathbf{h}(\mathbf{Y}, \mathbf{X}, \Theta)$ are of fundamental importance.

#### 3.4.3a Unbiasedness

One basic property of EFs that has been widely adopted in practice is that of *unbiasedness.* In the EE context, unbiasedness of an EF refers to the sampling characteristic

$$E_{\Theta}[\mathbf{h}(\mathbf{Y}, \mathbf{X}, \Theta)] = \mathbf{0}\,, \forall \Theta \in \Omega. \tag{3.4.9}$$

What purpose does unbiasedness of an EF serve? On an intuitive level, unbiasedness is a natural requirement to ensure that the solution for $\boldsymbol{\theta}$ obtained from the EEs is close to the true value $\boldsymbol{\theta}_0$ in the case in which "little variation" in the EFs is present. In the polar case in which the variance is zero, a biased (unbiased) EE would produce an incorrect (correct) value of $\boldsymbol{\theta}$ with probability 1 if the EEs can be solved uniquely for $\boldsymbol{\theta}$, which we henceforth tacitly assume is always the case (i.e., we are henceforth assuming that the EEs just-determine the unknown parameters). Furthermore, note that the case of "little variation" in the EF is intuitively an ideal that we seek because it appears logical to expect that if $\mathbf{h}(\cdot)$ is highly variable, then the solution of the EEs for $\boldsymbol{\theta}$ would be highly variable as well because the value of $\boldsymbol{\theta}$ is effectively the "adjustment factor" that aligns a value of $\mathbf{h}(\mathbf{y}, \mathbf{x}, \boldsymbol{\theta})$ with zero when solving the EEs. An unbiased EF is one way of guarding against the contradictory situation of having a good EE (with little variation) producing a largely incorrect value of $\boldsymbol{\theta}$.

There are conceptually deeper reasons why unbiasedness is a desirable EF characteristic. First of all, under appropriate regularity conditions, solutions to unbiased EEs represent consistent estimators of the parameters of the EEs. Essentially, when the EEs are defined via a sum of the contributions of $n$ individual data observations, as is most often the case in practice, laws of large numbers can be applied to ensure that a scaled version of the unbiased EEs converges to its zero expectation *iff* (with probability converging to 1) it is evaluated at the true parameter value $\boldsymbol{\theta}_0$. Thus, the solution value of $\boldsymbol{\theta}$ is drawn to $\boldsymbol{\theta}_0$ in the limit with probability limiting to 1. There is mounting Monte Carlo evidence in finite sample contexts that suggests that unbiased EFs result in EE estimators with superior finite sampling properties than biased EFs (Breslow [1990], Liang and Hanfelt [1994], and Liang and Zeger [1995]).

The unbiasedness criterion is also one component of a strong EE analogy with the classical theory of minimum variance unbiased estimators (MVUE) estimation in which one seeks an estimator within the unbiased class of estimators that has the smallest possible variance or covariance matrix. In the EE context, one seeks the EF from within the unbiased class of EFs that has the smallest possible variance, $\text{var}(\text{h}) = E_{\boldsymbol{\theta}}[\text{h}(\mathbf{Y}, \mathbf{X}, \boldsymbol{\theta})^2]$ or covariance matrix, $Cov(\mathbf{h}) = E_{\boldsymbol{\theta}}[\mathbf{h}(\mathbf{Y}, \mathbf{X}, \boldsymbol{\theta})\mathbf{h}(\mathbf{Y}, \mathbf{X}, \boldsymbol{\theta})']$. The rationale for seeking such an MVUE in the EE context parallels our previous remarks presented at the beginning of this subsection – an unbiased EE that also has little variation should provide a solution $\hat{\boldsymbol{\Theta}}_{EE}$ that is drawn more closely to $\boldsymbol{\theta}_0$ than a solution based on an EE that is biased and has large variation. However, it is also important to note that the estimators of parameters derived from unbiased EFs are not necessarily unbiased. Rather, many EE estimators are defined in terms of nonlinear functions of the data and are biased in finite samples.

### 3.4.3b Optimal Estimating Functions (OptEFs): The Scalar Case

An optimal estimating function, or OptEF, is an unbiased EF having the smallest variance or covariance matrix. A problem with implementing this concept of optimality is that the variance or covariance matrix of the EF $\mathbf{h}(\mathbf{Y}, \mathbf{X}, \boldsymbol{\Theta})$ can be arbitrarily changed by applying a scaling factors and/or multiplying by a full rank $k \times k$ matrix although not changing the implied EE estimator, or its sampling properties, at all. It is thus clear that some standardization of the EF is required for the OptEF concept to be operationally meaningful.

In the case of a scalar EF, Godambe (1960) was the first to suggest that the EF be standardized as

$$\mathrm{h}_s(\mathbf{Y}, \mathbf{X}, \theta) = \frac{\mathrm{h}(\mathbf{Y}, \mathbf{X}, \theta)}{E_\theta\left[\frac{\partial \mathrm{h}(\mathbf{Y}, \mathbf{X}, \theta)}{\partial \theta}\right]}, \tag{3.4.10}$$

so that the OptEF is then the unbiased EF that minimizes the variance of the *standardized* EF, that variance being defined as

$$\mathrm{var}(\mathrm{h}_s(\mathbf{Y}, \mathbf{X}, \theta)) = \frac{E_\theta[\mathrm{h}(\mathbf{Y}, \mathbf{X}, \theta)^2]}{\left\{E_\theta\left[\frac{\partial \mathrm{h}(\mathbf{Y}, \mathbf{X}, \theta)}{\partial \theta}\right]\right\}^2}. \tag{3.4.11}$$

It is clear that the variance of $\mathrm{h}_s(\mathbf{Y}, \mathbf{X}, \theta)$ is invariant to arbitrary scaling of $\mathrm{h}(\mathbf{Y}, \mathbf{X}, \theta)$ and leads to the same EE estimator, $\hat{\boldsymbol{\Theta}}_{EE}$, as $\mathrm{h}(\mathbf{Y}, \mathbf{X}, \theta)$.

In addition to being invariant to arbitrary scaling, the OptEF criterion of minimizing (3.4.11) has other properties that make it a useful optimality criterion within the EE framework. First, note that the denominator expectation term in (3.4.11) is the average gradient (averaged over the probability distribution of $(\mathbf{Y}, \mathbf{X})$) of the EF and, when evaluated at $\theta_0$, measures the average sensitivity of the EF to changes in the value of $\theta$ in the neighborhood of $\theta_0$. In minimizing (3.4.11), there is an incentive to make the denominator as large as possible and the numerator as small as possible to make the ratio a minimum. Thus, by attempting to minimize (3.4.11), we are pursuing a dual objective of decreasing the variance of the EF while increasing the expected sensitivity of its value to departures from the true value of $\theta$, both of which should improve the tendency for the solved value of $\theta$ to reside close to $\theta_0$. More concretely, it can be shown that the right-hand side of (3.4.11) represents the asymptotic variance of the (generally) consistent EE estimator derived from $h(\mathbf{Y}, \mathbf{X}, \theta)$ or, equivalently, from $h_s(\mathbf{Y}, \mathbf{X}, \theta)$; therefore, the criterion has an asymptotic justification of seeking the unbiased EF that produces the consistent EE estimator of $\theta$ with the smallest asymptotic variance.

In the special case in which $h(\mathbf{Y}, \mathbf{X}, \theta)$ is actually proportional to or is a scaled version of the log of the score or gradient function of a genuine likelihood function, then under the standard regularity conditions applied to ML estimation,

$$E_\theta\left[\frac{\partial \mathbf{h}(\mathbf{Y}, \mathbf{X}, \theta)}{\partial \theta}\right] \propto E_\theta\left[-\left(\frac{\partial^2 \ln L(\theta; \mathbf{Y}, \mathbf{X})}{\partial \theta^2}\right)\right] \text{ and}$$
$$E_\theta[h(\mathbf{Y}, \mathbf{X}, \theta)^2] \propto E_\theta\left[\left(\frac{\partial \ln L(\theta; \mathbf{Y}, \mathbf{X})}{\partial \theta}\right)^2\right], \tag{3.4.12}$$

where the expectations on the right-hand sides of the proportionality operators in (3.4.12) *are equal.* In this case, the OptEF criterion (3.4.11) becomes (note that the proportionality factors ultimately cancel):

$$\operatorname{var}(h_s(\mathbf{Y}, \mathbf{X}, \theta)) = \left[-E_\theta\left[\frac{\partial^2 \ln L(\theta; \mathbf{Y}, \mathbf{X})}{\partial \theta^2}\right]\right]^{-1}, \tag{3.4.13}$$

which is recognized as the ML variance and the Cramer-Rao Lower Bound (CRLB) for estimating the scalar $\theta$. This provides an OptEF *finite* sample justification for ML estimation in the case of estimating a scalar parameter $\theta$, and is analogous to the Gauss-Markov Theorem justification for LS estimation.

### 3.4.3c OptEFs: The Multivariate Case

The OptEF criterion can be extended to the multivariate unbiased EE framework in a natural way by replacing scalars with vectors and variances with covariance matrices. In particular, the multivariate OptEF criterion is stated in terms of the standardized vector EF

$$\mathbf{h}_s(\mathbf{Y}, \mathbf{X}, \boldsymbol{\Theta}) = \left(E_{\boldsymbol{\Theta}}\left[\frac{\partial \mathbf{h}(\mathbf{Y}, \mathbf{X}, \boldsymbol{\Theta})}{\partial \boldsymbol{\Theta}}\right]\right)^{-1} \mathbf{h}(\mathbf{Y}, \mathbf{X}, \boldsymbol{\Theta}). \tag{3.4.14}$$

The covariance matrix of $\mathbf{h}_s(\mathbf{Y}, \mathbf{X}, \boldsymbol{\Theta})$ is invariant to any arbitrary scaling or full rank linear transformation of the rows of $\mathbf{h}(\mathbf{Y}, \mathbf{X}, \boldsymbol{\Theta})$. The multivariate OptEF criterion is then to find the unbiased EF that minimizes, in the sense of symmetric positive definite matrix comparisons, the covariance matrix

$$
\begin{aligned}
&Cov(\mathbf{h}_s(\mathbf{Y},\mathbf{x},\boldsymbol{\theta}))\\
&= \left(E_{\boldsymbol{\theta}}\left[\frac{\partial \mathbf{h}(\mathbf{Y},\mathbf{x},\boldsymbol{\theta})}{\partial \boldsymbol{\theta}}\right]\right)^{-1} E_{\boldsymbol{\theta}}[\mathbf{h}(\mathbf{Y},\mathbf{X},\boldsymbol{\theta})\mathbf{h}(\mathbf{Y},\mathbf{X},\boldsymbol{\theta})']\\
&\times \left(E_{\boldsymbol{\theta}}\left[\frac{\partial \mathbf{h}(\mathbf{Y},\mathbf{X},\boldsymbol{\theta})}{\partial \boldsymbol{\theta}'}\right]\right)^{-1}
\end{aligned}
\tag{3.4.15}
$$

of the standardized EF (3.4.14). In addition to the invariance property of the OptEF measure, it can be shown, as in the scalar case, that the right-hand side of (3.4.15) represents the asymptotic covariance matrix of the (generally) consistent EE estimator derived from $\mathbf{h}_s(\mathbf{Y},\mathbf{X},\boldsymbol{\theta})$ or, equivalently, from $\mathbf{h}_s(\mathbf{Y},\mathbf{X},\boldsymbol{\theta})$; therefore, the criterion has an asymptotic justification of seeking the unbiased EF that produces the consistent EE estimator of $\boldsymbol{\theta}$ with the smallest asymptotic covariance matrix. The multivariate OptEF criterion can also be interpreted as providing for minimizing the covariance matrix of $\mathbf{h}(\mathbf{Y},\mathbf{X},\boldsymbol{\theta})$ (the middle expected value in (3.4.15)) and maximizing expected sensitivity of the EF value to departures from $\boldsymbol{\theta}_0$ (the leading and trailing expected values in (3.4.15)). However, unlike the scalar case, the interpretation is complicated due to the multiple directions from $\boldsymbol{\theta}_0$ in which the deviations can occur.

Analogous to the scalar case, in the special case in which $\mathbf{h}(\mathbf{Y},\mathbf{X},\boldsymbol{\theta})$ is actually proportional to or a scaled version of the log of the score or gradient vector function corresponding to a genuine likelihood function, it follows under the standard regularity conditions applied to ML estimation that

$$
\mathrm{E}_{\boldsymbol{\theta}}\left[\frac{\partial \mathbf{h}(\mathbf{Y},\mathbf{X},\boldsymbol{\theta})}{\partial \boldsymbol{\theta}}\right] \propto \mathrm{E}_{\boldsymbol{\theta}}\left[-\frac{\partial^2 \ln L(\boldsymbol{\theta};\mathbf{Y},\mathbf{X})}{\partial \boldsymbol{\theta}\,\partial \boldsymbol{\theta}'}\right]
\tag{3.4.16}
$$

and

$$
\begin{aligned}
&\mathrm{E}_{\boldsymbol{\theta}}[\mathbf{h}(\mathbf{Y},\mathbf{X},\boldsymbol{\theta})\mathbf{h}(\mathbf{Y},\mathbf{X},\boldsymbol{\theta})']\\
&\propto \mathrm{E}_{\boldsymbol{\theta}}\left[\frac{\partial \ln L(\boldsymbol{\theta};\mathbf{Y},\mathbf{X})}{\partial \boldsymbol{\theta}}\frac{\partial \ln L(\boldsymbol{\theta};\mathbf{Y},\mathbf{X})}{\partial \boldsymbol{\theta}'}\right],
\end{aligned}
\tag{3.4.17}
$$

where the expectations on the right-hand sides of (3.4.16) and (3.4.17) *are equal*. In this case, the OptEF criterion (3.4.15) becomes (note that the proportionality factors ultimately cancel):

$$
Cov(\mathbf{h}_s(\mathbf{Y},\mathbf{X},\boldsymbol{\theta})) = \left[-\mathrm{E}_{\boldsymbol{\theta}}\left[\frac{\partial^2 \ln L(\boldsymbol{\theta};\mathbf{Y},\mathbf{X})}{\partial \boldsymbol{\theta}\,\partial \boldsymbol{\theta}'}\right]\right]^{-1},
\tag{3.4.18}
$$

which is recognized as the ML covariance matrix and the CRLB for estimating the parameter vector $\boldsymbol{\theta}$. This provides an OptEF *finite* sample justification for ML estimation in the case of estimating a vector parameter $\boldsymbol{\theta}$, and is analogous to the Gauss-Markov Theorem justification for LS estimation.

The OptEF criterion in both the scalar and multivariate cases provides a general finite sample optimality result and associated finite sample justification for the ML approach to estimation. In particular, Godambe (1960) showed that (3.4.13) is in fact the lower bound for the variance of *any* standardized unbiased scalar EF $h_s(\mathbf{Y}, \mathbf{X}, \theta)$ under the standard CRLB regularity conditions. Godambe's approach can be generalized to the vector EF case, $\mathbf{h}_s(\mathbf{Y}, \mathbf{X}, \boldsymbol{\theta})$, leading to the result that (3.4.18) is the lower bound for the covariance matrix of *any* standardized unbiased vector EF under the standard CRLB regularity conditions (see Kale [1962] and Bhapkar [1997]).

It follows that an EE estimator based on an EF that is equal to the gradient of the log of the likelihood function is the OptEF estimator of $\boldsymbol{\theta}$. Therefore, the ML estimator (obtained via the solution to first-order conditions) is the OptEF estimator of $\boldsymbol{\theta}$. In practice, whenever the functional form of the likelihood function associated with a DSP can be correctly specified, the EE approach to estimation thus prescribes the ML estimator as the optimal (in finite samples) procedure for estimating the unknown parameter vector.

### 3.4.4 Inference in the Context of EE Estimation

The asymptotic normality of the EE estimator leads to the usual types of test and confidence region procedures being available for testing hypotheses and generating confidence regions about the value of a nonlinear (or linear) differentiable $(j \times 1)$ vector function, $\mathbf{c}(\boldsymbol{\theta})$, of the parameter vector. The following results can also be used for the LS, ML, and moments approached by an appropriate definition of the EFs. We note some of the traditional tests and develop them more completely in the chapters ahead as they are applied to particular problems.

#### 3.4.4a Wald (W) and Z Tests and Confidence Regions

The asymptotic normality of the EE estimator allows the $\mathbf{W}$ statistic

$$W = (\mathbf{c}(\hat{\boldsymbol{\theta}}_{EE}) - \mathbf{r})' \left( \left. \frac{\partial \mathbf{c}(\boldsymbol{\theta})}{\partial \boldsymbol{\theta}'} \right|_{\hat{\boldsymbol{\theta}}_{EE}} \hat{\Sigma}_{EE} \left. \frac{\partial \mathbf{c}(\boldsymbol{\theta})}{\partial \boldsymbol{\theta}} \right|_{\hat{\boldsymbol{\theta}}_{EE}} \right)^{-1} (\mathbf{c}(\hat{\boldsymbol{\theta}}_{EE}) - \mathbf{r})$$

$$\overset{a}{\sim} \textit{Chi-square}\,(j, 0) \textit{ under } H_0 \qquad (3.4.19)$$

to be used in the usual way to define asymptotically valid Chi-square tests of hypotheses of the form $H_0 : \mathbf{c}(\boldsymbol{\Theta}) = \mathbf{r}$, where $\hat{\boldsymbol{\Sigma}}_{\text{EE}}$ denotes a consistent estimator of the covariance matrix $\boldsymbol{\Sigma}$ of the asymptotic distribution. In general, within the current probability model context, a consistent estimator can be obtained using

$$\hat{E}\left[\left.\frac{\partial \mathbf{h}(\mathbf{Y}, \mathbf{X}, \boldsymbol{\theta})}{\partial \boldsymbol{\theta}}\right|_{\boldsymbol{\Theta}_0}\right] = \left.\frac{\partial \mathbf{h}(\mathbf{Y}, \mathbf{X}, \boldsymbol{\theta})}{\partial \boldsymbol{\theta}}\right|_{\hat{\boldsymbol{\Theta}}_{\text{EE}}} \tag{3.4.20}$$

and

$$\hat{E}\left[\mathbf{h}(\mathbf{Y}, \mathbf{X}, \boldsymbol{\theta}_0)\mathbf{h}(\mathbf{Y}, \mathbf{X}, \boldsymbol{\theta}_0)'\right] = n^{-1}\sum_{i=1}^{n} \mathbf{h}_*(\mathrm{Y}_i, \mathbf{X}_i, \hat{\boldsymbol{\Theta}}_{EE})\mathbf{h}_*(\mathrm{Y}_i, \mathbf{X}_i, \hat{\boldsymbol{\Theta}}_{EE})' \tag{3.4.21}$$

in the definition of the asymptotic covariance matrix, assuming that the EFs can be defined in terms of a sum of the contributions of $n$ observations as $\mathbf{h}(\mathbf{Y}, \mathbf{X}, \boldsymbol{\theta}) = n^{-1}\sum_{i=1}^{n} \mathbf{h}_*(\mathrm{Y}_i, \mathbf{X}_i, \boldsymbol{\theta})$ and the sample observations are independent (but not necessarily identically distributed).

The $Z$-statistic

$$Z = \frac{(\mathrm{c}(\hat{\boldsymbol{\Theta}}_{EE}) - \mathrm{r})}{\left(\left.\frac{\partial \mathrm{c}(\boldsymbol{\theta})}{\partial \boldsymbol{\theta}'}\right|_{\hat{\boldsymbol{\Theta}}_{\text{EE}}} \hat{\boldsymbol{\Sigma}}_{\text{EE}} \left.\frac{\partial \mathrm{c}(\boldsymbol{\theta})}{\partial \boldsymbol{\theta}}\right|_{\hat{\boldsymbol{\Theta}}_{\text{EE}}}\right)^{1/2}} \overset{a}{\sim} N(\delta, 1) \tag{3.4.22}$$

could also be used in the usual way to define tests of scalar inequality hypotheses of the form $H_0 : \mathrm{c}(\boldsymbol{\theta}) \leq \mathrm{r}$ or $H_0 : \mathrm{c}(\boldsymbol{\theta}) \geq \mathrm{r}$, where critical values would be based on quantiles of the standard normal distribution. Asymptotically valid confidence regions and confidence bounds based on either the $W$ or $Z$ tests can be constructed via duality with the hypothesis testing procedure.

#### 3.4.4b Generalized Score (Lagrange Multiplier-Type) Tests and Confidence Regions

In the context of EE estimation, there are alternatives to the $W$ statistics that can be used to test hypotheses of the form $\mathrm{H}_0 : \mathbf{c}(\boldsymbol{\theta}) = \mathbf{r}$, when the EEs can be interpreted as defining first-order conditions whose solution solves some E estimation problem. In these cases, the *generalized score statistic*, which is analogous to the score form of the usual Lagrange multiplier statistic, is given by (Qin and Lawless [1994]; Gallant [1987], section 3.5):

$$GS = \mathbf{h}(\mathbf{Y}, \mathbf{x}, \hat{\boldsymbol{\theta}}_{E_r})' \left[ \frac{\partial \mathbf{h}}{\partial \boldsymbol{\theta}} \bigg|_{\hat{\boldsymbol{\theta}}_{E_r}} \right]^{-1} \frac{\partial \mathbf{c}}{\partial \boldsymbol{\theta}} \bigg|_{\hat{\boldsymbol{\theta}}_{E_r}} \hat{\Phi}^{-1} \frac{\partial \mathbf{c}}{\partial \boldsymbol{\theta}'} \bigg|_{\hat{\boldsymbol{\theta}}_{E_r}} \left[ \frac{\partial \mathbf{h}}{\partial \boldsymbol{\theta}} \bigg|_{\hat{\boldsymbol{\theta}}_{E_r}} \right]^{-1} \mathbf{h}(\mathbf{Y}, \mathbf{X}, \hat{\boldsymbol{\theta}}_{E_r})$$

$$\overset{a}{\sim} \textit{Chi-square}\,(j, 0) \textit{ under } H_0, \tag{3.4.23}$$

where $\hat{\Phi} = \frac{\partial \mathbf{c}}{\partial \boldsymbol{\theta}'}|_{\hat{\boldsymbol{\theta}}_{E_r}} [\frac{\partial \mathbf{h}}{\partial \boldsymbol{\theta}}|_{\hat{\boldsymbol{\theta}}_{E_r}}]^{-1} [n^{-1} \sum_{i=1}^{n} \mathbf{h}_*(\mathrm{Y}_i, \mathbf{X}_i, \hat{\boldsymbol{\theta}}_{E_r}) \mathbf{h}_*(\mathrm{Y}_i, \mathbf{X}_i, \hat{\boldsymbol{\theta}}_{E_r})']$ $[\frac{\partial \mathbf{h}}{\partial \boldsymbol{\theta}}|_{\hat{\boldsymbol{\theta}}_{E_r}}]^{-1} \frac{\partial \mathbf{c}}{\partial \boldsymbol{\theta}}|_{\hat{\boldsymbol{\theta}}_{E_r}}$. Note that $\hat{\boldsymbol{\Theta}}_{E_r}$ refers to the *restricted* E estimator defined by constrained optimization under the restriction $\mathrm{H}_0 : \mathbf{c}(\boldsymbol{\theta}) = \mathbf{r}$, where the extremum objective function $\mathrm{m}(\mathbf{y}, \mathbf{X}, \boldsymbol{\theta})$ is implied by the partial differential equations $\mathbf{h}(\mathbf{y}, \mathbf{X}, \boldsymbol{\theta}) = \frac{\partial m(\mathbf{y}, \mathbf{X}, \boldsymbol{\theta})}{\partial \boldsymbol{\theta}}$. Again, the validity of the estimator $\hat{\Phi}$ in (3.4.23) assumes that the sample observations are independent, and the EFs can be defined in terms of a sum of $n$ contributions as $\mathbf{h}(\mathbf{Y}, \mathbf{X}, \boldsymbol{\theta}) = n^{-1} \sum_{i=1}^{n} \mathbf{h}_*(\mathrm{Y}_i, \mathbf{X}_i, \boldsymbol{\theta})$. Tests are conducted in the usual way based on the critical regions constructed from the central Chi-square distribution with degrees of freedom, *j*, which equals the number of functionally independent restrictions on $\boldsymbol{\theta}$ being tested. Confidence regions follow from duality with the hypothesis test.

We note that the generalized score test can be applied even in cases where an extremum objective function cannot be recovered from the partial differential equations $\mathbf{h}(\mathbf{y}, \mathbf{X}, \boldsymbol{\theta}) = \frac{\partial m(\mathbf{y}, \mathbf{X}, \boldsymbol{\theta})}{\partial \boldsymbol{\theta}}$. Details of this generalization can be found in Heyde and Morton (1993) and Heyde (1997, section 7.2 and chapter 9).

#### 3.4.4.c Pseudo-Likelihood Ratio Tests and Confidence Regions

Assuming that there exists a scalar function $\mathrm{m}(\mathbf{Y}, \mathbf{X}, \boldsymbol{\theta})$ such that $\Psi^{-1/2} \mathbf{h}(\mathbf{Y}, \mathbf{X}, \boldsymbol{\theta}) = \Psi^{-1/2} \frac{\partial m(\mathbf{Y}, \mathbf{X}, \boldsymbol{\theta})}{\partial \boldsymbol{\theta}} \xrightarrow{d} N(\mathbf{0}, \mathbf{I})$, where $\Psi = \mathit{Cov}(\mathbf{h}(\mathbf{Y}, \mathbf{x}, \boldsymbol{\theta}_0)) = E[\mathbf{h}(\mathbf{Y}, \mathbf{X}, \boldsymbol{\theta}_0) \mathbf{h}(\mathbf{Y}, \mathbf{X}, \boldsymbol{\theta}_0)']$ and $m(\mathbf{Y}, \mathbf{X}, \boldsymbol{\theta})$ is maximized at $\hat{\boldsymbol{\Theta}}_{\mathrm{EE}}$, then there exists an analog to the pseudo-likelihood ratio statistic of the form

$$PLR = 2(m(\mathbf{Y}, \mathbf{X}, \hat{\boldsymbol{\Theta}}_{EE}) - m(\mathbf{Y}, \mathbf{X}, \hat{\boldsymbol{\Theta}}_{EEr}))$$

$$\overset{a}{\sim} \textit{Chi-square}\,(j, 0) \textit{ under } H_0, \tag{3.4.24}$$

where again $\hat{\boldsymbol{\Theta}}_{\mathrm{E_r}}$ denotes the *restricted* E estimator calculated under the restriction $H_0 : \mathbf{c}(\boldsymbol{\theta}) = \mathbf{r}$. That is, in this context, the EE estimator is effectively equivalent to an E estimator that maximizes the estimation objective function $m(\mathbf{Y}, \mathbf{X}, \boldsymbol{\theta})$. Tests and confidence regions are again conducted in the usual way based on the asymptotic central Chi-square distribution. Additional details relating to the derivation and use of these and other test statistics for testing functional restrictions on the parameter vector, including discussion of the noncentral Chi-square distributions of these statistics under $H_a$, can be found in Heyde (1997, pp. 142–145) and Gallant (1987, section 3.5).

## 3.5 E Estimation with Instrumental Variables

In Section 2.5 of Chapter 2, we considered E estimation and inference relative to parametric and semiparametric linear models. In this section, we note in the context of the current chapter that estimates that use instruments in the context of linear structural models characterized by endogenous explanatory variables may be formulated as E estimators.

To illustrate the E estimator variants, consider a single structural equation that is contained within a system of structural equations and the linear statistical model $\mathbf{Y} = \mathbf{X}\boldsymbol{\beta} + \boldsymbol{\varepsilon}$. We observe a vector of sample outcomes $\mathbf{y} = (y_1, y_2, \cdots, y_n)'$ associated with this linear model, where $\mathbf{X}$ is a $(n \times k)$ matrix of stochastic explanatory variables, $\boldsymbol{\varepsilon}$ is an unobservable random noise vector with mean vector $\mathbf{0}$ and covariance matrix $\sigma^2\mathbf{I}_n$, and $\boldsymbol{\beta}$ is a $(k \times 1)$ vector of unknown parameters. If one or more of the regressors is correlated with the equation noise, then $\mathbf{E}\,[n^{-1}\mathbf{X}'\boldsymbol{\varepsilon}] \neq \mathbf{0}$ and the MOM-E estimator defined by

$$\hat{\boldsymbol{\beta}}_{mom} = \arg_{\boldsymbol{\beta}\in\mathbf{B}}[n^{-1}\mathbf{X}'(\mathbf{Y} - \mathbf{X}\boldsymbol{\beta}) = \mathbf{0}] \tag{3.5.1}$$

are biased and inconsistent, with unconditional expectation and probability limit given by $\mathrm{E}[\hat{\boldsymbol{\beta}}] \neq \boldsymbol{\beta}$ and $p\lim[\hat{\boldsymbol{\beta}}] \neq \boldsymbol{\beta}$.

In previous sections of this chapter, given a sampling process characterized by nonorthogonality of $\mathbf{X}$ and $\boldsymbol{\varepsilon}$, to avoid the use of strong distributional assumptions, we introduced additional information in the form of a $(n \times m)$, $m \geq k$, random matrix $\mathbf{Z}$ of instrumental variables whose elements are correlated with $\mathbf{X}$ but uncorrelated with $\boldsymbol{\varepsilon}$. This information is introduced into the statistical model resulting in the sample analog moment condition

$$\mathbf{h}(\mathbf{Y}, \mathbf{X}, \mathrm{Z}; \boldsymbol{\beta}) = n^{-1}[\mathbf{Z}'(\mathbf{Y} - \mathbf{X}\boldsymbol{\beta})] \xrightarrow{p} \mathbf{0} \tag{3.5.2}$$

that results from the orthogonality of instruments and model noise

$$\mathrm{E}[\mathbf{Z}'(\mathbf{Y} - \mathbf{X}\boldsymbol{\beta})] = \mathbf{0}. \tag{3.5.3}$$

If $m = k$, the sample moments (3.5.2) can be solved for the basic instrumental variable (IV)-E estimator

$$\hat{\beta}_{iv} = \arg_{\beta \in B}[n^{-1}\mathbf{Z}'(\mathbf{Y} - \mathbf{X}\beta) = \mathbf{0}]. \qquad (3.5.4)$$

When the usual regularity conditions are fulfilled, this IV estimator is consistent, asymptotically normally distributed, and an OptEF estimator (Godambe 1960; Heyde 1989; Mittelhammer, Judge, and Miller 2000).

When $m > k$, the vector of moment conditions overdetermines the model parameters and other IV-like estimation procedures are available, such as the well-known two-stage LS (2SLS) E estimator

$$\hat{\beta}_{2SLS} = (\mathbf{X}'\mathbf{P}_Z\mathbf{X})^{-1}\mathbf{X}'\mathbf{P}_Z\mathbf{Y}, \qquad (3.5.5)$$

where $\mathbf{P}_z = \mathbf{Z}(\mathbf{Z}'\mathbf{Z})^{-1}\mathbf{Z}'$ is the projection matrix for $\mathbf{Z}$. This estimator is equivalent to the estimator formed by applying the OptEF transformation $n(\mathbf{X}'\mathbf{Z}(\mathbf{Z}'\mathbf{Z})^{-1}\mathbf{Z}'\mathbf{X})^{-1}\mathbf{X}'\mathbf{Z}(\mathbf{Z}'\mathbf{Z})^{-1}$ to the moment conditions in (3.5.3) (Godambe, 1960; Judge et al., 1985; Heyde and Morton, 1998).

The GMM estimator (Hansen 1982) is another estimator that makes use of the information in (3.5.3). The GMM estimators minimize in an extremum context a quadratic form in the sample moment information

$$\begin{aligned}\hat{\beta}(\mathbf{W}) &= \arg\min_{\beta \in B}[(n^{-1}\mathbf{Z}'(\mathbf{Y}-\mathbf{X}\beta))'\mathbf{W}(n^{-1}\mathbf{Z}'(\mathbf{Y}-\mathbf{X}\beta))] \\ &= \arg\min_{\beta \in B}[n^{-2}(\mathbf{Y}-\mathbf{X}\beta)'\mathbf{ZWZ}'(\mathbf{Y}-\mathbf{X}\beta)]. \qquad (3.5.6)\end{aligned}$$

The GMM estimator can be shown to have optimal asymptotic properties if the weighting matrix **W** is appropriately defined. The optimal choice of **W** in the context of moment conditions (3.5.3) leads back to the definition of the 2SLS-OptEF estimator.

## 3.6 Summary and Forward

We have reviewed the use of moment-based information to obtain estimates and perform inference regarding the unknowns in an econometric model when that information is in the form of moment equations sufficient in number to either just-determine or overdetermine the unknowns in the model. In the former case, the (ordinary) method of moments involves solving a set of $k$ empirical moment equations for $k$ unknowns, the result being the MOM estimator for the unknowns. In the latter case, there are more empirical moment equations than unknowns, with the solution space for the unknowns then being the null set. In this case, a GMM solution is obtained by choosing values of the unknowns that solve the empirical moment equations as closely as possible, with closeness represented by a weighted Euclidean distance measure that indicates how close the moment equations are to being solved.

We also reviewed the EE approach to estimating the unknowns in an econometric model, which was seen to be a very general, virtually all-encompassing representation of estimators for the unknowns in a model. The approach subsumes the MOM and GMM methods as well as the ML and E estimation methods when first-order conditions are used to characterize the objective-optimizing values of the unknowns or, at least, when the optimal solution can be characterized functionally in terms of data and unknowns.

An important, and we believe pervasive, estimation context that arises in practice was not discussed in this chapter. Namely, the case in which there is insufficient information, in the way of moments, specification of the probability distribution underlying an ML objective, or EEs, to allow an estimate of the unknowns to be calculated. This is the case in which the unknowns are underdetermined by the sample information that is actually known and available to estimate them. This leads us to the very important general concept of *stochastic inverse problems* and solutions to them, which we introduce in the next chapter and that are a central focus for much of the rest of this volume.

## 3.7 Selected References

Bates, C. and H. White (1985), "A Unified Theory of Consistent Estimation for Parametric Models," *Econometric Theory*, 1, pp. 151–178.

Bhapkar, V. P. (1997), "Estimating Functions, Parital Sufficiency and Q-Sufficiency in the Presence of Nuisance Parameters," in *Selected Proceedings of the Symposium on Estimation Functions*, I. V. Basawa, V. P. Bodambe, and R. L. Taylor (Eds.), 31, Institute of Mathematical Statistics Lecture Notes–Monograph Series, Hayward, CA, pp. 83–104.

Breslow, N. (1990), "Tests of Hypothesis in Overdispersed Poisson Regression and Other Quasi-Likelihood Models," *Journal of the American Statistical Association*, 88, pp. 656–671.

Desmond, A. F. (1997), "Prediction Functions and Geostatistics," in *Selected Proceedings of the Symposium on Estimation Functions*, I. V. Basawa, V. P. Bodambe, and R. L. Taylor (Eds.), 31, Institute of Mathematical Statistics Lecture Notes–Monograph Series, Hayward, CA, pp. 353–368.

Engle, R. F., D. F. Hendry, and J.-F. Richard (1983), "Exogeneity," *Econometrica*, 21, pp. 277–304.

Fisher, R. A. (1935). "The Logic of Inductive Inference," *Journal of the Royal Statistical Society*, 98, 39–54.

Gallant, R. (1987), *Nonlinear Statistical Models*, New York: John Wiley and Sons.

Gallant, R. and H. White (1988), *A Unified Theory of Estimation and Inference for Nonlinear Dynamic Models*, Oxford, UK: Basil Blackwell.

Godambe, V. P. (1960), "An Optimum Property of Regular Maximum Likelihood Estimation," *Annals of Mathematics and Statistics*, 31, pp. 1208–1212.

Godambe, V. P. and C. C. Heyde (1987), "Quasi-Likelihood and Optimal Estimators," *International Statistical Review*, 55, pp. 231–244.

Godambe, V. P. (1991), "Orthogonality of Estimating Functions and Nuisance Parameters," *Biometrika*, 78, pp. 143–151.

Godambe, V. P. and B. K. Kale (1991), "Estimating Functions: An Overview," in V. P. Godambe (Ed.), *Estimating Functions*, Oxford, UK: Oxford University Press, pp. 3–20.

Godambe, V. P. (1997), "Estimating Functions: A Synthesis of Least Squares and Maximum Likelihood Methods," in *Selected Proceedings of the Symposium on Estimation Functions*, edited by I. V. Basawa, V. P. Godambe, and R. L. Taylor. Volume 32, Institute of Mathematical Statistics Lecture Notes–Monograph Series, Hayward, CA, pp. 5–16.

Hansen, L. (1982), "Large Sample Properties of Generalized Method of Moments Estimators," *Econometrica*, 50, pp. 1029–1054.

Heyde, C. C. (1997), "Avoiding the Likelihood," in *Selected Proceedings of the Symposium on Estimation Functions*, edited by I. V. Basawa, V. P. Godambe, and R. L. Taylor. Volume 32, Institute of Mathematical Statistics Lecture Notes–Monograph Series, Hayward, CA, pp. 35–42.

Heyde, C. C. (1994), "Quasi-Likelihood Approach to REML Estimating Equations," *Statistics and Probability Letters*, 21, pp. 381–384.

Heyde, C. C. (1989), "Quasi-Likelihood and Optimality for Estimating Functions: Some Current Unifying Themes," *Bulletin of the International Statistical Institute*, 53, Book 1, pp. 19–29.

Heyde, C. C. and R. Morton (1993), "On Constrained Quasi-Likelihood Estimation," *Biometrika*, 80, pp. 755–761.

Judge, G. G., W. E. Griffiths, R. Carter Hill, H. Lütkepohl, and T. C. Lee (1985), *The Theory and Practice of Econometrics*, 2nd Edition, New York: John Wiley and Sons.

Kale, B. K. (1962), "An Extension of Cramer-Rao Inequality for Statistical Estimation Functions," *Skandinavisk Aktuarietidsk Rift*, 45, pp. 60–89.

Liang, K. Y. and J. Hanfelt (1994), "On the Use of Quasi-Likelihood Methods in Teratological Experiments," *Biometrics*, 50, pp. 872–880.

Liang, K. Y. and S. L. Zeger (1995), "Inference Based on Estimating Functions in the Presence of Nuisance Parameters (with Discussion)," *Statistical Science*, 19, 158–199.

McCullagh, P. and J. A. Nelder (1989), *Generalized Linear Models, 2nd edition*, London: Chapman and Hall.

Mittelhammer, Ron C. (1996), *Mathematical Statistics for Economics and Business*, New York: Springer-Verlag.

Mittelhammer, R., G. Judge, and D. Miller (2000), *Econometric Foundations*. New York: Cambridge University Press.

Newey, W. K. and D. McFadden (1994), "Large Sample Estimation and Hypothesis Testing," in *Handbook of Econometrics*, edited by Robert F. Engle and Daniel L. McFadden, Volume 4, pp. 2111–2224.

Qin, J. and J. Lawless (1994), "Empirical Likelihood and General Estimating Equations," *The Annals of Statistics,* 22, pp. 300–325.
Vinod, H. (1997), "Using Godambe-Durbin Estimating Functions in Econometrics," in *Selected Proceedings of the Symposium on Estimating Equations,* Institute of Mathematical Statistics, pp. 215–238.
White, H. (1984), *Asymptotic Theory for Econometricians,* Orlando, FL: Academic Press.
White, H. (1994), *Estimation, Inference, and Specification Analysis,* New York: Cambridge University Press.

# PART II

# FORMULATION AND SOLUTION OF STOCHASTIC INVERSE PROBLEMS

In Part I, we reviewed the standard econometric enterprise where

i) the origin of observed data is characterized within a sufficiently constrained stochastic model formulation,
ii) assumptions are used to define the underlying data sampling process (DSP), and
iii) the model contains a sufficiently small number of unknowns so that information about them can be recovered-estimated by long-standing traditional econometric methods.

In this case, the econometric information recovery problem takes on the form of a well-posed just-determined or overdetermined problem where a solution exists, is unique, and there are a sufficient number of data observations to estimate the unknowns.

In Part II, we leave this convenient econometric-problem context built on assumptions and extremum estimation concepts and focus on the use of indirect noisy observations-data to recover information on unobserved, unobservable, and underdetermined unknown econometric model components. In this context, estimation and inference involves the solution of a stochastic inverse problem such as $(\mathbf{Y}, \mathbf{X}) \Rightarrow (\boldsymbol{\beta}, \sigma^2, \boldsymbol{\varepsilon})$. Maximum empirical likelihood and maximum empirical exponential likelihood estimators are introduced and we consider an econometric problem context in which

i) the conceptual model may be incomplete or incorrectly specified;
ii) the data underlying the econometric analysis are limited, partial, or incomplete;
iii) the conceptual model contains parameters or other components that are unknown and unobserved and are not subject to direct observation or measurement;

iv) the objective is the recovery of information on the unknown parameters or components;
v) the analyst uses indirect noisy measurements based on observable data and then solves the resulting stochastic inverse problem by mapping the indirect observations into information on the unobserved and unobservable unknowns;
vi) the models may be ill-posed or, in the context of traditional procedures, may be underdetermined and the solution not amenable to being written in closed form;
vii) the procedures used for estimation may not be optimal, and their properties may not even be precisely discernible;
viii) inferences are subject to errors and uncertainty; and
ix) finite sample results are seldom available.

Given this econometric-problem context, in Part II, we consider both solutions and new ways of thinking about the econometric-inverse problem described in items *i*) through *ix*).

FOUR

# A Stochastic-Empirical Likelihood Inverse Problem

## Formulation and Estimation

### 4.1 Introduction

A challenge in econometric analyses is that components of the econometric model cannot be observed directly. As a result, analysts must use indirect noisy observable data to recover information on these unobserved and unobservable model components. In many ways, this challenge is associated with a concept in systems and information theory called the *stochastic inverse problem*, which is the problem of recovering information about unknown and uncontrolled components of a model from indirect noisy observations on these components. This means the adjective *indirect* refers to the fact that although the observed data are considered to be directly influenced by the values of model components, the observations are not themselves the direct values of these components but rather only indirectly reflect the influence of the components. The relationship characterizing the effect of unobservable components on the observed data must be somehow inverted to recover information concerning the unobservable model components from the data observations. Thus, the analyst must use *indirect noisy observations* to recover information on the unobserved vector of parameters $\boldsymbol{\theta}$ and unobservable random components $\boldsymbol{\varepsilon}$ because the stochastic inverse problem generally involves both a systematic and a noise component. Consequently, the problem of recovering information about unknowns and unobservables $(\boldsymbol{\theta}, \boldsymbol{\varepsilon})$ from sample data observations $(\mathbf{y}, \mathbf{x})$, within the context of an econometric model $\mathbf{Y} = \boldsymbol{\eta}(\mathbf{X}, \boldsymbol{\varepsilon}, \boldsymbol{\theta})$, is referred to as an *inverse problem with noise* or as a *stochastic inverse problem*. A basis for the solution to this stochastic inverse problem is of the general form $(\mathbf{y}, \mathbf{x}) \Rightarrow (\boldsymbol{\theta}, \boldsymbol{\varepsilon})$, and the nature of the mapping implied by "$\Rightarrow$" is the topic that we pursue in this and subsequent chapters of this book. A stochastic inverse problem

(SIP) appears when one of the components, usually the noise component, is modeled as being stochastic.

The concept of a stochastic inverse problem is pervasive throughout economics-econometrics. Indeed, the basic problem of determining a density estimator is a stochastic inverse problem of probability theory. Another case in point is the current debate about experimental economics and the problem of identifying casual effects (Angrist and Pischke, 2010). *This causal effects debate involves the problem of determining the unknown and unobservable causes based on indirect noisy observations on economic effects.* In other words, the results or consequences (effects) are observed but not the underlying causes. Loosely speaking, this defines a stochastic inverse problem where the solution means the recovery of unobservable objects that contribute to defining causes from indirect noisy observations on the effects.

In many cases, the models that economists specify for analysis purposes contain unknown parameters that are unobserved and not accessible to direct measurement. This information-recovery situation is often formalized as follows: We observe outcomes of an economic variable $\mathcal{Y}$ that is thought to be influenced by outcomes of other variables $\mathcal{X}$, so the observed sample data are generated by outcomes of $[\mathcal{Y}, \mathcal{X}]$. The relationship between the elements of $[\mathcal{Y}, \mathcal{X}]$ is defined further by the specification of a stochastic model of the data sampling process (DSP). In the case of the classical linear model, this specification is given by

$$\mathcal{Y} = \mathcal{X}'\boldsymbol{\beta} + \varepsilon \tag{4.1.1}$$

along with the moment assumptions $E(\mathcal{Y}|\mathcal{X}) = \mathcal{X}'\boldsymbol{\beta}$. The parameter vector $\boldsymbol{\beta}$ is one component of $\boldsymbol{\theta}$, which also includes parameters relating to the variances and covariances of the random noise components $\varepsilon_i$, $i = 1, \ldots, n$ associated with multiple outcomes of $[\mathcal{Y}, \mathcal{X}]$. The relationship between $\mathcal{Y}$ and $\mathcal{X}$ depicted in (4.1.1) introduces the unknown and unobservable parameter $\boldsymbol{\beta}$, along with the unknown and observable noise variable $\varepsilon$, which is consistent with Chapter 2's $E(\varepsilon|\mathbf{X}) = 0$.

Because we cannot measure $\boldsymbol{\beta}$ or $\varepsilon$ directly in (4.1.1), to recover information on them we must use indirect noisy measurements on the observables – that is, on the outcomes of $[\mathcal{Y}, \mathcal{X}]$. In this context, consider the following linear additive stochastic inverse problem expressed in terms of the observed data $(\mathbf{y}, \mathbf{x})$, as

$$\mathbf{y} = \mathbf{x}\boldsymbol{\beta} + \mathbf{e}, \tag{4.1.2}$$

where $\mathbf{y} = (y_1, y_2, \ldots, y_n)'$ is an $n$-dimensional vector of observations (data) on $\mathcal{Y}$, $\boldsymbol{\beta}$ is an unobservable $k$ dimensional vector of unknowns, $\mathbf{x}$ is a known $(n \times k)$ linear operator based on outcomes of $\mathcal{X}$, and $\mathbf{e}$ is an $n$-dimensional outcome of the noise vector $\boldsymbol{\varepsilon} = [\varepsilon_1, \ldots, \varepsilon_n]'$ with a finite covariance matrix $\sigma^2\mathbf{I}_n$. Thus, we observe both $\mathbf{x}$ and $\mathbf{y}$ and wish to determine the unknown and unobservable parameter vector $\boldsymbol{\theta} = [\boldsymbol{\beta}, \sigma^2]$ and $\varepsilon$. This results in a stochastic inverse problem because we must recover $[\boldsymbol{\beta}, \sigma^2]$ and $\boldsymbol{\varepsilon}$ based only on indirect partial, sparse, or incomplete noisy information represented by $(\mathbf{y}, \mathbf{x})$.

One way to proceed is to convert (4.1.1)–(4.1.2) into a moment based on estimating equations (EEs) formulation where, as discussed in Chapter 3, the joint distribution of the underlying data is unspecified apart from a finite set of moment conditions or EEs. In this constraint-based context, there is insufficient information to recover $\boldsymbol{\beta}$ and $\boldsymbol{\varepsilon}$ using traditional procedures of mathematical inversion. To indicate the importance of stochastic inverse problems, in this chapter, we use the general linear model framework as a basis for identifying a data-based empirical likelihood (EL) function when only a finite set of indirect noisy estimating functions is used as the information base.

## 4.2 A Stochastic Linear Inverse Problem

Consider a DSP that results in observations on an $(n \times 1)$ vector $\mathbf{y} = [y_1, y_2, \ldots, y_n]' \in R^n$ and associated observations on an $n \times k$ matrix $\mathbf{x} \in R^{n \times k}$ whose elements are row-wise associated with the respective elements in $\mathbf{y}$. Clearly, without any further assumptions or constraints regarding the process by which such data came about, there are no explicit unknowns to speak of other than the entire DSP itself. Effectively, all that can be said at this point in the modeling process is that the numbers arose "somehow."

We now consider some basic assumptions about the DSP that can be made to proceed with a statistical analysis of the data. The assumptions define the basic linear model and are far from the only assumptions that can be made. However, they produce a well-defined stochastic inverse problem (SIP) to which elementary estimation and inference techniques can be applied to generate information about a finite set of unknowns. Of course, whether or not the assumptions are actually true is a matter of substantial concern in empirical practice, and various aspects of this issue will be dealt with in this and in the chapters to follow.

We begin by making the fundamental assumption that the observed data $\mathbf{y}$ and $\mathbf{x}$ arose as $n$ outcomes of random variables $\mathcal{Y}$ and $\mathcal{X}$ having some statistical distribution, so that the data relate to an SIP formulation. Additional structure on the DSP is formalized by stating that the outcomes in $\mathbf{Y}$ are related to the respective rows of $\mathbf{X}$ through the relationship

$$\mathbf{Y} = \mathbf{X}\boldsymbol{\beta} + \boldsymbol{\varepsilon}, \tag{4.2.1}$$

where outcomes of $\mathbf{Y}$ produce a $\mathbf{y}$-vector of noisy observations around values of $\mathbf{x}\boldsymbol{\beta}$ with $\mathbf{x}$ being an outcome of $\mathbf{X}$, $\boldsymbol{\beta}$ is a $k$-dimensional fixed vector of unknown and unobservable parameters representing coefficients multiplying the "explanatory variables" $\mathbf{X}$, and $\boldsymbol{\varepsilon}$ is a $(n \times 1)$ noise vector consisting of unobserved and unobservable random variables.

In the absence of any other assumptions, (4.2.1) frames an SIP in which the outcomes of the observable random variables $\mathbf{Y}$ and $\mathbf{X}$ are considered *indirect noisy observations* on the unknown and unobservable $\boldsymbol{\beta}$ and $\boldsymbol{\varepsilon}$. By indirect noisy observations, we mean that the observed values $\mathbf{y}$ and $\mathbf{x}$ are not direct observations on the values of $\boldsymbol{\beta}$ and $\boldsymbol{\varepsilon}$. Rather, $\mathbf{y}$ and $\mathbf{x}$ *indirectly* convey information about $\boldsymbol{\beta}$ and $\boldsymbol{\varepsilon}$ through the relation $\mathbf{e} = \mathbf{y} - \mathbf{x}\boldsymbol{\beta}$ that is implied by (4.2.1), where $\mathbf{e}$ denotes an outcome of $\boldsymbol{\varepsilon}$. The hope is to use these indirect noisy observations in some manner to solve the inverse problem and recover information about $\boldsymbol{\beta}$ and $\boldsymbol{\varepsilon}$. At this point in the definition of the inverse problem, the unknowns of the DSP that are of fundamental interest are the $k$ elements of the parameter vector $\boldsymbol{\beta}$ (which, if known, would then define the value of $\mathbf{e}$) and the probability distribution $F$ of the noise vector $\boldsymbol{\varepsilon}$.

The linear relationship $\mathbf{y} = \mathbf{x}\boldsymbol{\beta} + \mathbf{e}$ cannot be solved for unique values of the unknown $\boldsymbol{\beta}$ and $\mathbf{e}$ in terms of the observables $\mathbf{y}$ and $\mathbf{x}$ because the relationship is a system of $n$ equations in $(n + k)$ unknowns. Because neither $\boldsymbol{\beta}$ nor $\mathbf{e}$ is observable, there is no effective way of solving the equation system, $\mathbf{y} = \mathbf{x}\boldsymbol{\beta} + \mathbf{e}$, for one of $\boldsymbol{\beta}$ or $\mathbf{e}$ in terms of values of the other. There is also an *infinite* number of possibilities for the functional specification of $F$. In effect, the inverse problem of solving for $(\boldsymbol{\beta}, \mathbf{e})$ and $F$ in terms of $(\mathbf{y}, \mathbf{x})$ is underdetermined and ill-posed.

For the SIP to possess only a finite number of unknowns of interest, one needs to go beyond simply specifying the linear relationship (4.2.1) and be more specific regarding sampling characteristics of the random components of the model. We proceed by constraining the first- and second-order conditional moments of the elements in $\boldsymbol{\varepsilon}$, which is tantamount to constraining the first- and second-order conditional moments of $\mathbf{Y}$, given the linear functional relationship assumed in (4.2.1). The first-order moment assumptions that we make are $E(\boldsymbol{\varepsilon}|\mathbf{x}) = \mathbf{0}$, which implies and is implied by $E(\mathbf{Y}|\mathbf{x}) = \mathbf{x}\boldsymbol{\beta}$. If the outcomes of the $n$ elements in $\boldsymbol{\varepsilon}$ are independent and identically distributed (*iid*), it follows immediately that the value of all of the covariances between pairs of elements in $\boldsymbol{\varepsilon}$ are zero. Assuming further that the elements of $\boldsymbol{\varepsilon}$ all share the same variance value, $\sigma^2$, leads to the conclusion that the covariance matrix of the noise vector is given by $Cov(\boldsymbol{\varepsilon}|\mathbf{x}) = \sigma^2\mathbf{I}_n$. This assumption implies and is implied by $Cov(\mathbf{Y}|\mathbf{x}) = \sigma^2\mathbf{I}_n$, given the linear relationship $\mathbf{Y} = \mathbf{x}\boldsymbol{\beta} + \boldsymbol{\varepsilon}$. A final implication of the preceding assumptions is that the elements of $\mathbf{Y}$ are independent random variables, although they will generally not be identically distributed because the mean vector $E(\mathbf{Y}|\mathbf{x}) = \mathbf{x}\boldsymbol{\beta}$ will generally not be a vector of identical values. A summary of the DSP to this point is then given by

$$\mathcal{D} = \{(\mathbf{Y}, \boldsymbol{\varepsilon}), \mathbf{x}, \mathbf{Y} = \mathbf{x}\boldsymbol{\beta} + \boldsymbol{\varepsilon}, \{\mathrm{E}(\boldsymbol{\varepsilon}|\mathbf{x}) = \mathbf{0}_n, \\ Cov(\boldsymbol{\varepsilon}|\mathbf{x}) = \sigma^2\mathbf{I}_n, (\varepsilon_i|x_{i\cdot})'s \sim iid\}\}. \tag{4.2.2}$$

If the parametric family of probability distributions for $\boldsymbol{\varepsilon}$ is left unspecified, as in (4.2.2), then any probability distribution F that does not violate the stated specific *iid* and moment conditions can be considered a potential probability distribution for $\boldsymbol{\varepsilon}$. Any corresponding distribution for $\mathbf{Y}$, given by the distribution of $\mathbf{X}\boldsymbol{\beta} + \boldsymbol{\varepsilon}$, is then admissible as the probability distribution of $\mathbf{Y}$. In this eventuality, the model would be *semiparametric* in nature.

### 4.2.1 Addressing the Indeterminacy of Unknowns

The indeterminacy of $\boldsymbol{\beta}$ in the linear model (4.2.1), caused by the ill-posed nature of the SIP, is an instance of parameter indeterminacies that affect essentially all nontrivial econometric models used in practice. By far, the most widely adopted method for generating a unique SIP solution in such cases, and thus obtaining a unique value of model parameters, is to creatively introduce a metric or estimation objective function representing some estimation criteria that is assumed to be appropriate for the SIP at hand. Then, the parameter value that optimizes the metric or objective function value is chosen as the solution to the problem. As discussed in Chapters 2 and 3, estimators that are defined by optimizing an estimation metric or estimation objective function are called *extremum estimators* because they are characterized by the "extreme" value of the chosen metric or objective function. The most popular metrics for the case of the linear model have been the maximum likelihood (ML) approach in the case of parametric models, and the minimum sum of squared errors estimation metric leading to the least squares principle in semiparametric models. In the next section, we provide a *nonparametric* ML approach to this information-recovery problem.

## 4.3 Nonparametric ML Solutions to Inverse Problems

In this section, we focus on a statistical information-recovery problem involving the linear model $\mathbf{Y} = \mathbf{X}\boldsymbol{\beta} + \boldsymbol{\varepsilon}$, where the inverse problem is denoted in general terms by

$$(\mathbf{Y}, \mathbf{X}) \Rightarrow (\boldsymbol{\beta}, \sigma^2, \boldsymbol{\varepsilon}) \tag{4.3.1}$$

with moments $\mathrm{E}(\boldsymbol{\varepsilon}|\mathbf{X}) = \mathbf{0}_n$, and $Cov(\boldsymbol{\varepsilon}|\mathbf{X}) = \sigma^2\mathbf{I}_n$, where

i) the inverse problem is statistical in nature,
ii) sample information exists in the form of *indirect noisy observations*, and
iii) there is not enough information to specify the form of the underlying likelihood function.

*The eventual objective is a data-based nonparametric ML approach to estimation and inference. We call the approach nonparametric because no parametric functional form for the likelihood function is specified as part of the information known or assumed about the SIP.* We begin with a general introduction to the concept of nonparametric ML. We then introduce the method of EL, which provides a means of estimating a parametric likelihood from sample data in the absence of parametric functional specifications for the likelihood function. A comparison between EL and EE methods for estimating unknown parameters is provided. We then apply the EL principle to a simple problem of estimating the mean of a population. Finally, we use the EL concept to obtain a solution to the inverse problem (4.3.1) for the linear model.

### 4.3.1 Nonparametric ML

To motivate the search for a nonparametric ML estimate of a population distribution, we begin with the case of a simple *iid* random sample $\mathbf{Y} = (\mathrm{Y}_1, \mathrm{Y}_2, \ldots, \mathrm{Y}_n)'$ from some common population PDF $f(y; \boldsymbol{\theta})$, where $\boldsymbol{\theta} \in \Omega$ and the $\mathrm{Y}_i$'s are random scalars. Under the current assumptions, the true likelihood function for the parameter vector $\boldsymbol{\theta}$ can be stated as $L(\boldsymbol{\theta}; \mathbf{y}) \equiv \prod_{i=1}^{n} f(y_i; \boldsymbol{\theta})$. At this point, we have no parametric functional form specified for $f(y; \boldsymbol{\theta})$ in our probability model. Consider the SIP of using a random sample outcome $\mathbf{y} = (y_1, y_2, \ldots, y_n)$ to recover an estimate of the probability density function (PDF) of $\mathbf{Y}$. In this general *nonparametric* problem setting, we can define a nonparametric likelihood function whose arguments are not parameters but entire probability density or mass functions, $f(\cdot)$, as

$$L(f;\mathbf{y}) = \prod_{i=1}^{n} f(y_i). \tag{4.3.2}$$

Given a candidate for the *function* $f(y)$ in (4.3.2), the nonparametric likelihood function $L(f;\mathbf{y})$ indicates the likelihood that the candidate $f(\cdot)$ is the true population distribution underlying the random sample outcome, $\mathbf{y}$. The nonparametric ML (NPML) estimate of $f(y)$ is defined by

$$\hat{f}(y) = \text{argmax}_f\,[L(f;\mathbf{y})] = \text{argmax}_f \left[\prod_{i=1}^{n} f(y_i)\right]. \tag{4.3.3}$$

This is mathematically different than extremum problems that we examined previously because we are asking for the choice of *function*, $f$, and *not* the choice of a parameter vector, $\boldsymbol{\beta}$, which maximizes the likelihood function (4.3.2). *The feasible space for this maximization problem consists of all possible functions that satisfy the properties of probability density or mass functions.*

We can transform the maximization problem in (4.3.3) into a simpler parametric form by first observing that it is only the unknown values $p_i = f(y_i), i = 1, \ldots, n$ that matter in solving the ML problem in (4.3.3). We can then define an *empirical* probability mass function of the multinomial type that represents discrete probability masses assigned to each of the finite number of observed sample outcomes. In this context, all of the probability weights must be positive as $p_i > 0\ \forall\ i$ or the value of the joint likelihood for the observed sample is $\prod_{i=1}^{n} f(y_i) = 0$, which is a minimum as opposed to a maximum value of $L(f;\mathbf{y})$. Thus, the preceding ML problem, defined in (4.3.2)–(4.3.3), can be represented as a parametric ML problem of finding the optimal choice of $p_i$'s in a multinomial-type likelihood function in which each "type" of outcome occurs only once. This leads to the solution

$$(\hat{p}_1, \ldots, \hat{p}_n) = \arg\max_{\mathbf{p}} \left[\prod_{i=1}^{n} p_i\right] = \arg\max_{\mathbf{p}} \left[n^{-1}\sum_{i=1}^{n} \ln(p_i)\right], \tag{4.3.4}$$

subject to $\hat{p}_i > 0,\ \forall i$.

Transforming the problem into the parametric form (4.3.4) makes it apparent that the objective function of the maximization problem is unbounded because the $p_i$'s are unrestricted in value. Thus, (4.3.3) or

(4.3.4) has no solution unless a normalization condition, $\sum_{i=1}^{n} f(y_i) = \sum_{i=1}^{n} p_i = 1$, is imposed on the $p_i$'s.

By imposing the normalization condition on the $p_i$'s, the solution to the problem of finding the NPML estimate of $f(y)$ can then be defined in terms of the choice of $p_i$'s that maximize $n^{-1}\sum_{i=1}^{n}\ln(p_i)$, subject to the constraint $\sum_{i=1}^{n} p_i = 1$. The Lagrange function associated with this constrained optimization problem is given by

$$\ln(L(\mathbf{p},\eta)) \equiv n^{-1}\sum_{i=1}^{n}\ln(p_i) - \eta\left(\sum_{i=1}^{n} p_i - 1\right), \tag{4.3.5}$$

where the optimal $p_i$'s are given by $\hat{p}_i = n^{-1}\ \forall\ i$ and the optimal value of the Lagrange multiplier is $\hat{\eta} = 1$. Setting $\hat{p}_i = n^{-1}\ \forall\ y_i$ implies that the NPML estimate of the population probability distribution is

$$\hat{f}(y) = n^{-1}\sum_{i=1}^{n} I_{\{y_i\}}(y), \tag{4.3.6}$$

where $I_{\{y_i\}}(y) = 1$, if $y = y_i$, and $I_{\{y_i\}}(y) = 0$ otherwise; that is, $\hat{f}(y)$ equals the number of $y_i$'s equal to $y$, divided by $n$.

The NPML estimate of the *cumulative* probability distribution function associated with the PDF estimate (4.3.6) is given by

$$\hat{\mathrm{F}}(y) = n^{-1}\sum_{i=1}^{n} I_{(-\infty,y_i]}(y), \tag{4.3.7}$$

where $I_{(-\infty,y_i]}(y) = 1$, if $y \le y_i$, and $= 0$ otherwise. This means $\hat{\mathrm{F}}(y)$ is equal to the proportion of the sample outcomes whose values are $\le y$. This is recognized as the classical *empirical distribution function* estimate of the population cumulative distribution function.

### 4.3.2 Empirical Likelihood (EL) Function for $\boldsymbol{\theta}$

Whereas the NPML estimation approach leads to a useful estimate of the population cumulative distribution function $\mathrm{F}(y)$, we clearly have no basis at this point for defining either a likelihood function or an estimator for $\boldsymbol{\theta}$. It is perhaps obvious that because the likelihood (4.3.2) is devoid of parameters, it cannot be used to distinguish likely from unlikely values of a parameter vector $\boldsymbol{\theta}$. To do so, we must introduce some linkage between the data, $(y_1, y_2, \ldots, y_n)$; the population distribution $\mathrm{F}(y)$; and the parameter vector of interest, $\boldsymbol{\theta}$. *This linkage is accomplished through the use of unbiased estimating functions, to define estimating equation constraints on the NPML problem.* In effect, these constraints apply functional structure involving parameters to the data that then allow the extraction of additional informational content when maximizing the nonparametric likelihood. In particular, expectations of functions of the population random variable $Y \sim F(y)$ and $\theta$ that equal zero *iff* $\theta$ is the true value of the parameter (i.e., $E[\mathbf{h}(Y, \theta)] = \mathbf{0}$) is the basic form in which estimating function information is used. As defined in Chapter 3, the vector function $\mathbf{h}(Y, \theta)$ can be interpreted as an unbiased *estimating function.* The basic rationale for utilizing such constraints is as follows. For arbitrary choices of the parameter vector value $\theta$, the expected value of an estimating function will be some function of the chosen $\theta$, say $\mathbf{q}(\theta) = E[\mathbf{h}(Y, \theta)]$. Because the estimating function is unbiased, its expectation will, by definition, equal zero when $\theta$ equals the true value of the parameter. By setting the expected value of the estimating function to zero, one is then stating a valid functional constraint, $\mathbf{q}(\theta) = E[\mathbf{h}(Y, \theta)] = \mathbf{0}$, that can be used to help identify the true parameter vector if the estimating function is truly unbiased. In fact, if the number of functionally independent estimating functions in the vector $\mathbf{h}(Y, \theta)$ equals the number of parameters in the parameter vector $\theta$, $\mathbf{q}(\theta) = E[\mathbf{h}(Y, \theta)] = \mathbf{0}$ can be solved for the true value of $\theta$.

Although we have succeeded in establishing a method that conceptually links the parameters of interest, $\theta$, to the underlying population distribution, two fundamental and related problems are still unresolved. First, the constraints, $\mathbf{q}(\theta) = E[\mathbf{h}(Y, \theta)] = \mathbf{0}$, derived from the unbiased estimating functions, make no reference to the empirical probability weights, $\mathbf{p}$, and so do not represent any effective information or constraints on the choice of $\mathbf{p}$ in the NPML estimation problem. Furthermore, the expectations of the estimating functions cannot be calculated because $F(y)$ is unknown. Consequently, solving a system of expected value or moment equations for parameter values that is based on the expectation of estimating functions is not possible in practice. Both problems are resolved by representing expectations in terms of *empirical* probability weights applied to the $n$ *iid* observations, $\mathbf{h}(y_i, \theta)$, $i = 1, \ldots, n$ on the estimating functions and treating $E[\mathbf{h}(Y, \theta)] = \mathbf{0}$ as a valid structural constraint on the problem of maximizing the nonparametric likelihood (4.3.5). Because $F(y)$ is unknown, we can use a set of empirically estimated probability weights, say $\hat{p}_i$'s, in place of $F(y)$ as the probability distribution underlying the expectations that define the moment equations. In this case, the empirical representation of the moment constraints takes the form of the $(m \times 1)$ vector equation

$$E_{\mathbf{p}}[\mathbf{h}(Y, \theta)] = \sum_{i=1}^{n} p_i \mathbf{h}(y_i, \theta) = \mathbf{0}. \tag{4.3.8}$$

Note that the *empirical* moment constraints derived from the unbiased estimating functions *do* involve the empirical probabilities $\mathbf{p}$ explicitly and represent constraints on the choice of $\mathbf{p}$. This set of equations may be appended as a set of structural constraints on the constrained maximization problem represented by (4.3.5) and is one basis for solving the SIP

$$n^{-1}\ln(L_{\text{EL}}(\boldsymbol{\theta};\mathbf{y}))$$
$$\equiv \max_{\mathbf{p}}\left[n^{-1}\sum_{i=1}^{n}\ln(p_i)\ s.t.\ \sum_{i=1}^{n}p_i\mathbf{h}(y_i,\boldsymbol{\theta})=\mathbf{0}\text{ and }\sum_{i=1}^{n}p_i=1\right] \quad (4.3.9)$$

for the unobserved and unobservable $p_i$'s.

The constraints $p_i > 0\ \forall i$ are imposed implicitly by mathematical properties of the objective function of the optimization problem.[1] The Lagrange function associated with the constrained maximization problem can be represented as

$$L(\mathbf{p},\eta,\boldsymbol{\theta},\boldsymbol{\lambda}) \equiv \left[n^{-1}\sum_{i=1}^{n}\ln(p_i)-\eta\left(\sum_{i=1}^{n}p_i-1\right)-\boldsymbol{\lambda}'\sum_{i=1}^{n}p_i\mathbf{h}(y_i,\boldsymbol{\theta})\right]. \quad (4.3.10)$$

### 4.3.3 Comparing the Use of Estimating Functions in EE and EL Contexts

It is instructive at this point to highlight similarities and differences in the way estimating function information is used in the EL approach (4.3.10), compared to the EE approach of Chapter 3. In the EL case, the estimating function, $\mathbf{h}(\mathrm{Y},\boldsymbol{\theta})$, relates to the population random variable Y, and information about $\boldsymbol{\theta}$ conveyed by the estimating function is expressed and used in *expectation* or moment form $\mathrm{E}[\mathbf{h}(\mathrm{Y},\boldsymbol{\theta})]=\mathbf{0}$ to define constraints on the NPML problem that generates the EL function. The expectation, $\mathrm{E}[\mathbf{h}(\mathrm{Y},\boldsymbol{\theta})]=\mathbf{0}$, is unknown because $\mathrm{F}(y)$ is unknown. Therefore, an estimated empirical probability distribution is applied to observed sample outcomes of $\mathbf{h}(\mathrm{Y},\boldsymbol{\theta})$, $\mathbf{h}(y_i,\boldsymbol{\theta})$, $i=1,\ldots,n$ to define an empirical expectation, $\sum_{i=1}^{n}p_i\mathbf{h}(y_i,\boldsymbol{\theta})$, that approximates $E[\mathbf{h}(\mathrm{Y},\boldsymbol{\theta})]$. This can be used in forming an empirical moment equation as in (4.3.8). The empirical moment equation is ultimately the form in which sample information about the parameters of interest is represented and used in the definition of the EL. Note that the empirical moment equation depends not only

[1] Note that $\ln(p_i)\to-\infty$ as $p_i\to 0_+$, which effectively forces the solution for the probabilities to be positive.

on the sample data $\mathbf{y}$ and parameter vector $\boldsymbol{\theta}$ but also on the empirical probabilities $\mathbf{p}$. When viewed in the context of EE for $\boldsymbol{\theta}$, the system of $m$ EE, $\mathbf{h}_{\mathrm{EL}}(\mathbf{y}, \boldsymbol{\theta}, \mathbf{p}) \equiv \sum_{i=1}^{n} p_i \mathbf{h}(y_i, \boldsymbol{\theta}) = \mathbf{0}$, is generally underdetermined for identifying the $(k \times 1)$ vector $\boldsymbol{\theta}$ because there are $(n + k)$ unknowns, $(\boldsymbol{\theta}, \mathbf{p})$, in the system. Consequently, the inverse problem is ill-posed and no unique solution exists using the rules of logic. Such indeterminacy is solved by maximizing the EL, with respect to both $\boldsymbol{\theta}$ and $\mathbf{p}$, to obtain *maximum* EL estimates of the unknown parameters of interest.

In an EE context, the estimating functions themselves, and *not empirical expectations* of them, are used directly to define a system of equations, $\mathbf{h}(\mathbf{y}, \boldsymbol{\theta}) = \mathbf{0}$. Empirical probabilities, $\mathbf{p}$, are not involved. The solution of the EE for $\boldsymbol{\theta}$, $\hat{\boldsymbol{\theta}}_{\mathrm{EE}}(\mathbf{y})$, is the EE estimate of the parameter vector $\boldsymbol{\theta}$.

Despite the differing forms in which estimating function information is represented in the respective analyses, there is some notable degree of similarity in how estimating function information ultimately impacts an EE or EL analysis. Note that the EL empirical moment constraints, defined in terms of the conditional-on-$\boldsymbol{\theta}$ optimum empirical probability weights, are given by

$$\mathbf{h}_*(\mathbf{y}, \boldsymbol{\theta}) \equiv \mathrm{E}_{\hat{\mathbf{p}}}[\mathbf{h}(\mathrm{Y}, \boldsymbol{\theta})] \equiv \sum_{i=1}^{n} \hat{p}_i(\boldsymbol{\theta}, \mathbf{y})\mathbf{h}(y_i, \boldsymbol{\theta}) = \mathbf{0}. \quad (4.3.11)$$

These empirical moment constraints can be interpreted as an $(m \times 1)$ vector of EEs in the sense of the EE estimation context. *In effect, EL provides a method for forming a convex combination of* $(m \times 1)$ *estimating functions,* $\mathbf{h}(y_i, \boldsymbol{\theta}), i = 1, \ldots, n$.

Analogous to the EE estimation approach, one might consider solving the estimating equation (4.3.11) for $\boldsymbol{\theta}$ in terms of $\mathbf{y}$. Values of $\boldsymbol{\theta}$ that satisfy the EE (4.3.11) will surely exist because the value of $\mathbf{p}$ used in (4.3.11) and obtained by solving (4.3.9) necessarily satisfies the constraints $\sum_{i=1}^{n} p_i \mathbf{h}(y_i, \boldsymbol{\theta}) = \mathbf{0}$. However, (4.3.11) will generally not possess a unique solution for $\boldsymbol{\theta}$ but instead will be an identity in $\boldsymbol{\theta}$ for all values of $\boldsymbol{\theta}$ for which the EL in (4.3.9) is defined. That is, $\mathbf{p}$ is not fixed in (4.3.11) but rather is itself a function of $\boldsymbol{\theta}$ that changes in value to accommodate whatever $\boldsymbol{\theta}$ is in (4.3.9). We will see ahead that the maximum EL estimate of $\boldsymbol{\theta}$, obtained by maximizing (4.3.9) with respect to $\boldsymbol{\theta}$, defines empirical probability weights for (4.3.11), say $\mathbf{p}^*$, that define the *optimal* convex combination of estimating functions, $\mathbf{h}_*^*(\mathbf{y}, \boldsymbol{\theta}) \equiv \sum_{i=1}^{n} p_i^* \mathbf{h}(y_i, \boldsymbol{\theta}) = \mathbf{0}$. Within the class of estimators derived from linear combinations of the estimating functions $\mathbf{h}(\mathrm{Y}_i, \boldsymbol{\theta}), i = 1, \ldots, n$, the estimates of $\boldsymbol{\theta}$, obtained by solving these EEs for

$\boldsymbol{\theta}$, treating the optimal value $\mathbf{p}^*$ as *fixed*, are equal in asymptotic efficiency to the optimal estimating function (OptEF) estimate for $\boldsymbol{\theta}$. *Thus, in the final analysis, the EL and OptEF approaches to estimating $\boldsymbol{\theta}$ are thereby joined.*

### 4.3.4 The Functional Form of the EL Function

The value of the EL function evaluated at $\boldsymbol{\theta}_*$, $L_{EL}(\boldsymbol{\theta}_*;\mathbf{y})$ is the maximum empirical probability, $\prod_{i=1}^n p_i$, that can be assigned to the random sample outcome, $\mathbf{y}$, among all distributions of probability, $\mathbf{p}$, supported on the $y_i$'s and that satisfy the empirical moment equations, $\sum_{i=1}^n p_i\mathbf{h}(y_i, \boldsymbol{\theta}_*) = \mathbf{0}$. In effect, the EL function assigns the most favorable likelihood weight possible to each value of $\boldsymbol{\theta}_*$ from within the family of multinomial distributions supported on the data and that satisfy the moment equations. Note the comparison with an ordinary (parametric) likelihood function evaluated at $\boldsymbol{\theta}_*$, $L(\boldsymbol{\theta}_*;\mathbf{y})$, where the likelihood weight can be interpreted as the probability (or density value), $\prod_{i=1}^n f(y_i;\boldsymbol{\theta}_*)$, assigned to the sample outcome, $\mathbf{y}$, by the parametric family of PDFs, $f(y,\boldsymbol{\theta})$, $\boldsymbol{\theta}\in\Omega$, when $\boldsymbol{\theta}=\boldsymbol{\theta}_*$. In both the EL and parametric cases, the parameter vector, $\boldsymbol{\theta}$, indexes a family of probability distributions that, given a sample of data $\mathbf{y}$, can be interpreted as a likelihood function for $\boldsymbol{\theta}$ for which moment conditions, $E_{\mathbf{p}}[\mathbf{h}(Y,\boldsymbol{\theta}_*)]=\mathbf{0}$, hold (assuming the unbiasedness of $\mathbf{h}(Y,\boldsymbol{\theta})$).

We can now be considerably more precise about the functional form of the log-EL function defined in (4.3.9). In particular, we can solve for the optimal $\mathbf{p}$, $\eta$, and $\boldsymbol{\lambda}$ in the Lagrange form of the problem, (4.3.10), and then substitute optimal values for $\mathbf{p}$ back into the objective function in (4.3.9). This recovers a specific functional form for the EL function in terms of $\boldsymbol{\theta}$. The first-order conditions with respect to the $p_i$'s are

$$\frac{\partial \ln L(\mathbf{p},\eta,\boldsymbol{\theta},\boldsymbol{\lambda})}{\partial p_i}=\frac{1}{n}\frac{1}{p_i}-\sum_{j=1}^{m}\lambda_j h_j(y_i,\ \boldsymbol{\theta})-\eta=0,\ \forall i. \tag{4.3.12}$$

From the equality $\sum_{i=1}^n p_i\frac{\partial \ln L(\mathbf{p},\eta,\boldsymbol{\theta},\boldsymbol{\lambda})}{\partial p_i}=0$ and (4.3.11), it follows that

$$\sum_{i=1}^{n}p_i\frac{\partial \ln L(\mathbf{p},\eta,\boldsymbol{\theta},\boldsymbol{\lambda})}{\partial p_i}=\frac{1}{n}n-\eta=0 \tag{4.3.13}$$

so that $\eta=1$. The resulting unique optimal $p_i$ weights, implied by (4.3.12), can thus be expressed as a function of $\boldsymbol{\theta}$ and $\boldsymbol{\lambda}$ as

$$p_i(\boldsymbol{\theta},\boldsymbol{\lambda})=\left(n\left[\sum_{j=1}^{m}\lambda_j h_j(y_i,\ \boldsymbol{\theta})+1\right]\right)^{-1}. \tag{4.3.14}$$

We can use the solution for $\mathbf{p}$, given by (4.3.14), to solve for the Lagrange multipliers as a function of $\boldsymbol{\theta}$. Specifically, substituting (4.3.14) into the empirical moment equations (4.3.11) produces the following system of equations

$$\sum_{i=1}^{n} p_i \mathbf{h}(y_i, \boldsymbol{\theta}) = \sum_{i=1}^{n} n^{-1} \left[ \sum_{j=1}^{m} \lambda_j h_j(y_i, \boldsymbol{\theta}) + 1 \right]^{-1} \mathbf{h}(y_i, \boldsymbol{\theta}) = \mathbf{0} \qquad (4.3.15)$$

that $\boldsymbol{\lambda}$ must satisfy under general regularity conditions that will normally hold in practice. The solution, $\boldsymbol{\lambda}(\boldsymbol{\theta})$, is an implicit function of $\boldsymbol{\theta}$, which we denote in general by

$$\boldsymbol{\lambda}(\boldsymbol{\theta}) = \arg_{\lambda} \left[ \frac{1}{n} \sum_{i=1}^{n} \left[ \frac{1}{1 + \boldsymbol{\lambda}' \mathbf{h}(y_i, \boldsymbol{\theta})} \right] \mathbf{h}(y_i, \boldsymbol{\theta}) = \mathbf{0} \right]. \qquad (4.3.16)$$

Furthermore, the solution, $\boldsymbol{\lambda}(\boldsymbol{\theta})$, is continuous and differentiable in $\boldsymbol{\theta}$.

Substituting the optimal Lagrangian multiplier values $\boldsymbol{\lambda}(\boldsymbol{\theta})$ into the expression for the optimal $\mathbf{p}$ weights, $p_i(\boldsymbol{\theta}, \boldsymbol{\lambda})$, in (4.3.14) allows the empirical probabilities to be represented in terms of $\boldsymbol{\theta}$, as $p_i(\boldsymbol{\theta}) \equiv p_i(\boldsymbol{\theta}, \boldsymbol{\lambda}(\boldsymbol{\theta})) = (n[\sum_{j=1}^{m} \lambda_j(\boldsymbol{\theta}) h_j(y_i, \boldsymbol{\theta}) + 1])^{-1}$. Substitution of the optimal $\mathbf{p}(\boldsymbol{\theta})$ values into the (unscaled) objective function, $\sum_{i=1}^{n} \ln(p_i)$, in (4.3.9) yields the expression for the log-EL function evaluated at $\boldsymbol{\theta}$

$$\ln(L_{\mathrm{EL}}(\boldsymbol{\theta}; \mathbf{y})) = -\sum_{i=1}^{n} \ln(n[1 + \boldsymbol{\lambda}(\boldsymbol{\theta})' \mathbf{h}(y_i, \boldsymbol{\theta})]). \qquad (4.3.17)$$

Owen (1991) and Kolaczyk (1994) have shown that the maximum EL (MEL) approach can be applied to the stochastic linear model, and we demonstrate this possibility in Section 4.3.7 of this chapter.

### 4.3.5 Summary of the EL Concept

We have used indirect *noisy* observations in the forms of EE and the EL concept to provide a solution to an ill-posed SIP. The EL approach, in the case of *iid* data, may be summarized as follows. Assuming that $Y_1, Y_2, \ldots, Y_n$ are *iid* random variables with a common probability distribution $F$, we are interested in the values of some or all of the parameters, $\boldsymbol{\theta} \in R^k$, associated with $F$. Information relating to $\boldsymbol{\theta}$ and $F$ is summarized by a set of estimating functions relating to the population random variable Y as $\mathbf{h}(Y, \theta) = (h_1(Y, \theta), \ldots, h_m(Y, \theta))'$. The expectation of the estimating functions, $\mathbf{h}(Y, \theta)$, equals zero when evaluations occur at the true value of $\theta$ so that $E_\theta[\mathbf{h}(Y, \theta)] = \mathbf{0}$. *The log-EL function for* $\theta$ *is then defined as*

$$\ln(L_{EL}(\theta; \mathbf{y})) \equiv \max_{\mathbf{p}} \left[ \sum_{i=1}^{n} \ln(p_i) \; s.t. \sum_{i=1}^{n} p_i \mathbf{h}(y_i, \theta) = \mathbf{0} \text{ and } \sum_{i=1}^{n} p_i = 1 \right], \quad (4.3.18)$$

*where the* $p_i$*'s represent empirical probability weights assigned to the* $y_i$ *observations, and* $E_{\mathbf{p}}[\mathbf{h}(Y, \theta)] = \sum_{i=1}^{n} p_i \mathbf{h}(y_i, \theta) = \mathbf{0}$ *is the empirical representation of the moment equation* $E[\mathbf{h}(Y, \theta)] = \mathbf{0}$ *relating to the estimating functions.*

Given the characterization of the EL function in (4.3.18), the next question concerns estimation regarding the unknown parameter vector $\theta$. Analogous to the case of ML estimation in Chapter 2, we can define a maximum EL (MEL) estimator of $\theta$ by choosing the value of $\theta$ that maximizes the EL function (4.3.18), or maximizes the logarithm of the EL function, as

$$\hat{\theta}_{EL} = \text{argmax}_\theta[\ln(L_{EL}(\theta; \mathbf{Y}))]. \quad (4.3.19)$$

The MEL estimator is an extremum estimator with the log-EL function being the estimation objective function. The solution for $\hat{\theta}_{EL}$ is generally not obtainable in closed form because the $\boldsymbol{\lambda}(\theta)$ argument of the EL function is not a closed-form function of $\theta$. Consequently, numerical optimization techniques are required to obtain outcomes of the MEL estimator. These computational aspects will be discussed when we revisit additional MEL-like approaches in the chapters ahead and will be previewed in the simple case of estimating a population mean in the section ahead, together with Appendix 4.A.1. Also the asymptotic properties of (4.3.19) and issues such as MEL efficiency will be discussed and placed in perspective in Chapter 5.

### 4.3.6 Maximum Empirical Likelihood (MEL) Estimation of a Population Mean

In this section, we demonstrate the setup and properties of the MEL estimation approach for the case of estimating a population mean. To provide an illustration of computational issues attendant to many MEL estimation problems, we also provide a numerical illustration of this estimation problem in Appendix 4.A.1 of this chapter.

We begin with a random sample, $(Y_1, \ldots, Y_n)$, of scalars drawn from some population distribution, $F(y)$, assumed to have a finite mean. We introduce the scalar parameter $\theta$ to represent the unknown mean of $F(y)$. To formally identify $\theta$ as the mean of $F(y)$, we define the estimating function, $h(Y, \theta) = Y - \theta$, and then state the moment equation

$$E[h(Y, \theta)] = E[Y - \theta] = 0, \tag{4.3.20}$$

so $\theta = E[Y]$. Although in this case, we concentrate on the scalar case, we emphasize that, in general, it is possible for the number of EEs to exceed the dimension of the parameter vector of interest. Note that this estimation problem can also be solved from a method of moments (MOM) and/or estimating equation approach. The empirical counterpart to the population moment (4.3.20) is given by $\hat{E}[h(Y, \theta)] = \hat{E}[Y - \theta] = n^{-1} \sum_{i=1}^{n} [y_i - \theta] = 0$. Consequently, the MOM or estimating equation estimator of $\theta$ is $\hat{\theta}_{MOM} = \hat{\theta}_{EE} = n^{-1} \sum_{i=1}^{n} Y_i = \bar{Y}$.

Following the EL counterpart introduced in (4.3.10), the Lagrange function associated with the constrained maximization problem, which defines the scaled log-EL function, is given by

$$\ln(L(\mathbf{p}, \eta, \lambda)) \equiv \left[ n^{-1} \sum_{i=1}^{n} \ln(p_i) - \eta \left( \sum_{i=1}^{n} p_i - 1 \right) - \lambda \sum_{i=1}^{n} p_i (y_i - \theta) \right], \tag{4.3.21}$$

where $p_i > 0 \; \forall \; i$ is implicit in the structure of the optimization problem, as noted previously. The first-order conditions with respect to the $p_i$'s are

$$\frac{1}{np_i} - \lambda(y_i - \theta) - \eta = 0, \; i = 1, \ldots, n, \tag{4.3.22}$$

where $\lambda$ and $\eta$ are Lagrange multipliers. The first-order condition with respect to $\eta$ is precisely the same as (4.3.11), implying that $\eta = 1$. Substituting $\eta = 1$ in (4.3.22) yields a solution for $p_i$ given by

$$p_i(\theta, \lambda) = (n[1 + \lambda(y_i - \theta)])^{-1}, \tag{4.3.23}$$

which reflects (4.3.14) for the current problem. We can insert (4.3.23) and $\eta = 1$ into the Lagrange function of (4.3.21) to define the partially optimized function

$$n^{-1} \sum_{i=1}^{n} \ln(n^{-1}[1 + \lambda(y_i - \theta)]^{-1}) - \lambda \sum_{i=1}^{n} n^{-1}[1 + \lambda(y_i - \theta)]^{-1}(y_i - \theta). \tag{4.3.24}$$

Optimization of (4.3.24) with respect to $\lambda$ defines the Lagrange multiplier as a function of $\theta$ as

$$\lambda(\theta) = \arg_{\lambda}\left[\frac{1}{n}\sum_{i=1}^{n}\left[\frac{y_i - \theta}{1 + \lambda(y_i - \theta)}\right] = 0\right], \tag{4.3.25}$$

where (4.3.24) is the implementation of the general equation (4.3.16) for the current problem. *Note that $\lambda(\theta)$ is an implicit function of $\theta$ that cannot be expressed in closed form.* Substituting this solution for $\lambda$ into the expression $\sum_{i=1}^{n} \ln(p_i(\theta, \lambda)) = \sum_{i=1}^{n} \ln((n[1 + \lambda(y_i - \theta)])^{-1})$ and recalling (4.3.23) defines the log-EL function for $\theta$ as

$$\ln(L_{\text{EL}}(\theta; \mathbf{y})) = -\sum_{i=1}^{n} \ln(n[1 + \lambda(\theta)(y_i - \theta)]), \tag{4.3.26}$$

which we note is consistent with (4.3.17).

The MEL estimate of $\theta$ is found by maximizing the log-EL function (4.3.26) with respect to $\theta$. Regarding this maximization problem, note that the log-EL function is continuous, differentiable, and concave in $\theta$. Also, the feasible choices for $\theta$ must be in the interval $(y_S, y_L)$, where $y_S$ and $y_L$ are the smallest and largest values in the set of sample outcomes $(y_1, y_2, \ldots, y_n)$. In particular, given the empirical estimating equation constraint $\sum_{i=1}^{n} p_i y_i = \theta$, together with $\sum_{i=1}^{n} p_i = 1$ and $p_i > 0\,\forall i$, we see that the optimal value of $\theta$ must be a convex combination of the $y_i$'s.

Further, we demonstrate that the maximum of the EL or log-EL function is unique (in general as well as in the current problem) by considering the contradictory claim that $\mathbf{p}^*$ *and* $\mathbf{p}^{**}$ are *both* MEL probability distributions. The probability distribution $\mathbf{p}^0 = \alpha\mathbf{p}^* + (1-\alpha)\mathbf{p}^{**}$ then also satisfies the moment equation constraints, as $\sum_{i=1}^{n} p_i^0 \mathbf{h}(y_i, \theta) = \mathbf{0}$ for any $\alpha \in (0, 1)$. Due to the strict concavity of the natural logarithm, Jensen's Inequality implies $\ln(p_i^0) > \alpha \ln(p_i^*) + (1-\alpha)\ln(p_i^{**})\ \forall\ i$. Therefore, for the log-EL function of $\mathbf{p}^0$

$$\begin{aligned}\sum_{i=1}^{n} \ln(p_i^0) &> \alpha \sum_{i=1}^{n} \ln(p_i^*) + (1-\alpha)\sum_{i=1}^{n} \ln(p_i^{**}) \\ &= \sum_{i=1}^{n} \ln(p_i^*) = \sum_{i=1}^{n} \ln(p_i^{**}),\end{aligned} \tag{4.3.27}$$

it follows that the value of EL at $\mathbf{p}^0$ is larger than the common EL value at $\mathbf{p}^*$ and $\mathbf{p}^{**}$. Thus, we have a contradiction to the claim that $\mathbf{p}^*$ and $\mathbf{p}^{**}$ are both MEL probability distributions.

### 4.3.7 MEL Linear Model Estimation for Stochastic X

Owen (1991) and Kolaczyk (1994) demonstrated how the EL approach can be applied to the linear regression model. Whether or not the motivation for the linear model application is completely analogous to the approach presented in Section 4.3.3 depends on whether or not the explanatory variables are stochastic. When $\mathbf{X}$ is stochastic, the previous EL discussion directly applies to the regression case under the appropriate regularity conditions.

We now apply the EL principle to provide a solution to the inverse problem (4.3.1) for the linear model. Assume that the explanatory variable matrix, $\mathbf{X}$, is stochastic and nondegenerate, that $\mathbf{X}$ and $\boldsymbol{\varepsilon}$ are independent, that the conditional mean function for $\mathbf{Y}$ is given by $\mathrm{E}(\mathbf{Y}|\mathbf{x}) = \mathbf{x}\boldsymbol{\beta}$, and that $(\mathrm{Y}_i, \mathbf{X}[i,.])$, $i = 1, \ldots, n$ are *iid* random vectors.

Regarding the form of the estimating functions to use in the EL procedure, consider the $(k \times 1)$ vector function $\mathbf{h}((\mathrm{Y}_i, \mathbf{X}[i,.]), \boldsymbol{\beta}) = \mathbf{X}[i,.]'(\mathrm{Y}_i - \mathbf{X}[i,.]\boldsymbol{\beta})$ for any $i = 1, \ldots, n$. Note that under the prevailing assumptions, we can deduce that

$$\mathbf{E}(\mathbf{h}((\mathrm{Y}_i, [i,.]), \boldsymbol{\beta})) = \mathrm{E}(\mathbf{X}[i,.]'(\mathrm{Y}_i - \mathbf{X}[i,.]\boldsymbol{\beta})) = 0, \text{ for } i = 1, \ldots, n, \tag{4.3.28}$$

when $\boldsymbol{\beta}$ is the true value of the parameter vector $\boldsymbol{\beta}$ in the linear model $\mathbf{Y} = \mathbf{X}\boldsymbol{\beta} + \boldsymbol{\varepsilon}$. Consequently, the estimating functions are unbiased. Furthermore, the random vectors $\mathbf{Z}[.,i] \equiv \mathbf{X}[i,.]'(\mathrm{Y}_i - \mathbf{X}[i,.]\boldsymbol{\beta})$ for $i = 1, \ldots, n$ are *iid* random vectors under the prevailing assumptions because $(\mathrm{Y}_i, \mathbf{X}[i,.])$, $i = 1, \ldots, n$ are iid.

Given the definition of the EL function for $\boldsymbol{\beta}$, the scaled (by $n^{-1}$) log-EL is defined by solving a constrained maximization problem, expressed in Lagrange form as

$$n^{-1}\sum_{i=1}^{n}\ln(p_i) - \eta\left(\sum_{i=1}^{n}p_i - 1\right) - \boldsymbol{\lambda}'\sum_{i=1}^{n}p_i(\mathbf{x}[i,.]'(y_i - \mathbf{x}[i,.]\boldsymbol{\beta})), \tag{4.3.29}$$

where $p_i > 0\,\forall\, i$ is implicit in the structure of the optimization problem, as noted previously. The development of the optimal solution to the maximization problem in (4.3.29) leads to the functional form for the log-EL function given by

$$\ln(L_{\mathrm{EL}}(\boldsymbol{\beta}; \mathbf{y}, \mathbf{x})) = -\sum_{i=1}^{n}\ln(n[1 + \boldsymbol{\lambda}(\boldsymbol{\beta})'(\mathbf{x}[i,.]'(y_i - \mathbf{x}[i,.]\boldsymbol{\beta}))]). \tag{4.3.30}$$

The MEL estimator of $\boldsymbol{\beta}$ is then defined by

$$\hat{\boldsymbol{\beta}}_{\mathrm{EL}} = \arg\max_{\boldsymbol{\beta}}[\ln(L_{\mathrm{EL}}(\boldsymbol{\beta};\mathbf{y},\mathbf{x}))]. \tag{4.3.31}$$

As in the case of applying the EL procedure to estimating the population mean (Section 4.3.5), using the EL approach to estimate $\boldsymbol{\beta}$ in the linear regression model, based on the unbiased estimating functions (4.3.28), leads to a familiar functional form for $\hat{\boldsymbol{\beta}}_{\mathrm{EL}}$. In particular, note that $\hat{\mathbf{b}}_{\mathrm{EL}} = \hat{\mathbf{b}}_{\mathrm{LS}} = (\mathbf{x}'\mathbf{x})^{-1}\mathbf{x}'\mathbf{y}$ and $p_i = n^{-1}\ \forall\ i$, solve the estimating equation constraints in (4.3.29) and at the same time result in the maximum possible value of $n^{-1}\sum_{i=1}^{n}\ln(p_i)$, subject to the constraints $\sum_{i=1}^{n} p_i = 1$ and $p_i > 0\,\forall i$. That $n^{-1}\sum_{i=1}^{n}\ln(p_i)$ is maximized is apparent because $p_i = n^{-1}\ \forall\ i$ is in fact the solution for maximizing the EL, *unconstrained* by EEs. To see that the estimating equation constraints are satisfied when $p_i = n^{-1}$ and $\mathbf{b} = \hat{\mathbf{b}}_{\mathrm{LS}}$, note that

$$\begin{aligned}\sum_{i=1}^{n} p_i(\mathbf{x}[i,.]'(y_i - \mathbf{x}[i,.]\boldsymbol{\beta})) &= n^{-1}\sum_{i=1}^{n}(\mathbf{x}[i,.]'(y_i - \mathbf{x}[i,.]\hat{\mathbf{b}})) \\ &= n^{-1}(\mathbf{x}'\mathbf{y} - \mathbf{x}'\mathbf{x}\hat{\mathbf{b}}) = \mathbf{0},\end{aligned} \tag{4.3.32}$$

where the parenthetical expression to the right of the second equality in (4.3.32) is the set of normal equations that define the least squares estimator.

## 4.4 Epilogue

We had two objectives in this chapter. Our first objective was to define a stochastic inverse problem, note its ill-posed nature, and demonstrate an information theoretic solution. A second objective was to use the stochastic inverse problem framework to develop an operational basis for recovering an empirical data-based likelihood function from the underlying DSP. In the solution process, we made use of the concept of unbiased estimating functions to define a (empirical) likelihood function and an MEL estimator.

In this information-recovery process, we have followed Owen (1988, 1990, 1991), Qin and Lawless (1994), and Kolaczyk (1994), who demonstrate how the EL procedure can be used in the case of independent and/or *iid* data to define likelihood functions based on a particular multinomial probability distribution that is supported on the sample data. Nonparametric SIPs also appear in the statistics literature, and an article by Cavalier (2008) provides a good summary of how statisticians think about and analyze statistical inverse problems. In this literature, "regularization" methods are used to provide a meaningful solution, given the noise and ill-posed nature of the inverse problem. Their methods involve such concepts as adaptive estimation, oracle inequalities, and Stein's unbiased risk estimation, and the minimax approach is used to define notions of optimality. Finally, we note that the goodness-of-fit criterion $n^{-1}\sum_{i=1}^{n}\ln(p_i)$ that emerges in the EL formulation is the same as Burg (1972) relative entropy $\sum_{i=1}^{n} p_i^* \ln(p_i/p_i^*)$, where $p_i^* = 1/n$.

The focus of this chapter has been on defining a nonparametric stochastic inverse problem and developing an empirical likelihood estimation basis. In the next chapter, we continue to discuss the empirical likelihood method and provide a basis for inference.

## 4.5 Selected References


Angrist, J. and J. Pischke (2010), "The Credibility Revolution in Empirical Economics," *Journal of Economic Perspectives*, **24**:3–30.

Burg, J. (1972), "The Relationship between Maximum Entropy Spectra and Maximum Likelihood Spectra," *Geophysics*, **37**:375–376.

Cavalier, L. (2008), "Nonparametric Statistical Inverse Problems," *Inverse Problems*, **24**:1–19.

Kolaczyk, E. (1994), "Empirical Likelihood for Generalized Linear Models," *Statistica Sinica*, Vol. **4**, pp. 199–218.

Owen, A. (1988), "Empirical Likelihood Ratio Confidence Intervals for a Single Functional," *Biometrika*, Vol. **75**, pp. 237–249.

Owen, A. (1990), "Empirical Likelihood Ratio Confidence Regions," *The Annals of Statistics*, Vol. **18**, pp. 90–120.

Owen, A. (1991), "Empirical Likelihood for Linear Models," *The Annals of Statistics*, Vol. **19**, pp. 1725–1747.

Qin, J. and J. Lawless (1994), "Empirical Likelihood and General Estimating Equations," *The Annals of Statistics*, Vol. **22**, pp. 300–325.

Qin, J. and J. Lawless (1995), "Estimating Equations, Empirical Likelihood, and Constraints on Parameters," *Canadian Journal of Statistics*, Vol. **23**, pp. 145–159.


## APPENDIX 4. A NUMERICAL EXAMPLE: COMPUTING MEL ESTIMATES

The problem of estimating the mean of a population distribution from sample data has an easily obtained solution, and the problem of obtaining a MEL estimate of the mean was discussed in Section 4.3.6. Recall that the unconstrained MEL distribution is a discrete uniform distribution (least favorable prior) on the observations. In the population-mean problem, the MEL sample weights represent the discrete uniform distribution and the optimal estimator of the population mean parameter is simply $\bar{Y}$, the sample average. As such, the mean constraint is not binding and the optimal Lagrange multiplier $\lambda = 0$. As discussed in the text, the value of the Lagrange multiplier $\eta$ is known analytically to equal $\eta = 1$, and the condition can be imposed in the estimation process.

In more complicated models, MEL problems do not necessarily have simple analytical solutions. Numerical solutions methods are necessary, and there may be a number of different ways to numerically solve the MEL estimation problem. For demonstration purposes, the simple population-mean example is used here to serve as a benchmark for illustrating computing methods. In this example, the Newton-Raphson (NR) gradient search procedure is used to compute MEL estimates of $\theta$ and $\lambda$ in two different ways. One approach is to solve the first-order necessary conditions simultaneously for the unknown parameters, setting $\eta$ to its known value of 1, and concentrating out the optimal $p_i$'s as noted in (4.3.23)–(4.3.24). Using this solution method, $\theta$ and $\lambda$ are selected to minimize the squared Euclidean norm of the necessary conditions, where the GAUSS™ procedure EqSolve is used to compute the MEL solution values for $\theta$ and $\lambda$.

MEL solutions to more complicated problems may sometimes be easier to compute sequentially. That is, the user may fix a value of $\theta$ and then find the optimal $\lambda$ under the MEL criterion. Then, the optimal value of $\theta$ can be determined conditional on the preceding value of $\lambda$, and the sequential process is continued until convergence. To implement the sequential solution method, we use an application of the NR algorithm at each sequential conditional optimization step, again using GAUSS™ software.

Regarding the implementation details of this example, note that the fundamental problem to be solved is the maximization of the empirical log-likelihood function, which in Lagrange form is characterized by the optimization of

$$L(\mathbf{p}, \eta, \theta, \lambda) \equiv \left[ n^{-1} \sum_{i=1}^{n} \ln(p_i) - \eta \left( \sum_{i=1}^{n} p_i - 1 \right) - \lambda \sum_{i=1}^{n} p_i h(y_i, \theta) \right] \tag{A.4.1}$$

(recall [4.3.21]). This is recognized to be of the general form (4.3.10), with $\text{h}(y_i, \theta) = y_i - \theta, \forall i$. As indicated in (4.3.25), the necessary condition for optimization with respect to $\lambda$ is given by

$$\xi_1(\lambda, \theta) = n^{-1} \sum_{i=1}^{n} \left[ \frac{y_i - \theta}{1 + \lambda(y_i - \theta)} \right] = 0. \tag{A.4.2}$$

The necessary condition for optimization with respect to $\theta$ is given by

$$\xi_2(\lambda, \theta) = -n^{-1} \sum_{i=1}^{n} \left[ \frac{\lambda}{1 + \lambda(y_i - \theta)} \right] = 0. \tag{A.4.3}$$

Equations (A.4.2)–(A.4.3) may be solved simultaneously using the NR algorithm to minimize $\xi_1(\lambda, \theta)^2 + \xi_2(\lambda, \theta)^2$ (zeros are used as the starting values for both $\theta$ and $\lambda$). Also (A.4.3)–(A.4.4) may be solved sequentially, first solving (A.4.3) for $\lambda$ given a value of $\theta$ (using 0 as the starting value for $\theta$), then solving (A.4.4) for $\theta$ given the previously solved value of $\lambda$, and so on, iterating until convergence occurs.

Regarding the data used in this example, consider a simple location model for the DSP, in which

$$Y = \theta + \varepsilon,$$

where $\theta = 2$ and $\varepsilon$ is a standard normal noise component. The sample size is set to $n = 50$ and pseudo-random draws from this DSP are generated. The sample data outcome is given in Table A.4.1.

Table A.4.1. *Data for* $Y = 2 + \varepsilon$, $\varepsilon \sim N(0, 1)$

| | | | | |
|---|---|---|---|---|
| 3.9025 | 3.1129 | 2.8597 | 2.2940 | 1.1833 |
| 2.1889 | 3.3534 | 3.4589 | 2.2804 | 4.0063 |
| 3.1310 | 2.7769 | 2.8217 | 1.2417 | 2.4200 |
| 2.7767 | 2.1446 | 2.7261 | 2.6741 | 0.8538 |
| 3.5401 | 1.5701 | 1.5629 | 2.4431 | 1.4956 |
| 2.6310 | 2.0592 | −0.0830 | 3.7064 | 2.6267 |
| 2.9552 | 1.6646 | 1.9056 | 2.1022 | 2.9977 |
| 1.3593 | 0.0073 | 0.4511 | 2.5007 | 1.7911 |
| 2.2332 | 3.1325 | 0.2120 | 3.1800 | 2.5518 |
| 2.6773 | 3.4880 | 0.8828 | −1.4202 | 0.8573 |

The results for both the simultaneous and iterative numerical solutions to the MEL problem were identical, resulting in $\hat{\theta} = 2.18576$, which matches the calculated sample mean value. The simultaneous solution approach required only two iterations of the NR algorithm, whereas the sequential method required 27 iterations. Both NR-based solution methods resulted in $\hat{\lambda} = 0$, as expected, given the nonbinding nature of the mean constraint, as noted in Section 4.3.

FIVE

# A Stochastic Empirical Likelihood Inverse Problem

## Estimation and Inference

### 5.1 Introduction

In the preceding chapter, we defined a nonparametric stochastic inverse problem, noted its ill-posed nature, and demonstrated an information theoretic solution. We then used this framework to develop a basis for recovering an empirical data-based likelihood function from the underlying indirect noisy data sampling process (DSP). In the solution process, we used unbiased estimating functions to define an empirical likelihood function and the corresponding maximum empirical likelihood (MEL) estimator. In this chapter, we take up inference questions relating to the MEL estimator.

### 5.2 MEL Inference: *iid* Case

In Chapter 4, we demonstrated that, analogous to the case of maximum likelihood (ML) estimation, we can define a maximum *empirical* likelihood (MEL) estimator of $\boldsymbol{\theta}$ by choosing the value of $\boldsymbol{\theta}$ that maximizes the empirical likelihood (EL) function (4.3.9) or maximizes the logarithm of the EL function, as

$$\hat{\boldsymbol{\Theta}}_{\mathrm{EL}} = \operatorname{argmax}_{\theta}[\ln(\mathrm{L}_{\mathrm{EL}}(\boldsymbol{\theta}\,;\mathbf{Y}))]. \tag{5.2.1}$$

The MEL estimator is an extremum estimator with the log-EL function as the estimation objective function.

Regarding the asymptotic properties of $\hat{\boldsymbol{\Theta}}_{\mathrm{EL}}$, the usual consistency and asymptotic normality properties of extremum estimators hold for the MEL estimator under general regularity conditions. These properties may be established by invoking primitive conditions on the estimating equations. The regularity conditions relate to the differentiability of $\mathbf{h}(\mathrm{Y}, \boldsymbol{\theta})$ with respect to $\boldsymbol{\theta}$ and the bounded base of $\mathbf{h}(\cdot)$. If we assume that the row rank of $\mathrm{E}[\frac{\partial \mathbf{h}(Y,\theta)}{\partial \theta}|_{\theta_0}]$ equals the number of parameters in the vector $\theta$, these relatively mild conditions lead to the MEL estimator being *consistent* and *asymptotically normal* with limiting distribution

$$n^{1/2}(\hat{\Theta}_{\mathrm{EL}} - \theta_0) \xrightarrow{d} N(\mathbf{0}, \Sigma), \tag{5.2.2}$$

where

$$\Sigma = \left[\mathrm{E}\left[\frac{\partial \mathbf{h}(Y,\theta)}{\partial \theta}\bigg|_{\theta_0}\right](\mathrm{E}\,[\mathbf{h}(Y,\theta)\mathbf{h}(Y,\theta)'|_{\theta_0}])^{-1}\mathrm{E}\left[\frac{\partial \mathbf{h}(Y,\theta)}{\partial \theta'}\bigg|_{\theta_0}\right]\right]^{-1}. \tag{5.2.3}$$

The covariance matrix $\Sigma$ of the limiting normal distribution can be consistently estimated by

$$\hat{\Sigma} = \left[\left[\sum_{i=1}^{n} \hat{p}_i \frac{\partial \mathbf{h}(y_i,\theta)}{\partial \theta}\bigg|_{\hat{\theta}_{\mathrm{EL}}}\right]'\left[\sum_{i=1}^{n} \hat{p}_i \mathbf{h}(y_i,\hat{\theta}_{\mathrm{EL}})\mathbf{h}(y_i,\hat{\theta}_{\mathrm{EL}})'\right]^{-1} \times \left[\sum_{i=1}^{n} \hat{p}_i \frac{\partial \mathbf{h}(y_i,\theta)}{\partial \theta}\bigg|_{\hat{\theta}_{\mathrm{EL}}}\right]\right]^{-1}, \tag{5.2.4}$$

where the $\hat{p}_i$s are the MEL estimates of the empirical probability distribution $\mathbf{p}$, with $\theta$ replaced by $\hat{\theta}_{\mathrm{EL}}$ and $\boldsymbol{\lambda}$ replaced by $\hat{\boldsymbol{\lambda}}_{\mathrm{EL}} = \boldsymbol{\lambda}(\hat{\theta}_{\mathrm{EL}})$. An alternative consistent estimate can also be defined by using (5.2.4) with all of the $\hat{p}_i$s replaced by $n^{-1}$. This amounts to applying probability weights based on the empirical distribution function (EDF) instead of the empirical probability weights generated by the EL procedure. Because the latter incorporate the additional estimating function information, it is expected that these probability weight estimates are more efficient in finite samples. This assumes that the estimating function information is correct. Correct in this context refers to unbiased estimating functions. The limiting distribution of $\hat{\Theta}_{\mathrm{EL}}$ allows asymptotic hypothesis tests and confidence regions to be constructed.

### 5.2.1 MEL Efficiency Property

The MEL estimator has an important efficiency property and, in motivating this property, we obtain further insights into the workings of the MEL method of parameter estimation. On reviewing the definition of the scaled log-EL function and, in particular, the constraint information used in the definition, it is apparent that the MEL estimate $\hat{\theta}_{\mathrm{EL}}$ of $\theta$ may be obtained as the solution to the system of equations

$$\mathbf{h}_{\mathrm{EL}}(\mathbf{y}, \boldsymbol{\theta}) \equiv \sum_{i=1}^{n} \hat{p}_i \mathbf{h}(y_i, \boldsymbol{\theta}) = \mathbf{0}, \tag{5.2.5}$$

where $\hat{p}_i = p_i(\hat{\boldsymbol{\theta}}_{\mathrm{EL}}, \boldsymbol{\lambda}(\hat{\boldsymbol{\theta}}_{\mathrm{EL}}))$ is the optimal value of $p_i$ for $i = 1, \ldots, n$. Therefore, the MEL method of estimation can be viewed as a procedure for combining the collection of $(m \times 1)$ estimating functions $\mathbf{h}(y_i, \hat{\boldsymbol{\theta}})$, $i = 1, \ldots, n$, into a vector estimating equation, $\mathbf{h}_{\mathrm{EL}}(\mathbf{y}, \boldsymbol{\theta}) = \mathbf{0}$, that can be solved for an estimate of $\boldsymbol{\theta}$.

A natural question is whether the particular combination of the $n$ estimating functions, $\mathbf{h}(y_i, \hat{\boldsymbol{\theta}})$, $i = 1, \ldots, n$, used in the MEL approach, is in some sense the best combination. To demonstrate that it is best, consider the class of estimation procedures that can be defined by a linear combination of the estimating equation information

$$\mathbf{h}_\nu(\mathbf{y}, \boldsymbol{\theta}) \equiv \sum_{i=1}^{n} \mathbf{v}(\boldsymbol{\theta}) \mathbf{h}(y_i, \boldsymbol{\theta}) = \mathbf{0}, \tag{5.2.6}$$

where $\boldsymbol{\nu}(\boldsymbol{\theta})$ is a $(k \times m)$ real-valued matrix function such that the $(k \times 1)$ vector equation $\mathrm{h}_{\mathbf{v}}(\mathbf{y}, \boldsymbol{\theta}) = \mathbf{0}$ can be solved for the $(k \times 1)$ vector, $\boldsymbol{\theta}$, as $\hat{\boldsymbol{\theta}}_\nu(\mathbf{y})$. McCullagh and Nelder (1989, p. 341) demonstrate that the optimal choice of $\boldsymbol{\nu}$, in the sense of defining a consistent estimator with minimum asymptotic covariance matrix (in the class of estimators for $\boldsymbol{\theta}$ defined as solutions to [5.2.6]), is given by

$$\boldsymbol{\nu}(\boldsymbol{\theta}) = E\left[\frac{\partial \mathbf{h}(\mathrm{Y}, \boldsymbol{\theta})}{\partial \boldsymbol{\theta}}\right] Cov(\mathbf{h}(\mathrm{Y}, \boldsymbol{\theta}))^{-1}, \tag{5.2.7}$$

where Y denotes the random variable whose probability distribution is the common population distribution of the $\mathrm{Y}_i$s. Given the unbiased nature of the estimating equations, the optimal definition of $\boldsymbol{\nu}$ in (5.2.7) is such that $Cov(\mathbf{h}(\mathrm{Y}, \boldsymbol{\theta})) = \mathrm{E}[\mathbf{h}(\mathrm{Y}, \boldsymbol{\theta})\mathbf{h}(\mathrm{Y}, \boldsymbol{\theta})']$ and results in an estimator for $\boldsymbol{\theta}$ that has precisely the same asymptotic covariance matrix as that of the MEL estimator (5.2.3). Thus, as in (5.2.6), the MEL estimator is equivalent, in asymptotic distribution, to the most efficient estimator in the class of estimators defined via the solution to estimating equations formed by linear combinations of the unbiased estimating functions.

The asymptotic covariance matrix of the MEL estimator generally becomes smaller (by a positive semidefinite matrix) as the number of functionally independent estimating equations on which it is based increases

(Qin and Lawless, 1994). In practice, this means that the greater the number of *correct* (i.e., unbiased) estimating functions used, the more accurate the MEL estimator becomes in estimating $\boldsymbol{\theta}$. Thus, one should use as much information relating to valid estimating functions as is available when using the MEL estimator to estimate $\boldsymbol{\theta}$. We examine a test of the validity of estimating equations in a later section.

On obtaining the solution for $\hat{\boldsymbol{\theta}}_{\text{EL}}$, an estimate of the asymptotic variance of the MEL estimator can be obtained based on (5.2.4), or else (5.2.4), with the $\hat{p}_i$s replaced by $n^{-1}$. Following the former approach, which is at least as efficient as the latter in finite samples when valid moment constraints are used, and letting $\hat{p}_i = p_i(\hat{\theta}_{\text{EL}}, \lambda(\hat{\theta}_{\text{EL}})) = n^{-1}[1 + \lambda(\hat{\theta}_{\text{EL}})(y_i - \hat{\theta}_{\text{EL}})]^{-1}$, we have, in the case of estimating the mean of a population distribution, where $h(y_i, \theta) = y_i - \theta$, the following implementation of (5.2.4):

$$\hat{\Sigma} = \left[\left[\sum_{i=1}^{n} \hat{p}_i(-1)\right]\left[\sum_{i=1}^{n} \hat{p}_i(y_i - \hat{\theta}_{\text{EL}})^2\right]^{-1}\left[\sum_{i=1}^{n} \hat{p}_i(-1)\right]\right]^{-1}$$
$$= \sum_{i=1}^{n} \hat{p}_i(y_i - \hat{\theta}_{\text{EL}})^2. \tag{5.2.8}$$

The variance estimate can be interpreted as the expectation of $(\text{Y} - E_{\hat{\mathbf{p}}}\text{Y})^2$, treating the empirical probability distribution $\hat{\mathbf{p}} = (\hat{p}_1, \ldots, \hat{p}_n)'$ as the population distribution of Y. Thus, a natural estimate of variance evolves within the MEL context, where $\hat{\theta}_{\text{EL}} = E_{\hat{p}}(\text{Y}) = \sum_{i=1}^{n} p_i y_i$. If the $\hat{p}_i$s are replaced by $n^{-1}$, then (5.2.8) is simply the familiar ML-type estimate of the variance.

The purpose of the preceding discussion has been to illustrate and to clarify issues relating to the general problem of maximizing the MEL of $\boldsymbol{\theta}$, as well as estimating the asymptotic distribution of $\hat{\boldsymbol{\Theta}}_{\text{EL}}$. We now note that in the simple mean case, the solution for the MEL estimate is actually readily apparent via inspection of the Lagrange function, where the *unconstrained* maximum of $n^{-1}\sum_{i=1}^{n} \ln(p_i)$ is obtained by $p_i = n^{-1}\ \forall i$. This leads to the satisfaction of the estimating equation constraint and the solution $\hat{\theta}_{\text{EL}} = n^{-1}\sum_{i=1}^{n} y_i = \bar{y}$ for the MEL estimate. The asymptotic variance of the MEL estimator is estimated by $n^{-1}\sum_{i=1}^{n} (y_i - \bar{y})^2$. In the mean case, the EL method coincides with using the sample mean for the estimator of the population mean and the ML-type estimator of the variance. Note that $\lambda(\hat{\theta}_{\text{EL}}) = \lambda(\bar{y}) = 0$ follows from the fundamental fact that the estimating equation constraint is not constraining at the optimal MEL solution.

Table 5.3.1. *Estimated Mean and Variance of Three Estimators of* $\theta$*, from 1,000 Simulations*

| | Sample mean | | MEL | | ML estimator | |
|---|---|---|---|---|---|---|
| $n$ | Mean | Var | Mean | Var | Mean | Var |
| | | | N(0, 1), true value of $\theta = 0$ | | | |
| 10 | 0.004484 | 0.067624 | 0.006848 | 0.061824 | 0.006482 | 0.058516 |
| 20 | 0.000956 | 0.049740 | 0.001945 | 0.048108 | −0.002313 | 0.029835 |
| 30 | −0.005714 | 0.031004 | −0.005119 | 0.030921 | −0.004360 | 0.029835 |
| 40 | 0.000956 | 0.024572 | 0.002931 | 0.024221 | −0.000947 | 0.023431 |
| | | | N(1, 2), true value of $\theta = 1$ | | | |
| 10 | 1.004317 | 0.128445 | 0.946416 | 0.086383 | 0.966406 | 0.083193 |
| 20 | 0.995677 | 0.106569 | 0.952668 | 0.062353 | 0.972931 | 0.059177 |
| 30 | 1.006338 | 0.068629 | 0.968523 | 0.035759 | 0.984540 | 0.034930 |
| 40 | 1.015897 | 0.044045 | 0.984512 | 0.021883 | 0.994275 | 0.020584 |

## 5.3 Empirical Example of MEL Estimation Based on Two Moments

To provide some evidence regarding estimator performance, consider a sampling experiment first reported by Qin and Lawless (1994). In this experiment, the sample outcomes $y_1, y_2, \ldots, y_n$ are consistent with a model with first and second moments that satisfy $E[Y] = \theta$, $E[Y^2] = 2\theta^2 + 1$. One thousand samples of sizes 10, 20, 30, and 40 were generated from the population distribution $N(\theta, \theta^2 + 1)$ for two values of $\theta = 0, 1$. For each pair of sample sizes and $\theta$ values, the following three estimates of $\theta$ were obtained: (1) the sample mean (MEL using only first-moment information), (2) MEL based on both the first- and second-moment information, and (3) ML based on the normal distribution. The sample moment constraints in the MEL application were given by $\mathbf{h}(\mathbf{y}, \theta) = \sum_{i=1}^{n} p_i \begin{bmatrix} y_i - \theta \\ y_i^2 - 2\theta^2 - 1 \end{bmatrix} = \mathbf{0}$. The results for the estimated mean and variance of the three estimators of $\theta$ appear in Table 5.3.1.

As expected, the empirical variance of the MEL estimator lies between the sample mean (only first-moment information) and the parametric ML estimator. The sample mean is a semiparametric estimator based on less information than the semiparametric MEL estimator. The MEL estimator includes not only the first-order moment information but also the informative second-order moment information. The ML estimator is fully parametric and uses more information than either the sample mean or MEL estimator because it includes the precise parametric functional form of the underlying data sampling distribution. The empirical bias of MEL appears to be somewhat inferior to the other two estimators. However, the bias dissipates as sample size increases. Furthermore, the variance decreases as sample size increases and reflects the consistency of all of the estimators.

## 5.4 Hypothesis Tests and Confidence Regions: *iid* Case

In this section, we establish in an MEL context analogs to the usual likelihood ratio, Wald (W), Lagrange multiplier (LM), and Z-tests of hypotheses, relating to the value of a continuously differentiable function $\mathbf{c}(\boldsymbol{\theta})$ of the parameter vector. Confidence regions can be constructed in the usual way through duality with hypothesis tests. We also examine a method for testing the validity of the moment equations used in the definition of the MEL function. The test and confidence region methods developed in this section provide an inference base not only for this chapter but also for the chapters ahead.

### 5.4.1 Empirical Likelihood Ratio Tests and Confidence Regions for $\mathbf{c}(\boldsymbol{\theta})$

The MEL function $L_{EL}(\boldsymbol{\theta};\mathbf{y})$ bears a strong analogy to the ordinary likelihood function used in the ML procedure, when tests and confidence regions are constructed. However, now the tests and confidence regions are defined in terms of *empirical* likelihood ratios (ELR). Consider the test of the hypothesis $H_0 : \boldsymbol{\theta} = \boldsymbol{\theta}_0$ versus $H_0 : \boldsymbol{\theta} \neq \boldsymbol{\theta}_0$. The ELR

$$LR_{EL}(\boldsymbol{\theta}_0;\mathbf{Y}) = L_{EL}(\boldsymbol{\theta}_0;\mathbf{Y})/L_{EL}(\hat{\boldsymbol{\Theta}}_{EL};\mathbf{Y}) \tag{5.4.1}$$

is such that

$$-2\ln(LR_{EL}(\boldsymbol{\theta}_0;\mathbf{Y})) \overset{a}{\sim} \textit{Chi-square}\,(k,0) \text{ under } H_0, \tag{5.4.2}$$

when there are $m \geq k$ functionally independent empirical moment restriction used in the definition of the EL, and the value of the $(k \times 1)$ parameter vector $\boldsymbol{\theta}$ is set equal to the true value $\boldsymbol{\theta}_0$. Recall that *Chi-square*$(k, 0)$ denotes a Chi-square distribution with $k$ degrees of freedom and a noncentrality parameter of zero, that is, a central Chi-square distribution with $k$ degrees of freedom. An asymptotic level $\alpha$ test of $H_0$ is then defined by the rule

$$\textit{reject } H_0 : \boldsymbol{\theta} = \boldsymbol{\theta}_0 \text{ if } -2\ln(LR_{EL}(\boldsymbol{\theta}_0;\mathbf{y})) \geq \chi^2(1-\alpha, k, 0), \tag{5.4.3}$$

where $\chi^2(1-\alpha, k, 0)$ is the 100 $(1-\alpha)$% quantile of the central Chi-square distribution with $k$ degrees of freedom. An asymptotic 100 $(1-\alpha)$% confidence region for $\boldsymbol{\theta}$ can be defined in the usual way by applying the duality principle to the test procedure (5.4.3). This results in the set of $\theta_0$ values *not* rejected by the test.

The ELR can be used to construct other tests and confidence regions for subsets of the $\boldsymbol{\theta}$ vector. There is again a direct analogy to the generalized likelihood ratio (GLR) test in the ML context. Partition the parameter vector into two subvectors, as $\boldsymbol{\theta} = (\boldsymbol{\theta}_1' | \boldsymbol{\theta}_2')'$, where $\boldsymbol{\theta}_1$ is a $(q \times 1)$ vector and $\boldsymbol{\theta}_2$ is then $(k - q) \times 1$. To test the hypothesis $H_0 : \boldsymbol{\theta}_1 = \boldsymbol{\theta}_1^0$, one defines the ELR

$$\mathrm{LR}_{\mathrm{EL}}(\boldsymbol{\theta}_1^0; \mathbf{Y}) = \max_{\boldsymbol{\theta}_2} [L_{\mathrm{EL}}(\boldsymbol{\theta}_1^0, \boldsymbol{\theta}_2; \mathbf{Y}) / L_{\mathrm{EL}}(\hat{\boldsymbol{\theta}}_{\mathrm{EL}}; \mathbf{Y})], \tag{5.4.4}$$

in which case (again assuming $m \geq k$)

$$-2 \ln \left(L R_{\mathrm{EL}}(\boldsymbol{\theta}_1^0; \mathbf{Y})\right) \stackrel{a}{\sim} \textit{Chi-square}\,(q, 0) \text{ under } \mathrm{H}_0. \tag{5.4.5}$$

The test rule for $H_0 : \boldsymbol{\theta}_1 = \boldsymbol{\theta}_1^0$ is then

$$\textit{reject } H_0 \text{ if } \; -2 \ln \left(L R_{\mathrm{EL}}(\boldsymbol{\theta}_1^0; \mathbf{y})\right) \geq \chi^2(1 - \alpha, q, 0). \tag{5.4.6}$$

Among other things, this type of test can be used to examine whether certain parameters are irrelevant; that is, set $\boldsymbol{\theta}_1^0 = \mathbf{0}$ when conducting the test. Confidence regions for $\boldsymbol{\theta}_1$ can be constructed using the duality principle.

Extensions of the preceding tests and confidence region procedures to more general hypotheses of the form $\mathrm{H}_0 : \mathbf{c}(\boldsymbol{\theta}) = \mathbf{r}$ are also possible. In this case, the maximization of the numerator of the ELR is now constrained by the null hypothesis $\mathrm{H}_0 : \mathbf{c}(\boldsymbol{\theta}) = \mathbf{r}$ as

$$\mathrm{LR}_{\mathrm{EL}} = \max_{\boldsymbol{\theta}} [\mathrm{L}_{\mathrm{EL}}(\boldsymbol{\theta}; \mathbf{Y}) / \mathrm{L}_{\mathrm{EL}}(\hat{\boldsymbol{\Theta}}_{EL}; \mathbf{Y}) \text{ subject to } \mathbf{c}(\boldsymbol{\theta}) = \mathbf{r}], \tag{5.4.7}$$

and the degrees of freedom in the asymptotic Chi-square distribution equals the number of functionally independent restrictions, $j$, on the parameter vector, that is implied by $\mathbf{c}(\boldsymbol{\theta}) = \mathbf{r}$. The test and confidence region procedures then proceed in the usual way based on the asymptotic Chi-square $(j, 0)$ distribution of $-2 \ln(\mathrm{LR}_{\mathrm{EL}})$, under $\mathrm{H}_0$.

### 5.4.2 Wald Tests and Confidence Regions for $\mathbf{c}(\boldsymbol{\theta})$

It is possible to construct asymptotically valid MEL tests and confidence regions based on W statistics in the usual way, given the asymptotic normality of $\hat{\boldsymbol{\Theta}}_{EL}$. For example, to test the $j$ functionally independent nonlinear equality restrictions, $\mathbf{c}(\mathbf{\Theta}) = \mathbf{r}$, one could use the statistic

$$W = [\mathbf{c}(\hat{\mathbf{\Theta}}_{\mathrm{EL}}) - \mathbf{r}]' \left[ \frac{\partial \mathbf{c}(\mathbf{\Theta})}{\partial \mathbf{\Theta}} \bigg|_{\hat{\mathbf{\Theta}}_{\mathrm{EL}}} (n^{-1}\hat{\mathbf{\Sigma}}) \frac{\partial \mathbf{c}(\mathbf{\Theta})}{\partial \mathbf{\Theta}} \bigg|_{\hat{\mathbf{\Theta}}_{\mathrm{EL}}} \right]^{-1} [\mathbf{c}(\hat{\mathbf{\Theta}}_{\mathrm{EL}}) - \mathbf{r}]$$

$$\overset{a}{\sim} \textit{Chi-square}\,(\mathbf{j}, \mathbf{0}) \text{ under } \mathrm{H}_0 \tag{5.4.8}$$

where $\hat{\mathbf{\Sigma}}$ is defined in (5.2.4). The asymptotic level $\alpha$ test rule for $\mathrm{H}_0 : \mathbf{c}(\mathbf{\Theta}) = \mathbf{r}$ is

$$\textit{reject } \mathrm{H}_0 \text{ if } w \geq \chi^2(1-\alpha, j, 0). \tag{5.4.9}$$

A confidence region for $\mathbf{c}(\mathbf{\Theta})$, with asymptotic level $100(1-\alpha)\%$ confidence, can be based on duality with the W hypothesis test, where the confidence region would be the set of $\mathbf{r}$ vectors *not* rejected by the W test (5.4.8).

### 5.4.3 Lagrange Multiplier Tests and Confidence Regions for $\mathbf{c}(\mathbf{\Theta})$

Lagrange multiplier tests of the hypothesis $\mathrm{H}_0 : \mathbf{c}(\mathbf{\Theta}) = \mathbf{r}$ can be defined in terms of the LM $\boldsymbol{\xi}$ of the *constrained*, by $\mathrm{H}_0$, MEL problem. The LM test may be expressed in Lagrange form by

$$n^{-1}\ln(L_{EL}(\mathbf{\Theta}\,;\mathbf{y})) + \boldsymbol{\xi}'(\mathbf{c}(\mathbf{\Theta}) - \mathbf{r}), \tag{5.4.10}$$

and under $\mathrm{H}_0$

$$n^{1/2}\hat{\boldsymbol{\xi}} \xrightarrow{d} N\left(\mathbf{0}, \left[ \frac{\partial \mathbf{c}(\mathbf{\Theta})}{\partial \mathbf{\Theta}'} \bigg|_{\theta_0} \Sigma \frac{\partial \mathbf{c}(\mathbf{\Theta})}{\partial \mathbf{\Theta}} \bigg|_{\theta_0} \right]^{-1}\right). \tag{5.4.11}$$

Therefore, it follows that

$$n\hat{\boldsymbol{\xi}}' \left[ \frac{\partial \mathbf{c}(\mathbf{\Theta})}{\partial \mathbf{\Theta}'} \bigg|_{\theta_0} \Sigma \frac{\partial \mathbf{c}(\mathbf{\Theta})}{\partial \mathbf{\Theta}} \bigg|_{\theta_0} \right] \hat{\boldsymbol{\xi}} \xrightarrow{d} \textit{Chi-square}\,(j, 0) \text{ under } H_0, \tag{5.4.12}$$

where, as usual, $j$ is the number of functionally independent constraints on $\mathbf{\Theta}$ implied by $\mathrm{H}_0 : \mathbf{c}(\mathbf{\Theta}) = \mathbf{r}$. An operational LM statistic is obtained from (5.4.12) by replacing $\mathbf{\Theta}_0$ with the constrained MEL estimate $\hat{\mathbf{\Theta}}_{EL}^{c}$ and replacing $\mathbf{\Sigma}$ *by* $\hat{\mathbf{\Sigma}}$, with all estimates derived from the constrained MEL procedure. The test is then conducted in the usual way based on critical values obtained from the Chi-square($j$, 0) distribution. Confidence regions can be derived from the hypothesis tests based on duality.

### 5.4.4 Z-Test of Inequality Hypotheses for the Value of $\mathbf{c}(\mathbf{\Theta})$

Given the asymptotic normality of $\hat{\mathbf{\Theta}}_{\mathrm{EL}}$, it is possible to construct asymptotically valid tests of scalar inequality hypotheses and to define confidence bounds based on Z-statistics. For example, to test the nonlinear inequality restrictions, $c(\Theta) \leq r$, one could use the test statistic

$$Z = \frac{c(\hat{\Theta}_{EL}) - r}{\left[\frac{\partial c(\theta)}{\partial \theta'}\big|_{\hat{\Theta}_{EL}} (n^{-1}\hat{\Sigma}) \frac{\partial c(\theta)}{\partial \theta}\big|_{\hat{\Theta}_{EL}}\right]^{1/2}} \overset{a}{\sim} N(\delta, 1), \tag{5.4.13}$$

where $\hat{\Sigma}$ is defined in (5.2.4) and

$$\delta = \frac{c(\theta_0) - r}{\left[\frac{\partial c(\theta)}{\partial \theta'}\big|_{\Theta_0} \Sigma \frac{\partial c(\theta)}{\partial \theta}\big|_{\Theta_0}\right]^{1/2}}. \tag{5.4.14}$$

The asymptotic level $\alpha$ test rule for $H_0 : c(\theta) \leq r$ is

$$\textit{reject } H_0 \text{ if } z \geq z(1-\alpha), \tag{5.4.15}$$

where $z(1-\alpha)$ is the $100(1-\alpha)\%$ quantile of the standard normal distribution. Reversing inequalities defines a test of the hypothesis $H_0 : c(\theta) \geq r$. Confidence bounds for $c(\theta)$, with asymptotic level $100(1-\alpha)\%$ confidence, can be based on duality with the Z-tests, where the confidence region is the set of r values *not* rejected by the Z-test.

### 5.4.5 Testing the Validity of Moment Equations

Because moment-estimating equations are used as a link to the data, another MEL test of interest concerns the validity of the moment equations, $H_0 : E[\mathbf{h}(\mathbf{Y}, \theta)] = \mathbf{0}$. This is equivalent to testing the *unbiasedness* of the estimating functions used in the EL approach. Two natural ways of testing this hypothesis are through the ELR test and the LM test.

The MEL ratio test of moment equation validity is defined analogous to the way GLR tests of functional restrictions would be tested. Recall from Chapter 4 that if the estimating equation restrictions are removed from the optimization, then the EL is optimized at $\hat{p}_i = n^{-1}\ \forall i$. This is coincident with the classical EDF of the data. The value of the unrestricted EL function is then $L^*_{EL} = n^{-n}$. In addition, note that $L_{EL}(\hat{\theta}_{EL}; \mathbf{Y})$ is the maximum MEL possible, *subject to the estimating equation restrictions.* As one might anticipate, a test of the $m$ estimating equation restrictions can be conducted based on the ELR statistic

$$LR_{EL}(\mathbf{Y}) = L_{EL}(\hat{\Theta}; \mathbf{Y})/L^*_{EL}. \tag{5.4.16}$$

If the moment constraints are correct,

$$-2\ln(LR_{EL}(\mathbf{Y})) \overset{a}{\sim} \textit{Chi-square}\,(m-k, 0). \tag{5.4.17}$$

The asymptotic $\alpha$-level ELR test of the validity of the moment restrictions may be conducted as

$$\text{reject } \mathrm{H}_0 : E[\mathbf{h}(Y, \boldsymbol{\theta})] = \mathbf{0} \text{ if } -2\ln(LR_{\mathrm{EL}}(\mathbf{y})) \geq \chi^2(1-\alpha, m-k, 0). \tag{5.4.18}$$

It is also possible to devise an LM test of the validity of the estimating equation restrictions. This follows because the LMs, associated with the moment constraints in the definition of the MEL estimator, are such that

$$n^{1/2}\boldsymbol{\lambda}(\hat{\boldsymbol{\Theta}}_{\mathrm{EL}}) \xrightarrow{d} N(\mathbf{0}, \Psi), \tag{5.4.19}$$

where

$$\Psi = [\mathrm{E}[\mathbf{hh}'|_{\boldsymbol{\theta}_0}]]^{-1}\left[\mathbf{I}_{\mathrm{m}} - \mathbf{E}\left[\frac{\partial \mathbf{h}}{\partial \boldsymbol{\theta}}\bigg|_{\boldsymbol{\theta}_0}\right]' \Sigma\, \mathrm{E}\left[\frac{\partial \mathbf{h}}{\partial \boldsymbol{\theta}}\bigg|_{\boldsymbol{\theta}_0}\right][E[\mathbf{hh}'|_{\boldsymbol{\theta}_0}]]^{-1}\right], \tag{5.4.20}$$

and $\Sigma$ is as defined in (5.2.3). Note that $\Psi$ is a $(\mathrm{m} \times \mathrm{m})$ matrix of rank $(m-k)$, and so the limiting distribution in (5.4.21) is a *singular* normal distribution. The asymptotic covariance matrix, $\Psi$, can be estimated by replacing $\Sigma$ with $\hat{\Sigma}$, defined in (5.2.4), and making analogous substitutions. Finally, the LM test of the validity of the estimating equations is based on the LM statistic:

$$LM = n\boldsymbol{\lambda}(\hat{\boldsymbol{\Theta}}_{\mathrm{EL}})'\hat{\Psi}^{-}\boldsymbol{\lambda}(\hat{\boldsymbol{\Theta}}_{\mathrm{EL}}) \sim \textit{Chi-square}\,(m-k, 0) \text{ under } \mathrm{H}_0, \tag{5.4.21}$$

where $H_0$ is the hypothesis that the restrictions are valid and $\hat{\Psi}^{-}$ is the generalized inverse of $\hat{\Psi}$. Because of the degree of singularity in the distribution of $\boldsymbol{\lambda}(\hat{\boldsymbol{\Theta}}_{\mathrm{EL}})$, the degrees of freedom are $(m-k)$. The test rule is

$$\text{reject } \mathrm{H}_0 \text{ if } lm \geq \chi^2(1-\alpha, m-k, 0)\,. \tag{5.4.22}$$

For completeness, we note that MEL-based testing and confidence regions, when $\mathbf{X}$ is stochastic, proceed analogous to methods developed in the preceding sections.

### 5.4.6 MEL Testing and Confidence Intervals for Population Mean

In this section, we continue the illustration concerning the population mean begun in Chapter 4 and examine testing and confidence interval generation within the MEL context. Suppose we were interested in testing the hypothesis that the population distribution had a zero mean, so that

$H_0 : \theta = 0$. The ELR in (5.4.1) may be used to test this hypothesis. The ELR test statistic is specified as

$$-2\ln(LR_{\mathrm{EL}}(0)) = 2\sum_{i=1}^{n} \ln(1+\lambda(0)y_i)\,. \tag{5.4.23}$$

To see this, note that

$$2\ln(L_{\mathrm{EL}}(\hat{\theta}_{\mathrm{EL}};\mathbf{y})) = -2\sum_{i=1}^{n} \ln(n[1+\lambda(\hat{\theta}_{\mathrm{EL}})(y_i-\hat{\theta}_{\mathrm{EL}})]) = -2n\ln(n) \tag{5.4.24}$$

because $\lambda(\hat{\theta}_{\mathrm{EL}}) = \lambda(\overline{y}) = 0$. The test statistic is calculated by first solving for $\lambda$ in (5.4.23), with $\theta = 0$, and then substituting the solution value for $\lambda(0)$. The hypothesis $H_0 : \theta = 0$ may also be tested based on the asymptotic result that $\hat{\theta}_{\mathrm{EL}} = \overline{\mathrm{Y}} \overset{a}{\sim} N(\mu, \sigma^2/n)$. The W test (5.4.10)–(5.4.11) for this problem is based on the statistic

$$W = \overline{\mathrm{Y}}'[S^2/n]^{-1}\overline{\mathrm{Y}} \overset{a}{\sim} \textit{Chi-square}\,(1,0) \text{ under } \mathrm{H}_0, \tag{5.4.25}$$

with the test rule

$$\text{reject } \mathrm{H}_0 \text{ if } \mathrm{w} \geq \chi^2(1-\alpha, 1, 0), \tag{5.4.26}$$

where $S^2 = n^{-1}\sum_{i=1}^{n}(\mathrm{Y}_i - \overline{\mathrm{Y}})^2$. In either the ELR or W context, confidence regions for $\mu$ may be obtained in the usual way via duality.

For the problem of estimating and testing the population mean, the estimating equations (5.4.8) just identify the unknown parameters; therefore, the validity of the estimating equation (5.4.8) *cannot* be tested with either the ELR test (5.4.20) or the LM test (5.4.24). However, we can conduct tests regarding hypothesized values of the location parameter, $\theta = \theta_0$.

### 5.4.7 Illustrative MEL Confidence Interval Example

Qin and Lawless use an experiment to compare three methods of obtaining confidence intervals for $\boldsymbol{\theta}$. One method (ELR) obtains confidence intervals using the ELR statistic and the Chi-square approximation. The second method is based on a Z-statistic and the limiting normal distribution and is referred to as normal confidence interval, or NCI. The third method (GLR) uses the parametric GLR statistic based on the normal distribution $\mathrm{N}(\theta, \theta^2+1)$. The average confidence interval length and empirical coverage probability for 1,000 samples and sample sizes of 30 and 60 are given in Table 5.4.1.

Table 5.4.1. *Average Length (AVL) and Empirical Coverage (ECV) for Three Confidence Interval Methods, from 1,000 Simulations*

| | | 90% | | 95% | |
|---|---|---|---|---|---|
| | | AVL | ECV | AVL | ECV |
| | | $n = 30$ | | | |
| N(0,1) | ELR | 0.55064 | 85.8% | 0.65714 | 92.4% |
| | NCI | 0.56965 | 86.0% | 0.67889 | 92.0% |
| | GLR | 0.60197 | 89.6% | 0.72441 | 94.3% |
| N(1,2) | ELR | 0.56698 | 83.3% | 0.67737 | 89.2% |
| | NCI | 0.56863 | 84.3% | 0.67767 | 90.1% |
| | GLR | 0.61489 | 88.3% | 0.73900 | 93.6% |
| | | $n = 60$ | | | |
| N(0,1) | ELR | 0.41535 | 89.5% | 0.49611 | 95.4% |
| | NCI | 0.41291 | 89.2% | 0.49210 | 94.9% |
| | GLR | 0.42549 | 90.8% | 0.50950 | 96.1% |
| N(1,2) | ELR | 0.41200 | 88.6% | 0.49267 | 94.1% |
| | NCI | 0.40933 | 89.0% | 0.48782 | 93.2% |
| | GLR | 0.42845 | 91.3% | 0.51265 | 96.1% |

In general, the two MEL methods yield coverage probability less than nominal coverages. As might be expected, the GLR approach, based on the correct parametric likelihood, yields intervals that are close to the nominal coverage probability. Also, note that the average length of the MEL confidence intervals compares favorably to the alternatives, being the shortest in half of the cases examined, and always shorter than GLR intervals.

## 5.5 Concluding Comments

In this chapter, we extended the method of MEL estimation to include inference. *This significantly enlarges the scope of procedures available for solving stochastic inverse problems in cases where full probability distribution specifications are not available.* At this point, a few generalizations that emerge from the works of Owen (1991), Qin and Lawless (1994, 1995), and Kolaczyk (1994) are useful in comparing alternative approaches to estimation and inference.

In terms of inference, the MEL point estimates will be the same in linear models under classical assumptions, but the corresponding likelihood ratio curves and confidence regions need not be the same. The MEL method only requires that the estimating functions have zero expectations. This means the estimating function must only be unbiased and thus imparts a degree of robustness to the MEL approach. In the fully parametric case using parametric methods of analysis, if the variance function (of parameters) is functionally misspecified, the normal approximation to estimators is still valid, but the Chi-square approximation and associated confidence limits of the usual test statistics are not valid. In general, under MEL, if the variance is misspecified, there will be a loss of efficiency but, over a large class of linear, nonlinear, and semiparametric models, test statistics and confidence regions are still valid.

Finally, we note that MEL shares the sampling properties of various nonparametric methods based on resampling of the data, such as the bootstrap. However, in contrast to the resampling methods, MEL works by optimizing a continuously differentiable function, which makes it amenable to imposing side constraints on the parameters that add information to the data.

Chapters 4 and 5 relating to the MEL approach to estimation and inference raise a number of issues that we underscore here. First, why would one use the parametric ML concept when knowledge of the parametric family of probability distributions underlying the DSP, and thus the likelihood function, is generally unknown? On a related note, what are the estimation and inference implications of achieving first-order asymptotic statistical results analogous to parametric methods but that do not rely on a generally unknown parametric specification of the likelihood function? The number of unknowns in DSPs analyzed in practice generally exceeds the number of data points available. Thus, unique solutions for the unknowns are not possible in the absence of using some estimation criteria that, when applied, determines a choice of the unknowns given the data available. The ML approach is based on the assumption of perfect knowledge of the functional form of the probability distribution underlying the DSP and chooses an estimate of the associated finite number of unknown parameters using the estimation criteria of maximizing the likelihood function, implied by that generally unknown probability distribution. Alternatively, MEL begins by representing the probability distribution of the DSP, and thus the likelihood function of the unknowns, fully nonparametrically, and then proceeds to choose the probability weights for the data that satisfy certain fundamental moment relationships among the random variables of the DSP. In practice, moment relationships hold more generally and are less prone to misspecification than the full parametric probability distribution underlying the DSP. Consequently, the probability distribution and the likelihood function implied by the MEL approach are less prone to misspecification, and estimation and inference based on the EL should be more accurate.

In closing, asymptotically, the ELR statistic allows us to test hypotheses and construct confidence intervals. However, small sample behavior of this statistic may be problematic. If the sample mean is not inside the convex hull of the sample, the statistic is undefined. For a discussion of this problem, see Emerson (2009). Also, we note that the set of data supported probability mass functions that satisfy the empirical estimating equations may be empty for some models and finite data samples. For discussion of the empty-set problem, see Grendar and Judge (2010).

## 5.6 Selected References

DiCiccio, T. and J. Romano (1990), "Nonparametric Confidence Limits by Resampling Methods and Least Favorable Families," *International Statistical Review*, **58**:59–76.

DiCiccio, T. J., P. Hall, and J. Romano (1989), "Comparison of Parametric and Empirical Likelihood Functions," *Biometrika*, **76**:465–476.

Emerson, S. (2009), "Small Sample Performance and Calibration of the Empirical Likelihood Method," Dissertation, Department of Statistics, Stanford University (Google accessible).

Grendar, M. and G. Judge (2010), "The Empty Set Problem of Maximum Empirical Likelihood Methods," *Electronic Journal of Statistics*, **3**:1542–1555.

Hall, P. (1990), "Pseudo-Likelihood Theory for Empirical Likelihood," *The Annals of Statistics*, **18**:121–140.

Kolaczyk, E. (1994), "Empirical Likelihood for Generalized Linear Models," *Statistica Sinica*, **4**:199–218.

McCullagh, P. and J. A. Nelder (1989), *Generalized Linear Models*, 2nd ed., London: Chapman and Hall.

Mittelhammer, R., G. Judge, and D. J. Miller (2000), *Econometric Foundations*, Cambridge: Cambridge University Press.

Owen, A. (1988), "Empirical Likelihood Ratio Confidence Intervals for a Single Functional," *Biometrika*, **75**:237–249.

Owen, A. (1990), "Empirical Likelihood Ratio Confidence Regions," *Annals of Statistics*, **18**:90–120.

Owen, A. (1991), "Empirical Likelihood for Linear Models," *Annals of Statistics*, **19**:1725–1747.

Qin, J. and J. Lawless (1994), "Empirical Likelihood and General Estimating Equations," *Annals of Statistics*, **22**:300–325.

Qin, J. and J. Lawless (1995), "Estimating Equations, Empirical Likelihood, and Constraints on Parameters," *Canadian Journal of Statistics*, **23**:145–159.

SIX

# Kullback-Leibler Information and the Maximum Empirical Exponential Likelihood

## 6.1 Introduction

In this chapter, we continue to build on the extremum (E) estimation and estimating equations (EE) concepts introduced in Chapter 3 and the maximum empirical likelihood (MEL) approach demonstrated in Chapters 4 and 5. Our focus is on methods of estimation and inference involving stochastic inverse problems of the form $(\mathbf{Y}, \mathbf{X}) \Rightarrow (\boldsymbol{\beta}, \sigma^2, \boldsymbol{\varepsilon})$. In this context, in this chapter we introduce the Kullback-Leibler Information Criterion (KLIC) and the maximum empirical exponential likelihood (MEEL) function and estimator.

### 6.1.1 Solutions to Systems of Estimating Equations and Kullback-Leibler Information

The procedures examined in the previous three chapters involved solutions relating to systems of estimating equations (EEs). In both the MEL and EE contexts, the EEs were empirical analogs to expectation relations of the type $\mathrm{E}[\mathbf{h}(\mathbf{Y}, \mathbf{X}, \boldsymbol{\theta})] = \mathbf{0}$. Estimators for $\boldsymbol{\theta}$, defined by the solution to moment equations, subsume a large collection of familiar estimation procedures that include linear and nonlinear least squares. The idea of basing an estimator definition on the solution to EEs can be applied quite generally to extremum problems, as demonstrated in Chapter 3.

In the MEL procedure, developed in Chapter 4, the focus was on a vector of EEs whose dimension, $m$, is at least as large as the dimension of the unknown parameter vector $\boldsymbol{\theta}$. The EEs were defined as empirical analogs to population moments, $\mathrm{E}[\mathbf{h}(Y, \mathbf{X}, \boldsymbol{\theta})] = \mathbf{0}$. In the transition to empirical specifications of the moment conditions, a vector of $n$ unknown nonnegative weights, $\mathbf{p} = (p_1, p_2, \ldots, p_n)'$, was introduced, yielding the empirical moment equations, $\sum_{i=1}^{n} p_i \mathbf{h}(y_i, \mathbf{x}_{i\cdot}, \boldsymbol{\theta}) = \mathbf{0}$. This $m$-dimensional vector moment equation, coupled with the adding-up restriction, $\sum_{i=1}^{n} p_i = 1$, was sufficient to determine only $(m+1)$ of the $(n+k)$ unknowns, $(\boldsymbol{\theta}, \mathbf{p})$. This leaves $(n+k-(m+1))$ of the unknowns undetermined. The under-determined nature of the system of moment equations was resolved in Chapter 4 by the introduction of an estimation objective function, $n^{-1}\sum_{i=1}^{n} \ln(p_i)$, which was maximized, subject to the moment equation constraints, to determine the $(n+k)$ unknowns, $(\boldsymbol{\theta}, \mathbf{p})$. Relatedly, constrained estimation of $n^{-1}\sum_{i=1}^{n} \ln(p_i)$ for *given* values of $\boldsymbol{\theta}$ resulted in a maximum value function, $\sum_{i=1}^{n} \ln(p_i(\boldsymbol{\theta}))$, which was interpreted as an *empirical log-likelihood function* for $\boldsymbol{\theta}$. The resulting MEL estimator was defined by maximizing this empirical log-likelihood function with respect to $\boldsymbol{\theta}$. When the number of moment constraints, $m$, exceeds the number of unknown parameters, $k$, the MEL approach defines the optimal combination of the moment equations and duplicates the asymptotic efficiency of the most efficient EEs estimator. *Recall that the efficient EE estimator is obtained from the most efficient set of* k *estimating equations that can be constructed from the information contained in linear combinations of the set of* m *moment equations.*

To provide perspective on where we have been and where we are going with respect to the concept of EEs and *the general notion of an empirical representation of likelihood*, we return to a general stochastic inverse problem context and the interesting and challenging task of recovering unobservables from observables. *Indeed, progress in previous chapters has been measured by how and "how well" we solved such inverse problems involving indirect noisy observations.* In many cases in economics, we use unobservable probabilities to characterize information contained in observables (data). If we can *define a set of consistent probability values with the observables* of the problem, then the issue becomes how to use these probabilities to provide a basis for estimation and inference for the remaining unknowns of direct interest. *In this stochastic inverse problem situation, we have reversed the process of modeling data information via probabilities and have used the data information to recover values of the probabilities, which we then subsequently use for estimation and inference purposes.* One can then view the recovered probability values as *inverse probabilities*, that is, the probability weight solutions to a stochastic inverse problem.

In Chapter 4, we considered the case of a finite and a discrete (in terms of unknown probability weights) stochastic inverse problem, involving *iid* outcomes, $y_1, \ldots, y_n$, which were observed along with *empirical* moment conditions. We used an estimation objective function together with observed data to define a profile likelihood function and corresponding inverse probabilities; that is, we defined an empirical likelihood function associated with an empirical probability distribution (Owen, 1990). By choosing the criterion of maximizing the empirical likelihood function, we identified a basis for recovering the unobservable inverse probabilities and defined a solution to the estimation and inference problem relating to unknown parameters of the stochastic inverse problem.

The act of maximizing the empirical likelihood function and producing the MEL estimator results is *one* way to define an empirical likelihood estimator that has good first-order asymptotic properties. In contrast to the traditional MEL formulation and solution, in this chapter we take a more general approach and examine an alternative estimation objective function for deriving solutions to sets of EEs. This approach has been called various names in the literature, including *relative* entropy, *cross* entropy, *discriminant information*, and the *Kullback-Leibler* (KL) *information criterion*. We adopt the latter name in recognition of Kullback and Leibler (1951), whose seminal article stimulated the development and use of the criterion in the statistics literature. The KL approach subsumes the MEL as a special case and encompasses the maximum entropy principle and the MEEL function for use in solving stochastic inverse problems.

## 6.2 Kullback-Leibler Information Criterion (KLIC)

Kullback-Leibler information is a measure of the discrepancy between two probability distributions, say, $\mathbf{p}(\mathbf{y})$ and $\mathbf{w}(\mathbf{y})$. The KL information in $\mathbf{p}(\mathbf{y})$ relative to $\mathbf{w}(\mathbf{y})$, which is referred to in the physics literature as the entropy of $\mathbf{p}$ *relative to* $\mathbf{w}$, is defined in the discrete case by

$$\mathrm{KL}(\mathbf{p}, \mathbf{w}) = \sum_{y} p(y) \ln(p(y)/w(y)) \tag{6.2.1}$$

and in the continuous case by

$$\mathrm{KL}(\mathbf{p}, \mathbf{w}) = \int_{y} p(y) \ln(p(y)/w(y)) dy. \tag{6.2.2}$$

In the discrete case, we denote KL information alternatively as $\mathrm{KL}(\mathbf{p}, \mathbf{w}) = \sum_i p_i \ln(p_i/w_i)$, where $\mathbf{p}$ and $\mathbf{w}$ denote the vectors of finite or countable probability weights implied by the discrete distributions $\mathbf{p}(\mathbf{y})$ and $\mathbf{w}(\mathbf{y})$. The distribution in the second position, $\mathbf{w}$, of the argument list in $\mathrm{KL}(\mathbf{p}, \mathbf{w})$

is called the *reference distribution* and often in practice is specified as a uniform distribution $\mathbf{w} = 1/n$. The first distribution in the argument list, $\mathbf{p}$, is usually referred to as the *subject distribution.*

The KL information in $\mathbf{w}(\mathbf{y})$ relative to $\mathbf{p}(\mathbf{y})$, denoted as $\text{KL}(\mathbf{w}, \mathbf{p})$, is obtained by reversing the roles of the reference and subject distributions; that is, $\mathbf{p}$ and $\mathbf{w}$ are reversed in (6.2.1)–(6.2.2). Note that the KL information metric is not symmetric in $\mathbf{p}$ and $\mathbf{w}$ so that, in general, $\text{KL}(\mathbf{w}, \mathbf{p}) \neq \text{KL}(\mathbf{p}, \mathbf{w})$. Consequently, KL is not a true measure of the distance between $\mathbf{p}$ and $\mathbf{w}$ and is referred to instead as a *pseudodistance function* or as a *discrepancy function.* For our purposes, this property is not particularly important because the reference distribution is usually taken to be fixed in noisy estimation problems. We are only concerned in our stochastic inverse problem with choosing the subject distribution $\mathbf{p}$ that minimizes KL discrepancy, subject to solving the moment equations. This results in an estimate of $\mathbf{p}$ that is as close as possible to the reference distribution $\mathbf{w}$ (i.e., as close to the reference distribution as the moment equations, and the noisy data will permit, where closeness is measured in KL pseudodistance).

The KLIC for our stochastic inverse problem has a number of useful statistical properties relating to sufficient statistics, information additivity, and hypothesis testing, and the interested reader is directed to Kullback and Leibler (1951) and Kullback (1959, 1987), as well as the discussion later in this chapter for details. Our principal interest is in the noisy discrete case. For our immediate purposes, it is useful to note that $\text{KL}(\mathbf{p}, \mathbf{w}) \geq 0$ for every $\mathbf{p} \geq \mathbf{0}$, and $\text{KL}(\mathbf{p}, \mathbf{w}) = 0$ *iff* $\mathbf{p} = \mathbf{w}$. Furthermore, $\text{KL}(\mathbf{p}, \mathbf{w})$ is a strictly convex function of the elements of $\mathbf{p}$. The latter property follows directly from an examination of the second-order derivative matrix of $\text{KL}(\mathbf{p}, \mathbf{w})$, with respect to $\mathbf{p}$, and recalling that $p_i \in [0, 1], \forall i$. Note that $w \ln(w)$ is *defined* to be 0 when $\text{w} = 0$. The closer $\text{KL}(\mathbf{p}, \mathbf{w})$ is to zero, the more similar is the distribution $\mathbf{p}(\mathbf{y})$ relative to $\mathbf{w}(\mathbf{y})$, and the distributions coincide when $\text{KL}(\mathbf{p}, \mathbf{w}) = 0$. The greater the value of $\text{KL}(\mathbf{p}, \mathbf{w})$, the greater the discrepancy between the distributions $\mathbf{p}(\mathbf{y})$ and $\mathbf{w}(\mathbf{y})$.

We can interpret the KL information value, as we do later in this chapter, as the expectation of a log-likelihood ratio, and it is in this context that Kullback (1959) and Gokhale and Kullback (1978) used it to discriminate between distributional hypotheses relating to the probability distributions of observed indirect noisy data. To illustrate, let $\boldsymbol{\theta}_1$ and $\boldsymbol{\theta}_2$ be two alternative values of the parameter vector leading to two alternative discrete probability distribution characterizations, $f(y; \boldsymbol{\theta}_1)$ and $f(y; \boldsymbol{\theta}_2)$, for the distribution of $Y$. Consider in this context the KL information in $f(y; \boldsymbol{\theta}_1)$ relative to

$f(y;\theta_2)$, given by

$$\begin{aligned}\mathrm{KL}(f(y;\theta_1), f(y;\theta_2)) &= \sum_y [\ln(f(y;\theta_1)/f(y;\theta_2))]\, f(y;\theta_1)\\ &= \mathrm{E}_{\theta_1}[\ln(L(\theta_1;\mathrm{Y})/L(\theta_2;\mathrm{Y}))],\end{aligned} \tag{6.2.3}$$

where $\mathrm{E}_{\theta_1}$ denotes an expectation taken with respect to the distribution $f(y;\theta_1)$. It is apparent that the KL information in (6.2.3) can be interpreted as a mean log-likelihood ratio, where averaging is done using weights provided by the subject distribution. Interpreting $\ln(f(y;\theta_1)/f(y;\theta_2)) = \ln(L(\theta_1;y)/L(\theta_2;y))$ as the information in the data outcome $y$ in favor of the hypothesis $\theta_1$ relative to $\theta_2$, Kullback then interprets (6.2.3) as the *mean information* provided by sample data in favor of $\theta_1$, relative to $\theta_2$, *under the assumption that* $\theta_1$ *is actually true.* The KL information criterion can be defined in a way that subsumes the MEL objective function as a special case and this relationship is demonstrated in Appendix 6.A.1.

### 6.2.1 Relationship between Maximum Empirical Exponential Likelihood (MEEL) and KL Information

It is interesting to consider what would happen if we used a uniform distribution for the reference distributions in defining the KL-information objective function in solving the empirical moment equations. In this case, the objective is to minimize the KL-discrepancy between the subject distribution and the classical empirical distribution function on the data. The result is the MEEL criterion pseudodistance measure, and this pseudodistance measure is also known in the literature as the *maximum entropy* criterion (Jaynes 1957a, 1957b, 1963, 1984; Golan et al. 1996). In place of the MEL criterion, the entropy metric provides an alternative basis for determining the sample weights, or inverse probabilities. In particular, if we minimize KL information, subject to the empirical moment constraints, $\sum_{i=1}^n p_i \mathbf{h}(y_i, \mathbf{x}_{i\cdot}, \theta) = \mathbf{0}$, and the normalization constraints, $\sum_{i=1}^n p_i = 1$, the KL-information criterion is defined as

$$\mathrm{KL}(\mathbf{p}, n^{-1}\mathbf{1}_n) = \sum_{i=1}^n p_i \ln(np_i) = \sum_{i=1}^n p_i \ln(p_i) + \ln(n), \tag{6.2.4}$$

where $\mathbf{p} = (p_1, p_2, \ldots, p_n)'$ denotes probability weights on the noisy sample observations. Minimizing KL information is clearly equivalent to *maximizing* $-\sum_{i=1}^{n} p_i \ln(p_i)$, which is precisely the Shannon-Jaynes information (entropy) measure.

The particular KL-information criterion defined in (6.2.4) may be interpreted as a measure of the degree of uncertainty in a discrete probability distribution, $\mathbf{p} = (p_1, p_2, \ldots, p_n)'$. The criterion takes on its maximal value of $\log(n)$; thus, the KL-information criterion takes its minimum value, when the distribution is maximally dispersed and thus uniformly distributed on the $y_i$s. Therefore, $-\sum_{i=1}^{n} p_i \ln(p_i)$ is maximized when $\mathbf{p}$ is maximally uninformative, with regard to discriminating between likely and unlikely outcomes among $y_1, y_2, \ldots, y_n$. The KL function (6.2.4) takes on its maximum value of 0, if the distribution is maximally informative, in that $\mathbf{p}$ is degenerate on one particular $y_i$ value; that is, $p_i = 1$ and $p_j = 0$, $\forall i \neq j$, where $0 \ln(0) \equiv 0$.

### 6.2.1a Objective of MEEL

Now consider interpreting the objective of MEEL or, equivalently, minimizing $\mathrm{KL}(\mathbf{p}, n^{-1}\mathbf{1}_n)$, defined in (6.2.4). In the absence of any constraints, other than the standard normalization, $\sum_{i=1}^{n} p_i = 1$, it follows immediately that $p_i = n^{-1}$, $\forall i$ are the optimal choices of the $p_i$s. Therefore, as in the case of the MEL, under the minimum $\mathrm{KL}(n^{-1}\mathbf{1}_n, \mathbf{p})$ criterion, the solution for the $p_i$s is drawn toward the maximally uninformative uniform distribution. If the minimization of $\mathrm{KL}(\mathbf{p}, n^{-1}\mathbf{1}_n)$ is constrained by $m$ moment equations, then the objective can again be interpreted as choosing the $p_i$s to be as maximally uninformative as the moment equations (the links to the data) will allow. The objective is consistent with the goal of not wanting to assert more about the distribution of the noisy $\mathrm{Y}_i$s than is known via the moment equations' links to the data. Extraneous information is "minimized out" using the $\mathrm{KL}(\mathbf{p}, n^{-1}\mathbf{1}_n)$ criterion, just as it is for the MEL criterion. In effect, one is making use of all of the information available for the problem (i.e., the moment constraints and uniform reference distribution), but one is also avoiding the unintentional introduction of empty or unsubstantiated informational assumptions.

What is the difference between MEL and MEEL *for obtaining empirical probability or likelihood weights* or, equivalently, for a stochastic inverse problem, what is the difference between minimizing $\mathrm{KL}(n^{-1}\mathbf{1}_n, \mathbf{p})$ and $\mathrm{KL}(\mathbf{p}, n^{-1}\mathbf{1}_n)$? The difference lies in the calibration of the mean information provided by sample data for and against the uniform and the **p** distribution of probabilities on the $y_i$s. In the MEL or, equivalently, $KL(n^{-1}\mathbf{1}_n, \mathbf{p})$ case, *averaging is performed with respect to the predata empirical distribution function weights* $n^{-1}$ for each $Y_i$. Then, assuming the uniform distribution to be true, the mean information is interpreted in the context of the expected information in favor of the uniform distribution relative to the postdata estimated probability distribution **p**. In the MEEL or $KL(\mathbf{p}, n^{-1}\mathbf{1}_n)$ case, *averaging is performed with respect to the postdata probability distribution* **p**. Thus, assuming the **p** distribution to be true, the mean information is interpreted in the context of the expected information in favor of the **p**-distribution relative to the predata empirical distribution function (EDF) weights, $n^{-1}$, for each $Y_i$.

Heuristically, the MEEL or $KL(\mathbf{p}, n^{-1}\mathbf{1}_n)$ criteria would seem the more appealing of the two approaches because it weights discrepancies between the uniform and **p** distributions, using estimates of the probabilities of the $y_i$s, which are based on observed data information rather than on a priori uniform weights. Assuming that the moment equation information is valid, one would then anticipate that the expected log-likelihood ratio, or mean sample information in favor/against the uniform distribution, is estimated more efficiently in the MEEL approach because it is calculated with respect to probability weights inferred from a larger data-enriched information base. Consequently, in this chapter, we focus on the MEEL estimation objective function

$$KL(\mathbf{p}, n^{-1}\mathbf{1}_n) = \sum_{i=1}^{n} p_i \left[\ln(p_i) - \ln\left(\frac{1}{n}\right)\right] \tag{6.2.5}$$

instead of the MEL estimation objective function

$$KL(n^{-1}\mathbf{1}_n, \mathbf{p}) = \sum_{i=1}^{n} \frac{1}{n}\left[\ln\left(\frac{1}{n}\right) - \ln(p_i)\right], \tag{6.2.6}$$

which is, except for an additive constant, the negative of the traditional log-MEL objective function. *In Section 6.3.1, we draw an interesting connection between MEEL and a likelihood function based on the data.* A numerical illustration of the estimation of the probability distribution associated with a data sampling process based on both the MEL and MEEL estimation objectives is provided in Appendix 6.A.1 of this chapter.

## 6.3 The General MEEL Alternative Empirical Likelihood Formulation

If we use MEEL as a basis for estimating the $p_i$s of the multinomial likelihood function, the corresponding problem of estimating the unknown probability weights becomes

$$\underset{\mathbf{p}}{\text{Max}} \quad S(\mathbf{p}) \equiv -\sum_{i=1}^{n} p_i \ln p_i, \tag{6.3.1}$$

subject to

$$\sum_{i=1}^{n} p_i h_j(y_i, \boldsymbol{\theta}) = 0 \qquad j = 1, 2, \ldots, m \tag{6.3.2}$$

and

$$\sum_{i=1}^{n} p_i = 1 \text{ and } p_i \geq 0 \quad \forall i. \tag{6.3.3}$$

On close examination of the problem formulation, it is evident that except for the estimation objective function, the form of the stochastic inverse problem and the basis for the MEEL solution closely mirror the problem form and solution for MEL discussed in Chapter 4.

### 6.3.1 The MEEL Estimator and Alternative Empirical Likelihood

The Lagrangian form of the MEEL problem for a given value of $\boldsymbol{\theta}$ and first-order conditions with respect to $p_i$ are

$$L(\boldsymbol{\theta}; \mathbf{p}, \boldsymbol{\lambda}, \eta) = -\sum_{i=1}^{n} p_i \ln p_i - \sum_{j=1}^{m} \lambda_j \left[ \sum_{i=1}^{n} p_i h_j(y_i, \boldsymbol{\theta}) \right] + \eta \left( 1 - \sum_{i=1}^{n} p_i \right), \tag{6.3.4}$$

$$\frac{\partial L}{\partial p_i} = -\ln p_i - 1 - \sum_{j=1}^{m} \lambda_j h_j(y_i, \boldsymbol{\theta}) - \eta = 0. \tag{6.3.5}$$

The optimal MEEL $p_i$s, expressed as a function of $\theta$, are

$$\hat{p}_i(\theta) = \frac{\exp\left[-\sum_{j=1}^{m} \hat{\lambda}_j(\theta) h_j(y_i, \theta)\right]}{\sum_{i=1}^{n} \exp\left[-\sum_{j=1}^{m} \hat{\lambda}_j(\theta) h_j(y_i, \theta)\right]}, \tag{6.3.6}$$

where the $\hat{\lambda}_j(\theta)$s are the $m$ optimal Lagrange multipliers associated with the $m$ moment constraints. The inequality constraints, $p_i > 0\ \forall i$, are implicitly enforced by the structure of the optimization problem. This MEEL solution, with the $p_i$s expressed in an *exponential* form, should be compared with the MEL solution $\hat{p}_i(\theta) = n^{-1}[\sum_{j=1}^{m} \hat{\lambda}_j(\theta) h_j(y_i, \theta) + 1]^{-1}$ for the $p_i$s developed in (4.3.14). The MEEL objective function is strictly concave for linear constraints, the Hessian matrix for $\mathbf{p}$ is negative definite, and the solution $\hat{\mathbf{p}}$ is unique and optimal. The MEEL estimator for the parameter vector $\theta$ is defined as

$$\hat{\theta}_{\text{MEEL}} = \arg\max_{\theta} \left[L_{\text{MEEL}}(\theta; \mathbf{Y})\right], \tag{6.3.7}$$

where

$$L_{\text{MEEL}}(\theta; \mathbf{Y}) \equiv L(\theta; \hat{\mathbf{p}}(\theta), \hat{\boldsymbol{\lambda}}(\theta), \hat{\eta}(\theta)). \tag{6.3.8}$$

As is apparent from (6.3.4), the estimation objective function, $L_{\text{MEEL}}(\theta; \mathbf{Y})$, which is optimized to produce the MEEL estimate of the parameters, is *not* a likelihood function per se. The MEEL-based alternative to MEL, for representing an empirical *likelihood* for $\theta$, is given by the function $L_{\text{ME}}(\theta; \mathbf{y}) = \prod_{i=1}^{n} \hat{p}_i(\theta)$, where the definition of $\hat{p}_i(\theta)$ is based on (6.3.6) instead of the MEL definition of these empirical probabilities. An *empirical maximum likelihood estimator* (EML), which would generally differ from the MEEL estimator defined in (6.3.7), can be defined by maximizing $L_{\text{ME}}(\theta; \mathbf{y})$ as $\hat{\theta}_{\text{ME}} = \arg\max_{\theta} [L_{\text{ME}}(\theta; \mathbf{y})]$. We will discuss this matter further in Chapters 7 and 8, where we investigate an entire family of information-theoretic-type EML solutions for the stochastic inverse problem.

### 6.3.2 MEEL Asymptotics

Under general regularity conditions, including

i) the random sample outcome $(y_1, y_2, \ldots y_n)$ represents $n$ independent realizations of a random variable $\mathcal{Y}$ with probability distribution $F(\mathcal{y}; \theta)$,

ii) there exists a unique value of the $(k \times 1)$ parameter vector, $\boldsymbol{\theta}_0$, such that $\mathrm{E}[\mathbf{h}(\mathcal{Y}, \boldsymbol{\theta}_0)] = \mathbf{0}$, and
iii) $\mathbf{h}(\cdot)$ consists of $m \geq k$ functionally independent coordinate functions,

the MEEL estimator for $\boldsymbol{\theta}$ is consistent and asymptotically normally distributed. Consequently, asymptotic tests and confidence regions can be developed based on asymptotic normality of the estimator analogous to the MEL case in Chapter 5. In fact, Imbens (1997) demonstrates that under regularity conditions analogous to those assumed in the MEL context, the limiting distributions of the MEEL and MEL estimators for $\boldsymbol{\theta}$ are *identical*. The main regularity conditions, in addition to those listed previously, are that $\mathbf{h}(\mathcal{Y}, \boldsymbol{\theta})$ must be twice continuous differentiable with respect to $\boldsymbol{\theta}$, the first and second derivatives of $\mathbf{h}$ must all be bounded in a neighborhood of the true parameter value, $\boldsymbol{\theta}_0$, and the row rank of the $(k \times m)$ matrix, $\mathrm{E}[\frac{\partial \mathbf{h}(\mathcal{Y}, \boldsymbol{\theta})}{\partial \boldsymbol{\theta}}|_{\theta_0}]$, must equal the number of parameters in the $(k \times 1)$ vector $\boldsymbol{\theta}$. These are relatively mild conditions that lead to the MEEL estimator being *consistent* and *asymptotically normal* with limiting distribution

$$n^{1/2}(\hat{\boldsymbol{\theta}}_{\mathrm{MEEL}} - \boldsymbol{\theta}_0) \xrightarrow{d} N(\mathbf{0}, \Sigma), \tag{6.3.9}$$

where

$$\Sigma = \left[ \mathrm{E}\left[ \frac{\partial \mathbf{h}(\mathcal{Y}, \boldsymbol{\theta})}{\partial \boldsymbol{\theta}} \bigg|_{\boldsymbol{\theta}_0} \right] (\mathrm{E}[\mathbf{h}(\mathcal{Y}, \boldsymbol{\theta})\mathbf{h}(\mathcal{Y}, \boldsymbol{\theta})'|_{\boldsymbol{\theta}_0}])^{-1} \mathrm{E}\left[ \frac{\partial \mathbf{h}(\mathcal{Y}, \boldsymbol{\theta})}{\partial \boldsymbol{\theta}'} \bigg|_{\boldsymbol{\theta}_0} \right] \right]^{-1} \tag{6.3.10}$$

The covariance matrix $\Sigma$ of the limiting normal distribution can be consistently estimated by the estimator

$$\hat{\Sigma} = \left[ \left[ \sum_{i=1}^{n} \hat{p}_i \frac{\partial \mathbf{h}(y_i, \boldsymbol{\theta})}{\partial \boldsymbol{\theta}} \bigg|_{\hat{\boldsymbol{\theta}}_{\mathrm{MEEL}}} \right] \left[ \sum_{i=1}^{n} \hat{p}_i \mathbf{h}(y_i, \hat{\boldsymbol{\theta}}_{\mathrm{MEEL}}) \mathbf{h}(y_i, \hat{\boldsymbol{\theta}}_{\mathrm{MEEL}})' \right]^{-1} \times \left[ \sum_{i=1}^{n} \hat{p}_i \frac{\partial \mathbf{h}(y_i, \boldsymbol{\theta})}{\partial \boldsymbol{\theta}} \bigg|_{\hat{\boldsymbol{\theta}}_{\mathrm{MEEL}}} \right]' \right]^{-1}, \tag{6.3.11}$$

where the $\hat{p}_i$s are the MEEL estimates of the empirical probability distribution $\mathbf{p}$. An alternative consistent estimate can be defined by using (6.3.11), with all of the $\hat{p}_i$s replaced by $n^{-1}$. This amounts to applying probability weights based on the EDF instead of the empirical probability weights generated by the MEEL procedure. Because the MEEL estimates incorporate the additional moment equation information, these probability weight estimates should be more efficient in finite samples. *This assumes that the moment equation information is accurate or, equivalently, that the estimating functions on which the moment equations are based are unbiased.*

### 6.3.3 MEEL Inference

The asymptotic normal distribution of $\hat{\boldsymbol{\Theta}}_{\text{MEEL}}$ permits asymptotic hypothesis tests and confidence regions to be constructed. The asymptotic testing and confidence region procedures for the MEEL case are analogous to those developed for the MEL estimator based on its asymptotic normal distribution. The only essential differences in practice are that the MEL estimates of $\boldsymbol{\theta}$, $\mathbf{p}$, and $\boldsymbol{\lambda}$ are replaced by MEEL estimates in the test and confidence region formulas. We review the basic formulas ahead (Kitamura and Stutzer 1997; Imbens et al. 1998).

#### 6.3.3a Testing $\text{H}_0 : \mathbf{c}(\boldsymbol{\theta}) = \mathbf{r}$

The usual triad of asymptotically valid Wald, Lagrange multiplier, and pseudolikelihood ratio test procedures is available to test the validity of functional restrictions on the parameters of the probability model. All of the test statistics have the usual central Chi-square distribution, Chi-square($j$,0), under the null hypothesis, where $j$ denotes the number of functionally independent hypotheses represented by $\mathbf{c}(\boldsymbol{\theta}) = \mathbf{r}$. The tests are conducted by comparing the outcome of the test statistic with the $100(1-\alpha)\%$ quantile of the Chi-square($j$,0) distribution, producing an asymptotic level–$\alpha$ test of the hypothesis. The Wald (W), Lagrange multiplier (LM), and pseudolikelihood ratio (PLR) statistics are defined as follows:

$$W = [\mathbf{c}(\hat{\boldsymbol{\Theta}}_{\text{MEEL}}) - \mathbf{r}]' \left[ \left.\frac{\partial \mathbf{c}}{\partial \boldsymbol{\theta}'}\right|_{\hat{\boldsymbol{\Theta}}_{\text{MEEL}}} (n^{-1}\hat{\boldsymbol{\Sigma}}) \left.\frac{\partial \mathbf{c}}{\partial \boldsymbol{\theta}}\right|_{\hat{\boldsymbol{\Theta}}_{\text{MEEL}}} \right]^{-1} [\mathbf{c}(\hat{\boldsymbol{\Theta}}_{\text{MEEL}}) - \mathbf{r}], \tag{6.3.12}$$

$$\text{LM} = \left[ n^{-1} \sum_{i=1}^{n} \mathbf{h}(Y_i, \hat{\boldsymbol{\Theta}}^c_{\text{MEEL}}) \right]' \left[ \hat{\Psi}^{-1} \left(n^{-1}\hat{\boldsymbol{\Sigma}}\right)^{-1} \hat{\Psi}^{-1} \right] \times \left[ n^{-1} \sum_{i=1}^{n} \mathbf{h}(Y_i, \hat{\boldsymbol{\Theta}}^c_{\text{MEEL}}) \right], \tag{6.3.13}$$

$$\text{PLR} = 2\text{n}[\ln(\text{L}_{\text{MEEL}}(\hat{\boldsymbol{\Theta}}_{\text{MEEL}}; \mathbf{Y})) - \ln(\text{L}_{\text{MEEL}}(\hat{\boldsymbol{\Theta}}^c_{\text{MEEL}}; \mathbf{Y}))], \tag{6.3.14}$$

where

$$\hat{\Psi} = \hat{Cov}(\mathbf{h}(\mathcal{Y};\boldsymbol{\theta})) = n^{-1}\sum_{i=1}^{n}\mathbf{h}(Y_i;\hat{\boldsymbol{\theta}}_{\text{MEEL}})\mathbf{h}(Y_i;\hat{\boldsymbol{\theta}}_{\text{MEEL}})' \quad (6.3.15)$$

and $\hat{\boldsymbol{\Theta}}^{c}_{\text{MEEL}}$ denotes the constrained MEEL estimator that satisfies the restriction $\text{H}_0 : \mathbf{c}(\boldsymbol{\theta}) = \mathbf{r}$, and $\hat{\boldsymbol{\Sigma}}$ is as defined in (6.3.11).

#### 6.3.3b Testing $\text{H}_0 : c(\boldsymbol{\theta}) \leq r$ or $\text{H}_0 : c(\boldsymbol{\theta}) \geq r$

It is possible to construct asymptotically valid tests of scalar inequality hypotheses and define confidence bounds based on $Z$-statistics in the usual way given the asymptotic normality of $\hat{\boldsymbol{\Theta}}_{\text{MEEL}}$. For example, to test the nonlinear inequality restrictions $c(\boldsymbol{\theta}) \leq r$, one could use the statistic

$$Z = \frac{c(\hat{\boldsymbol{\Theta}}_{\text{MEEL}}) - r}{\left[\frac{\partial c(\boldsymbol{\theta})}{\partial \boldsymbol{\theta}'}\Big|_{\hat{\boldsymbol{\Theta}}_{\text{MEEL}}}(n^{-1}\hat{\Sigma})\frac{\partial c(\boldsymbol{\theta})}{\partial \boldsymbol{\theta}}\Big|_{\hat{\boldsymbol{\Theta}}_{\text{MEEL}}}\right]^{1/2}} \overset{a}{\sim} N(\delta, 1), \quad (6.3.16)$$

where

$$\delta = \frac{c(\boldsymbol{\Theta}_0) - r}{\left[\frac{\partial c(\boldsymbol{\theta})}{\partial \boldsymbol{\theta}'}\Big|_{\Theta_0}\Sigma\frac{\partial c(\boldsymbol{\theta})}{\partial \boldsymbol{\theta}}\Big|_{\Theta_0}\right]^{1/2}}. \quad (6.3.17)$$

The asymptotic level $\alpha$ test rule for $\text{H}_0 : c(\boldsymbol{\theta}) \leq r$ is

$$\textit{reject}\ \text{H}_0 \text{ if } z \geq z(1-\alpha), \quad (6.3.18)$$

where $z(1–\alpha)$ is the $100(1-\alpha)\%$ quantile of the standard normal distribution. Reversing inequalities defines a test of the hypothesis $\text{H}_0 : c(\boldsymbol{\theta}) \geq r$.

#### 6.3.3c Testing the Validity of Moment Equations

Another test of interest in the MEEL context is the test of the validity of moment equations, $\text{H}_0 : \text{E}[\mathbf{h}(\mathcal{Y}, \boldsymbol{\theta})] = \mathbf{0}$. This is equivalent to testing the *unbiasedness* of the estimating functions used in the MEEL approach. Imbens et al. (1998) and Kitamura and Stutzer (1997) provide a variety of tests for the validity of moment equations. Two such tests parallel the likelihood ratio and LM tests presented previously in the MEEL context.

A pseudolikelihood ratio–type asymptotic Chi-square test of the moment equations can be based on a suitably scaled version of the KL information criterion, as

$$K = 2n(\text{KL}(\hat{\mathbf{p}}, n^{-1}\mathbf{1}_n)) \overset{a}{\sim} \textit{Chi-square}(m-k, 0) \text{ under } \text{H}_0. \quad (6.3.19)$$

The test is based on the KL-information discrepancy between estimates of the probability weights that satisfy the moment restrictions (the subject distribution) and the standard empirical distribution function probability weights $n^{-1}\ \forall i$ (the reference distribution). As in the MEEL case, the test is only available if there are more functionally independent moment equations than parameters to be estimated.

Regarding a LM-type test of the moment equations, Imbens et al. (1998) examine three alternatives and find that in Monte Carlo simulations, the following variant is superior:

$$\text{LM} = n\hat{\boldsymbol{\lambda}}'\,\mathbf{R}\,\boldsymbol{\lambda} \overset{a}{\sim} \textit{Chi-square}\,(m-k, 0) \text{ under } \text{H}_0, \tag{6.3.20}$$

where

$$\mathbf{R} = \left[\sum_{i=1}^{n} \hat{p}_i \mathbf{h}_i \mathbf{h}'_i\right] \left[\sum_{i=1}^{n} \hat{p}_i^2 \mathbf{h}_i \mathbf{h}'_i\right]^{-1} \left[\sum_{i=1}^{n} \hat{p}_i \mathbf{h}_i \mathbf{h}'_i\right], \tag{6.3.21}$$

$\mathbf{h}_i \equiv \mathbf{h}(\text{Y}_i, \hat{\boldsymbol{\theta}})$, and $\mathbf{R}$ is a robust estimator of the covariance matrix of the moment functions (Imbens et al. 1998, 341). The test is available only in the case in which the number of moment equations exceeds the number of parameters being estimated. Using either the K or LM statistic, the test is conducted in the usual way by rejecting $\text{H}_0$, if the outcome of the statistic exceeds the $100(1-\alpha)\%$ quantile of the Chi-square($m$-$k$,0) distribution.

### 6.3.3d Confidence Regions

Confidence regions and bounds for model parameters can be conducted in the usual way based on duality with hypotheses tests. In particular, the set of null hypotheses values *not* rejected by the respective $\alpha$-level hypothesis test represents an asymptotic confidence region with asymptotic confidence level $(1-\alpha)$.

## 6.3.4 Contrasting the Use of Estimating Functions in EE and MEEL Contexts

It may be useful at this point to note similarities and differences in the way estimating function information is used in the MEEL and EE approaches. In this regard, arguments analogous to those presented in Section 4.3.3 relating to the MEL problem context apply here. We emphasize that, asymptotically, the MEEL approach provides an optimal method of combining estimating function information in the same way as the MEL procedure does. This view is supported by the fact that, asymptotically, the MEEL and MEL estimators share precisely the same asymptotic distribution, but in a large deviation context a different rate function. In fact, the only essential difference between the two approaches is the values of the weights used, in finite samples, to form the estimating equations.

## 6.4 Combining Estimation Equations under Kullback-Leibler Loss

Given where econometric models come from, there are many uncertainties surrounding their makeup. The correct components of the model are unknown. In this section, we follow Judge and Mittelhammer (2007) and focus on the uncertainty regarding the appropriate set of estimating equations and consider competing sets of estimating equations that provide a link to the data. Using KL loss and the MEEL divergence measure, we suggest a formulation that adapts naturally to a set of competing EEs and that has improved sampling performance under KL loss.

### 6.4.1 Combating Model Uncertainty: General Combining Formulations

In the context of an overdetermined traditional constraint set, we consider two or more plausible sets of estimating equations, and associated estimators, that are potentially consistent with an underlying data sampling process. We seek, within a KL loss objective, a basis for choosing a combination of EEs and associated estimators that best satisfies the joint constraint set.

Assume that just two data sampling processes are considered to be plausible alternative descriptions of the stochastic mechanism by which a given observed set of data may have come about. Also assume that the two data sampling processes imply population-estimating equations, or moment conditions, of the form

$$\mathbf{E}\mathbf{h}_1(\mathbf{Y}, \mathbf{X}, \mathbf{Z}, \boldsymbol{\beta}) = \mathbf{0} \text{ and } \mathbf{E}\mathbf{h}_2(\mathbf{Y}, \mathbf{X}, \mathbf{Z}, \boldsymbol{\beta}) = \mathbf{0} \tag{6.4.1}$$

with empirical counterparts of the form $\mathbf{h}_1(\mathbf{Y}, \mathbf{X}, \mathbf{Z}, \boldsymbol{\beta}) = \mathbf{0}$ and $\mathbf{h}_2(\mathbf{Y}, \mathbf{X}, \mathbf{Z}, \boldsymbol{\beta}) = \mathbf{0}$. This leads to two competing estimators for the parameter vector $\boldsymbol{\beta}$ and a solution based on the sample counterparts of the estimating equations. If orthogonality between a set of instrumental variables and the noise term of a model is maintained through estimating equations of the form $\mathbf{h}_1(\mathbf{Y}, \mathbf{X}, \mathbf{Z}, \boldsymbol{\beta}) = \mathbf{Z}'(\mathbf{Y} - \mathbf{X}\boldsymbol{\beta})$, and if $m = k$, then the instrumental variable estimator, $\tilde{\boldsymbol{\beta}} = (\mathbf{Z}'\mathbf{X})^{-1}\mathbf{Z}'\mathbf{Y}$, is implied for solving $\mathbf{h}_1(\mathbf{Y}, \mathbf{X}, \mathbf{Z}, \boldsymbol{\beta}) = \mathbf{0}$. Alternatively, if the orthogonality condition between regressors and the noise term of the model is used in specifying estimating equations of the form $\mathbf{h}_2(\mathbf{Y}, \mathbf{X}, \mathbf{Z}, \boldsymbol{\beta}) = \mathbf{X}'(\mathbf{Y} - \mathbf{X}\boldsymbol{\beta})$, then the least squares estimator of the parameters $\hat{\boldsymbol{\beta}} = (\mathbf{X}'\mathbf{X})^{-1}\mathbf{X}'\mathbf{Y}$ results for solving $\mathbf{h}_2(\mathbf{Y}, \mathbf{X}, \mathbf{Z}, \boldsymbol{\beta}) = \mathbf{0}$.

In general terms, the estimation objective is to choose the parameter estimate that maximizes the empirical likelihood of the data information, expressed in terms of a combined set of EEs. Using KL loss and the MEEL pseudodistance measure, the estimation problem may be defined as

$$\max_{\mathbf{p},\alpha} \left\{ -\sum_{i=1}^{n} \mathbf{p}_i \ln(\mathbf{p}_i) \right\} \tag{6.4.2}$$

*subject to*

$$\mathrm{E}_{\mathbf{p}}\mathbf{h}_1(\mathbf{Y}, \mathbf{X}, \mathbf{Z}, \bar{\boldsymbol{\beta}}) = \mathbf{0}, \; \mathrm{E}_{\mathbf{p}}\mathbf{h}_2(\mathbf{Y}, \mathbf{X}, \mathbf{Z}, \bar{\boldsymbol{\beta}}) = \mathbf{0}, \tag{6.4.3}$$

$$\bar{\boldsymbol{\beta}} = \boldsymbol{\alpha} \odot \hat{\boldsymbol{\beta}}_1 + (\mathbf{1}_k - \boldsymbol{\alpha}) \odot \hat{\boldsymbol{\beta}}_2, \; \boldsymbol{\alpha} \in \times_{j=1}^{k} [0, 1], \tag{6.4.4}$$

$$\mathbf{p} \geq \mathbf{0}, \text{ and } \mathbf{1}_n'\mathbf{p} = 1, \tag{6.4.5}$$

where $\mathrm{E}_{\mathrm{p}}(\cdot)$ denotes an empirical expectation taken with respect to the empirical probability distribution implied by the empirical probability weight-distribution, $\mathbf{p}$, and $\hat{\boldsymbol{\beta}}_1$ and $\hat{\boldsymbol{\beta}}_2$ represent the respective estimators derived from the two sets of moment equations, $\mathbf{E}[\mathbf{h}_1(\mathbf{Y}, \mathbf{X}, \mathbf{Z}, \boldsymbol{\beta})] = \mathbf{0}$ and $\mathbf{E}[\mathbf{h}_2(\mathbf{Y}, \mathbf{X}, \mathbf{Z}, \boldsymbol{\beta})] = \mathbf{0}$, with $\odot$ denoting the Hadamard (elementwise) product operator. In effect, the estimator of $\boldsymbol{\beta}$ is the particular value of the parameter vector, chosen from within the elementwise-convex feasible space of alternatives $\{\boldsymbol{\beta} : \boldsymbol{\beta} = \boldsymbol{\alpha} \odot \hat{\boldsymbol{\beta}}_1 + (\mathbf{1}_k - \boldsymbol{\alpha}) \odot \hat{\boldsymbol{\beta}}_2, \mathbf{0}_k \leq \boldsymbol{\alpha} \leq \mathbf{1}_k\}$ that maximizes the negative of the KL measure, given the data, and subject to meeting the combined sets of empirical moment conditions (6.4.3). The estimation problem assigns the minimum KL to the empirical sets of moment conditions and estimator defined by the combination. The ultimate probability distribution $\mathbf{p}$ is effectively the empirical probability distribution of the observed data outcomes that best represents, in terms of the KL measure, the joint distribution of the data and rationalizes the full set of moment conditions considered plausible for the underlying data sampling process. The parameter $\boldsymbol{\alpha}$ provides a basis for weighting the contributions of each alternative estimator and is influenced by how much the data support each model (Judge and Mittelhammer, 2004; Judge and Bock, 1978).

### 6.4.2 Example: A Combined Estimator

In this section, we consider the case of two alternative data sampling processes and assume that these alternatives are spawned from a classical linear statistical model context, $\mathbf{Y} = \mathbf{X}\boldsymbol{\beta} + \boldsymbol{\varepsilon}$, in which there is uncertainty regarding whether the noise term of the model is orthogonal to the regressors. Let $\mathbf{Z}$ be an $n \times m$ matrix of instruments $m > k$ leading to the overdetermined set of estimating equations $\mathbf{h}_1(\mathbf{Y}, \mathbf{X}, \mathbf{Z}, \boldsymbol{\beta}) = \mathbf{Z}'(\mathbf{Y} - \mathbf{X}\boldsymbol{\beta})$. This set of estimating equations would be appropriate for the case in which one or more regressors are not orthogonal to the noise term. An asymptotically optimal estimator derived from this set of moment conditions is given by the familiar 2SLS estimator

$$\hat{\boldsymbol{\beta}}_{2sls} = [(\mathbf{X}'\mathbf{Z})(\mathbf{Z}'\mathbf{Z})^{-1}(\mathbf{Z}'\mathbf{X})]^{-1}(\mathbf{X}'\mathbf{Z})(\mathbf{Z}'\mathbf{Z})^{-1}\mathbf{Z}'\mathbf{Y}. \tag{6.4.6}$$

Alternatively, under the assumption of orthogonality between regressors and noise, a plausible set of estimating equations that could be assumed to apply to the data sampling process is given by $\mathbf{h}_2(\mathbf{Y}, \mathbf{X}, \mathbf{Z}, \boldsymbol{\beta}) = \mathbf{X}'(\mathbf{Y} - \mathbf{X}\boldsymbol{\beta})$. These estimating equations just determine the parameter vector, leading directly to the familiar least squares estimator:

$$\hat{\boldsymbol{\beta}}_{ols} = [\mathbf{X}'\mathbf{X}]^{-1}\mathbf{X}'\mathbf{Y}. \tag{6.4.7}$$

Given the two alternative sets of estimating equations, consider the following empirical likelihood combination (ELC) estimator that combines, under a MEEL estimation objective measure, the EE from (6.4.6) and (6.4.7) into one overdetermined set of moment conditions

$$\max_{\mathbf{p},\alpha} \left\{ -\sum_{i=1}^{n} p_i \ln(p_i) \right\} \tag{6.4.8}$$

subject to

$$\sum_{i=1}^{n} p_i \mathbf{Q}'_{i.}(y_i - \mathbf{x}_{i.}\bar{\boldsymbol{\beta}}(\boldsymbol{\alpha})) = \mathbf{0}, \tag{6.4.9}$$

$$\bar{\boldsymbol{\beta}}(\boldsymbol{\alpha}) = \boldsymbol{\alpha} \odot \hat{\boldsymbol{\beta}}_{2sls} + (\mathbf{1}_k - \boldsymbol{\alpha}) \odot \hat{\boldsymbol{\beta}}_{ols}, \ \boldsymbol{\alpha} \in \times_{j=1}^{k}[0, 1] \tag{6.4.10}$$

and

$$\mathbf{p} \geq \mathbf{0}, \ \mathbf{1}'_n\mathbf{p} = 1. \tag{6.4.11}$$

In (6.4.9), $\mathbf{Q}$ denotes a matrix chosen from the variables in $\mathbf{Z}$ and $\mathbf{X}$, with any overlapping duplicates removed.

The Lagrange form of the preceding MEEL problem is given by

$$L(\mathbf{p}, \boldsymbol{\lambda}, \boldsymbol{\alpha}, \eta) = -\sum_{i=1}^{n} p_i \ln(p_i) - \boldsymbol{\lambda}' \sum_{i=1}^{n} p_i \mathbf{Q}'_{i.}$$

$$(y_i - \mathbf{x}_{i.}(\boldsymbol{\alpha} \odot \hat{\boldsymbol{\beta}}_{2sls} + (\mathbf{1}_n - a) \odot \hat{\boldsymbol{\beta}}_{ols})) - \eta\left(\sum_{i=1}^{n} p_i - 1\right). \quad (6.4.12)$$

The first-order conditions for (6.4.12) leads, conditional on the values $\boldsymbol{\alpha}$ and $\boldsymbol{\lambda}$, to the following solution for $p_i$:

$$p_i(\boldsymbol{\lambda}, \boldsymbol{\alpha}) = \frac{\exp(\boldsymbol{\lambda}'\mathbf{Q}'_{i.}(y_i - \mathbf{x}_{i.}(\boldsymbol{\alpha} \odot \hat{\boldsymbol{\beta}}_{2sls} + (\mathbf{1}_n - \boldsymbol{\alpha}) \odot \hat{\boldsymbol{\beta}}_{ols})))}{\sum_{j=1}^{n} \exp(\boldsymbol{\lambda}'\mathbf{Q}'_{i.}(y_j - \mathbf{x}_{j.}(\boldsymbol{\alpha} \odot \hat{\boldsymbol{\beta}}_{2sls} + (\mathbf{1}_n - \boldsymbol{\alpha}) \odot \hat{\boldsymbol{\beta}}_{ols})))}. \quad (6.4.13)$$

The $p_i(\boldsymbol{\lambda}, \boldsymbol{\alpha})$ solution for the $p_i$s can be used to form a concentrated Lagrange representation:

$$L_c(\boldsymbol{\lambda}, \boldsymbol{\alpha}) = -\sum_{i=1}^{n} p_i(\boldsymbol{\lambda}, \boldsymbol{\alpha}) \ln(p_i(\boldsymbol{\lambda}, \boldsymbol{\alpha}))$$

$$- \boldsymbol{\lambda}' \sum_{i=1}^{n} p_i(\boldsymbol{\lambda}, \boldsymbol{\alpha})\mathbf{Q}'_{i.}(y_i - \mathbf{x}_{i.}\, \bar{\boldsymbol{\beta}}(\boldsymbol{\alpha}).) \quad (6.4.14)$$

The solution $\hat{\boldsymbol{\alpha}}$, obtained from solving either (6.4.12) or (6.4.14), results in the estimator $\bar{\boldsymbol{\beta}}(\hat{\boldsymbol{\alpha}}) \equiv \hat{\boldsymbol{\alpha}} \odot \hat{\boldsymbol{\beta}}_{2sls} + (\mathbf{1}_k - \hat{\boldsymbol{\alpha}}) \odot \hat{\boldsymbol{\beta}}_{ols}$; that is, the MEEL estimator of $\boldsymbol{\beta}$ based on element-wise convex combinations of the estimators $\hat{\boldsymbol{\beta}}_{2sls}$ and $\hat{\boldsymbol{\beta}}_{ols}$. This solution $\bar{\boldsymbol{\beta}}(\hat{\boldsymbol{\alpha}})$ corresponds to the minimum possible KL divergence, or maximum entropy, based on both the data and the moment constraints postulated to hold across the two plausible models of the data sampling process.

Except for the introduction of the additional convexity constraint that $\bar{\boldsymbol{\beta}}(\boldsymbol{\alpha}) = \boldsymbol{\alpha} \odot \hat{\boldsymbol{\beta}}_1 + (\mathbf{1}_k - \boldsymbol{\alpha}) \odot \hat{\boldsymbol{\beta}}_2$, the exponential empirical likelihood problem (6.4.8)–(6.4.11) parallels closely the standard definition of MEEL problems considered in the previous sections of this chapter and the basis for establishing consistency.

### 6.4.2a Finite Sample Performance

A relevant question for empirical practice is how the preceding ELC estimator actually performs in sample sizes normally found in practice. The finite sample probability distribution of the ELC estimator is generally intractable.

Consequently, Judge and Mittelhammer (2007) used extensive sampling experiments to identify and compare the repeated sampling performance of the ELC estimator. From the results of their sampling experiments, it appears that the objective of an estimator that would adapt naturally to plausible constraint sets was achieved.

#### 6.4.2b Implications

The combined (ELC) estimator is designed to adapt naturally to whatever set of EEs–moment constraint conditions are specified as being plausible for the data sampling process analyzed. The ELC optimization formulation avoids usually necessary testing-tuning-nuisance parameters in problems of this type. The ELC estimates are asymptotically normally distributed and test statistics with the usual limiting Chi-square distribution can be defined under familiar regularity conditions.

In a structural equation context, the Judge and Mittelhammer (2007) sampling experiments support the conclusion that notable risk gains may be achieved from using the ELC estimation principle, when there is uncertainty with respect to nonorthogonality and other model characteristics. In general, in the structural equation context, the ELC estimator appears more robust than traditional estimation methods based on a single set of moment conditions, derived from a single postulated data sampling process, such as 2SLS. Traditional model discovery procedures focus on the identification of a single statistical model-estimator to represent the information in a sample of data. These results imply, given uncertainty regarding the relevant set of EEs, that the statistical cost of choosing a single estimator or set of EEs can be notable in terms of estimation risk and invalid inferences.

## 6.5 An Informative Reference Distribution

In Section 6.4, in implementing the MEEL estimation objective, the KL information measure was applied using a reference distribution with uniform probabilities $n^{-1}$. In addition to the $m$ moment constraints, there may exist, in the form of a vector $\mathbf{p}^{o}$, additional information relating to the unknown convexity weights or probabilities $\mathbf{p}$. Extending the MEEL framework, the estimation objective function may be reformulated to minimize the cross exponential empirical likelihood (CEEL) or KL information discrepancy between $\mathbf{p}$ and $\mathbf{p}^{o}$. Thus, the problem may be cast in terms of minimizing CEEL now consistent with the information in the moment restrictions and the prior probabilities $\mathbf{p}^{o}$.

Regarding MEL formulations of Chapter 4 in which restrictions are empirical moment equations, if we use the CEEL variant of the MEEL criterion, the extremum problem of recovering likelihood weights $p_i > 0$ can be expressed as

$$\min_{\mathbf{p}} \mathrm{KL}(\mathbf{p}, \mathbf{p}^o) \equiv \min_{\mathbf{p}} \left[ \sum_{i=1}^{n} p_i \ln(p_i / p_i^o) \right]$$
$$= \min_{\mathbf{p}} \left[ \sum_{i=1}^{n} p_i \ln p_i - \sum_{i=1}^{n} p_i \ln p_i^o \right], \qquad (6.5.1)$$

subject to the empirical moment conditions

$$\sum_{i=1}^{n} p_i\, h_j(y_i, \boldsymbol{\theta}) = 0,\ j = 1, \ldots, m \qquad (6.5.2)$$

and the adding-up constraint on the sum of the nonnegative empirical probability weights

$$\sum_{i=1}^{n} p_i = 1. \qquad (6.5.3)$$

In this case, the discrepancy between the empirical and prior sample weights is measured by the empirical moment-constrained KL information. Forming the Lagrangian function for the problem (6.5.1)–(6.5.3), the optimal solution to the problem is

$$\hat{p}_i(\boldsymbol{\theta}) = \frac{p_i^o \exp\left(\sum_{j=1}^{m} \hat{\lambda}_j h_j(y_i, \boldsymbol{\theta})\right)}{\sum_{i=1}^{n} p_i^o \exp(\sum_{j=1}^{m} \hat{\lambda}_j h_j(y_i, \boldsymbol{\theta}))}, \qquad (6.5.4)$$

where the $\hat{\lambda}_j$s are the optimal LMs associated with the moment constraints and the $\hat{p}_i(\boldsymbol{\theta})$s are the optimal empirical weights that can be used to form an empirical likelihood function for $\boldsymbol{\theta}$. If the prior probability weights are uniform, that is, $p_i^0 = n^{-1}, \forall i$, then the CEEL solution (6.5.4) is identical to the MEEL solution (6.3.6), after accounting for the change in sign in the LMs (i.e., $\hat{\boldsymbol{\lambda}}_{\mathrm{CEEL}} = -\hat{\boldsymbol{\lambda}}_{\mathrm{MEEL}}$ ). In contrast to the traditional MEL or MEEL formulation, by using the CEEL formalism, information can be introduced through the reference distribution $\mathbf{p}^o$ that can affect the likelihood weights. The inverse probabilities in (6.5.4) are a function of the data, the prior distribution, and a normalizing constant.

## 6.6 Concluding Remarks

At this point, we have examined the MEL and MEEL estimation objective functions for solving empirical moment-type EEs for estimators of $\boldsymbol{\theta}$. In these two cases, we simultaneously obtain estimates of empirical probability or likelihood weights for the sample outcomes. In each case, we can define an empirical likelihood for $\boldsymbol{\theta}$, based on the value $L(\boldsymbol{\theta}) = \prod_{i=1}^{n} p_i(\boldsymbol{\theta})$, where $p_i(\boldsymbol{\theta})$ denotes the optimum empirical probability weights obtained from employing either the MEL or MEEL criteria, constrained by empirical moment constraints of the general form, $\sum_{i=1}^{n} p_i(\boldsymbol{\theta})\mathbf{h}(y_i, \boldsymbol{\theta}) = \mathbf{0}$, and the normalization restriction, $\sum_{i=1}^{n} p_i(\boldsymbol{\theta}) = 1$.

Under the standard regularity conditions used to establish the asymptotic properties of each of the estimators, the MEL and MEEL estimators are *asymptotically equivalent.* That is, they both lead to consistent estimators of $\boldsymbol{\theta}$ with the same asymptotic normal distributions (Imbens, 1997; Imbens et al., 1998). Thus, a choice between the estimators cannot be based on their asymptotic distributions. This asymptotic equivalence has the practical benefit that any test or confidence region procedure that applies to one of the estimation contexts based on the estimator's asymptotic normal distribution applies to both estimation contexts. In applications, one simply inserts the appropriate MEL or MEEL estimates into test or confidence region formulas to obtain operational asymptotically valid inference procedures. The asymptotic equivalence also implies that the MEL and MEEL estimators share the same asymptotic efficiency property.

Furthermore, the MEL and MEEL procedures provide the means for directly estimating the population distribution of the $Y_i$s. In particular, an EDF-like estimate of the cumulative distribution function is given by

$$\hat{F}(y_0) = \sum_{i=1}^{n} \hat{p}_i I_{(-\infty, y_i]}(y_0), \tag{6.6.1}$$

where $\hat{\mathbf{p}}$ is either the MEL or MEEL estimate of $\mathbf{p}$. By taking *correct* estimating equations into account, the MEL and MEEL estimators of the CDF of the population distribution are generally more efficient than the standard EDF estimator (Imbens 1997, 365) and, in any case, are no less efficient. Moreover, the estimator (6.6.1) is in fact the *efficient* semiparametric estimator of the CDF, based on the estimating equations, $\mathrm{E}[\mathbf{h}(\mathcal{Y}, \boldsymbol{\theta})] = \mathbf{0}$ (Imbens, 1997, theorem 2).

In addition, both the MEEL and MEL approaches can be viewed as being based on minimizing the weighted average discrepancies between the logs of the estimated probabilities, $\hat{p}_i$, and empirical frequency weights, $n^{-1}$.

However, to represent the expected discrepancy as accurately as possible, it would appear advisable to weight the discrepancies using an efficient MEEL $\hat{p}_i$ estimate based on the data rather than the inefficient $n^{-1}$ estimates represented by the EDF weights. On this basis, the MEEL approach is favored over the MEL approach.

Finally, Imbens et al. (1998) show that the MEEL estimator is more robust against misspecification of the moment equations than is the MEL estimator. Thus, if there is considerable uncertainty regarding the validity of the moment equations, the use of the MEEL estimator may be preferred to the MEL estimator.

Given the current state of affairs, it would appear that the MEEL approach is to be recommended in cases characterized by independent data observations. The apparently less robust MEL approach appears to be a viable competitor in cases in which there is substantial confidence in the validity of the moment restrictions and we are dealing with independent data observations.

In this chapter, we demonstrated that MEL is not the only stochastic "semiparametric likelihood" approach. Like traditional empirical likelihood, a MEEL-based likelihood can be defined and applied to any reasonable set of estimating functions and, in some cases, this offers a superior alternative. It shares properties with various nonparametric methods based on resampling, such as the bootstrap, yet it offers a simple formulation based on an estimation objective function to be optimized subject to side constraints. Conceptually, the nonlinear solution to the stochastic inverse problem is simple and generally tractable. Unlike the traditional empirical likelihood approach, MEEL permits the introduction, in the reference distribution, of information concerning the unknown likelihood function weights. The linkages between the concepts developed in Chapters 3, 4, 5, and 6 have many statistical implications for the process of econometric estimation and inference.

In the next chapter, we demonstrate that the MEL, MEEL, and CEEL estimation objective functions may be embedded in a family of goodness-of-fit power divergence measures and pursue the interesting implications of this for estimation and inference.

## 6.7 Reader Idea Checklist

1. In the context of the preceding chapters and extremum estimation, what is the importance of the distance-divergence measures in the analysis of probability models?

2. What is the fundamental idea underlying the Kullback-Leibler information measure and what is its importance and usefulness as a distance measure? What is the potential importance of KL information in providing a basis for comparing two competing statistical models?
3. What are the major differences in the MEL and MEEL approaches to estimation and inference? What are the similarities?
4. We hope that the last three chapters may have changed the way you think about the problem of estimation and inference. If so, what are the changes in your thinking and in the corresponding statistical implications? If not, why not?
5. What are the potential statistical implications of the differences in the likelihood weights obtained from the MEL and MEEL estimation objective functions?
6. What are inverse probabilities when referring to a stochastic inverse problem?

## 6.8 Selected References

Brown, L. D. (1986), *Fundamentals of Statistical Exponential Families*, Hayward, CA: Institute of Mathematical Statistics.

Csiszar, I. (1991), "Why Least Squares and Maximum Entropy? An Axiomatic Approach to Inference for Linear Inverse Problems," *Annals of Statistics*, **19**:2032–2066.

Gokhale, D. V. and S. Kullback (1978), *The Information in Contingency Tables*, New York: Marcel Dekker.

Golan, A., G. G. Judge, and D. Miller (1996), *Maximum Entropy Econometrics: Robust Estimation with Limited Data*, New York: John Wiley & Sons.

Good, I. J. (1963), "Maximum Entropy for Hypothesis Formulation, Especially for Multidimensional Contingency Tables," *Annals of Mathematical Statistics*, **34**:911–934.

Imbens, G. (1997), "One-Step Estimators for Over-Identified Generalized Method of Moment Models," *Review of Economic Studies*, **64**:359–383.

Imbens, G., R. Spady, and P. Johnson (1998), "Information Theoretic Approaches to Inference in Moment Condition Models," *Econometrica*, **66**:333–357.

Jaynes, E. T. (1957a), "Information Theory and Statistical Mechanics," *Physics Review*, **106**:620–630.

Jaynes, E. T. (1957b), "Information Theory and Statistical Mechanics II," *Physics Review*, **108**:171–190.

Jaynes, E. T. (1963), "Information Theory and Statistical Mechanics," in K. W. Ford (Ed.), *Statistical Physics* (pp. 181–218), New York: W. A. Benjamin.

Jaynes, E. T. (1984), "Prior Information and Ambiguity in Inverse Problems," in D. W. McLaughlin (Ed.), *Inverse Problems* (pp. 151–166), Providence, RI: American Mathematical Society.

Judge, G. G. and Bock, M. E. (1978), *The Statistical Implications of Pre-Test and Stein-Rule Estimators in Econometrics*, Amsterdam: North-Holland.

Judge, G. G. and Mittelhammer, R. (2004), "A Semiparametric Like Basis for Combining Estimators under Quadratic Loss," *Journal of American Statistical Association*, **99**:479–487.

Judge, G. G. and Mittelhammer, R. (2007), "Estimation and Inference in Case of Competing Sets of Estimating Equations," *Journal of Econometrics*, **138**:513–531.

Kitamura, Y. and M. Stutzer (1997), "An Information-Theoretic Alternative to Generalized Method of Moments Estimation," *Econometrica*, **65**:861–874.

Kullback, S. (1987), "Letter to the Editor: The Kullback-Leibler Distance," *American Statistician*, **41**:340–341.

Kullback, S. (1959), *Information Theory and Statistics*, New York: John Wiley & Sons.

Kullback, S. and R. A. Leibler (1951), "On Information and Sufficiency," *Annals of Mathematical Statistics*, **22**:79–86.

Mittelhammer, R., Judge, G., and Miller, D. (2000). *Econometric Foundations*, New York: Cambridge University Press, 835 pages.

Owen, A. (1990), "Empirical Likelihood Ratio Confidence Regions," *Annals of Statistics*, **18**:90–120.

Shannon, C. E. (1948), "A Mathematical Theory of Communication," *Bell System Technical Journal*, **27**:379–423.

## APPENDIX 6.A RELATIONSHIP BETWEEN THE MAXIMUM EMPIRICAL LIKELIHOOD (MEL) OBJECTIVE AND KL INFORMATION

The KL information criterion may be defined in a way that subsumes the MEL estimation objective function as a special case. Establishing this relationship between the MEL approach and the KL information criterion provides us with an alternative rationale for the MEL estimation objective function, $n^{-1}\sum_{i=1}^{n}\ln(p_i)$.

Consider the KL information criterion when the *reference* distribution is some discrete distribution $p(y)$, having discrete and finite support $\mathbf{y} \in \Gamma$, and the *subject* distribution is $w(y) = n^{-1}\ \forall y \in \Gamma$. In this context, KL information is given by

$$\mathrm{KL}(n^{-1}\mathbf{1}_n, \mathbf{p}) = \sum_{i=1}^{n} \frac{1}{n} \ln\left(\frac{1}{n} / p(\mathbf{y}_i)\right) = -n^{-1}\sum_{i=1}^{n} \ln(p_i) - \ln(n), \tag{6.A.1}$$

where recall that $\mathbf{1}_n$ represents a $(n \times 1)$ vector of ones so that $n^{-1}\mathbf{1}_n = [n^{-1}, \ldots, n^{-1}]'$ denotes a discrete uniform distribution, $n$ is the number of elements in $\Gamma$, $\mathbf{p} = (p_1, p_2, \ldots, p_n)'$, and $p_i \equiv p(y_i)$. Because $n$ is a constant in (6.A.1), it is apparent that minimizing (6.A.1) is equivalent to maximizing the scaled (by $n^{-1}$) log-MEL objective function, $n^{-1}\sum_{i=1}^{n}\ln(p_i)$. Consequently, for the case at hand, maximizing empirical likelihood is equivalent to minimizing KL information.

To see the additional rationale we have gained for solving systems of estimating equations via the MEL principle, recall the fundamental rationale for the MEL objective function. The MEL objective function was originally specified as $\prod_{i=1}^{n} p_i$ to provide an empirical representation of the joint PDF of a random sample of independent random variables. The function $\prod_{i=1}^{n} p_i$ thus has the natural interpretation of representing the joint PDF value of the independent random variables outcomes, $y_1, y_2, \ldots y_n$. Maximizing $\prod_{i=1}^{n} p_i$ or, equivalently, maximizing $n^{-1}\sum_{i=1}^{n}\ln(p_i)$, subject to $m$ moment equations and the normalization restriction, $\sum_{i=1}^{n} p_i = 1$, effectively chooses the $p_i$s so as to assign the *maximum joint probability* possible to the *observed* set of sample outcomes $(y_1, y_2, \ldots y_n)$ from *among all possible probability assignments* consistent with the moment equations.

Now consider interpreting the objective of minimizing KL-information as given by (6.2.4). In the absence of any constraints other than the normalization restriction, $\sum_{i=1}^{n} p_i = 1$, we know by the previously discussed properties of KL-information that $\text{KL}(n^{-1}\mathbf{1}_n, \mathbf{p})$ will be minimized when $p(y) = n^{-1}\ \forall\ y \in \Gamma$. Thus, the objective of minimizing $\text{KL}(n^{-1}\mathbf{1}_n, \mathbf{p})$ has the effect of drawing the $p_i$s toward the maximally uninformative uniform distribution on $\Gamma$. If minimizing $\text{KL}(n^{-1}\mathbf{1}_n, \mathbf{p})$ is constrained by $m$ moment equations and the normalization restriction $\sum_{i=1}^{n} p_i = 1$, then the objective can be interpreted as choosing the $p_i$s to be as *maximally uninformative* as the estimating equation information will permit. In effect, the objective is consistent with the goal of not wanting to assert more about the distribution of the $Y_i$s than is known from the moment equations. Regarding the set of distributions, $\mathbf{p}$, that satisfy the moment equations, some distributions will assign probabilities to the sample outcomes that can be much different from the uniform distribution weights defined by the subject distribution. In effect, these distributions provide additional or extraneous information about the sample outcomes that is not justified by the available information (i.e., the information contained in the moment equations and subject distribution). By selecting $\mathbf{p}$ to minimize KL $(n^{-1}\mathbf{1}_n, \mathbf{p})$, we effectively remove extraneous information in the MEL-KL solution. Given the equivalence of the maximum MEL and minimum KL-information criteria, this "maximally uninformative $\mathbf{p}$" interpretation of the KL principle can be used as a motivation for the MEL principle as well.

*We emphasize that the MEL-KL equivalence holds only when the uniform distribution is used as the subject distribution in defining the KL-information function.* From our previous discussion of the KLIC in Section 6.2.1, where we interpreted KL information as an expected log-likelihood ratio, we know that minimizing KL $(n^{-1}\mathbf{1}_n, \mathbf{p})$ can be interpreted as minimizing the mean information provided by sample data in favor of the uniform distribution relative to $p(\mathbf{y})$ *under the assumption that the uniform distribution is true.* In this case, we are effectively calibrating our mean information measure in terms of the standard empirical distribution function weights, $n^{-1}$. This may be a reasonable thing to do under *iid* sampling from a population distribution. *In this case, we are choosing the reference distribution that minimizes mean information in favor of the empirical distribution weights.* This interpretation is, of course, consistent with the idea of drawing the reference distribution as close as possible to the subject (uniform) distribution, which will concomitantly minimize the expected log-likelihood ratio. We note that the lack of symmetry in the KL function is not a problem for MEL-KL estimation because we are holding the *subject* distribution fixed.

## APPENDIX 6.B NUMERICAL ILLUSTRATION OF MEEL AND MEL ESTIMATION OF A PROBABILITY DISTRIBUTION

The purpose of this example is to compare the MEL and MEEL estimators for the population mean and, in particular, compare the probability distributions for the data estimated under each estimation objective. This numerical example is a continuation of the problem considered in Appendix 4.A.2 of Chapter 4.

Two fundamental estimation problems to be solved, stated in Lagrange form, are the maximization of

$$L_{\mathrm{MEL}}(\mathbf{p}, \eta, \theta, \lambda) \equiv \left[ n^{-1} \sum_{i=1}^{n} \ln(p_i) - \eta \left( \sum_{i=1}^{n} p_i - 1 \right) - \lambda \sum_{i=1}^{n} p_i (y_i - \theta) \right] \tag{6.B.1}$$

and

$$L_{\mathrm{MEEL}}(\mathbf{p}, \eta, \theta, \lambda) \equiv \left[ - \sum_{i=1}^{n} p_i \ln(p_i) - \eta \left( \sum_{i=1}^{n} p_i - 1 \right) - \lambda \sum_{i=1}^{n} p_i (y_i - \theta) \right]. \tag{6.B.2}$$

Regarding the data used in this example, we are again considering a simple location model for the data sampling process in which

$$Y = \theta + \varepsilon,$$

where $\theta = 0$ and $\varepsilon$ is a standard normal noise component. The sample size is set to $n = 50$ and pseudorandom draws from this DSP are generated. The sample data outcome is given in Table B.2.1.

The results for the MEL and MEEL estimates of $\theta$ were $\hat{\theta}_{\text{MEL}} = 0.0958$ and $\hat{\theta}_{\text{MEEL}} = 0.0949$. The empirical probability distributions, resulting from the MEL and MEEL estimation procedures, are plotted together with the true underlying $N(0, 1)$ distribution in the graph that follows.

Table B.2.1. *Data for* $Y = \varepsilon$, $\varepsilon \sim N(0, 1)$

| | | | | |
|---|---|---|---|---|
| −2.1707 | −0.7609 | −0.1780 | 0.4111 | 1.0841 |
| −1.8620 | −0.7283 | −0.0428 | 0.4290 | 1.0908 |
| −1.7350 | −0.6856 | −0.0095 | 0.5284 | 1.1381 |
| −1.4936 | −0.5891 | −0.0094 | 0.5284 | 1.2694 |
| −1.1863 | −0.3894 | 0.0474 | 0.5573 | 1.3468 |
| −1.1802 | −0.3631 | 0.1011 | 0.5652 | 1.3973 |
| −1.0532 | −0.2637 | 0.1198 | 0.7155 | 1.5051 |
| −0.9636 | −0.2142 | 0.1341 | 0.7665 | 1.5210 |
| −0.8460 | −0.2135 | 0.1463 | 0.8827 | 1.8383 |
| −0.8225 | −0.1895 | 0.2875 | 1.0443 | 3.8755 |

MEL and MEEL EDFs vs. Normal CDF

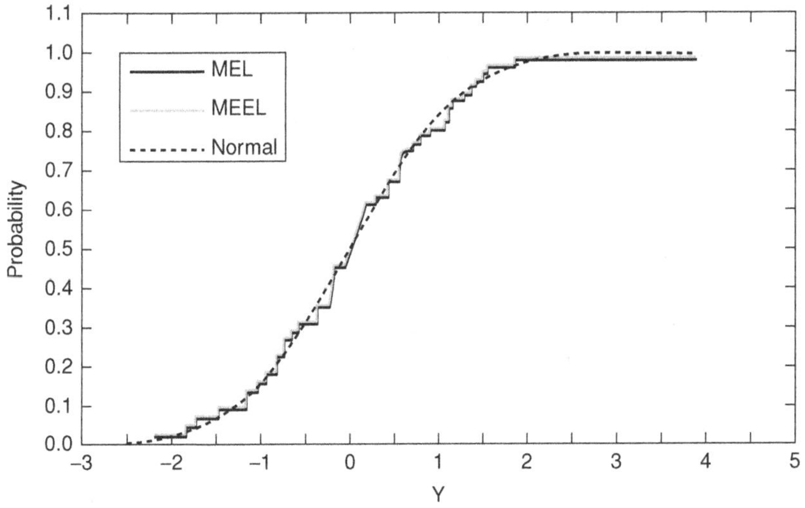

## APPENDIX 6.C SHANNON'S ENTROPY – SOME HISTORICAL PERSPECTIVE

In developing the concept of maximum entropy, Shannon began by defining a measure of information content called "self-information," or "surprisal," of a message $m$, which he defined as

$$\tau(m) = \log_b\left(\frac{1}{p(m)}\right) = -\log_b(p(m)), \tag{6.C.1}$$

where $p(m)$, $m \in \mathrm{M}$ is the probability that message $m$ is chosen from all possible choices in the message space M. The base of the logarithm only affects the units in which the measured information content is expressed. If the logarithm is base 2, which is how Shannon chose the base in his seminal work, then the measure of information is expressed in units of *bits*; whereas if $b = e$, that is, a natural logarithm is used, then the information is defined in terms of *nats*. The use of the natural logarithm is more common in econometrics and so we proceed henceforth using natural logarithms $\ln(\cdot) = \log_e(\cdot)$.

Regarding the intuition underlying Shannon's notion of *surprisal* or *self-information*, $\tau(m) = -\ln(p(m))$, first note that information is transferred to a recipient only if the recipient did not already possess the information. Any message whose content is already known by the recipient contains no real information. This is reflected in (6.C.1), where a certain message – that is, one that has probability 1 so that $p(m) = 1$ – results in $\tau(m) = 0$, indicating *no information* was received.

The *entropy* of a (discrete) message space M, measures the amount of uncertainty that exists about the message that will be chosen. This uncertainty is defined as the average or expected self-information or surprisal value of a message $m$ arising from the message space M, as

$$S = -\sum_{m \in \mathrm{M}} p(m)\ln(p(m)). \tag{6.C.2}$$

The averaging or expectation operation is taken with respect to the probability distribution defined on the messages, $m$, in the message space, M. Note that entropy is maximized so that there is a maximal uncertainty associated with the message space if the probability distribution is uniform on the messages in the message space.

As discussed in this chapter, the application of maximum entropy is more general than the original messaging context in which Shannon conceived the information concept. In particular, if $\{p_1, p_2, \ldots, p_n\}$ denotes any discrete probability distribution on the $n$ possible outcomes of a random variable $Y$, then Shannon's entropy can be defined as

$$S = -\sum_{i=1}^{n} p_i \ln(p_i), \qquad (6.C.3)$$

where $S$ in this case measures the uncertainty associated with the outcome of the random variable. The outcome is maximally uncertain when the probability distribution of $Y$ is the uniform distribution. Shannon's axioms and the maximum entropy principle are important foundation stones for pure ill-posed inverse information-theoretic methods.

# PART III

# A FAMILY OF MINIMUM DISCREPANCY ESTIMATORS

In Part II, to avoid an explicit specification of both the joint probability distribution of the data sampling process underlying the observed data and the associated likelihood function, a possible sample distribution function is chosen from the multinomial family that assigns probability weight $p_i$ to observation $y_i$. Under this concept, likelihood weights, $\mathbf{p}$, supported on the sample data, are used to reduce a problem characterized by an infinite dimensional set of unknowns to a finite dimensional one. Based on this idea, alternative divergence measures, maximum empirical likelihood (MEL) and maximum empirical exponential likelihood (MEEL), were proposed and a basis for estimation and inference was developed. In Part III, we use goodness-of-fit measures proposed by Cressie and Read (CR) to specify a family of divergence measures that subsumes MEL and MEEL and that may be used to characterize data sampling process outcomes. In this context, the CR objective can be interpreted as a generalized divergence measure that leads to a generalized likelihood function concept and an associated empirical maximum likelihood method of estimation and inference.

In Chapter 7, we demonstrate how the CR objective leads to likelihood functions that span a rich space of data sampling processes. In Chapter 8, we illustrate empirical implementation and performance characteristics of the minimum power divergence estimation and inference procedures.

SEVEN

# The Cressie-Read Family of Divergence Measures and Empirical Maximum Likelihood Functions

## 7.1 Introduction

Given Chapters 4 and 6, the reader may be expecting another empirical likelihood (EL)-like functional or divergence measure to be introduced in this chapter. However, we do even more. We provide an entire family of likelihood functionals-divergence measures that includes the maximum empirical likelihood (MEL) and maximum empirical exponential likelihood (MEEL) formulations discussed in Chapters 4 and 6.

We remind the reader that in Chapter 4 we started the pursuit of the solution to a stochastic inverse problem that was based on indirect noisy observations. In this context, we noted in Chapter 2 that when the functional form of the likelihood function is known, the maximum likelihood concept provides an appealing basis for estimation and inference. However, if sufficient information about the underlying data sampling process is not available to specify the functional form of the likelihood function, parametric maximum likelihood (ML) methods are fragile and lose their attractive optimal statistical characteristics. In econometrics, information about the underlying data sampling process is usually partial and incomplete. Consequently, estimation and inference over the past two decades has, as demonstrated in Chapter 3, proceeded under semiparametric formulations in the sense that the joint probability distribution of the data is unspecified, apart from a finite set of theoretical moment conditions or conditional moment restrictions.

In Chapter 4, we noted that a way of avoiding an explicit functional specification of the likelihood is to use an estimation method that is still likelihood based but that does not assume a specific parametric member of the family of probability distributions to represent the underlying data sampling process. To achieve this objective, we noted that one such possibility is to use an information theoretic concept where, given a set of random observations $\{Y_1, Y_2, \ldots, Y_n\}$, a possible sample distribution function is chosen from the multinomial family that assigns probability weight $p_i$ to observation $Y_i$. Under this concept, likelihood weights, **p**, supported on the sample of observed data outcomes, are used to reduce the infinite dimensional problem of nonparametric likelihood estimation to a finite dimensional one. Building on this idea, in Chapter 6, an alternative divergence measure, MEEL, was proposed. In this chapter, to avoid the constant drip, drip, drip of alternative individual divergence measures, we propose a family of divergence measures that subsumes those introduced in Chapters 4 and 6 and leads to likelihood functions that span a rich space of data sampling processes.

### 7.1.1 Family of Likelihood Functions

In pursuing an entire family of divergence measures that may be used as a basis for characterizing the outcomes of the sampling processes, we start with the family of goodness-of-fit measures proposed by Cressie and Read (1983) and Read and Cressie (1988). Cressie and Read (CR) were interested in developing a family of test statistics and proposed the following power divergence–goodness-of-fit family of measures:

$$I(\mathbf{p}, \mathbf{q}, \gamma) = \frac{1}{\gamma(\gamma+1)} \sum_{i=1}^{n} p_i \left[ \left( \frac{p_i}{q_i} \right)^{\gamma} - 1 \right], \tag{7.1.1}$$

where $\gamma$ is a parameter that indexes members of the CR family, $p_i$s represent the subject probability distribution, and the $q_i$s are interpreted as reference probabilities that also satisfy the usual probability distribution characteristics of $q_i \in (0, 1), \forall i$, and $\sum_{i=1}^{n} q_i = 1$. The CR family of power divergences are defined through a class of additive convex functions.

The CR family has a rich "goodness-of-fit" and "family of power divergences" statistical base. For example, given particular values of $\gamma$, the divergence measures in (7.1.3) correspond to well-known test statistics, including the Pearson Chi-square statistic, $\chi^2$ $(\gamma = 1)$, the log-likelihood ratio statistic $(\gamma = 0)$, the Freeman-Tukey statistic $(\gamma = -1/2)$, the modified log-likelihood ratio statistic $(\gamma = 1)$, and the Neyman-modified statistic $(\gamma = -2)$. Overall, the CR power divergence measure encompasses a substantial family of test statistics and, correspondingly, a broad family of likelihood functions. In addition, the CR normalization factor exhibits proper convexity for all values of $\gamma$ and embodies the required probability system characteristics, such as additivity and invariance with respect to a monotonic transformation of the divergence measures.

In the context of extremum metrics, first introduced in Chapter 3, the general Cressie and Read (1984) family of power divergence statistics represents a flexible family of pseudodistance measures from which to derive empirical probabilities. The CR statistic contains a parameter $\gamma$ that indexes a set of empirical goodness-of-fit (empirical divergence) measures and estimation criteria. As $\gamma$ varies, the resulting estimators that minimize power divergence exhibit qualitatively different sampling behavior. Using theoretical data moments as constraints, a solution to the stochastic inverse problem, based on the optimized value of $I(\mathbf{p}, \mathbf{q}, \gamma)$, will be demonstrated as a basis for representing a range of data sampling processes.

To place the CR family of power divergence statistics in an entropy perspective we note, in Appendix 7B, corresponding Gibbs (1981), Renyi (1961, 1970) and Tsallis (1988) families of entropy functionals–divergence measures. As demonstrated by Gorban, Gorban, and Judge (2010), over defined ranges of the divergence measures, the CR and entropy families are equivalent.

## 7.2 The Cressie-Read (CR) Power Divergence Family

As a basis for motivating the CR family, consider the following well-known linear econometric model: Let $\mathcal{Y}$ be a random variable and $\mathcal{X}$ be a $k$ dimension random vector and assume that $\mathcal{Y}$ and $\mathcal{X}$ are linked via $\mathcal{Y} = g(\mathcal{X}, \boldsymbol{\beta}) + \varepsilon$. Given the possibility of this general formulation, consider a simple semiparametric linear statistical model manifestation of it in the form $\mathcal{Y} = \mathcal{X}\boldsymbol{\beta} + \varepsilon$. Assume that we observe a vector of sample outcomes $\mathbf{y} = (y_1, y_2, \ldots, y_n)'$, associated with this linear model represented by $\mathbf{y} = \mathbf{x}\boldsymbol{\beta} + \mathbf{e}$, where $\mathbf{x}$ is an $(n \times k)$ matrix of outcomes of stochastic explanatory variables, $\mathbf{e}$ is an unobservable outcome of the random noise vector with mean vector $\mathbf{0}$ and covariance matrix $\sigma^2\mathbf{I}_n$, and $\boldsymbol{\beta} \in \mathbf{B}$ is a $(k \times 1)$ vector of unknown parameters. If one or more of the right-hand side $\mathbf{x}_{.j}$s are correlated with the equation noise, then $\mathrm{E}[n^{-1}\mathbf{X}'\varepsilon] \neq \mathbf{0}$ or $\mathrm{plim}[n^{-1}\mathbf{X}'\varepsilon] \neq \mathbf{0}$. This means the traditional Gauss-Markov–based procedures or, equivalently, the Chapter 3 method of moments (MOM) estimator defined by $\hat{\boldsymbol{\beta}}_{\mathrm{mom}} = \arg_{\boldsymbol{\beta} \in \mathrm{B}}[\mathbf{X}'(\mathbf{Y} - \mathbf{X}\boldsymbol{\beta}) = \mathbf{0}]$ are biased and inconsistent, with unconditional expectation and probability limit given by $\mathrm{E}[\hat{\boldsymbol{\beta}}] \neq \boldsymbol{\beta}$ and $\mathrm{plim}[\hat{\boldsymbol{\beta}}] \neq \boldsymbol{\beta}$. Given a sampling process characterized by nonorthogonality of $\mathbf{X}$ and $\varepsilon$, to avoid the use of strong distributional assumptions, it is conventional to introduce additional information in the form of an

$(n \times m)$, $m \geq k$, random matrix, $\mathbf{Z}$, of instrumental variables whose elements are correlated with $\mathbf{X}$ but uncorrelated with $\varepsilon$. This information is introduced into the statistical model by specifying the sample analog moment condition

$$\mathbf{h}(\mathbf{Y}, \mathbf{X}, \mathbf{Z}; \boldsymbol{\beta}) = n^{-1}[\mathbf{Z}'(\mathbf{Y} - \mathbf{X}\boldsymbol{\beta})] \xrightarrow{p} \mathbf{0}, \tag{7.2.1}$$

where the orthogonality between $\mathbf{Z}$ and the model noise is defined by

$$\mathrm{E}[\mathbf{Z}'(\mathbf{Y} - \mathbf{X}\boldsymbol{\beta})] = \mathbf{0}. \tag{7.2.2}$$

When the usual moment regularity conditions are fulfilled, this estimator is consistent, asymptotically normal distributed, and optimal estimating function (OptEF) estimator (Godambe 1960; Heyde 1989; Mittelhammer, Judge, and Miller, 2000).

If the vector of moment conditions overdetermines the model parameters, one possibility is the estimator formed by following Godambe (1960), Judge et al. (1985), Heyde and Morton (1998), and applying the optimal estimating function (OptEF) transformation $(\mathbf{X}'\mathbf{Z}(\mathbf{Z}'\mathbf{Z})^{-1}\mathbf{Z}'\mathbf{X})^{-1}\mathbf{X}'\mathbf{Z}(\mathbf{Z}'\mathbf{Z})^{-1}$ to the moment conditions in (7.2.2). The generalized method of moments (GMM) estimator (Hansen, 1982; Lindsay and Qu, 2003), which minimizes a quadratic form in the sample moment information, is another popular estimator that makes use of the information in (7.2.2).

In contrast to traditional moment-based estimators, *the information theoretic approach permits the investigator to employ likelihood-type methods for model estimation and inference, without having to choose a specific parametric family of probability densities on which to base the likelihood function.* As noted in Section 7.1.1, although there are several rich equivalent families of divergences, our focus is on the general and flexible power-divergence family of statistics introduced by Cressie and Read (1984) and Read and Cressie (1988) and defined in (7.1.3).

In a linear econometric model context, if we use (7.1.3) as the goodness-of-fit criterion and (7.2.2) as the moment-estimating function information, the estimation problem based on the CR divergence measure (CRDM) can be formulated as the following extremum-type estimator for $\boldsymbol{\beta}$, for any given choice of the $\gamma$ parameter:

$$\hat{\boldsymbol{\beta}}(\gamma) = \underset{\boldsymbol{\beta} \in B}{\arg\max} \left[ \ell_E(\boldsymbol{\beta}; \gamma) = \max_{\mathbf{p}} \left\{ - I(\mathbf{p}, \mathbf{q}, \gamma) \mid \sum_{i=1}^{n} p_i \mathbf{Z}'_{i\cdot}(Y_i - \mathbf{X}_{i\cdot}\boldsymbol{\beta}) = \mathbf{0}, \sum_{i=1}^{n} p_i = 1, p_i \geq 0 \, \forall i \right\} \right]. \tag{7.2.3}$$

This class of estimation procedures will be referred to as *minimum power divergence* (MPD) estimation, and we will examine the details of this solution to the stochastic inverse problem in Section 7.4.

The *family* of power divergence statistics defined by (7.1.1) is symmetric in the choice of which set of probabilities is considered as the first and second arguments of the function (7.2.3). In particular, whether the statistic is designated as $I(\mathbf{p}, \mathbf{q}, \gamma)$ or $I(\mathbf{q}, \mathbf{p}, \gamma)$, *the same collection* of members of the family of divergence measures are ultimately spanned, when considering all of the possibilities for $\gamma \in (-\infty, \infty)$. This point, which is discussed by Osterreicher (2002) and Osterreicher and Vajda (2003), is demonstrated in Appendix 7A as Proposition 1.

## 7.3 Three Main Variants of $I(\mathrm{p}, \mathrm{q}, \gamma)$

In this section, we pay particular attention to the three integer variants of $I(\mathbf{p}, \mathbf{q}, \gamma)$ and the associated empirical likelihood functions $\ell_{\mathrm{E}}(\boldsymbol{\beta}; \gamma)$. For expository purposes, in this section, all are based on the reference distribution specification $\mathbf{q} = n^{-1}\mathbf{1}_n$, where, as before, $\mathbf{1}_n$ denotes an $n \times 1$ vector of unit values. This choice of the reference distribution is tantamount to choosing the classical empirical distribution function (EDF) as the target empirical likelihood function. Although there are literally a countably infinite number of alternatives, defined through the choice of $\gamma$ and the reference distribution $\mathbf{q}$, these three discrete CR alternatives have received the most attention in the literature and have been virtually the only variants that have been investigated empirically to date. Later, in Chapters 10 and 11, we investigate how one can use the entire family of CR divergence measures, and not just individual choices of the measure, to address estimation and inference problems.

In going forward, we use the abbreviated notation $\mathrm{CR}(\gamma) \equiv I(\mathbf{p}, \mathbf{q}, \gamma)$, where the arguments $\mathbf{p}$ and $\mathbf{q}$ are tacitly understood to be evaluated at relevant vector values. In the two special cases, where $\gamma = 0$ or $-1$, the notations $CR(0)$ and $CR(-1)$ are to be interpreted as the continuous limits, $\lim_{\gamma \to 0} \mathrm{CR}(\gamma)$ and $\lim_{\gamma \to -1} \mathrm{CR}(\gamma)$, respectively.

The specification CR(−1) leads to the traditional empirical log-likelihood (MEL) objective function, $n^{-1} \sum_{i=1}^{n} \ln(p_i)$, and the maximum empirical likelihood estimate of $\boldsymbol{\beta}$. The specification CR(0) leads to the empirical exponential likelihood objective function, $-\sum_{i=1}^{n} p_{\mathrm{i}} \ln(p_{\mathrm{i}})$, and the MEEL estimator of $\boldsymbol{\beta}$. Finally, CR(1) defines the log Euclidean or least squares likelihood function, $\frac{n}{2}(\sum_{i=1}^{n} (p_i^2 - \frac{1}{n})) \propto (\mathbf{p}-\mathrm{n}^{-1}\mathbf{1}_n)'(\mathbf{p}-n^{-1}\mathbf{1}_n)$, leading to the maximum log Euclidean likelihood (MLEL), or least squares empirical likelihood estimate of $\boldsymbol{\beta}$. This estimator is related (see Chapter 3) to an updating variant of the GMM estimator, where the unknown covariance matrix is handled internally to the estimation problem (Brown and Chen 1998). The limiting forms $\gamma \to 0$ or $\gamma \to -1$ of the CR statistic are used, and the $\gamma = 1$ result is immediate from the definition of CR(1).

## 7.4 Minimum Power Divergence and Empirical Maximum Likelihood (EML) Estimation

If the traditional MEL criterion (CR($-1$)) is used to solve the stochastic inverse problem, this coincides with the estimation objective of MPD with power parameter $\gamma = -1$. A solution in this case involves finding the feasible weights $\hat{\mathbf{p}}$ that maximizes, conditional on the moment constraints, the joint empirical log-likelihood assigned to the observed set of sample observations. *In the sense of objective function analogies, the choice of $\gamma = -1$ defines an empirical analog to the classical maximum likelihood approach, where no explicit functional form for the likelihood function is assumed known or specified at the outset of the estimation problem.*

The CR(0) criterion of maximizing, $-\sum_{i=1}^{n} p_i \ln(p_i)$, is equivalent to defining an estimator by *minimizing* the Kullback-Leibler (KL) information criterion, $\sum_{i=1}^{n} p_i \ln(p_i/n^{-1})$, when the reference distribution is specified to be uniform. If this type of stochastic inverse problem is interpreted in the KL context, this estimation objective finds the feasible weights, $\hat{\mathbf{p}}$, that define the minimum value of all possible *expected log-likelihood ratios*, consistent with the structural moment constraints (Mittelhammer, Judge, and Miller, 2000). The expectations are based on the $\hat{\mathbf{p}}$ distribution, and the log-likelihood ratio has the restricted (by moment constraints) likelihood in the numerator and the unrestricted (i.e., uniform distribution) likelihood in the denominator.

The CR(1) solution seeks feasible weights, $\hat{\mathbf{p}}$, that minimize the Euclidean distance of $\mathbf{p}$ from the uniform probability distribution, with the square of the Euclidean distance being $(\mathbf{p} - n^{-1}\mathbf{1}_n)'(\mathbf{p} - n^{-1}\mathbf{1}_n)$. The constrained optimum data weights are nonnegative in the solutions to the CR(0) and CR(–1) cases. However, negative weights are not ruled out by the CR(1) functional specification and the solution is therefore not automatically restricted to the convex hull of the data. In this case, constraints need to be imposed on the solution.

With regard to MPD ($CR(\gamma)$ family) estimation, under the usual assumed regularity conditions when establishing the asymptotics of traditional structural equation estimators, all of the MPD estimators of $\boldsymbol{\beta}$ obtained by optimizing the $p_i$s are consistent, asymptotically normally distributed, and asymptotically efficient relative to the optimal estimating function (OptEF) estimator (Baggerly 1998). The solution to the constrained optimization problem (6.2.6) yields optimal estimates $\hat{\mathbf{p}}(\gamma)$ and $\hat{\boldsymbol{\beta}}(\gamma)$ that cannot, in general, be expressed in closed form and, thus, must be obtained using numerical methods. For applications in which the reference distribution is specified as $q_i = n^{-1}\ \forall i$, *any* of the estimation objective functions contained in the Cressie-Read family achieve *unconstrained* (by moment equations) optima, when the value of the empirical probability distribution is set to $\mathbf{p} = n^{-1}\mathbf{1}_n$.

It is only the case of $\gamma = -1$ where MPD estimation actually coincides with the maximum likelihood principle for estimating the unknown parameters contained in the stochastic inverse problem. This outcome results because, for this value of the power divergence parameter, the objectives of minimum power divergence and maximum likelihood are identical. For other values of $\gamma$, the power divergence measure *does not* equate to the maximum likelihood objective, for example, the estimation objective relates to *expected log-likelihood ratios when* $\gamma = 0$. However, when $\gamma \neq -1$, one can nonetheless construct a maximum likelihood estimation objective by using the functional representation of the observation probabilities, $\mathbf{p}(\boldsymbol{\theta})$, implied in the solution to the MPD problem, to form the likelihood of the sample data as $L(\boldsymbol{\theta}) = \prod_{i=1}^{n} p_i(\boldsymbol{\theta})$ and then estimate $\boldsymbol{\theta}$ by maximizing $L(\boldsymbol{\theta})$. In effect, this approach uses the *functional form* of the probability distribution $\mathbf{p}$ that minimizes power divergence relative to whatever reference distribution is specified (e.g., the EDF in the case where a uniform distribution is used). At this point, one then chooses the unknown parameter vector $\boldsymbol{\theta}$ of that distribution to maximize the likelihood of the sample data. Henceforth, we refer to this estimation approach as *empirical maximum likelihood* (EML).

We will discuss the EML approach to solving a stochastic inverse problem in Chapter 10, where we analyze the binary response problem. In that context, EML behaves in an analogous way to classical ML in almost all respects except that no functional form of the likelihood function is specified at the outset of the estimation problem. This EML-type estimation coincides perfectly with MPD estimation when $\gamma = -1$. *However, the EML concept allows for ML to be applied more broadly to the functional forms of probability distributions implied by the entire class of MPD problems for the full range of choices of* $\gamma \in (-\infty, \infty)$.

## 7.5 Inference

Inference methods, including hypothesis testing and confidence region estimation, for the CR family bear a strong analogy to inference methods used in traditional ML and GMM approaches. In terms of the MEL-type inference, Owen (1988, 1991) demonstrated that an analog of Wilks's theorem for likelihood ratios, specifically, $-2\ln(\mathrm{LR}) \overset{a}{\sim} \chi_j^2$, holds for the empirical likelihood CR(−1)approach, where $j$ denotes the number of functionally independent restrictions on the parameter space. Baggerly (1998) explained that this calibration remains applicable when the likelihood is replaced with any properly scaled member of the Cressie-Read family of power divergence statistics (7.1.1). In this context, the empirical likelihood ratio (LR) for testing the linear combinations hypothesis, $\mathbf{c}\boldsymbol{\beta} = \mathbf{r}$, when $rank\,(\mathbf{c}) = j$, is given for the CR( − 1) case by

$$\mathrm{LR}_{\mathrm{CR}(-1)}(\mathbf{y}) = \frac{\max_{\boldsymbol{\beta}}\left[\ell_E\,(\boldsymbol{\beta}, \gamma \to -1)\ \text{ s.t. } \mathbf{c}\boldsymbol{\beta} = \mathbf{r}\right]}{\max_{\boldsymbol{\beta}}\,\ell_E\,(\boldsymbol{\beta}, \gamma \to -1)}, \tag{7.5.1}$$

and

$$-\,2\ln\left(LR_{CR(-1)}\,(y)\right) \overset{n}{\sim} \mathit{Chi\text{-}square}(j, 0), \tag{7.5.2}$$

under $\mathrm{H_o}$ when $m \geq k$.

An analogous pseudo-LR approach can be applied, mutatis mutandis, to other members of the Cressie-Read family. One can also base tests of $\mathbf{c}\boldsymbol{\beta} = \mathbf{r}$ on the Wald criterion in the usual way. This proceeds by using the inverse of the asymptotic covariance matrix of $\mathbf{c}\hat{\boldsymbol{\beta}}_{MPD}$ as the weight matrix of a quadratic form in the vector $\mathbf{c}\hat{\boldsymbol{\beta}}_{MPD} - \mathbf{r}$, where $\hat{\boldsymbol{\beta}}_{MPD}$denotes an MPD estimator of $\boldsymbol{\beta}$. Alternatively, one may construct tests based on the Lagrange multipliers (LM) associated with the constraints $\mathbf{c}\boldsymbol{\beta} = \mathbf{r}$ imposed on the MPD-type optimization problem. Confidence region estimates may be obtained from hypothesis test outcomes in the usual way based on duality. The validity of the moment conditions (7.2.1)–(7.2.2) can be assessed by using a variation of the preceding testing methodology, which we examine in more detail ahead.

### 7.5.1 Test Statistics

We next discuss two different inference contexts that include testing the validity of the moment constraints and testing hypotheses and generating confidence intervals for parameters of the structural model.

### 7.5.1a Moment Validity Tests

Regarding the validity of the moment restrictions, Wald quadratic form-type of tests, often referred to as average moment tests, may be calculated for all members of the CR family. The Wald test statistics are specified as

$$\begin{aligned} Wald = & (\mathbf{1}_n'(\mathbf{Z} \odot (\mathbf{Y} - \mathbf{X}\hat{\boldsymbol{\beta}})))'[(\mathbf{Z} \odot (\mathbf{Y} - \mathbf{X}\hat{\boldsymbol{\beta}}))'(\mathbf{Z} \odot (\mathbf{Y} - \mathbf{X}\hat{\boldsymbol{\beta}}))]^{-1} \\ & \times (\mathbf{1}_n'(\mathbf{Z} \odot (\mathbf{Y} - \mathbf{X}\hat{\boldsymbol{\beta}}))), \end{aligned} \tag{7.5.3}$$

where $\hat{\boldsymbol{\beta}}$ is the estimator of the $\boldsymbol{\beta}$ vector and $\odot$ denotes the *generalized* Hadamard (elementwise) product operator. Under the null hypothesis of moment validity, the Wald statistic has an asymptotic Chi-square distribution, with degrees of freedom equal to the degree, $m - k$, of over identification of the parameter vector. Rather than using classical sample moments in defining the Wald statistic, one could also substitute $\mathbf{Z} \odot \mathbf{p}$, for $\mathbf{Z}$ in (7.5.3). This yields a test statistic based on sample moments formed from the MEL probability distribution and has the same asymptotic Chi-square distribution. Pseudolikelihood ratio (LR)–type tests of moment validity can also be calculated for members of the CR family. The respective test statistics for the MEEL and MEL procedures are $\mathrm{LR}_{\mathrm{EEL}} = 2n(\mathbf{p}'\ln(\mathbf{p}) + \ln(n))$ and $\mathrm{LR}_{\mathrm{EL}} = -2(\mathbf{1}_n'\ln(\mathbf{p}) + n\ln(n))$, respectively.

In the case of MLEL, the pseudolikelihood ratio statistic is derived as a special case of the generalized empirical likelihood (GEL) class of procedures identified by Newey and Smith (2000, p. 8) and given by

$$\begin{aligned} LR_{LEL} &= n\left(1 - n^{-1}\mathbf{1}_{\mathrm{n}}'\left[(\mathbf{Z} \odot (\mathbf{Y} - \mathbf{X}\boldsymbol{\beta}))\left(\frac{\boldsymbol{\lambda}}{\eta}\right)\right]^2\right) \\ &= n\left(1 - \left(\frac{2}{\eta}\right)^2 n\sum_{i=1}^{n} p_i^2\right). \end{aligned} \tag{7.5.4}$$

The $\mathbf{p}$ weights, $\boldsymbol{\beta}$ vector, Lagrange multipliers $\boldsymbol{\lambda}$ on the moment constraints, and $\eta$ on the adding up condition for the $p_i$s are replaced by their respective MEL-type estimates. All of the pseudo-LR-type test statistics follow the same asymptotic Chi-square distribution as the Wald statistics of moment validity. Another set of moment validity tests can be based on the Lagrange multipliers of the moment constraints. In the case of the MEEL-type test statistic, note the following quadratic form in the Lagrange multiplier vector that incorporates a robust estimator of the covariance matrix of the moment constraints

$$\begin{aligned} \mathrm{LM}_{\mathrm{EEL}} = & n\boldsymbol{\lambda}'[(\mathbf{h}(\boldsymbol{\beta}) \odot \mathbf{p})'\mathbf{h}(\boldsymbol{\beta})][(\mathbf{h}(\boldsymbol{\beta}) \odot \mathbf{p})'(\mathbf{h}(\boldsymbol{\beta}) \odot \mathbf{p})]^{-1} \\ & \times [(\mathbf{h}(\boldsymbol{\beta}) \odot \mathbf{p})'\mathbf{h}(\boldsymbol{\beta})]\boldsymbol{\lambda}, \end{aligned} \tag{7.5.5}$$

where $\mathbf{h}(\boldsymbol{\beta}) \equiv (\mathbf{Z} \odot (\mathbf{Y} - \mathbf{X}\boldsymbol{\beta}))$ and $\mathbf{p}$, $\boldsymbol{\lambda}$, and $\boldsymbol{\beta}$ are estimated on the basis of the MEEL method. In the case of the MEL and MLEL methods, one can instead use LM tests that are based on equivalences with GEL tests implied by the asymptotic results of Newey and Smith (2000, p. 8). Both of these LM tests are based on the statistic

$$\mathrm{LM} = n\boldsymbol{\lambda}'(\boldsymbol{\Omega}^{-1} - \boldsymbol{\Omega}^{-1}\mathbf{G}'\mathbf{V}\mathbf{G}\boldsymbol{\Omega}^{-1})^{-}\boldsymbol{\lambda}, \tag{7.5.6}$$

where $\boldsymbol{\Omega} \equiv n^{-1}(\mathbf{Z} \odot (\mathbf{Y} - \mathbf{X}\boldsymbol{\beta}))'(\mathbf{Z} \odot (\mathbf{Y} - \mathbf{X}\boldsymbol{\beta}))$, $\mathbf{G} \equiv n^{-1}\mathbf{X}'\mathbf{Z}$, $\mathbf{V} \equiv (\mathbf{G}\boldsymbol{\Omega}^{-1}\mathbf{G}')^{-1}$, and the values of $\boldsymbol{\beta}$ and $\boldsymbol{\lambda}$ are replaced by either MEEL or MLEL estimates. Under the null hypothesis, all of the LM tests are asymptotically Chi-square distributed with degrees of freedom equal to $m - k$.

#### 7.5.1b Tests of Parameter Restrictions

A test of the significance of the parameters of the moment-based model can be based on the usual asymptotic normally distributed $Z$-statistic and, concomitantly, by duality, confidence region coverage of the parameters can also be inferred. The test statistic for all of the estimation procedures examined has the familiar form

$$Z = \frac{\hat{\beta}_i}{\widehat{std}(\hat{\beta}_i)} \overset{a}{\sim} N(0,1) \text{ under } \mathrm{H}_0 : \beta_i = 0. \tag{7.5.7}$$

The associated confidence interval estimate is $(\hat{\beta}_i - z_\tau \widehat{std}(\hat{\beta}_i), \hat{\beta}_i + z_\tau \widehat{std}(\hat{\beta}_i))$, where $z_\tau$ denotes the $100\tau\%$ quantile of the standard normal distribution. In (7.5.7), $\hat{\beta}_i$ and $\widehat{std}(\hat{\beta}_i)$ can be appropriate estimates of the parameter and the estimated standard error, based on any estimation procedure that produces estimates that follow the asymptotic normal distribution. The respective estimates of the standard errors, used in the test and confidence interval procedures, are obtained as the square roots of the appropriate diagonal elements of the asymptotic covariance matrices, such as those for 2SLS-OptEF, or GMM. These EL-type estimators may be defined, respectively, as

$$AsyCov(\hat{\mathbf{B}}_{2\mathrm{sls}}) = \hat{\sigma}^2(\mathbf{X}'\mathbf{Z}(\mathbf{Z}'\mathbf{Z})^{-1}\mathbf{Z}'\mathbf{X})^{-1}, \tag{7.5.8}$$

$$AsyCov(\hat{\mathbf{B}}_{\mathrm{GMM}}) = \hat{\sigma}^2(\mathbf{X}'\mathbf{Z}\mathbf{Z}'\mathbf{X})^{-1}(\mathbf{X}'\mathbf{Z}(\mathbf{Z}'\mathbf{Z})^{-1}\mathbf{Z}'\mathbf{X})(\mathbf{X}'\mathbf{Z}\mathbf{Z}'\mathbf{X})^{-1} \tag{7.5.9}$$

and

$$\begin{aligned} AsyCov(\hat{\mathbf{B}}_{\text{EL-type}}) = {} & [(\mathbf{X}'(\mathbf{Z} \odot \hat{\mathbf{p}}))[((\mathbf{Z} \odot (\mathbf{Y} - \mathbf{X}\hat{\mathbf{B}})) \odot \hat{\mathbf{p}})' \\ & \times (\mathbf{Z} \odot (\mathbf{Y} - \mathbf{X}\hat{\mathbf{B}}))]^{-1}((\mathbf{Z} \odot \hat{\mathbf{p}})'\mathbf{X})]^{-1}, \end{aligned} \tag{7.5.10}$$

where $\hat{\sigma}^2$ is the usual consistent estimate of the equation noise variance, and $\hat{\mathbf{p}}$ and $\hat{\mathbf{B}}$ are the appropriate estimates obtained from applications of the estimation procedure.

## 7.6 Concluding Remarks

Given a stochastic econometric model satisfying linear constraints with unknown parameters, we cast the estimation problem as how to best estimate the response coefficients when one's prior knowledge consists only of the values of expectations of moment functions of the sample information. Rather than approach choosing the estimation criterion in an ad hoc manner, we ask the basic question of how best to make use of the sample information and use the Cressie-Read discrepancy statistic as a basis for identifying a family of potential distance-divergence measures. The CR measure of divergence includes in its family of estimators the empirical likelihood (MEL), the Kullback-Leibler (KL)-MEEL, and the Euclidean likelihood estimation alternatives. The CR divergence measures are not true distance measures. In fact, for a *given* value of $\gamma$, they are not symmetric under the interchange of the two distributions $\mathbf{p}$ and $\mathbf{q}$ being compared. However, as demonstrated in Appendix 7.A, precisely the same *family* of divergence measures is defined when viewed across all possibilities for $\gamma \in (-\infty, \infty)$, regardless of which of the distributions is used as the reference distribution and which is used as the subject distribution. Thus, if one were to allow the entire family to be used as candidates for generating a likelihood in any estimation or inference problem, the problem of choice of the reference and subject distributions is mitigated. We investigate this issue further in Chapters 10 and 11.

Some of the useful functional characteristics of the CR divergence measures are i) first and second derivatives of the CR function with respect to $\gamma$ exist; and ii) the derivatives are smoothly differentiable and permit a definition of the Hessian of the CR statistic. The CR divergence measure, as a function of $\gamma$, is strictly convex and has a well-defined minimum for a given $\mathbf{p}$ vector. A global minimum value exists relative to the closed and bounded choices of $\mathbf{p}$ and $\gamma$ and, if $\gamma$ is confined to a fixed interval, the entire set of $\mathbf{p}$ and $\gamma$ is closed and bounded. Furthermore, the CR objective function is continuous and differentiable in *all* its arguments and a global optimum exists. If there are no data-moment constraints on the choices of the $\mathbf{p}$ and $\gamma$ arguments, the global optimum is not unique and the resulting ridge of $\gamma$ values are all optimal.

Implicit differentiation can be used to define the appropriate derivatives of the probabilities with respect to the explanatory variables. The derivatives are flexible in the sense that they are functions of the sample data and not dependent on parameters other than the data-determined Lagrange multipliers. The optimal member of the class of CR-based estimators avoids tuning parameter choice or nuisance parameter estimation, such as the unknown covariance components, in the case of the traditional GMM estimator, or regularization methods used in traditional stochastic inverse problems. From an asymptotic standpoint, the range of estimators from the CR($\gamma$) family under usual regularity conditions is consistent and asymptotically normal and efficient. Finally, the EML concept permits ML methods to be applied broadly to the entire class of MPD problems.

## 7.7 Selected References

Baggerly, K. A. (1998), "Empirical Likelihood as a Goodness of Fit Measure," *Biometrika* **85**:535–547.

Baggerly, K. A. (2001), "Studentized Empirical Likelihood and Maximum Entropy: Empirical t," Working paper, Department of Statistics, Rice University.

Boltzmann, L. (1872), "Weitere Studien uber das Warmegleichgewicht unter Gasmolekulen," *Sitzungsberichte der keiserlichen Akademie der Wissenschaften*, **66**:275–370. Translation.

Boltzmann, L. (2003), "Further Studies on the Thermal Equilibrium of Gas Molecules," in S. G. Brush and N. S. Hall (Ed.), *Kinetic Theory of Gases: An Anthology of Classic Papers with Historical Commentary* (pp. 362–368), London: Imperial College Press.

Brown, B. and S. Chen (1998), "Combined Least Squares Empirical Likelihood," *Annals of Institute of Statistical Mathematics*, **60**:697–714.

Corcoran, S. A. (2000), "Empirical Exponential Family Likelihood Using Several Moment Conditions," *Statistica Sinica*, **10**:545–557.

Cotofrei, P. (2003), "A Possible Generalization of the Empirical Likelihood," Computer Sciences, University of "A.I. Cuza," Iasi, Romania.

Cressie, N. and T. Read (1984), "Multinomial Goodness of Fit Tests," *Journal of Royal Statistical Society of Series B*, **46**:440–464.

Gibbs, J. W. (1981), *Elementary Principles in Statistical Mechanics*, New York: Ox Bow Press.

Godambe, V. (1960), "An Optimum Property of Regular Maximum Likelihood Estimation," *Annals of Mathematical Statistics*, **31**:1208–1212.

Golan, A., G. G. Judge, and D. Miller (1996), *Maximum Entropy Econometrics*, New York: John Wiley and Sons.

Gorban, A., P. Gorban, and G. Judge (2010), "Entropy: The Markov Ordering Approach," *Entropy*, **5**:1145–1193.

Grunwald, P. and A. David (2004), "Game Theory, Maximum Entropy, Minimum Discrepancy and Robust Bayesian Decision Theory," *Annals of Statistics*, **32**:1367–1433.

Hansen, L. P. (1982), "Large Sample Properties of Generalized Method of Moments Estimators," *Econometrica*, **50**:1029–1054.

Haubold, H., A. Mathai, and R. Saxena (2004), "Boltzmann-Gibbs Entropy versus Tsallis Entropy," *Astrophysics and Space Sciences*, **290**:241–245.

Heyde, C. (1989), "Quasi-Likelihood and Optimality of Estimating Functions: Some Current and Unifying Themes," *Bulletin of International Statistical Institute*, **1**:19–29.

Heyde, C. and R. Morton (1998), "Multiple Roots in General Estimating Equations," *Biometrika*, **85**:954–959.

Huber, P. J. (1981), *Robust Statistics*, New York: John Wiley and Sons.

Imbens, G. W., R. H. Spady, and P. Johnson (1998), "Information Theoretic Approaches to Inference in Moment Condition Models." *Econometrica*, **66**:333–357.

Jaynes, E. T. (1957), "Information Theory and Statistical Mechanics," *Physics Review*, **106**: 620–630.

Jaynes, E. T. (1957), "Information Theory and Statistical Mechanics. II." *Physics Review*, **108**:171–190.

Judge, G., R. Hill, W. Griffiths, H. Lutkepohl, and T. Lee (1985), *The Theory and Practice of Econometrics*. New York: John Wiley and Sons.

Koenker, R. and G. Bassett, Jr. (1978), "Regression Quantiles," *Econometrica*, **46**:33–50.

Kullback, S. and Leibler, R. A. (1951), "On Information and Sufficiency," *Annals of Mathematica Statistics*, **22**:79–86.

Lindsay, B. and A. Qu (2003), "Inference Functions and Quadratic Score Tests," *Statistical Science*, **18**:394–410.

Mittelhammer, R. and G. Judge (2002), "Endogeneity and Moment Based Estimation under Squared Error Loss," in A. Ullah, A. Wan, and A. Chaturvedi (Eds.), *Handbook of Applied Econometrics and Statistical Inference*, New York: Marcel Dekker, pp. 347–370.

Mittelhammer, R. C. and G. G. Judge (2003), "Some Empirical Evidence on EL-Weighted Combinations of Structural Equation Estimators," *Journal of Agricultural and Applied Economics*, **35**: 91–101.

Mittelhammer, R., G. G. Judge, and D. Miller (2000), *Econometric Foundations*, Cambridge: Cambridge University Press.

Mittelhammer, R., G. G. Judge, and R. Schoenberg (2004)."Empirical Evidence Concerning the Finite Sample Performance of EL-Type Structural Equation Estimation and Inference Methods," in *Festschrift in Honor of Thomas Rothenberg*, D. K. Andrews and J. H. Stock (Eds.) New York: Cambridge University Press, pp. 282–305.

Newey, W. K. and R. G. Smith (2000), "Asymptotic Bias and Equivalence of GMM and GEL Estimators," MIT Working Paper.

Osterreicher, F. (2002), *Csiszar's f-Divergencies-Basic Properties.* Salzburg: Institute of Mathematics, University of Salzburg, Austria.

Osterreicher, F. and I. Vajda (2003), "A New Class of Metric Divergences on Probability Spaces and Its Applicability in Statistics," *Annals of the Institute of Statistical Mathematics*, **55**:639–653.

Owen, A. (1988), "Empirical Likelihood Ratio Confidence Intervals for a Single Functional." *Biometrika*, **75**:237–249.

Owen, A. (1991), "Empirical Likelihood for Linear Models," *Annals of Statistics*, **19**:1725–1747.

Owen, A. (2001), *Empirical Likelihood.* New York: Chapman and Hall.

Qin, J. (2000), "Combining Parametric and Empirical Likelihood Data," *Biometrika*, **87**:484–490.

Qin, J. and J. Lawless (1994), "Empirical Likelihood and General Estimating Equations," *Annals of Statistics*, **22**(l):300–325.

Read, T. R. and N. A. Cressie (1988), *Goodness of Fit Statistics for Discrete Multivariate Data.* New York: Springer Verlag.

Renyi, A. (1961), "On Measures of Entropy and Information," in Proceedings of the 4th Berkeley Symposium on Mathematics, Statistics and Probability 1960, Berkeley, CA, USA, 20 June–30 July 1960; Berkeley: University of California Press, **1**:547–561.

Renyi, A. (1970), *Probability Theory.* Amsterdam, The Netherlands: North-Holland.

Shannon, C. E. (1948), "A Mathematical Theory of Communication," *Bell System Technical Journal,* **27**:379–423, 623–656.

Topsoe, F. (1979), "Informational Theoretical Optimization Techniques," *Kybernetika,* **15**:8–27.

Tsallis, C. (1988), "Possible Generalization of Boltzmann-Gibbs Statistics," *Journal of Statistical Physics,* **52**:479–487.

Walley, P. (1991), *Statistical Reasoning with Imprecise Probabilities.* London: Chapman and Hall.

Wolpert, D. and D. R. Wolf (1995), "Estimating Functions of Probability Distributions from a Finite Set of Data," *Physical Review E* **6**:6841–6852.

## APPENDIX 7.A PROPOSITIONS, PROOFS, AND DEFINITIONS

**Proposition 1:** *Subject-Reference Distribution Symmetry in the CR Family of Power Divergence Statistics*

Let $\mathbf{p}$ and $\mathbf{q}$ denote two $n$-element probability distributions such that $\mathbf{p} \gg \mathbf{0}$, $\mathbf{q} \gg \mathbf{0}$ and $\mathbf{1}'_n\mathbf{p} = \mathbf{1}'_n\mathbf{q} = 1$. Define the family of CR divergence statistics, indexed by the parameter, $\gamma$, alternatively as

$$I(\mathbf{p}, \mathbf{q}, \gamma) = \frac{1}{\gamma(\gamma+1)} \sum_{i=1}^{n} p_i \left[ \left( \frac{p_i}{q_i} \right)^{\gamma} - 1 \right] \tag{7.A.1}$$

or

$$I(\mathbf{q}, \mathbf{p}, \gamma) = \frac{1}{\gamma(\gamma+1)} \sum_{i=1}^{n} q_i \left[ \left( \frac{q_i}{p_i} \right)^{\gamma} - 1 \right]. \tag{7.A.2}$$

Then

$$\text{a) } I(\mathbf{p}, \mathbf{q}, \alpha) = I(\mathbf{q}, \mathbf{p}, -(1+\alpha)) \ \forall \alpha \neq 0 \ \text{ or } \ -1 \tag{7.A.3}$$

and

$$\text{b) } \lim_{\alpha \to 0 \text{ or } -1} I(\mathbf{p}, \mathbf{q}, \alpha) = \lim_{\alpha \to 0 \text{ or } -1} I(\mathbf{q}, \mathbf{p}, -(1+\alpha)). \tag{7.A.4}$$

***Proof:***

*Part a:* Evaluating the two discrepancy measures at $\alpha$ and $-(1+\alpha)$, respectively, when $\alpha \neq 0$ or $-1$ yields

$$I(\mathbf{p}, \mathbf{q}, \alpha) = \frac{1}{\alpha(\alpha+1)} \sum_{i=1}^{n} p_i \left[ \left( \frac{p_i}{q_i} \right)^{\alpha} - 1 \right]$$
$$= \frac{1}{\alpha(\alpha+1)} \left( \left[ \sum_{i=1}^{n} p_i^{\alpha+1} q_i^{-\alpha} \right] - 1 \right), \tag{7.A.5}$$

$$I(\mathbf{q}, \mathbf{p}, -(1+\alpha)) = \frac{1}{-(1+\alpha)(1-(1+\alpha))} \sum_{i=1}^{n} q_i \left[ \left( \frac{q_i}{p_i} \right)^{-(1+\alpha)} - 1 \right]$$
$$= \frac{1}{\alpha(\alpha+1)} \left( \left[ \sum_{i=1}^{n} p_i^{\alpha+1} q_i^{-\alpha} \right] - 1 \right), \tag{7.A.6}$$

which demonstrates the validity of part a).

*Part b:* First examine the case where $\alpha \to 0$. Applying l'Hôpital's rule to evaluate the limits yields

$$\lim_{\alpha \to 0} I(\mathbf{p}, \mathbf{q}, \alpha) = \lim_{\alpha \to 0} \frac{\sum_{i=1}^{n} p_i \left[ \left( \frac{p_i}{q_i} \right)^{\alpha} - 1 \right]}{\alpha(\alpha+1)}$$
$$= \lim_{\alpha \to 0} \left[ \frac{\sum_{i=1}^{n} p_i \left( \frac{p_i}{q_i} \right)^{\alpha} \ln \left( \frac{p_i}{q_i} \right)}{2\alpha + 1} \right]$$
$$= \sum_{i=1}^{n} p_i \ln \left( \frac{p_i}{q_i} \right), \tag{7.A.7}$$

and

$$\lim_{\alpha \to 0} I(\mathbf{q}, \mathbf{p}, -(1+\alpha)) = \lim_{\gamma \to -1} I(\mathbf{q}, \mathbf{p}, \gamma)$$
$$= \lim_{\gamma \to -1} \frac{\sum_{i=1}^{n} q_i \left[ \left( \frac{q_i}{p_i} \right)^{\gamma} - 1 \right]}{\gamma(\gamma+1)}$$
$$= \lim_{\gamma \to -1} \left[ \frac{\sum_{i=1}^{n} q_i \left( \frac{q_i}{p_i} \right)^{\gamma} \ln \left( \frac{q_i}{p_i} \right)}{2\gamma + 1} \right]$$
$$= \sum_{i=1}^{n} p_i \ln \left( \frac{p_i}{q_i} \right), \tag{7.A.8}$$

which demonstrates the result when $\alpha \to 0$.

Now examine the case in which $\alpha \to -1$. Again applying l'Hôpital's rule to evaluate the limits yields

$$\begin{aligned}
\lim_{\alpha \to -1} I(\mathbf{p}, \mathbf{q}, \alpha) &= \lim_{\alpha \to -1} \frac{\sum_{i=1}^{n} p_i \left[ \left( \frac{p_i}{q_i} \right)^{\alpha} - 1 \right]}{\alpha(\alpha+1)} \\
&= \lim_{\alpha \to -1} \left[ \frac{\sum_{i=1}^{n} p_i \left( \frac{p_i}{q_i} \right)^{\alpha} \ln\left( \frac{p_i}{q_i} \right)}{2\alpha + 1} \right] \\
&= \sum_{i=1}^{n} q_i \ln\left( \frac{q_i}{p_i} \right), \qquad (7.A.9)
\end{aligned}$$

and

$$\begin{aligned}
\lim_{\alpha \to -1} I(\mathbf{q}, \mathbf{p}, -(1+\alpha)) = \lim_{\gamma \to 0} I(\mathbf{q}, \mathbf{p}, \gamma) &= \lim_{\gamma \to 0} \frac{\sum_{i=1}^{n} q_i \left[ \left( \frac{q_i}{p_i} \right)^{\gamma} - 1 \right]}{\gamma(\gamma+1)} \\
&= \lim_{\alpha \to 0} \left[ \frac{\sum_{i=1}^{n} q_i \left( \frac{q_i}{p_i} \right)^{\gamma} \ln\left( \frac{q_i}{p_i} \right)}{2\gamma + 1} \right] \\
&= \sum_{i=1}^{n} q_i \ln\left( \frac{q_i}{p_i} \right), \qquad (7.A.10)
\end{aligned}$$

which demonstrates the result when $\alpha \to -1$.

For a discussion of the symmetry issue in a somewhat different context, see Osterreicher (2002).

**Proposition 2:**

$$\begin{aligned}
\lim_{\gamma \to 0} I(\mathbf{p}, n^{-1}\mathbf{1}_n, \gamma) &= \lim_{\gamma \to 0} \left[ \frac{\sum_{i=1}^{n} \mathrm{p}_i [(\frac{\mathrm{p}_i}{n^{-1}})^{\gamma} - 1]}{\gamma(\gamma+1)} \right] \\
&= \sum_{i=1}^{n} p_i \ln(p_i) + \ln(n) \qquad (7.A.11)
\end{aligned}$$

***Proof:*** Applying l'Hôpital's rule to the ratio of terms yields

$$\lim_{\gamma \to 0} \left[ \frac{\sum_{i=1}^{n} p_i (n p_i)^{\gamma} \ln(n p_i)}{2\gamma + 1} \right] = \sum_{i=1}^{n} p_i \ln(p_i) + \ln(n) \qquad (7.A.12)$$

because $\sum_{i=1}^{n} p_i = 1$.

**Proposition 3:**

$$\lim_{\gamma \to -1} I(\mathbf{p}, n^{-1}\mathbf{1}_n, \gamma) = \lim_{\gamma \to -1} \left[ \frac{\sum_{i=1}^{n} p_i[(\frac{p_i}{n^{-1}})^{\gamma} - 1]}{\gamma(\gamma+1)} \right]$$
$$= -\sum_{i=1}^{n} n^{-1} \ln(p_i) - \ln(n) \qquad (7.A.13)$$

***Proof:*** Applying l'Hôpital's rule to the ratio of terms yields

$$\lim_{\gamma \to -1} \left[ \frac{\sum_{i=1}^{n} p_i (n p_i)^{\gamma} \ln(n p_i)}{2\gamma + 1} \right] = -\sum_{i=1}^{n} n^{-1} \ln(p_i) - \ln(n) \quad (7.A.14)$$

because $\sum_{i=1}^{n} p_i = 1$.

**Definition 1: Hessian of $I(\mathbf{p}, n^{-1}\mathbf{1}_n, \gamma)$**

Let $\boldsymbol{\xi} = [\frac{\mathbf{p}}{\gamma}]$. Then

$$\frac{\partial^2 I(\mathbf{p}, n^{-1}\mathbf{1}_n, \gamma)}{\partial \boldsymbol{\xi}\, \partial \boldsymbol{\xi}'} = \left[ \begin{array}{c|c} \frac{\partial^2 I(\mathbf{p}, n^{-1}\mathbf{1}_n, \gamma)}{\partial \mathbf{p}\, \partial \mathbf{p}'} & \frac{\partial^2 I(\mathbf{p}, n^{-1}\mathbf{1}_n, \gamma)}{\partial \mathbf{p}\, \partial \lambda} \\ \hline \frac{\partial^2 I(\mathbf{p}, n^{-1}\mathbf{1}_n, \gamma)}{\partial \gamma\, \partial \mathbf{p}'} & \frac{\partial^2 I(\mathbf{p}, n^{-1}\mathbf{1}_n, \gamma)}{\partial \gamma^2} \end{array} \right], \quad (7.A.15)$$

where

$$\frac{\partial^2 I(\mathbf{p}, n^{-1}\mathbf{1}_{\mathrm{n}}, \gamma)}{\partial \mathbf{p}\, \partial \mathbf{p}'} = n^{\gamma} \begin{bmatrix} p_1^{\gamma-1} & 0 & \cdots & 0 \\ 0 & p_2^{\gamma-1} & \cdots & 0 \\ 0 & 0 & \ddots & \vdots \\ 0 & 0 & \cdots & p_2^{\gamma-1} \end{bmatrix} = n^{\gamma}(\mathbf{I}_n \odot \mathbf{p}^{\gamma-1}), \quad (7.A.16)$$

$$\frac{\partial^2 I(\mathbf{p}, n^{-1}\mathbf{1}_{\mathrm{n}}, \gamma)}{\partial \gamma^2} = \left[ \sum_{i=1}^{n} n^{\gamma} p_i^{\gamma+1} \left[ \frac{(\ln(np_i))^2}{\gamma(\gamma+1)} - \frac{2(2\gamma+1)\ln(np_i)}{(\gamma(\gamma+1))^2} + \frac{6\gamma(\gamma+1)+2}{(\gamma(\gamma+1))^3} \right] \right] - \frac{6\gamma(\gamma+1)+2}{(\gamma(\gamma+1))^3}, \quad (7.A.17)$$

and

$$\frac{\partial^2 I(\mathbf{p}, n^{-1}\mathbf{1}_n, \gamma)}{\partial \mathbf{p}\, \partial \gamma} = \left( \frac{n^{\gamma}}{\gamma^2} \right) [\mathbf{p}^{\gamma} \odot (\gamma \ln(n\mathbf{p}) - \mathbf{1}_n)]. \quad (7.A.18)$$

## APPENDIX 7.B ENTROPY FAMILIES

In this chapter, we used the CR power divergence measure

$$\mathrm{CR}(\gamma) = I(\mathbf{p}, \mathbf{q}, \gamma) = \frac{1}{\gamma(1+\gamma)} \sum_{i=1}^{N} \left( p_i \left[ \left( \frac{p_i}{q_i} \right)^{\gamma} - 1 \right] \right) \tag{7.B.1}$$

to define a family of likelihood CDF functions. Other attractive sets of nonparametric divergence measures include the Tsallis ($T$) and Renyi ($R$) entropy families of distribution functions (Renyi, 1961, 70; Tsallis, 1988; Haubold et al., 2004). Gorban, Gorban, and Judge (2010) demonstrate that the Renyi (1961, 1970) family of entropic functionals (R)

$$R_{\gamma} = \frac{1}{\gamma} \ln \left[ \sum_{i=1}^{n} p_i \left( \frac{p_i}{q_i} \right)^{\gamma} \right]; (\gamma > -1, \gamma \neq 0), \tag{7.B.2}$$

and the CR family of divergence functions are equivalent. The relationship between the two families may be expressed as $\gamma(1+\gamma)\mathrm{CR} = \exp(-R_{\gamma}) - 1$, where $\gamma$ is an arbitrary and unspecified parameter. The difference between the families is not important in divergence applications. In addition, they note that there is a one-to-one relation between the CR and the Tsallis ($T$) (1988) family of concave entropy functions

$$T_{\gamma} = \left( 1 - \sum_{i=1}^{N} (p_i/q_i)^{\gamma} \right) / (1-\gamma); \left( \text{limit } p \to 0 = -\sum_{i=1}^{n} p_i \ln(p_i/q_i) \right). \tag{7.B.3}$$

In Chapter 11, we will build on this base of entropy functionals and introduce a family of concave functions, which satisfy additivity and trace conditions and can produce nonexponential probability distributions.

EIGHT

# Cressie-Read-MPD-Type Estimators in Practice

## Monte Carlo Evidence of Estimation and Inference Sampling Performance

### 8.1 Introduction

We began developing the concept of empirical likelihood in Chapter 4, and we introduced a number of explicit formulations of minimum power divergence (MPD)-type estimators and inference procedures in Chapter 7 that can be applied to an array of econometric models used in empirical practice. These procedures dealt with data sampling processes that were of the linear model variety and encompassed the problem of structural equation modeling, whereby one or more right-hand-side explanatory variables were nonorthogonal to the noise term of the model. The procedures were thus applicable to the general linear model context, as well as to simultaneous equations models and other models that contain right-hand-side endogenous variables. Before proceeding to other data sampling processes that can be addressed using MPD-type methods, we devote this chapter to illustrate empirical implementation and performance characteristics of these MPD-type estimation and inference procedures, using a data sampling context that emulates problems encountered in applied econometric analysis.

The finite sample properties of the MPD-type estimators and associated inference procedures delineated in Chapter 7 cannot be derived from a direct evaluation of closed functional forms applied to distributions of random variables. This is similar to the case of finite sample probability distributions of traditional two-stage least squares (2SLS) and generalized method of moments (GMM) estimators, which are also generally intractable in closed form. Consequently, we use Monte Carlo (MC) sampling experiments to examine and compare the finite sample performance of competing estimators and inference methods. Although these results are specific to the collection of particular MC experiments analyzed, the wide-ranging reported sampling evidence provides an indication of the types of relative performance that can occur over a range of scenarios for which the unknown parameters of a model are moderately well identified.

## 8.2 Design of Sampling Experiments

Consider a data sampling process of the following form:

$$Y_{i1} = Z_{i1}\beta_1 + Y_{i2}\beta_2 + e_i = \mathbf{X}_{i.}\boldsymbol{\beta} + \varepsilon_i \tag{8.2.1}$$

$$Y_{i2} = \sum_{j=1}^{5} \pi_j Z_{ij} + v_i = \mathbf{Z}_{i.}\pi + v_i, \tag{8.2.2}$$

where $\mathbf{X}_{i.} = (Z_{i1}, Y_{i2})$ and $i = 1, 2, \ldots, n$. In the sampling experiment, the two-dimensional vector of unknown parameters $\boldsymbol{\beta}$ in (8.2.1) is set equal to the vector $[-1, 2]'$. The outcomes of the $(6 \times 1)$ random vector, $[Y_{i2}, \varepsilon_i, Z_{i1}, Z_{i2}, Z_{i3}, Z_{i4}]$, are *iid* from a multivariate normal distribution, with a zero mean vector and standard deviations uniformly set to five for the first two random variables and two for the remaining random variables and $Z_{i5} \equiv 1$, $\forall i$. Also, various other conditions relating to the correlations among the six scalar random variables are assumed. The values of the $\pi_j$'s in (8.2.2) are determined by the regression function between $Y_{i2}$ and $[Z_{i1}, Z_{i2}, Z_{i3}, Z_{i4}, Z_{i5}]$, which is itself a function of the covariance specification relating to the marginal normal distribution associated with the $(5 \times 1)$ random vector $[Y_{i2}, Z_{i1}, Z_{i2}, Z_{i3}, Z_{i4}]$. Thus, the $\pi_j$'s generally change as the scenario postulated for the correlation matrix of the sampling process changes. In this sampling design, the outcomes of $[Y_{i1}, V_i]$ are calculated by applying (8.2.1)–(8.2.2) to the outcomes of, $[Y_{i2}, Z_{i1}, Z_{i2}, Z_{i3}, Z_{i4}, Z_{i5}]$.

Regarding the sampling scenarios simulated for these MC experiments, sample sizes of $n = 50$, 100, and 250 are examined. The outcomes of $\varepsilon_i$ were generated independently of the vector $[Z_{i1}, Z_{i2}, Z_{i3}, Z_{i4}]$ so that the correlations between $\varepsilon_i$ and the $Z_{ij}$'s were zero. This fulfills a fundamental condition for $[Z_{i1}, Z_{i2}, Z_{i3}, Z_{i4}]$ to be considered a set of valid instrumental variables for estimating the unknown parameters in (8.2.1). Regarding the degree of nonorthogonality and identifiability in (8.2.1), correlations of 0.25, 0.50, and 0.75 between the random variables $Y_{i2}$ and $\varepsilon_i$, are used to simulate moderately to relatively strongly correlated nonorthogonal relationships between the explanatory variable $Y_{i2}$ and the equation noise $\varepsilon_i$.

For each sample size, alternative scenarios are examined relating to both the degree of correlation existing between each of the random instruments

Table 8.2.1. *Monte Carlo experiment definitions, with* $\boldsymbol{\beta} = [-1, 2]'$, $\sigma_{\varepsilon_i} = \sigma_{Y_{2i}} = 5$, *and* $\sigma_{Z_{ij}} = 2$, $\forall i$ and $j = 1, \ldots, 5$

| Experiment Number | $\rho_{y_{2i},\varepsilon_i}$ | $\rho_{y_{2i},z_{i,1}}$ | $\rho_{y_{2i},z_{ij};j>1}$ | $\rho_{z_{ij},z_{ik}}$ | $R^2_{Y_1,\hat{Y}_1}$ | $R^2_{Y_2,\hat{Y}_2}$ |
|---|---|---|---|---|---|---|
| 1 | 0.25 | 0.25 | 0.25 | 0 | 0.84 | 0.25 |
| 2 | 0.25 | −0.25 | 0.25 | 0.5 | 0.86 | 0.40 |
| 3 | 0.50 | 0.25 | 0.25 | 0 | 0.89 | 0.25 |
| 4 | 0.50 | −0.25 | 0.25 | 0.5 | 0.90 | 0.40 |
| 5 | 0.75 | 0.25 | 0.25 | 0 | 0.95 | 0.25 |
| 6 | 0.75 | −0.25 | 0.25 | 0.5 | 0.94 | 0.40 |
| 7 | 0.50 | 0.1 | 0.5 | 0.25 | 0.89 | 0.53 |
| 8 | 0.50 | 0.1 | 0.5 | 0.5 | 0.89 | 0.50 |
| 9 | 0.50 | 0.1 | 0.5 | 0.75 | 0.89 | 0.68 |
| 10 | 0.50 | 0.5 | 0.1 | 0.75 | 0.89 | 0.53 |

*Note:* $\rho_{y_{2i},\varepsilon_i}$ denotes the correlation between $Y_{2i}$ and $e_i$ and measures the degree of nonorthogonality; $\rho_{y_{2i},z_{ij}}$ denotes the common correlation between $Y_{2i}$ and each of the four random instrumental variables, the $Z_{ij}$'s; $\rho_{z_{ij},z_{ik}}$ denotes the common correlation between the four random instrumental variables; $R^2_{Y_1,\hat{Y}_1}$ denotes the population squared correlation between $\mathbf{Y}_1$ and $\hat{\mathbf{Y}}_1 = \mathbf{X}\beta$; and $R^2_{Y_2,\hat{Y}_2}$ denotes the population squared correlation between $\mathbf{Y}_2$ and $\hat{\mathbf{Y}}_2 = \mathbf{Z}\pi$.

in the matrix $\mathbf{Z}$ and the $\mathbf{Y}_2$ variable, and the levels of collinearity existing among the instrumental variables themselves. By varying the degrees of intercorrelation among the variables, the overall correlation of the instrumental variables with $\mathbf{Y}_2$ is affected and contributes to determining the overall effectiveness of the set of instruments in predicting values of the endogenous $\mathbf{Y}_2$. The joint correlation between $\mathbf{Y}_2$ and the set of instruments ranges from a relatively low 0.25 to a relatively strong 0.68.

The major characteristics of each sampling scenario are delineated in Table 8.2.1. In general, the scenarios range from relatively weak but independent instruments to stronger but more highly multicollinear instruments. All models have a relatively strong signal component in the sense that the squared correlation between the dependent variable $\mathbf{Y}_1$ and the explanatory variables $(\mathbf{Z}_{.1}, \mathbf{Y}_2)$ ranges between 0.84 and 0.95. In total, there are 10 different MC experimental designs in combination with the 3 different sample sizes. This resulted in 30 different sampling scenarios in which to observe estimator and inference behavior.

The sampling results reported in Section 8.3 are based on 5,000 MC repetitions. This was sufficient to produce stable estimates of the empirical mean squared error (MSE) of two types: (i) expressed in terms of the mean of the empirical squared Euclidean distance between the true parameter vector $\boldsymbol{\beta}$ and $\hat{\boldsymbol{\beta}}$ (measuring parameter estimation risk), and (ii) the MSE between $\mathbf{y}$ with $\hat{\mathbf{y}}$ (measuring predictive risk). We also examined (iii) the average estimated bias in the estimates, Bias $(\hat{\boldsymbol{\beta}}) = \mathrm{E}[\hat{\boldsymbol{\beta}}]$-$\boldsymbol{\beta}$, and (iv) the average estimated variances, $\mathrm{Var}(\hat{\beta}_i)$.

Regarding inference performance, we (i) compare the empirical size of 10 alternative tests of moment equation validity with the typical nominal target size of 0.05, (ii) examine the empirical coverage probability of confidence interval estimators based on a target coverage probability of 0.99, (iii) compare the empirical expected lengths of confidence intervals, and (iv) examine the power of significance tests associated with the different estimation methods.

## 8.3 Sampling Results

We report MSE results for the entire parameter vector $\boldsymbol{\beta}$ but limit our reporting of bias, variance, hypothesis test, and confidence region performance to the structural parameter $\beta_2$. The results for the remaining structural parameters are qualitatively similar. Some computational issues relating to the solutions of the MPD-type estimation and inference procedures examined here, as well as the numerical approaches used to obtain solutions, are discussed in Appendix 8.A of this chapter.

### 8.3.1 Estimator MSE Performance

The simulated MSE associated with estimating the $\boldsymbol{\beta}$ vector are presented in Figure 8.3.1. The results are expressed relative to the MSE of the 2SLS estimator, and scenarios are numbered sequentially to represent the 10 sampling scenarios in Table 8.2.1, for each of the sample sizes 50, 100, and 250. A number of general patterns is evident from the sampling results. First, the 2SLS estimator dominates the other four estimators in terms of parameter MSE, with the exception of the smallest sample size and scenario 5, in which case the maximum exponential empirical likelihood (MEEL) estimator is marginally superior to all others. Second, the MSEs of the GMM estimator are very close to the MEEL estimator across all scenarios, but MEEL is actually MSE superior to GMM in only a few cases. Third, there is a general order ranking of the MSEs of the MPD-type estimators, whereby generally MSE(MEEL) < MSE(MEL) < MSE(MLEL) (MEL denotes maximum empirical likelihood and MLEL denotes maximum log Euclidean likelihood). However, differences in MSE performance among these estimators are small at $n = 100$ and practically indistinguishable at $n = 250$. Fourth, the MSE differences between *all* of the estimators dissipate as the sample size increases, with the differences being negligible at the largest sample size $n = 250$.

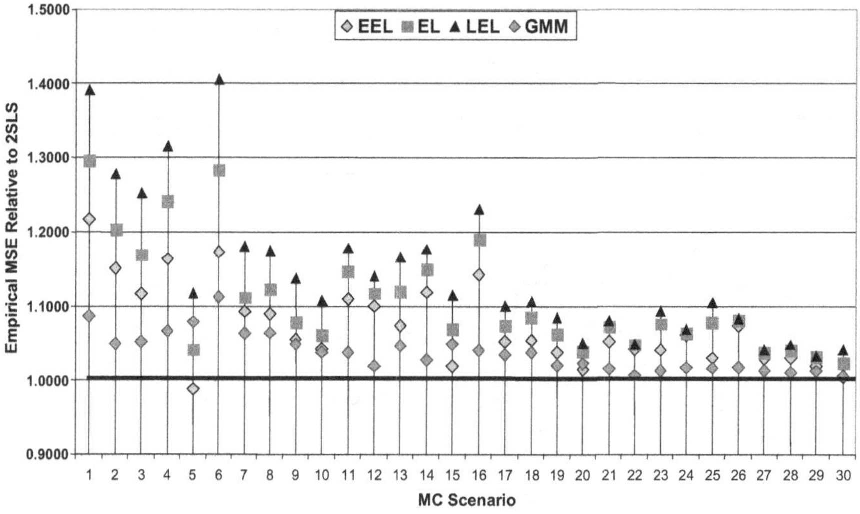


Figure 8.3.1. Parameter Vector Relative-to-2SLS MSE.

### 8.3.2 Bias and Variance

Empirical bias and variance results for the estimators of $\beta_2$ are presented in Figures 8.3.2 and 8.3.3. Again, some general estimator performance patterns emerge. The MPD-type estimators, as a group, generally tend to be less biased than either the 2SLS or GMM estimators. However, the MEL

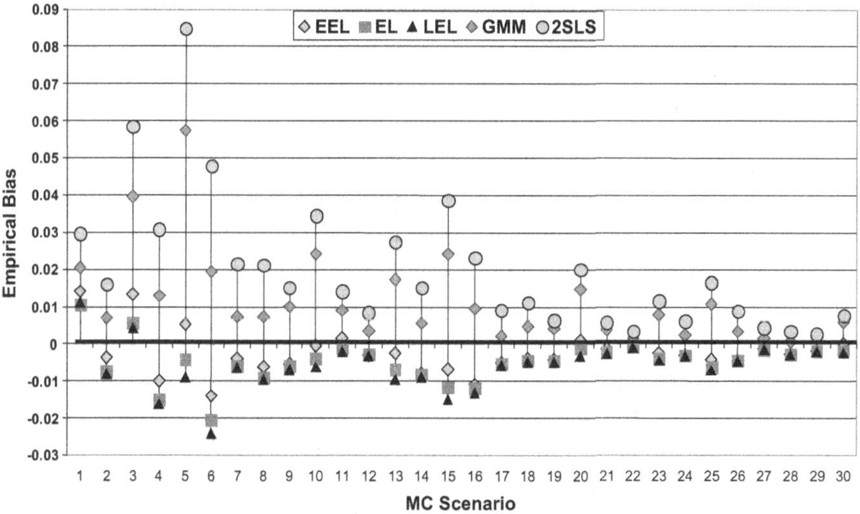


Figure 8.3.2. Bias in Estimating $\beta_2 = 2$.

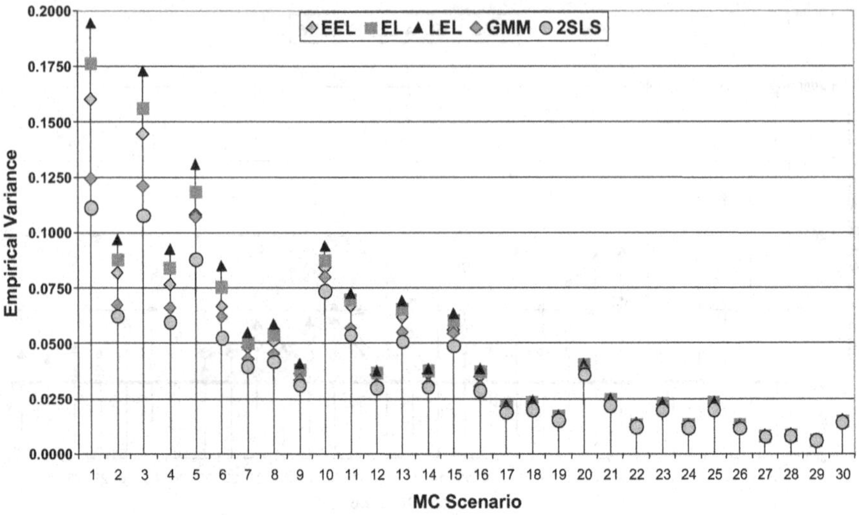


Figure 8.3.3. Variance in Estimating $\beta_2 = 2$.

estimators also tend to exhibit more variation than the traditional estimators. These performance patterns are most evident for the small sample size ($n = 50$). The volatility in bias, across MC scenarios, is notably more pronounced for 2SLS and GMM than for the empirical likelihood (EL) estimators, whereas just the opposite is true regarding volatility in variance measures across sampling scenarios. Again, this performance pattern is notably more pronounced for the smallest sample size than for the larger sample sizes. Regarding comparisons among MPD-type estimators, the MEEL estimator tends to be the least variable among the three MEL alternatives. The ranking of variability tends to be of the order var(MEEL) $<$ var(MEL) $<$ var(MLEL). The ranking of relative bias performance among the MEL estimators is less distinct. For the smallest sample size, each of the MPD-type estimators exhibits least bias for at least one sampling scenario. For larger sample sizes, the MEEL estimator more often than not has the smallest bias. However, there are exceptions for some scenarios and, in any case, the bias of all of the MPD-type estimators tends to be small, bordering on inconsequential for most of the scenarios when sample sizes are $n = 100$ or larger. For the largest sample size ($n = 250$), both bias and variance tends to be quite small for all of the estimators considered, although in a relative sense, the traditional estimators continued to have notably larger bias for most scenarios than any of the MPD-type estimators.

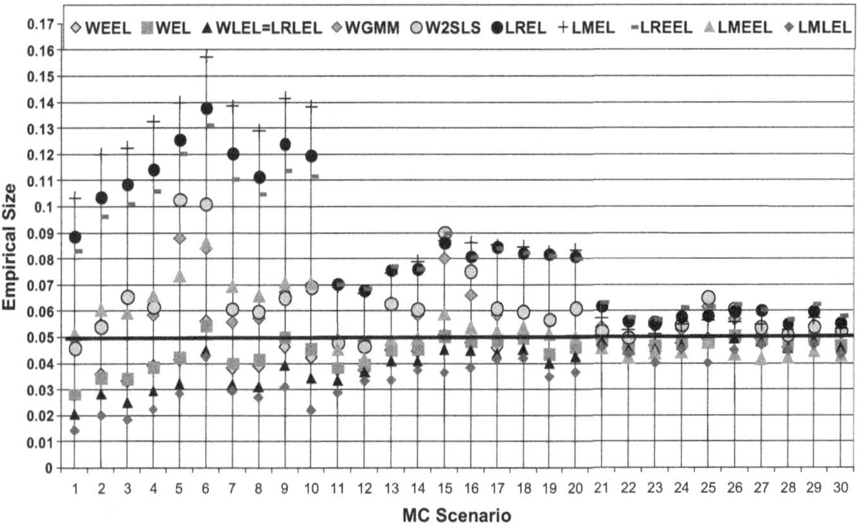


Figure 8.3.4. Size of Moment Validity Test, Target = 0.05.

## 8.3.3 Prediction MSE

Judged in the context of generating predictions closest in expected Euclidean distance to actual dependent variable outcomes, the 2SLS and GMM estimators were superior to the MPD-type estimators across the majority of sampling scenarios and, in any case, were never worse. However, if one intended to use estimated residuals to generate an estimate of the model noise variance, the MPD-type methods exhibited MSE measures that were closer in proximity to the true noise variance of $\sigma^2 = 25$. Among the EL-type methods, the general rank ordering of prediction MSE was MSE(MEEL) < MSE(MEL) < MSE(MLEL).

## 8.3.4 Size of Moment Validity Tests

Figure 8.3.4 presents empirical sizes of the 10 different tests of moment validity described in Section 7.5. The target size of the test was set to the typical 0.05 level and, when $n = 250$, all of the tests are generally within $\pm 0.01$ of this level across all MC scenarios. However, a number of the test procedures, most notably the likelihood ratio (LR) tests for MEEL and MEL, the LaGrange multiplier (LM) test for MEL, and to a lesser extent the Wald-Average Moment Test for 2SLS and GMM were more variable and notably distant from the target test size when $n = 50$. The most consistent tests in terms of average proximity to the true test size across sampling

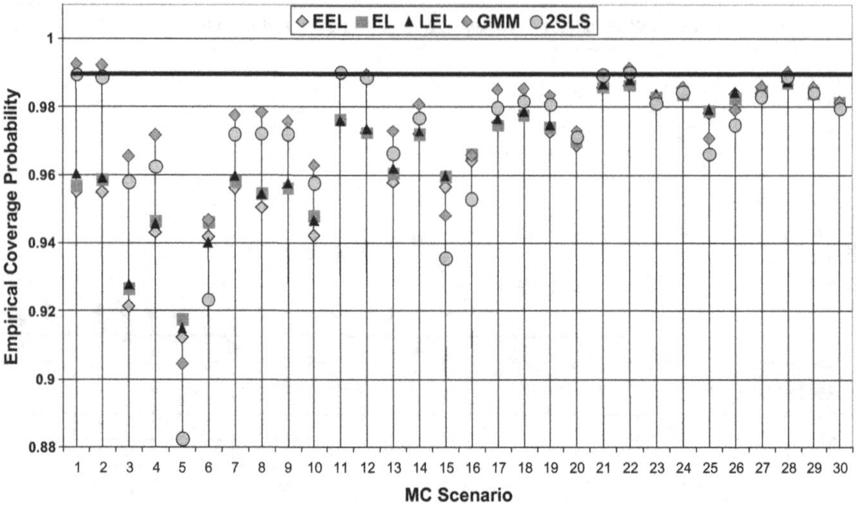


Figure 8.3.5. Confidence Interval Coverage Probability for $\boldsymbol{\beta}_2$, Target = 0.99.

scenarios were the Wald-Average Moment Tests for all three of the MPD-type estimators. In addition, the LM tests in the case of MEEL and MLEL were reasonably accurate when $n \geq 100$. As noted in the literature, for a subset of the scenarios, the size of the tests based on the traditional 2SLS and GMM methods were substantially distant from target size.

### 8.3.5 Confidence Interval Coverage and Expected Length

Figure 8.3.5 displays results relating to the empirical coverage probability of confidence intervals for the $\beta_2$ parameter, where target coverage is 0.99. Except for two scenarios involving the 2SLS and GMM methods, all of the confidence intervals are generally within 0.01 of the target coverage for the large sample size of $n = 250$. Again, with the preceding two exceptions noted relating to the traditional estimators, coverage is generally within 0.03 of target for the sample size of $n = 100$. Coverage degrades significantly for the small sample size of $n = 50$, with the traditional estimators generally having better coverage, although they exhibited the worst coverage performance for two sampling scenarios. Moreover, the traditional methods exhibited more volatility across sampling scenarios than MPD-type methods. The coverage results observed for the MPD-type methods are consistent with observations in the literature that the MPD-type methods consistently underachieve target coverage probability under the asymptotic Chi-square calibration

(Baggerly, 2001). In most cases, the traditional inference procedures also underachieved target coverage.

In the case of expected confidence interval length, a clearer relative performance pattern was apparent. In particular, the general relative ranking of confidence interval (CI) length among the five alternative estimators was given by the following ordering of empirical average lengths: CI(MEEL) < CI(MEL) < CI(MLEL) < CI(2SLS) < CI(GMM). As expected, differences in length were most pronounced at the smallest sample size, in some cases exceeding 15%, but differences dissipated to effectively negligible levels when $n = 250$.

### 8.3.6 Test Power

All test procedures exhibited substantial power in rejecting the false null hypothesis $H_o : \beta_2 = 0$, where all rejection probabilities were in the range of 0.92 or higher. Among the MPD-type methods, the relative power performance ranking was Power(MEEL) > Power(MEL) > Power(MLEL). When comparing power performance to traditional methods, it was generally the case that 2SLS exhibited the highest test power, followed by either MEEL or GMM. The powers of the last two procedures were, in any case, always very close to each other. The differences in power dissipated substantially for the higher sample sizes, and when $n = 250$, there was effectively no difference in power between any of the procedures, with all procedures achieving the ideal power of 1.

## 8.4 Summary Comments

In statistical models consisting of linear structural equations, the 2SLS and GMM estimators have long been the estimator of choice when the number of moment conditions-IV variables exceeded the number of unknown response parameters in the equation in question. Both the 2SLS and GMM estimators solve the problem of overidentification by defining particular rank-$k$ linear combinations of the moment conditions. In contrast, the nontraditional MPD-type estimator transforms the overdetermined moments problem into a set of equations that is solvable for the model parameters by imposing a functional dependence on the moment equations through the choice of sample observation weights. Although both the traditional and MPD-type estimators perform well in terms of first-order asymptotics, questions persist about their small sample bias and variance performance in estimation, and their coverage, interval width, and power characteristics in terms of inference.

Given these questions and corresponding conjectures that appear in the literature, in this chapter, we provided some empirical evidence concerning the relative sampling performance of 2SLS, GMM, and MPD-type methods by simulating a wide range of sampling processes and observing empirical sampling behavior of the estimators and associated inference procedures. Although sampling results are never definitive, the base results presented in this chapter examine a range of data sampling processes and provide insights into the relative sampling performance of different types of general moment-based estimators for a range of data sampling processes. Some distinct and interesting estimation and inference properties that were observed are as follows:

i) The MPD-type estimators tend to exhibit less bias and more variance than the traditional estimators.
ii) In terms of MSE, the 2SLS estimator is generally superior but, at a sample size of 100 or more, all estimators exhibit similar MSE performances.
iii) In terms of accurate size of moment tests, the MPD-type inference methods are superior, based on the average moment (or Wald) statistics, across all sample sizes. For sample sizes of 100 or more, the LM tests also do reasonably well, especially in the case of MEEL and MLEL. For a sample size of 250, all of the moment tests are in the neighborhood of the correct size.
iv) On confidence interval coverage, the traditional estimators perform somewhat erratically across differing data sampling processes, until the highest sample size is reached. However, the MPD-type methods are similar to one another in interval coverage performance and exhibit a more orderly convergence to the correct coverage.
v) Test power for significance tests is very high for a sample size of 100 and is essentially 1 and ideal across all significance tests for sample size 250.

Speculating further about the observed results, both the 2SLS and EL-type methods begin with the same ill-posed, overidentified set of moment conditions but transform them in differing ways into well-posed systems of solvable equations for the parameters. The 2SLS approach applies an optimal (in the optimal estimating function, OptEF, sense) linear transformation to the moment conditions that has a unique solution. This OptEF transformation can be derived analytically – its functional form is completely known – and it does not depend on any of the $\boldsymbol{\beta}$ or $\sigma^2$ parameters to be estimated. Even though the unknown variance parameter $\sigma^2$ does appear in the explicit OptEF transformation, it is a redundant scale factor that can be eliminated when the optimal transform matrix is applied. However, the MPD-type methods introduce *n* additional unknown parameters to resolve the overdetermined nature of the moment equations. These parameters must be estimated from the data and act as slack variables that scale the sample observation components of the moment conditions to define a functionally dependent set of equations, with rank equal to the dimension of the $\boldsymbol{\beta}$ parameter vector.

The particular set of transformed moment conditions that is solved for $\boldsymbol{\beta}$ in MPD-type methods is, in a sense, determined by an arbitrary choice of pseudodistance measure (some member of the Cressie-Read family). This begs the question of the optimal choice of the $\gamma$ parameter and thereby the choice of MPD-type method to apply in a given estimation or inference problem. We address the issue of the choice of $\gamma$ in Chapters 10 and 11.

## 8.5 Selected References


Baggerly, K. A. (1998), "Empirical Likelihood as a Goodness of Fit Measure," *Biometrika* **85**:535–547.

Baggerly, K. A. (2001), *Studentized Empirical Likelihood and Maximum Entropy: Empirical t*, Working Paper, Department of Statistics, Rice University.

Bertsekas, D. P. (1995), *Nonlinear Programming*, Belmont, MA: Athena Scientific.

Bound, J., Jaeger, D., and Baker, R. (1995), "Problems with Instrumental Variable Estimation When the Correlation between the Instruments and the Endogenous Variables Is Weak," *Journal of the American Statistical Association* **90**:443–450.

Corcoran, S. A. (2000), "Empirical Exponential Family Likelihood Using Several Moment Conditions," *Statistica Sinica* **10**:545–557.

Cressie, N. and Read, T. (1984), "Multinomial Goodness of Fit Tests," *Journal of Royal Statistical Society of Series B* **46**:440–464.

Godambe, V. (1960), "An Optimum Property of Regular Maximum Likelihood Estimation," *Annals of Mathematical Statistics* **31**:1208–1212.

Golan, A., Judge, G. G., and Miller, D. (1996), *Maximum Entropy Econometrics*. New York: John Wiley and Sons.

Hansen, L. P. (1982), "Large Sample Properties of Generalized Method of Moments Estimators," *Econometrica* **50**:1029–1054.

Heyde, C. (1989), "Quasi-Likelihood and Optimality of Estimating Functions: Some Current and Unifying Themes," *Bulletin of International Statistical Institute* **1**:19–29.

Heyde, C. and Morton, R. (1998), "Multiple Roots in General Estimating Equations," *Biometrika* **85**(4):954–959.

Imbens, G. W., Spady, R. H., and Johnson, P. (1998), "Information Theoretic Approaches to Inference in Moment Condition Models," *Econometrica* **66**:333–357.

Jacoby, S. L. S., Kowalik, J. S., and Pizzo, J. T. (1972), *Iterative Methods for Nonlinear Optimization Problems*, New York: Prentice Hall, 1972.

Judge, G., Hill, R., Griffiths, W., Lutkepohl, H., and Lee, T. (1985), *The Theory and Practice of Econometrics.* New York: John Wiley and Sons.

Kullback, S. (1959), *Information Theory and Statistics.* New York: John Wiley and Sons.

Maddala, G. S. and Jeong, J. (1992), "On the Exact Small Sample Distribution of the Instrumental Variable Estimator," *Econometrica* **60**:181–183.

Mittelhammer, R. C. and G. J. Judge (2003), "Finite Sample Performance of the Empirical Likelihood Estimator under Endogeneity," in *Computer Aided Econometrics*, edited by D. Giles, New York: Marcel Dekker, Inc., pp. 149–174.

Mittelhammer, R. C. and G. J. Judge (2002), "Endogeneity and Biased Estimation under Squared Error Loss," in *Handbook of Applied Econometrics and Statistical Inference*, edited by Alan Wan, Aman Ullah, and Anoop Chaturvedi, Marcel Dekker, Inc., pp. 347–369.

Mittelhammer, R. and G. Judge (2003), "Some Empirical Evidence on EL-Weighted Combinations of Structural Equation Estimators," *Journal of Agricultural and Applied Economics*, **35**: 91–101.

Mittelhammer, R., Judge, G., and Miller, D. (2000), *Econometric Foundations*, Cambridge: Cambridge University Press.

Nelder, J. A. and Mead, R. (1965), "A Simplex Method for Function Minimization," *Computer Journal* **7**:308–313.

Nelson, C. R. and Startz, R. (1990), "Some Further Results on the Exact Small Sample Properties of the Instrumental Variable Estimator," *Econometrica* **58**:967–976.

Newey, W. K. and Smith, R. J. (2000), "Asymptotic Bias and Equivalence of GMM and GEL Estimators," MIT Working Paper.

Owen, A. (1988), "Empirical Likelihood Ratio Confidence Intervals for a Single Functional," *Biometrika* **75**, 237–249.

Owen, A. (1991), "Empirical Likelihood for Linear Models," *The Annals of Statistics* **19**(4):1725–1747.

Owen, A. (2001), *Empirical Likelihood.* New York: Chapman and Hall.

Qin, J. and Lawless, J. (1994), "Empirical Likelihood and General Estimating Equations," *The Annals of Statistics* **22**(l):300–325.

Read, T. R. and Cressie, N.A. (1988), *Goodness of Fit Statistics for Discrete Multivariate Data.* New York: Springer Verlag.

Stock, J. H. and Wright, J. H. (2000), "GMM with Weak Identification," *Econometrica* **68**(5):1055–1096.

## APPENDIX 8.A COMPUTATIONAL ISSUES AND NUMERICAL APPROACH

As noted in Chapters 4 and 5, the computation of solutions to MPD-type constrained optimization problems can present numerical challenges. This is especially true in the neighborhood of the solution to such problems because the gradient matrix associated with the moment constraints will approach an ill-conditioned state. This occurs by design in these types of problems because the fundamental method by which MPD-type methods resolve the overdetermined nature of the empirical moment conditions, $\Sigma_{i=1}^{n} p_i \mathbf{z}'_{i.}(y_i - \mathbf{x}_{i.}\boldsymbol{\beta}) = \mathbf{0}$, is to choose sample weights that ultimately transform the $m$ moment equations into a functionally dependent, lower rank ($k < m$) system of equations, capable of being solved uniquely for the parameters. This creates instability in gradient-based constrained optimization algorithms regarding the representation of the feasible spaces and feasible directions for such problems. Moreover, attempting to solve the optimization problems in primal form is complicated by the dimensionality of the problem, where there are as many $p_i$ sample weights as there are sample observations and requires that explicit constrained optimization methods be used to enforce the moment conditions and the convexity properties of the sample weights.

Given these complications, it has been suggested in the literature that it may be advantageous, at least in the MEL and MEEL cases, to use a dual penalty function method for enforcing the moment constraints, whereby a penalty-augmented objective function is optimized within the context of an unconstrained optimization problem. Although the penalty-function approach appeared to perform well for the range of applications examined by Imbens, Spady, and Johnson (1998), the algorithm failed (nonconvergence) frequently when applied to the IV-based moment-constrained problems examined in this chapter.

The computational approach used here for solving the MPD-type problems consisted of concentrating out the Lagrange multiplier vector and scalars, $\boldsymbol{\lambda}$ and $\eta$, on the moment constraints and the adding-up condition on the $p_i$'s, respectively, expressing $\boldsymbol{\lambda}$ and $\eta$ as a function of the $\boldsymbol{\beta}$ vector (in the case of MEEL and MEL, the optimal $\eta$ is simply the scalar 1). The actual process of concentrating out the Lagrange multipliers cannot be accomplished in closed form and requires a numerical nonlinear equation–solving procedure. However, solving the system of equations was quite stable and efficient. The resulting concentrated Lagrange representations of the MPD-type estimation problems were optimized with respect to the choice of $\boldsymbol{\beta}$, leading to the parameter estimates.

More specifically, in the first step of the computational procedure, the Lagrange multiplier vector $\boldsymbol{\lambda}$ was expressed as a function of $\boldsymbol{\beta}$ by using the empirical moment conditions and the weight representation for the vector $\mathbf{p}(\boldsymbol{\beta}, \boldsymbol{\alpha})$ as

$$\boldsymbol{\lambda}(\boldsymbol{\beta}) \equiv \arg_{\lambda}[(\mathbf{Z} \odot (\mathbf{Y} - \mathbf{X}\boldsymbol{\beta}))'\mathbf{p}(\boldsymbol{\beta}, \boldsymbol{\alpha}) = \mathbf{0}]. \qquad (8.A.1)$$

The solution was determined numerically using the NLSYS nonlinear equation solver in the GAUSS mathematical programming language

(Aptech Systems, Black Diamond, Washington). Regarding the Lagrange multiplier $\eta$, the first-order conditions for either the MEL or MEEL estimation problems imply that $\eta(\boldsymbol{\beta}) \equiv 1$. In the case of the MLEL problem, $\eta(\boldsymbol{\beta})$ can be defined by substituting the value of $\boldsymbol{\lambda}(\boldsymbol{\beta})$ into the definition of $\eta(\boldsymbol{\alpha}, \boldsymbol{\beta})$ yielding

$$\eta(\boldsymbol{\beta}) \equiv \left(2 - n^{-1} \sum_{i=1}^{n} \boldsymbol{\lambda}(\boldsymbol{\beta})' \mathbf{z}_{i.}' (y_i - \mathbf{x}_i \boldsymbol{\beta})\right). \tag{8.A.2}$$

In the second step relating to optimization, the concentrated Lagrange function can be represented as

$$\begin{aligned} L_*(\boldsymbol{\beta}) &\equiv L(\mathbf{p}(\boldsymbol{\beta}, \boldsymbol{\lambda}(\boldsymbol{\beta})), \mathrm{b}, \boldsymbol{\lambda}(\boldsymbol{\beta}), \eta(\boldsymbol{\beta})) \\ &\equiv \phi(\mathbf{p}(\boldsymbol{\beta}, \boldsymbol{\lambda}(\boldsymbol{\beta}))) - \boldsymbol{\lambda}(\boldsymbol{\beta})' \sum_{i=1}^{n} p_i(\boldsymbol{\beta}, \boldsymbol{\lambda}(\boldsymbol{\beta}))\, \mathbf{z}_{i.}' (y_i - \mathbf{x}_i \boldsymbol{\beta}) \\ &\quad - \eta(\boldsymbol{\beta}) \left( \sum_{i=1}^{n} p_i(\boldsymbol{\beta}, \boldsymbol{\lambda}(\boldsymbol{\beta})) - 1 \right). \end{aligned} \tag{8.A.3}$$

The value of $L_*(\boldsymbol{\beta})$ is then optimized (maximized for MEL, minimized for MEEL and MLEL) with respect to the choice of $\boldsymbol{\beta}$, where $\phi(\bullet)$ can denote any of the estimation objective functions in the Cressie-Read family. The algorithm used to accomplish the optimization step was based on a Nelder-Meade polytope-type direct search procedure written by the authors and implemented in the GAUSS programming language (Nelder and Meade,1965; Jacoby, Kowalik, and Pizzo,1972; and Bertsekas,1995) using the values 0.5, 0.5, and 1.1, respectively, for the reflection, contraction, and expansion coefficients. The Nelder-Meade approach is especially well suited for this problem because it requires only that the function itself be evaluated at trial values of the $\boldsymbol{\beta}$ vector and does not require calculation of the numerical derivatives of the first or second order used by gradient-based search algorithms, which were inaccurate and unstable in the current context for reasons mentioned previously in this appendix.

# PART IV

# BINARY–DISCRETE CHOICE MINIMUM POWER DIVERGENCE (MPD) MEASURES

Continuing with the Cressie-Read family of divergence measures, in Part IV we identify a new class of probability distributions and associated likelihood functions for the binary response model. MPD estimators, as well as empirical maximum likelihood (EML) estimators, for the binary response model are specified, asymptotic properties are assessed, and sampling experiments are used to illustrate finite sample performance. The resulting MPD class of distributions and associated estimators subsume the conventional logit model-estimator.

# NINE

# Family of MPD Distribution Functions for the Binary Response-Choice Model

## 9.1 Introduction

Continuing in the context of Chapter 7, in this chapter the Cressie-Read family of minimum power divergence (MPD) measures is used to identify a new class of probability distributions (PDFs) and associated statistical models for the binary response model. We present MPD estimators for the binary response-choice models and examine the asymptotic properties of the estimators. In Chapter 10, we illustrate finite sample performance of the estimators, based on extensive sampling experiments, and examine the empirical maximum likelihood (EML) alternative to MPD estimation, whereby the MPD class of probability distributions is used to form a likelihood function subsequently maximized with respect to the unknown parameters of the distribution. The large MPD class of distributions subsumes the conventional logit distribution and, under the EML approach, subsumes the logit maximum likelihood (ML) estimator. *The MPD class of distributions, under both MPD and EML estimation objectives, forms the basis for a vast set of parametric estimation alternatives.*

The applied statistics literature is replete with analyses of binary response data-models, which include the important analysis of discrete choice models in econometrics. *The objective is to predict unobserved and unobservable probabilities from indirect noisy observations.* Traditionally, the estimation and inference methods used in empirical analyses of binary response converts this fundamentally *ill-posed stochastic inverse problem* into a well-posed one that can be analyzed via conventional parametric statistical methods. This is accomplished by imposing a parametric functional form on the underlying data sampling distribution. Typical distributional choices in empirical analyses of binary response models (BRMs) have been either the normal or logit cumulative distribution function (CDF). This representation is followed by maximum likelihood estimation and inference applied to a specific parametric statistical model. The negative statistical implications–consequences associated with following traditional parametric estimation and inference approaches, when the assumed statistical model is suspect, are well known.

In attempts to mitigate model misspecification issues, a variety of semiparametric models and estimators for the BRM have arisen in the literature from a generation of econometricians (e.g., Ichimura, 1993; Klein and Spady, 1993; Gabler, Laisney, and Lechner, 1993; Gozalo and Linton, 1994; Manski, 1975; Horowitz, 1992; Han, 1987; Cosslet, 1983; Wang and Zhou, 1993). These semiparametric methods tend to be of either the "regression-estimating equation" or "maximum likelihood" variety. Each uses some form of nonparametric-regularization or semiparametric estimate of the probability that the binary response variable takes the value $y_i = 1$, conditioned on the outcome of explanatory or response variables. On the basis of asymptotic performance comparisons, among those estimators for which asymptotics are tractable and well developed, it is found that many of the estimators do not achieve $\sqrt{n}$ consistency. Moreover,

i) intricate regularity assumptions are often necessary to achieve semiparametric performance results;
ii) unknown population distributions and/or distribution scores must be replaced with stochastic approximations, when forming "optimal" estimating equations or likelihood functions underlying the definition of estimators;
iii) values of tuning, bandwidth, and/or trimming parameters must be chosen in the specification of estimators; and
iv) finite sample performance can be quite variable.

Consequently, it is not possible to definitively rule out many semiparametric alternatives when considering empirical analyses of data underlying BRMs.

Against this background, to provide a solution for this stochastic inverse problem, in this chapter we use information-theoretic (IT) methods to define a flexible new collection of BRM CDFs. These members constitute a complete class of potential probability distributions, satisfying standard error orthogonality conditions. The resulting class of statistical models and associated likelihood functions are both consistent with parametric specifications of the binary response model and are minimally power divergent from any possible reference distribution for the Bernoulli probabilities. The associated estimators, whose finite sample properties we investigate in Chapter 10, represent a large set of alternatives to traditional logit and probit methods, as well as to conventional semiparametric methods of analysis. The new class of probability distributions is interesting in its own right and, as we saw in Chapters 4 through 7, has potential for use in statistical models outside of the BRM family.

## 9.2 The Statistical Model Base

To provide a base for the statistical models ahead, in this section we review parametric and nonparametric BR models and estimation alternatives.

### 9.2.1 Parametric

Assume that on trial $i = 1, 2, \ldots, n$, one of two alternatives is observed to occur for each of the independent binary random variables $Y_i$, $i = 1, 2, \ldots, n$, with $p_i$, $i = 1, \ldots, n$ representing the probabilities of observing successes ($y_i = 1$) on each respective trial. The value of $p_i$ is represented by the linear index model[1]

$$p_i = P(y_i = 1 \mid \mathbf{x}_{i\cdot}) = F(\mathbf{x}_{i\cdot}\boldsymbol{\beta}), \tag{9.2.1}$$

where $F(\cdot)$ is some CDF and $\mathbf{x}_{i\cdot}$, $i = 1, \ldots, n$ are independent outcomes of a $(1 \times k)$ random vector of explanatory variables.[2] When the parametric family of probability density functions underlying the binary response model is assumed known (e.g., logit or probit), one can define the specific functional form of the log-likelihood and use traditional maximum likelihood (ML) approaches as a basis for estimation and inference relative to the unknown $\beta$ and the response probabilities $F(\mathbf{x}_{i\cdot}\boldsymbol{\beta})$. If the particular choice of the parametric functional form for the distribution is also *correct*, then the usual ML properties of consistency, asymptotic normality, and efficiency hold (McFadden, 1974, 1984; Train, 2003). For seminal work with Bayesian binary response models, see Zellner and Rossi (1984). For a review of conventional binary response models and a literature review, see Green (2007).

1 A presentation of similar concepts to those discussed in this chapter that are cast in the context of nonlinear indices can be found in Mittelhammer and Judge (2011).

2 We remind the reader that as in other chapters, capital letters denote random variables and lowercase letters denote observed values or outcomes. An exception will be the use of $\varepsilon$ to denote a random variable and $e$ to denote an outcome of the random variable, and the use of $F$ and $f$ to denote a CDF and PDF, respectively. Boldface type denotes a vector or matrix, whereas nonbold denotes scalars.

In contrast to historical empirical practice, we assume that the CDF in (9.2.1) is neither based on nor restricted to the conventional logit and probit parametric families. Estimation is based on the new MPD-class of CDFs implemented by either solving for an extremum of a Cressie-Read power divergence measure in terms of response coefficients (i.e., MPD estimation) or by applying standard maximum likelihood (i.e., EML estimation) methods to the new class of CDFs.

More to the point, we recognize the stochastic inverse nature of the problem and seek a class of CDFs that are congruent with basic and generally applicable conditions relating to the binary response model. These conditions include:

i) a generally applicable nonparametric statistical model specification of the Bernoulli outcomes reflecting signal and noise components,
ii) a simple orthogonality condition between response variables and the noise components,
iii) minimum divergence between members of the CDF class and any possible reference distribution for the Bernoulli probabilities, underlying the binary response model.

The resultant class of CDFs contains a flexible collection of CDFs that subsumes the logistic distribution as a special case, and the overall approach provides an alternative statistical rationale for the specification of a logit model of binary response.

### 9.2.2 Nonparametric Stochastic Inverse Problem Representation

Seeking to minimize the use of unknown information concerning model components, we begin by characterizing the $n \times 1$ vector of nondegenerate Bernoulli random variables, **Y**, by the universally applicable stochastic representation

$$\mathbf{Y} = \mathbf{p} + \varepsilon, \quad \text{where } \mathrm{E}(\boldsymbol{\varepsilon}) = \mathbf{0} \quad \text{and } \mathbf{p} \in \mathop{\times}_{i=1}^{n} (0, 1). \qquad (9.2.2)$$

The specification in (9.2.2) implies only that the expectation of the random vector **Y** is some mean vector of Bernoulli probabilities **p** and that the outcomes of **Y** are decomposed into means and noise terms. The noise term outcomes each have dichotomous support and, if **Y** is a random vector of nondegenerate binary random variables, the specification (9.2.2) is always true.

The Bernoulli probabilities in (9.2.1) are allowed to depend on the values of explanatory variables contained in the $(n \times k)$ matrix $\mathbf{X}$, whose $i^{\text{th}}$ row is $\mathbf{X}_{i\cdot}$, through some general conditional expectation or linear model relationship

$$\mathrm{E}\,(\mathbf{Y} \mid \mathbf{X}) = \mathbf{p}\,(\mathbf{X}) = [p_1\,(\mathbf{X}_{1\cdot})\,|p_2\,(\mathbf{X}_{2\cdot})\,|\ldots|p_n\,(\mathbf{X}_{n\cdot})]', \qquad (9.2.3)$$

where the conditional orthogonality condition, $E\,[\mathbf{X}'(\mathbf{Y} - \mathbf{p}(\mathbf{X})) \mid \mathbf{X}] = \mathbf{0}$, is implied. Note that the functional form of the relationship $\mathbf{p}(\mathbf{X})$ is left unspecified at this point. This underscores the substantial generality and nonparametric nature of the model specification. An application of the iterated expectation theorem leads to the unconditional orthogonality condition

$$\mathrm{E}[\mathbf{X}'(\mathbf{Y} - \mathbf{p}(\mathbf{X}))] = \mathbf{0}. \qquad (9.2.4)$$

The information employed to this point represents a minimal set of statistical model assumptions for representing the unknown Bernoulli probabilities in the binary response model. This formulation assumes only that some general relationship exists between regressor variables $\mathbf{X}$ and the Bernoulli random variables $\mathbf{Y}$ and, at this point, there is virtually no risk of model misspecification. Moreover, it is clear that the empirical moments

$$n^{-1}(\mathbf{x}'(\mathbf{y} - \mathbf{p}(\mathbf{x}))) = \mathbf{0} \qquad (9.2.5)$$

cannot possibly be used in isolation to identify the Bernoulli probabilities. This follows because, regardless of their number, $\mathbf{p}(\mathbf{x}) = \mathbf{y}$ always solves the set of moment constraints. In addition, *there are more unknowns than estimating equations because all that has been assumed to this point is that* $\mathbf{p}(\mathbf{x})$ *is an unknown nonparametric vector function, varying over a function space.* Thus, the problem consists of $n$ unknown values. Consequently, the system of equations (9.2.5) is underdetermined and will not provide a unique interior solution for the probability vector $\mathbf{p}$. In the face of this, we seek an extremum basis for choosing among the infinite number of solutions for $\mathbf{p}$.

## 9.3 Minimum Power Divergence Class of CDFs for the Binary Response Model

Given sampled binary outcomes from (9.2.1), we use $k < n$ empirical moment representations of the orthogonality conditions, $n^{-1}\mathbf{x}'(\mathbf{y} - \mathbf{p}) = \mathbf{0}$, to connect the data space to the unknown-unobservable probabilities. At this stage, an infinite feasible set of probabilities satisfy both (9.2.1) and the empirical representation of (9.2.2). To proceed in the face of this stochastic inverse problem, an estimation criterion is needed to address the undetermined nature of $(n-k)$ of the elements in $\mathbf{p}$. In the sections ahead, we develop such a criterion based on the general principle of MPD estimation.

### 9.3.1 Applying MPD to Conditional Bernoulli Probabilities

Instead of restricting the feasible set for $\mathbf{p}$ by assuming some specific ad hoc functional distribution form, we specify this as an extremum problem and characterize the conditional Bernoulli probabilities by minimizing, as in Chapter 7, some member of the family of generalized Cressie-Read (CR) power divergence measures (Cressie and Read, 1984; Read and Cressie, 1988; Mittelhammer, Judge, and Miller, 2000). In this context, the extremum problem takes the form

$$\min_{p_{ij}'s}\left\{\sum_{i=1}^{n}\left(\frac{1}{\gamma(\gamma+1)}\sum_{j=1}^{2}p_{ij}\left[\left(\frac{p_{ij}}{q_{ij}}\right)^{\gamma}-1\right]\right)\right\}, \tag{9.3.1}$$

$$\text{subject to: } \sum_{j=1}^{2}p_{ij}=1,\ p_{ij}\geq 0,\quad \forall i,j \tag{9.3.2}$$

$$\sum_{j=1}^{2}q_{ij}=1,\ q_{ij}\geq 0,\quad \forall i,j \tag{9.3.3}$$

$$n^{-1}(\mathbf{x}'(\mathbf{y}-\mathbf{p}))=\mathbf{0}. \tag{9.3.4}$$

The Bernoulli process underlying the binary outcomes for each observation is characterized by the probabilities $\{p_{i1}, p_{i2}\}$, which are conditioned on the value of $\mathbf{x}_{i.}$ as $p_{i1}=E(Y \mid \mathbf{x}_{i.})$, $\forall i$, and, in general, $\mathbf{p}=\mathrm{E}(\mathbf{Y}\mid\mathbf{x})$. The parenthetical component $(\frac{1}{\gamma(\gamma+1)}\sum_{j=1}^{2}p_{ij}[(\frac{p_{ij}}{q_{ij}})^{\gamma}-1])$ in the estimation objective function refers to the CR power divergence of the conditional Bernoulli probability distribution $\{p_{i1}, p_{i2}\}$, from any respective *reference* Bernoulli distribution $\{q_{i1}, q_{i2}\}$. *Regarding the interpretation of the CR divergence measure in this application, this parenthetical component is proportional to the weighted average deviation of* $(\frac{p}{q})^{\gamma}$ *from 1, with the Bernoulli probabilities* $\{p_{i1}, p_{i2}\}$ *being the weights* applied to the corresponding probability ratios $(\frac{p_{i1}}{q_{i1}})^{\gamma}$ and $(\frac{p_{i2}}{q_{i2}})^{\gamma}$. The CR divergence measure is strictly convex in the $p_{ij}$s and assumes an unconstrained unique global minimum when $p_{ij}=q_{ij}$, $\forall i$ and $j$.

The constraints (9.3.2) and (9.3.3) are necessary conditions required for the $p_{ij}$s and $q_{ij}$s to be interpreted as probabilities in this binary response application and for the collection of the $n$ conditional Bernoulli probability distributions, $\{p_{i1}, p_{i2}\}$, $i=1,\ldots,n$, to represent proper probability distributions. Note that in this application, unlike the MPD applications found in previous chapters, there is no adding-up condition on probabilities imposed across the $n$ sample observations. The $n$ adding up conditions are legitimate and necessarily applied across the two probabilities that correspond to each of the $n$ conditional Bernoulli distributions, but no such adding-up condition is applicable *across* the *n conditional* probability distributions.

The constraint (9.3.4) is the empirical implementation of the moment condition $\mathrm{E}(\mathbf{X}'(\mathbf{Y}-\mathbf{p}))=\mathbf{0}$. There may be additional sample and/or non-sample information about the data sampling processes that is known. If so, this type of constraint can be introduced and imposed in the constraint set. However, as argued previously, the constraints in the estimation problem defined herein represent a minimalist set of data and model specification information to impose on the behavior of dichotomous outcomes, under the assumption that the Bernoulli probabilities underlying the problem are functionally related to some set of response variables **X**.

### 9.3.2 Conditional Reference Probabilities

The reference probabilities **q**, specified in the MPD estimation objective (9.3.1), may originate from a number of sources. If no information is available concerning $q_{i1}, q_{i2}$, the usual course of action is to specify them as the discrete uniform distribution $q_{i1}=q_{i2}=.5\ \forall i$.

Another potential source of reference information is the sample mean $\bar{y}$, which represents a sample-based estimate of the *unconditional* Bernoulli probabilities $P(y=1)$ *and* $P(y=0)$; that is, $\{\hat{p},1-\hat{p}\}=\{\bar{y},1-\bar{y}\}$. Given this sample average of $y$ outcomes, one can make use of an MPD-type divergence measure to construct an empirical distribution representing inverse *conditional* probabilities associated with the observed-sample mean $\bar{y}$. Moreover, the feasible space to this stochastic inverse problem can be viewed as a statement about the collection of empirical conditional probability distributions that are compatible with observed sample outcomes. For an explicit example, using the case of $\gamma=0$, we could select the empirical reference probabilities that maximize

$$H(\mathbf{p})=-\sum_{i=1}^{n}(q_i \ln(q_i)) \tag{9.3.5}$$

subject to

$$n^{-1}\sum_{i=1}^{n}q_i=\bar{y}, \tag{9.3.6}$$

$$q_i\in(0,1),\quad \forall i, \tag{9.3.7}$$

where we have defined $q_i \equiv q_{i1}$ *and* $(1 - q_i) \equiv q_{i2}$. Note that (9.3.6) follows directly from the idea that the sample average of the conditional probabilities $(p_i = E(Y \mid \mathbf{x}_{i\cdot}))$, taken with respect to a random sample of $\mathbf{x}_{i\cdot}$s, is a sample moment-type estimate of the unconditional probability, $p = E(Y)$.

The Lagrangian for the problem is

$$L = H(\mathbf{p}) + \lambda \left( \bar{y} - n^{-1} \sum_{i=1}^{n} q_i \right), \tag{9.3.8}$$

and as in Chapter 7, the inequality constraints (9.3.7) are imposed by the nature of the estimation objective function in this case. Also note that there is no adding-up condition imposed in (9.3.5)–(9.3.7) because the $q_i$s in the current context are *conditional* probabilities, and not unconditional probabilities that must sum to unity. Given that $y \in \{0, 1\}$, the constraint set is nonempty and compact and because $H$ is strictly concave, there is a unique, interior solution to the problem. The first-order conditions for this stochastic inverse problem of generating reference probabilities are

$$q_i = \exp(-(1 + n^{-1}\lambda)), \quad i = 1, \ldots, n, \tag{9.3.9}$$

and

$$\sum_{i=1}^{n} \exp(-(1 + n^{-1}\lambda)) = n\bar{y}. \tag{9.3.10}$$

The solution of the first-order conditions is straightforward and leads to the conclusion that $q_i = \bar{y}, \ \forall i$ is the solution for the conditional reference probabilities for every observation. Note that the constraint (9.3.6) is the only information used in deriving this conditional reference distribution. This information will generally lead us to modify the distribution of probabilities on the outcome space when these reference probabilities are used in the MPD estimation problem (9.3.1). In fact, it can be shown that any of the divergence measures in the CR family could have been used in place of the objective function in (9.3.5), and the solution to the stochastic inverse reference probability problem would have been precisely the same.

Although not often available in empirical practice, if one had repeated observations on Y, say, $y_{ik}$, $k = 1, \ldots, n_i$, for each of the $\mathbf{x}_{i\cdot}$ values on which the Bernoulli probabilities are being conditioned, an alternative straightforward means of obtaining reference probabilities would be to define $q_i = n_i^{-1} \sum_{k=1}^{n_i} y_{ik}$, $i = 1, \ldots, n$ as the reference probabilities. Each of the conditional reference probabilities defined this way would then be the result of a minimum variance unbiased as well as consistent and efficient estimate of their values. Note, in effect, the MPD problem (9.3.5)–(9.3.7) posed previously is a way to solve the stochastic inverse problem created for the reference probabilities when there are no repeated observations on Y for each of the $x_i$.

There may be additional sample and/or nonsample information that is *a priori* available and, if so, this type of information can be imposed in either the reference distribution or in the constraint set of the MPD problem. The overall implication of the extremum formulation (9.3.5)–(9.3.7) is that the value of $\mathbf{p}$ is chosen from among an infinite number of possible solutions so as to be both consistent with the sample moment equations, $n^{-1}\mathbf{x}'(\mathbf{y}-\mathbf{p}) = \mathbf{0}$, and *minimally divergent* from any reference distribution $\mathbf{q}$. If $\mathbf{q}$ happens to satisfy the moment conditions, so that $n^{-1}\mathbf{x}'(\mathbf{y}-\mathbf{q}) = \mathbf{0}$, then $\mathbf{p} = \mathbf{q}$. Otherwise, the solution is a shrinkage-type rule, where the solution for $\mathbf{p}$ is as minimally divergent from $\mathbf{q}$ as the sample data, in the form of moment constraints, will allow. Pardo (2006) provides, in a range of statistical model contexts, a discussion of the use of minimum divergence measures for estimation. This approach implies departure from the need to define-assume a particular fully specified parametric distributional structure underlying the Bernoulli probabilities and reduces the possibility of statistical-econometric model misspecification.

### 9.3.3 The Class of CDFs Underlying $p$

The Lagrange form of the divergence minimization problem (9.3.5)–(9.3.7), for given $\gamma$ and $q_i \in (0, 1)$, $i = 1, \ldots, n$, is

$$L(\mathbf{p}, \boldsymbol{\lambda}) = \sum_{i=1}^{n} \frac{\left(p_i\left(\left(\frac{p_i}{q_i}\right)^{\gamma} - 1\right) + (1-p_i)\left(\left(\frac{1-p_i}{1-q_i}\right)^{\gamma} - 1\right)\right)}{\gamma(\gamma+1)} + \boldsymbol{\lambda}'\mathbf{x}'(\mathbf{y}-\mathbf{p}), \tag{9.3.11}$$

$$\text{s.t. } p_i \in [0, 1], \quad i = 1, \ldots, n, \tag{9.3.12}$$

where the premultiplier $n^{-1}$, on the moment constraints, is henceforth suppressed. The $p_i$'s can be expressed as functions of the explanatory variables and Lagrange multipliers by solving the first-order conditions (FOCs) with respect to $\mathbf{p}$. In the event that inequality constraints are binding, the FOCs can be adjusted by the complementary Kuhn-Tucker

(1951) slackness conditions. The FOCs with respect to the $p_i$ values in the problem imply

$$\frac{\partial L}{\partial p_i} = \mathbf{0} \Rightarrow \left\{ \begin{array}{c} \left(\left(\frac{p_i}{q_i}\right)^{\gamma} - \left(\frac{1-p_i}{1-q_i}\right)^{\gamma}\right) - \mathbf{x}_{i.}\boldsymbol{\lambda}\gamma \\ \left(\ln\left(\frac{p_i}{q_i}\right) - \ln\left(\frac{1-p_i}{1-q_i}\right)\right) - \mathbf{x}_{i.}\boldsymbol{\lambda} \end{array} \right\} = 0 \quad \text{for } \gamma \left\{ \begin{array}{c} \neq 0 \\ = 0 \end{array} \right\}. \tag{9.3.13}$$

When $\gamma \leq 0$, the solutions are strictly interior to the inequality constraints because the range of the strictly monotonic and continuous functions of $p_i \in [0, 1]$ in (9.3.13), $\ln(\frac{p_i}{q_i}) - \ln(\frac{1-p_i}{1-q_i})$ and $(\frac{p_i}{q_i})^{\gamma} - (\frac{1-p_i}{1-q_i})^{\gamma}$, encompass the entire real line. The range is compact otherwise, and corner point solutions are possible. Accounting for the inequality constraints in (9.3.12), when $\gamma > 0$, the first-order condition in (9.3.13), together with the complementary slackness conditions, allows $p_i$ to be expressed as the following functions of $\mathbf{x}_{i.}\boldsymbol{\lambda}$:

$$\begin{aligned} p(\mathbf{x}_{i.}\boldsymbol{\lambda}; q_i, \gamma) &= \arg_{p_i}\left[\left(\left(\frac{p_i}{q_i}\right)^{\gamma} - \left(\frac{1-p_i}{1-q_i}\right)^{\gamma}\right) = \mathbf{x}_{i.}\boldsymbol{\lambda}\gamma\right] \quad \text{for } \gamma \neq 0 \\ &= \arg_{p_i}\left[\ln\left(\frac{p_i}{q_i}\right) - \ln\left(\frac{1-p_i}{1-q_i}\right) = \mathbf{x}_{i.}\boldsymbol{\lambda}\right] \quad \text{for } \gamma = 0 \end{aligned} \tag{9.3.14}$$

$$= \left\{ \begin{array}{c} 1 \\ \left(\arg_{p_i}\left[\left(\left(\frac{p_i}{q_i}\right)^{\gamma} - \left(\frac{1-p_i}{1-q_i}\right)^{\gamma}\right)\right] = \mathbf{x}_{i.}\boldsymbol{\lambda}\gamma\right) \\ 0 \end{array} \right\} \quad \text{for } \gamma > 0$$

$$\text{and } \mathbf{x}_{i.}\boldsymbol{\lambda} \left\{ \begin{array}{c} \geq \gamma^{-1} q_i^{-\gamma} \\ \in \left(-\gamma^{-1}(1-q_i)^{-\gamma}, \gamma^{-1} q_i^{-\gamma}\right) \\ \leq -\gamma^{-1}(1-q_i)^{-\gamma} \end{array} \right\}$$

The class of CDFs defined in (9.3.14) are henceforth referred to as the MPD-class of distributions for the binary response problem. This class of CDFs characterize a unique and complete set of distributions that is consistent with the empirical orthogonality conditions and minimally divergent from any choice of reference distributions, $\mathbf{q}$, for the Bernoulli probabilities. Although the CDFs are defined only as *implicit* functions of $\mathbf{x}_{i.}\boldsymbol{\lambda}$, for almost all $\gamma$, numerical representations of the functional relationship between $p_i$ and $\mathbf{x}'_{i.}\boldsymbol{\lambda}$ can, because of the strict monotonicity of $p_i$ in $\mathbf{x}_{i.}\boldsymbol{\lambda}$, be determined in a straightforward manner.

Explicit closed-form solutions for the CDFs exist for $p(\mathbf{x}_{i.}\boldsymbol{\lambda}; q_i, \gamma)$ on a Lebesque measure zero set of $\gamma$ values that includes the set of all integers. Some examples are given in (9.3.15)–(9.3.17).

$$p\,(\mathbf{x}_{i.}\boldsymbol{\lambda}; q_i, -1) = \left\{ \begin{matrix} \left( .5 + \dfrac{[(\mathbf{x}_{i.}\boldsymbol{\lambda})^2 + (4q_i - 2)(\mathbf{x}_{i.}\boldsymbol{\lambda}) + 1]^{.5} - 1}{2\mathbf{x}_{i.}\boldsymbol{\lambda}} \right) \\ .5 \end{matrix} \right\} \text{ if } \mathbf{x}_{i.}\boldsymbol{\lambda} \left\{ \begin{matrix} \neq 0 \\ = 0 \end{matrix} \right\}, \tag{9.3.15}$$

$$p\,(\mathbf{x}_{i.}\boldsymbol{\lambda}; q_i, 0) = \frac{q_i \exp\,(\mathbf{x}_{i.}\boldsymbol{\lambda})}{(1 - q_i) + q_i \exp\,(\mathbf{x}_{i.}\boldsymbol{\lambda})}, \tag{9.3.16}$$

$$p(\mathbf{x}_{i.}\boldsymbol{\lambda}; q_i, 1) = \left\{ \begin{matrix} 1 \\ (q_i + q_i(1 - q_i)\mathbf{x}_{i.}\boldsymbol{\lambda}) \\ 0 \end{matrix} \right\} \text{ for } \mathbf{x}_{i.}\boldsymbol{\lambda} \left\{ \begin{matrix} \geq q_i^{-\gamma} \\ \in (-(1 - q_i)^{-\gamma},\ q_i^{-\gamma}) \\ \leq -(1 - q_i)^{-\gamma} \end{matrix} \right\}. \tag{9.3.17}$$

Computationally, one very stable, accurate, and relatively efficient method for determining the value of $p_i$ associated with $\mathbf{x}_{i.}\boldsymbol{\lambda}$ is through the interval bisection applied to the closed-form *inverse CDFs,* defined in (9.3.14). Effectively, this means searching over $p_i \in [0, 1]$ until the inverse image matches $\mathbf{x}_{i.}\boldsymbol{\lambda}$. This method is used in finite sampling results presented in Chapter 10.

A nice feature of the CR family is that when $\gamma = 0$ and the reference distribution is $q_i = 0.5$, the functional form for $p_i$ in (9.3.16) coincides with the standard logistic binary response model. When $\gamma = 1$, the CDF in (9.3.17) subsumes the linear probability model.

### 9.3.4 Properties of the MPD Class of Probability Distribution Functions

We use the notation MPD$(q, \gamma)$ to denote a specific member of the MPD-class of distributions identified by particular values of $q$ and $\gamma$. A vast array of symmetric as well as left- and right-skewed probability density

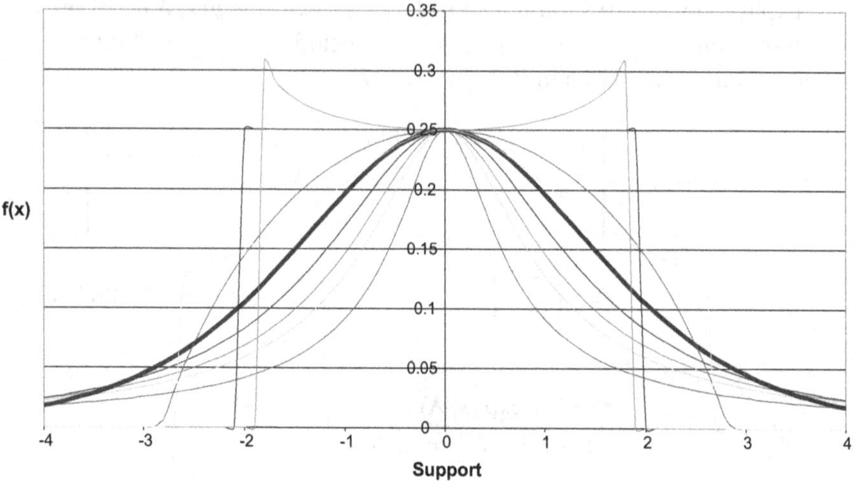


Figure 9.3.1. PDFs for $q = -0.5$ and $\gamma = -3, -1.5, -1, -0.5, 0, 0.5, 1, 1.5,$ and 3.

functions is contained within the MPD-class of PDFs. To illustrate the range of possibilities, graphs of some members of the class are presented in Figures 9.3.1 and 9.3.2. These graphs do much to suggest the possible wide range of distributional-likelihood possibilities as $\gamma$ and $q$ take on different values.

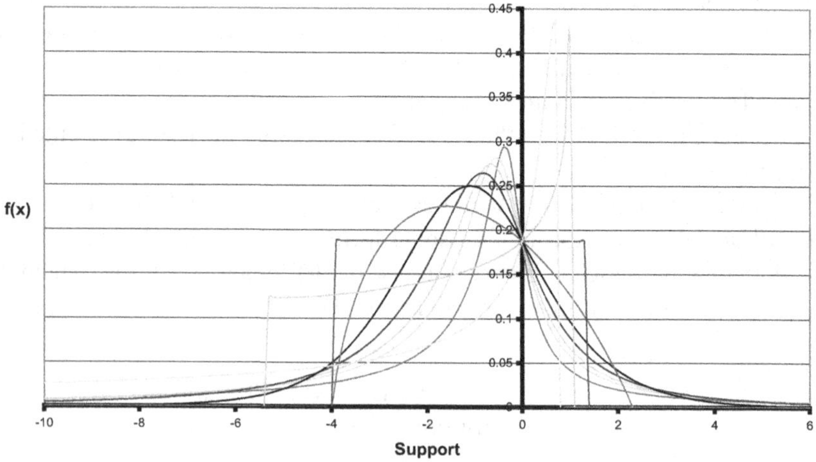


Figure 9.3.2. PDFs for $q = -0.75$ and $\gamma = -3, -1.5, -1, -0.5, 0, 0.5, 1, 1.5,$ and 3.

### 9.3.4a Moments

The existence of moments and their values in the MPD-class of distributions depends on the $\gamma$ parameter. The case of $\gamma = 0$ is a limiting case that defines a family of logistic distributions and can be handled explicitly. For other $\gamma$ cases, consider the general definition of the expectation of $g(W)$ with respect to MPD$(q, \gamma)$. Implicit differentiation of (9.3.14) with respect to $w = \mathbf{x}_{i.}\lambda$ implies the following general representation of the MPD-class of probability densities for nonzero $\gamma$:

$$f(w; q, \gamma) = \frac{1}{q^{-\gamma}F(w; q, \gamma)^{\gamma-1} + (1-q)^{-\gamma}(1-F(w; q, \gamma))^{\gamma-1}} \quad \text{for} \quad w \in \Upsilon(q, \gamma), \tag{9.3.18}$$

where $F(w; q, \gamma)$ denotes the cumulative distribution function and $\Upsilon(q, \gamma)$ denotes the appropriate support of the distribution. As indicated in (9.3.18), the support depends on $q$ and $\gamma$ if $\gamma > 0$ and $\Upsilon(q, \gamma) = R$ otherwise. Expectations can be defined as

$$E(g(W)) = \int_{w \in \Upsilon(q,\gamma)} \frac{g(w)}{q^{-\gamma}F(w; q, \gamma)^{\gamma-1} + (1-q)^{-\gamma}(1-F(w; q, \gamma))^{\gamma-1}} dw. \tag{9.3.19}$$

As demonstrated in Appendix 9.A.1, the expectation of $g(W)$ may be defined in the computationally more convenient form

$$E\left(g\left(W\right)\right) = \int_0^1 g\left(\gamma^{-1}\left(\left(\frac{p_i}{q_i}\right)^{\gamma} - \left(\frac{1-p_i}{1-q_i}\right)^{\gamma}\right)\right) dp. \tag{9.3.20}$$

When $\gamma > 0$, moments of all orders exist for densities in the MPD-class. This follows immediately from the fact that the integrand in

$$E(W^{\delta}) = \int_0^1 \left(\gamma^{-1}\left(\left(\frac{p}{q}\right)^{\gamma} - \left(\frac{1-p}{1-q}\right)^{\gamma}\right)\right)^{\delta} dp \tag{9.3.21}$$

is bounded for each positive integer-valued $\delta$, $q \in (0, 1)$, and each finite positive-valued $\gamma$. In terms of the first moment, the means of the probability densities are obtained by evaluating the integral (9.3.21) for $\delta = 1$ and yields the result

$$E\left(W\right) = \frac{q^{-\gamma} - (1-q)^{-\gamma}}{\gamma\left(\gamma+1\right)}. \tag{9.3.22}$$

The second moment around the origin is obtained by solving (9.3.21) when $\delta = 2$ as

$$E(W^2) = \gamma^{-2}\left[\frac{q^{-2\gamma} + (1-q)^{-2\gamma}}{1+2\gamma} - 2q^{-\gamma}(1-q)^{-\gamma}B(\gamma+1, \gamma+1)\right], \tag{9.3.23}$$

where $B(a, b) = \frac{\Gamma(a)\Gamma(b)}{\Gamma(a+b)}$ and $\Gamma(\alpha) = \int_0^\infty w^{\alpha-1}e^{-w}dw$ are the well-known beta and gamma functions, respectively. The variance of the distribution follows in the usual way by subtracting the square of (9.3.22) from (9.3.23).

The integral in (9.3.21) is divergent for any choice of $\delta \geq 1$ for distributions in the MPD-class with $\gamma \leq -1$, so these distributions do not have moments defined of any order. Moments do exist for values of $\gamma \in (-1, 0)$; however, only a finite number of moments exist and how high an order of moment exists depends on the value of $\gamma$. If $\gamma > -1$, the mean of the distribution exists and its functional representation in terms of $\gamma$ and $q$ is precisely the same as in (9.3.23). If $\gamma > -\frac{1}{2}$, the second moment about the origin and thus the variance exist, and the first two moments have exactly the same functional forms as in (9.3.22) and (9.3.23), respectively. In general, the moment of order $\delta$ exists provided that $\gamma > -\delta^{-1}$. In this case, it is identical in functional form to the corresponding moment in the subclass of MPD-class distributions for which $\gamma > 0$.

#### 9.3.4b Concavity of $\ln(F(w; q, \gamma))$ and $\ln(1 - F(w; q, \gamma))$ in $w$

It is useful for estimation purposes to identify curvature properties of both $\ln(F(w; q, \gamma))$ and $\ln(1 - F(w; q, \gamma))$. From the work of Pratt (1981), if these logarithmic functions of the CDF are concave in $w$, it follows that the log-likelihood based on the CDF, with arguments $w_i \equiv \mathbf{x}_{i.}\beta$, $i = 1, \ldots, n$ is concave in $\beta$. In fact, both logarithmic functions are concave in $w$ for any $q \in (0, 1)$, so long as the MPD distribution is such that $\gamma \leq 1$. When $\gamma > 1$, one or both of $\ln(F(w; q, \gamma))$ and $\ln(1 - F(w; q, \gamma))$ will not be concave, depending on the value of $q$ (see Appendix 9.6.2).

### 9.4 Summary and Extensions

Representing sample information underlying binary response outcomes through moment conditions $E[\mathbf{X}'(\mathbf{Y} - \mathbf{p})] = \mathbf{0}$, the CR family of power divergence measures is used to identify a new class of statistical models and associated CDFs for characterizing binary response outcomes. The MPD class of distributions contains a vast array of symmetric and skewed probability distributions for modeling binary response problems and subsumes the traditional logistic distribution as a special case. Moreover, it is a complete class of candidate distributions for the binary response model in the sense of being the distributions that are minimally power divergent from *any* reference distribution for the binary responses and that satisfy the sample data moment restrictions.

It is straightforward to extend the univariate distribution formulations of this chapter to their multivariate counterparts. For example, one such extension, which subsumes the multivariate logistic distribution as a special case, begins with a multinomial specification of the minimum power divergence estimation problem in Lagrange form as

$$L(\mathbf{p}, \lambda) = \sum_{i=1}^{n} \left( \frac{1}{\gamma(\gamma+1)} \sum_{j=1}^{m} p_{ij} \left[ \left( \frac{p_{ij}}{q_{ij}} \right)^{\gamma} - 1 \right] \right) + \sum_{j=1}^{m} \lambda_j' \mathbf{x}'(y_j - p_j) + \sum_{i=1}^{n} \eta_i \left( \sum_{j=1}^{m} p_{ij} - 1 \right). \quad (9.4.1)$$

Solving first-order conditions with respect to the $p_{ij}$s leads to the standard multivariate logistic distribution, when the reference distributions are uniform.

One of the remaining question concerns how to make use of the reference distribution, $\mathbf{q}$, to take into account known or estimable characteristics of the Bernoulli probabilities. Consideration of alternative conditional moment formulations and their effect on efficiency of the resultant estimators provides another set of interesting research. Aspects of these and other issues, such as a more robust basis for estimator choice in a given loss context, are the subject of chapters ahead.

## 9.5 Selected References

Cosslett, S. R. (1983), "Distribution-Free Maximum Likelihood Estimation of the Binary Choice Model," *Econometrica*, **51**:765–782.

Cressie, N. and T. Read (1984), "Multinomial Goodness of Fit Tests," *Journal of the Royal Statistical Society, Series B*, **46**:440–464.

Gabler, S., F. Laisney, and M. Lechner (1993), "Seminonparametric Estimation of Binary Choice Models with an Application to Labor Force Participation," *Journal of Business and Economic Statistics*, **11**:61–80.

Gozalo, P. L. and O. Linton (1994), *Local Nonlinear Least Squares Estimation Using Parametric Information Nonparametrically.* Discussion Paper No. 1075, Cowles Foundation, Yale University.

Green, W. (2007), "Discrete Choice Modeling," in T. Mills and K. Patterson (Eds.), *Handbook of Econometrics*, Vol. 2, *Applied Econometrics*, Part 4.2, London: Palgrave.

Han, A. K. (1987), "Nonparametric Analysis of a Generalized Regression Model," *Journal of Econometrics*, **35**:303–316.

Horowitz, J. L. (1992), "A Smoothed Maximum Score Estimator for the Binary Response Model," *Econometrica*, **60**:505–531.

Ichimura, H. (1993), "Semiparametric Least Squares (SLS) and Weighted SLS Estimation of Single-Index Models," *Journal of Econometrics*, **58**:71–120.

Klein, R. W. and R. H. Spady (1993), "An Efficient Semiparametric Estimator for Binary Response Models," *Econometrica*, **61**:387–421.

Kuhn, H. W. and A. W. Tucker (1951), "Non-linear Programming," in *Proc. 2 Berkeley Symp. on Mathematical Statistics and Probability* (pp. 481–492). Berkeley: University of California Press.

Manski, C. F. (1975), "The Maximum Score Estimation of the Stochastic Utility Model of Choice," *Journal of Econometrics*, **3**:205–228.

McFadden, D. (1974), "Conditional Logit Analysis of Qualitative Choice Behavior," in P. Zarembka (Ed.), *Frontiers of Econometrics* (pp. 105–142), New York: Academic Press.

McFadden, D. (1984), "Qualitative Response Models," in Z. Griliches and M. Intriligator (Eds.), *Handbook of Econometrics 2* (pp. 1395–1457), Amsterdam: North Holland.

Mittelhammer, R. and G. Judge (2011), "A Family of Empirical Likelihood Functions and Estimators for the Binary Response Model," *Journal of Econometrics*, doi:10.1016/j.jeconom.2011.04.002.

Mittelhammer, R., G. Judge, and D. Miller (2000), *Econometric Foundations*, New York: Cambridge University Press.

Pardo, L. (2006), *Statistical Inference Based on Divergence Measures*, Boca Raton, FL: Chapman and Hall.

Pratt, J. W. (1981), "Concavity of the Log Likelihood," *Journal of the American Statistical Association*, **76**:103–106.

Read, T. R. and N. A. Cressie (1988), *Goodness of Fit Statistics for Discrete Multivariate Data*, New York: Springer Verlag.

Train, K. (2003), *Discrete Choice Methods with Simulation*, New York: Cambridge University Press.

Wang, W. and M. Zhou (1993), "Iterative Least Squares Estimator of Binary Choice Models: Semiparametric Approach." Department of Statistics Technical Report No. 346, University of Kentucky.

Zellner, A. and P. Rossi (1984), "Bayesian Analysis for Dichotomous Response Models," *Journal of Econometrics*, **25**:365–393.

## APPENDIX 9.A ADDITIONAL PROPERTIES OF MPD DISTRIBUTIONS

### 9.A.1 Alternative form of $\mathbf{E}(g(\mathbf{W}))$

Make a change of variable in (9.3.19) via the transformation $p = F(w; q, \gamma)$ so that $w = F^{-1}(p; q, \gamma)$ and $\frac{\partial w}{\partial p} = \frac{\partial F^{-1}(p;q,\gamma)}{\partial p}$, where $F^{-1}(p; q, \gamma)$ denotes the inverse function associated with the CDF. It follows that the expectation can be represented as

$$\mathrm{E}\left(g\left(\mathrm{W}\right)\right) = \int_0^1 g\left(F^{-1}\left(p;q,\gamma\right)\right) dp. \tag{9.A.1}$$

Note that (9.A.1) involves the *closed form* inverse CDF function given by

$$w = F^{-1}(p;q,\gamma) = \gamma^{-1}\left(\left(\frac{p_i}{q_i}\right)^{\gamma} - \left(\frac{1-p_i}{1-q_i}\right)^{\gamma}\right) \text{ for } p \in (0,1). \tag{9.A.2}$$

Assuming the expectation of $g(\mathrm{W})$ exists, (9.6.1) can then be represented as

$$E\left(g\left(\mathrm{W}\right)\right) = \int_0^1 g\left(\gamma^{-1}\left(\left(\frac{p_i}{q_i}\right)^{\gamma} - \left(\frac{1-p_i}{1-q_i}\right)^{\gamma}\right)\right) dp. \tag{9.A.3}$$

### 9.A.2 Concavity of $\ln(F(w;q,\gamma))$ and $\ln(1-F(w;q,\gamma))$

Given that

$$\frac{\partial^2 \ln\left(F\right)}{\partial w^2} = \frac{1}{F}\frac{\partial^2 F}{\partial w^2} - \left(\frac{\partial F}{\partial w}\right)^2 \frac{1}{F^2} \tag{9.A.4}$$

and

$$\frac{\partial^2 \ln\left(1-F\right)}{\partial w^2} = -\frac{1}{\left(1-F\right)}\frac{\partial^2 F}{\partial w^2} - \left(\frac{\partial F}{\partial w}\right)^2 \frac{1}{\left(1-F\right)^2}, \tag{9.A.5}$$

it follows that $\ln(F(w;q,\gamma))$ and $\ln(1-F(w;q,\gamma))$ are concave for $w$ in the support of the distribution *iff*, respectively,

$$F\left[\frac{\frac{\partial^2 F}{\partial w^2}}{\left(\frac{\partial F}{\partial w}\right)^2}\right] \leq 1 \quad \text{and} \quad -\left(1-F\right)\left[\frac{\frac{\partial^2 F}{\partial w^2}}{\left(\frac{\partial F}{\partial w}\right)^2}\right] \leq 1. \tag{9.A.6}$$

Based on implicit differentiation of the CDF, it follows that

$$F\left[\frac{\frac{\partial^2 F}{\partial w^2}}{\left(\frac{\partial F}{\partial w}\right)^2}\right] = F\left(1-\gamma\right) \times \left[\frac{\left(\frac{1-q}{q}\right)\left(\frac{F}{q}\right)^{\gamma-2} - \left(\frac{q}{1-q}\right)\left(\frac{1-F}{1-q}\right)^{\gamma-2}}{q\left(\frac{1-F}{1-q}\right)^{\gamma-1} + \left(1-q\right)\left(\frac{F}{q}\right)^{\gamma-1}}\right] \tag{9.A.7}$$

and

$$-(1-F)\left[\frac{\frac{\partial^2 F}{\partial w^2}}{\left(\frac{\partial F}{\partial w}\right)^2}\right] = -(1-F)(1-\gamma)$$
$$\times\left[\frac{\left(\frac{1-q}{q}\right)\left(\frac{F}{q}\right)^{\gamma-2} - \left(\frac{q}{1-q}\right)\left(\frac{1-F}{1-q}\right)^{\gamma-2}}{q\left(\frac{1-F}{1-q}\right)^{\gamma-1} + (1-q)\left(\frac{F}{q}\right)^{\gamma-1}}\right]. \quad (9.A.8)$$

Numerical analysis of the values of (9.A.7) and (9.A.8) for values of $q \in (0, 1)$ and for support points of $F$, that is, for $F \in [0, 1]$, reveals that both terms are $\leq 1$ for $\gamma \leq 1$. One or both of (9.A.7) and (9.A.8) will be $> 1$ if $\gamma > 1$. Thus, $\ln(F(w; q, \gamma))$ and $\ln(1 - F(w; q, \gamma))$ will both be concave in $w$ given that $\gamma \leq 1$, and one or both terms will fail to be concave if $\gamma > 1$.

TEN

# Estimation and Inference for the Binary Response Model Based on the MPD Family of Distributions

## 10.1 Introduction

In this chapter, we use the family of minimum power divergence (MPD) distributions that was introduced in Chapter 9 and identify an associated new family of estimators for binary response-choice models based on the implied likelihood models. As discussed in Chapter 9, the large MPD class of distributions subsumes the conventional logit distribution and forms the basis for a very large set of parametric estimation alternatives. Finite sample properties of the MPD estimators, as well as empirical maximum likelihood (EML) estimators and an alternative nonlinear least squares estimator based on the MPD class of distributions (NLS-MPD), are demonstrated through extensive sampling experiments.

As noted in the previous chapter, the estimation and inference methods that have been traditionally used in empirical analyses of binary response converts the fundamentally ill-posed binary response model (BRM) stochastic inverse problem into a well-posed one that can be analyzed via conventional parametric statistical methods. In the past, this has often been accomplished by assuming that either a probit or logit cumulative distribution function (CDF) underlies the binary response and then applying maximum likelihood (ML) estimation and inference to a specific parametric statistical model. We noted in Chapter 9 the attendant negative statistical consequences that may result when the assumed statistical model is suspect.

In this chapter, we use the large class of statistical models and estimators associated with the Cressie-Read MPD family of distributions and present a large set of alternatives to traditional logit and probit methods and conventional semiparametric methods of analysis. Establishing $\sqrt{n}$ consistency, as well as asymptotic normality and efficiency in this new class of statistical models, is accomplished using traditional regularity conditions. Consistent estimates of the asymptotic covariance matrices of the estimators are presented and can form the basis for the usual asymptotic Chi-square tests of hypotheses. The finite sample properties of the estimators are illustrated by sampling experiments and suggest these estimators' substantial promise for empirical econometric practice.

## 10.2 MPD Solutions for p and λ as Estimators in Binary Response Models

In this section, we consider the direct use of the MPD solutions for p and $\lambda$ obtained from (9.3.1)–(9.3.4) in Chapter 9, that is, MPD estimation, as a basis for estimating the unknowns underlying binary response probabilities. As demonstrated in Chapter 9, a divergence-minimizing estimate of $\boldsymbol{\lambda}$ can be determined by incorporating the functional representation of $p(\mathbf{x}_{i.}\boldsymbol{\lambda})$ into the first-order conditions with respect to $\boldsymbol{\lambda}$. The resulting optimal $\boldsymbol{\lambda}$ solves the (scaled) sample moment equations

$$\boldsymbol{\lambda}_{\text{MPD}} = \mathbf{arg}_{\lambda}\{\mathbf{x}'(\mathbf{y} - \mathbf{p}(\mathbf{x}\boldsymbol{\lambda})) = \mathbf{0}\}. \tag{10.2.1}$$

The estimated value of $\mathbf{p}$, which is a function of the sample data, follows directly by substitution. We let $\widehat{\text{MPD}}(q, \gamma)$ indicate the MPD solution for given values of $q$ and $\gamma$.

As in all Lagrange-form optimization problems, $\boldsymbol{\lambda}$ reflects the marginal change in the objective function with respect to a marginal change in the constraint equations. In the current context, the $k \times 1$ vector, $\boldsymbol{\lambda}$, can be thought of as representing the "relative contribution" of each of the $k$ data constraints to the minimized divergence value. The polar case, $\lambda_i = 0$, indicates that the $i$th data constraint is nonbinding and redundant and adds no informational value to that already contained in the reference distribution for those probabilities. It is not apparent from general Lagrange multiplier theory that $\boldsymbol{\lambda}$ can actually be interpreted as an estimate of the parameter vector $\boldsymbol{\beta}$, underlying the linear index representation of the Bernoulli probabilities depicted in (9.2.1)–(9.2.3). In the next section, we motivate this interpretation.

### 10.2.1 Interpreting λ as an Estimator of β

Suppose one could actually use the true conditional population moments in the MPD estimation problem as $n^{-1}(\mathbf{E}(\mathbf{x}'\ (\mathbf{y} - \mathbf{p}))) = n^{-1}(\mathbf{x}'(\mathbf{F}(\mathbf{x}\boldsymbol{\beta}) - \mathbf{p})) = \mathbf{0}$, where $\mathbf{F}(\mathbf{x}\boldsymbol{\beta})$ represents the $n \times 1$ vector of actual CDFs defining the Bernoulli probabilities. The Lagrange form of the problem would then be

$$L(\mathbf{p},\boldsymbol{\lambda}) = \sum_{i=1}^{n}\left(\frac{1}{\gamma(\gamma+1)}\left[p_i\left(\frac{p_i}{q_i}\right)^{\gamma} + (1-p_i)\left(\frac{1-p_i}{1-q_i}\right)^{\gamma} - 1\right]\right)$$

$$+\boldsymbol{\lambda}'[n^{-1}\mathbf{x}'(\mathbf{F}(\mathbf{x}\boldsymbol{\beta})-\mathbf{p})],\ 0 \le p_i, q_i \le 1, \forall i \qquad (10.2.2)$$

The first-order conditions with respect to **p** would be precisely as indicated in (9.3.13) of Chapter 9 and lead to the same representations of the optimal **p** expressed in terms of $\boldsymbol{\lambda}$; that is, the same $\mathbf{p}(\mathbf{x}\lambda)$ vector of probabilities represented by (9.3.14).

Now suppose further that the probability model is specified correctly, in the sense that the MPD distribution matches the functional form of the true underlying probability distribution, $\mathbf{F}(\mathbf{x}\boldsymbol{\beta})$. The first-order conditions with respect to $\boldsymbol{\lambda}$ imply that

$$\mathbf{H}(\boldsymbol{\beta},\boldsymbol{\lambda}) \equiv n^{-1}\mathbf{x}'(\mathbf{F}(\mathbf{x}\boldsymbol{\beta}) - \mathbf{F}(\mathbf{x}\boldsymbol{\lambda})) = \mathbf{0}. \qquad (10.2.3)$$

In this case, it is apparent that one solution for $\boldsymbol{\lambda}$ is given directly by $\boldsymbol{\lambda} = \boldsymbol{\beta}$. That this is the unique solution to the problem follows from the Implicit Function Theorem, which can be used to demonstrate that (10.2.3) determines $\boldsymbol{\lambda}$ as a function of $\boldsymbol{\beta}$ in the neighborhood of $\boldsymbol{\beta}$. By this theorem, if the Jacobian of the $k$ constraints in (10.2.3), with respect to the $k \times 1$ vector $\boldsymbol{\lambda}$, is nonsingular when evaluated at $\boldsymbol{\lambda} = \boldsymbol{\beta}$, then such a functional relationship exists. The Jacobian is given by

$$\left.\frac{\partial \mathbf{H}(\boldsymbol{\beta},\boldsymbol{\lambda})}{\partial \boldsymbol{\lambda}}\right|_{\boldsymbol{\beta}=\tau} = -n^{-1}\mathbf{x}'(\mathbf{f}(\mathbf{x}\boldsymbol{\beta}) \odot \mathbf{x}) = -n^{-1}\sum_{i=1}^{n} f(\mathbf{x}_{i.}\boldsymbol{\beta})\,\mathbf{x}_{i.}'\mathbf{x}_{i.}, \qquad (10.2.4)$$

where $\mathbf{f}(\mathbf{x}\boldsymbol{\beta})$ is the vector of true underlying probability density function values. The Jacobian is negative definite and nonsingular under the mild assumption that there are $k$ or more rows of **x** that are not linearly independent and for which $f(\mathbf{x}_{i.}\boldsymbol{\beta}) > 0$. It follows that $\boldsymbol{\lambda}$ equals $\boldsymbol{\beta}$ in the solution to (10.2.3). Using observable sample moments in place of unobservable population moments, as $n^{-1}\mathbf{x}'(\mathbf{Y} - \mathbf{F}(\mathbf{x}\boldsymbol{\lambda})) = n^{-1}\mathbf{x}'(\mathbf{F}(\mathbf{x}\boldsymbol{\beta}) - \mathbf{F}(\mathbf{x}\boldsymbol{\lambda}) + \boldsymbol{\varepsilon}) = \mathbf{0}$, the solution for $\boldsymbol{\lambda}$ is then interpretable as a random variable estimating $\boldsymbol{\beta}$, which is consistent under familiar regularity conditions that include $n^{-1}\mathbf{x}'\boldsymbol{\varepsilon} \xrightarrow{p} \mathbf{0}$.

It can be shown under general regularity conditions that the estimator of $\hat{\boldsymbol{\lambda}}$ is asymptotically normally distributed. The limiting distribution of the estimator is defined by $n^{1/2}(\hat{\boldsymbol{\lambda}} - \boldsymbol{\beta}) \xrightarrow{d} N(\mathbf{0}, \mathbf{A}^{-1}\mathbf{V}\mathbf{A}^{-1})$, where $\mathbf{A} = \frac{\partial \mathbf{G}(\boldsymbol{\lambda})}{\partial \boldsymbol{\lambda}} \equiv E(f(\mathbf{X}_{1.}\boldsymbol{\beta})\mathbf{X}_{1.}'\mathbf{X}_{1.})$ and $\mathbf{V} = E(F(\mathbf{X}_{1.}\boldsymbol{\beta})(1 - F(\mathbf{X}_{1.}\boldsymbol{\beta}))\mathbf{X'}_{1.}\mathbf{X}_{1.})$. This result enables the usual hypothesis testing methodology that is relevant to asymptotic normal distribution theory.

### 10.2.2 Estimating the Marginal Probability Effects of Changes in Response Variables

In empirical work, the effect that changes in response variables have on the probabilities of the discrete choices being realized is often a focal point of analysis. Estimates of these marginal probability effects, represented by $\partial p_i/\partial x_{ij}$ for the $j$th response variable and the $i$th binary response probability, are straightforwardly defined in the case of the fully parametric logit and probit models as

$$\text{Logit:} \quad \frac{\partial \hat{p}_i}{\partial x_{ij}} = \frac{\exp(\mathbf{x}_{i.}\hat{\boldsymbol{\beta}})}{[1+\exp(\mathbf{x}_{i.}\hat{\boldsymbol{\beta}})]^2}\hat{\beta}_j \tag{10.2.5}$$

$$\text{Probit:} \quad \frac{\partial \hat{p}_i}{\partial x_{ij}} = \phi(\mathbf{x}_{i.}\hat{\boldsymbol{\beta}})\hat{\beta}_j, \tag{10.2.6}$$

where $\phi(\cdot)$ is the standard normal probability density function.

In the case of the MPD-class of estimators, marginal probability effects are derived by differentiating the appropriate definition of $p_i(\mathbf{x}_{i.}\boldsymbol{\lambda})$, with respect to the response variables used in defining the linear index, and yield the following:

$$\gamma < 0: \quad \frac{\partial p_i}{\partial x_{ij}} = \frac{\lambda_j}{\left(q_i^{-\gamma} p_i^{\gamma-1} + (1-q_i)^{-\gamma}(1-p_i)^{\gamma-1}\right)}, \tag{10.2.7}$$

$$\gamma = 0: \quad \frac{\partial p_i}{\partial x_{ij}} = \frac{q_i(1-q_i)^{-1}\exp(\mathbf{x}_{i.}\boldsymbol{\lambda})}{[1+q_i(1-q_i)^{-1}\exp(\mathbf{x}_{i.}\boldsymbol{\lambda})]^2}\lambda_j, \tag{10.2.8}$$

$$\gamma > 0: \quad \frac{\partial p_i}{\partial x_{ij}} = \left\{\begin{matrix} 0 \\ \left(\dfrac{\lambda_j}{(q_i^{-\gamma} p_i^{\gamma-1} + (1-q_i)^{-\gamma}(1-p_i)^{\gamma-1})}\right) \\ 0 \end{matrix}\right\} \text{ for } p_i \left\{\begin{matrix} \geq 1 \\ \in (0,1) \\ \leq 0 \end{matrix}\right\}. \tag{10.2.9}$$

The derivative in (10.2.8) is recognized as being identical in functional form to the logit derivative defined in (10.2.5), when $q_i = 0.5$. Moreover, the solution for $\lambda_{MPD}$ and the logit estimate of $\beta$ are in fact identical when $q_i = 0.5$ because the first-order conditions to both estimation problems coincide.

## 10.3 Asymptotic Estimator Properties

Asymptotic properties are one basis for evaluating the performance of the $\widehat{\text{MPD}}(q, \gamma)$ class of estimators. In this discussion, it will be useful to represent the first-order conditions with respect to the Lagrange multipliers for random $\mathbf{X}$ as

$$\begin{aligned} \mathbf{G}_n(\boldsymbol{\lambda}) &= n^{-1} \sum_{i=1}^{n} \mathbf{X}_i'(\mathrm{F_c}(\mathbf{X}_{i.}\boldsymbol{\beta}) - p(\mathbf{X}_{i.}\boldsymbol{\lambda}) + \varepsilon_i) \\ &= n^{-1} \sum_{i=1}^{n} \mathbf{G}_{ni}(\boldsymbol{\lambda}) = \mathbf{0}, \end{aligned} \quad (10.3.1)$$

where $\mathrm{Y_i} \equiv \mathrm{F_c}(\mathbf{X}_{i.}\boldsymbol{\beta}) + \varepsilon_i$ and, $\mathrm{F_c}(\cdot)$ denotes the true underlying CDF. Main results are presented next. Additional details are provided in the Appendix 10.A.

Asymptotic results are based on the following standard assumptions:

i) *The observations* $(y_i, \mathbf{x}_{i.})$, $i = 1, \ldots, n$, *are* iid *random realizations of the random row vector* $(\mathrm{Y}, \mathbb{X})$;
ii) $\mathbf{G}_n(\boldsymbol{\beta}) \rightarrow \mathbf{0}$, *with probability 1;*
iii) *All* $\mathbf{G}_n(\boldsymbol{\lambda})$ *are continuously differentiable with probability 1 in a neighborhood N of* $\boldsymbol{\beta}$, *and the associated Jacobians,* $\frac{\partial \mathbf{G}_n(\boldsymbol{\lambda})}{\partial \boldsymbol{\lambda}}$, *converge uniformly to a nonstochastic limit,* $\frac{\partial \mathbf{G}(\boldsymbol{\lambda})}{\partial \boldsymbol{\lambda}}$, *that is nonsingular at* $\boldsymbol{\lambda} = \boldsymbol{\beta}$; *and*
iv) $n^{1/2}\mathbf{G}_n(\boldsymbol{\beta}) \xrightarrow{d} N(\mathbf{0}, \mathbf{V})$.

Given these standard regularity conditions, the following two theorems establish the consistency and asymptotic normality of the $\widehat{\text{MPD}}(\mathrm{q}, \gamma)$ estimation approach.

**Theorem 1:** *Under assumptions (i)–(iii), the* $\widehat{\text{MPD}}(\mathrm{q}, \gamma)$ *estimator* $\hat{\boldsymbol{\lambda}} = \arg_{\boldsymbol{\lambda}}[\mathbf{G}_n(\boldsymbol{\lambda}) = \mathbf{0}]$ *is a consistent estimator of* $\boldsymbol{\beta}$.

**Theorem 2:** *Under assumptions (i)–(iv), the* $\widehat{\text{MPD}}(\mathrm{q}, \gamma)$ *estimator* $\hat{\boldsymbol{\lambda}} = \arg_{\boldsymbol{\lambda}} [\mathbf{G}_n(\boldsymbol{\lambda}) = \mathbf{0}]$ *is asymptotically normally distributed, with limiting distribution* $n^{1/2}(\hat{\boldsymbol{\lambda}} - \boldsymbol{\beta}) \xrightarrow{d} N(\mathbf{0}, \mathbf{A}^{-1}\mathbf{V}\mathbf{A}^{-1})$, *where* $\mathbf{A} = \frac{\partial \mathbf{G}(\boldsymbol{\lambda})}{\partial \boldsymbol{\lambda}} \equiv \mathrm{E}(\mathrm{f}(\mathbf{X}_{1.}\boldsymbol{\beta})\mathbf{X}_{1.}'\mathbf{X}_{1.})$ *and* $\mathbf{V} = \mathrm{E}(\mathrm{F}(\mathbf{X}_{1.}\boldsymbol{\beta})(1 - \mathrm{F}(\mathbf{X}_{1.}\boldsymbol{\beta}))\mathbf{X}_{1.}'\mathbf{X}_{1.})$.

Consistency of $\mathbf{p}_{\text{MPD}} = \mathbf{p}(\mathbf{x}\boldsymbol{\lambda}_{\text{MPD}})$ follows from the continuity of $\mathbf{p}(\mathbf{x}\boldsymbol{\lambda})$ in $\boldsymbol{\lambda}$. Asymptotic normality of $\mathbf{p}_{\text{MPD}} = \mathbf{p}(\mathbf{x}\boldsymbol{\lambda}_{\text{MPD}})$, including a representation of the asymptotic covariance matrix of the distribution, follows from the fact that $\mathbf{p}(\mathbf{x}\boldsymbol{\lambda})$ is continuously differentiable in $\boldsymbol{\lambda}$. Application of the delta method may be used to derive the asymptotic results.

### 10.3.1 Asymptotic Inference

On the basis of normal distribution theory and the asymptotic results of the previous subsections, usual hypothesis tests hold in large samples. The principal issue in empirical application is how to define the sample approximations to the covariance matrices associated with the asymptotic distributions. Given the definition of the covariance matrix in Theorem 2, a consistent estimator of the Jacobian matrix $\mathbf{A} = \frac{\partial \mathbf{G}(\boldsymbol{\lambda})}{\partial \boldsymbol{\lambda}} \equiv E(f(\mathbf{X}_{1.}\boldsymbol{\beta})\mathbf{X}_{1.}'\mathbf{X}_{1.})$ is defined by

$$\hat{\mathbf{A}} = n^{-1}\sum_{i=1}^{n} f(\mathbf{X}_{i.}\hat{\boldsymbol{\lambda}})\mathbf{X}_{i.}'\mathbf{X}_{i.} \tag{10.3.2}$$

and a consistent estimator of $\mathbf{V} = E(F(\mathbf{X}_{1.}\boldsymbol{\beta})(1 - F(\mathbf{X}_{1.}\boldsymbol{\beta}))\mathbf{X}_{1.}'\mathbf{X}_{1.})$ is defined by

$$\hat{\mathbf{V}} = n^{-1}\sum_{i=1}^{n} F(\mathbf{X}_{i.}\hat{\boldsymbol{\lambda}})(1 - F(\mathbf{X}_{i.}\hat{\boldsymbol{\lambda}}))\mathbf{X}_{i.}'\mathbf{X}_{i.}. \tag{10.3.3}$$

From this base, it follows that a Wald-type statistic for testing the $J$ linear restrictions $\text{H}_0 : \mathbf{C}\boldsymbol{\beta} = \mathbf{r}$ is given by

$$n(\mathbf{C}\hat{\boldsymbol{\lambda}} - \mathbf{r})'[\mathbf{C}\mathbf{A}^{-1}\mathbf{V}\mathbf{A}^{-1}\mathbf{C}']^{-1}(\mathbf{C}\hat{\boldsymbol{\lambda}} - \mathbf{r}) \xrightarrow{d} \chi_J^2 \text{ under } \text{H}_0. \tag{10.3.4}$$

Hypotheses relating to the value of $p(\mathbf{z}'\boldsymbol{\beta})$, where $\mathbf{z}$ is a vector of variate response values, can be based on an application of the delta method. This means

$$p(\mathbf{z}'\hat{\boldsymbol{\lambda}}) \overset{a}{\sim} N(p(\mathbf{z}'\boldsymbol{\beta}),\ n^{-1}f(\mathbf{z}'\hat{\boldsymbol{\lambda}})^2\mathbf{z}'\mathbf{A}^{-1}\mathbf{V}\mathbf{A}^{-1}\mathbf{z}). \tag{10.3.5}$$

Thus, under the $\text{H}_0 : p(\mathbf{z}'\boldsymbol{\beta}) = p_o$,

$$\frac{n(p(\mathbf{z}'\hat{\boldsymbol{\lambda}}) - p_o)}{(f(\mathbf{z}'\hat{\boldsymbol{\lambda}})^2\mathbf{z}'\hat{\mathbf{A}}^{-1}\hat{\mathbf{V}}\hat{\mathbf{A}}^{-1}\mathbf{z})^{1/2}} \overset{a}{\sim} N(0, 1) \text{ under } \text{H}_0. \tag{10.3.6}$$

## 10.4 Estimation Alternatives

Before evaluating the small sample properties of the MPD-estimation solution to the stochastic inverse problem of binary response, we note that the consistency and asymptotic normality of the MPD solutions rely on appropriate choices of $q$ and $\gamma$. This is fully analogous to the specification issue involved when choosing either the normal or logistic distribution in probit or logit analyses. The MPD class of CDFs provides a large and flexible family of distributions from which to choose a characterization of Bernoulli binary response probabilities. To provide an operational basis for mitigating the unknown sampling distribution problem, one possibility is an ML approach in which the optimal distributional choice, from among all of the members of the MPD class, is nested in the estimation process. This results in a highly flexible and distributionally robust approach for estimating BRMs that can be consistent, asymptotically normal, and efficient, in the absence of knowledge of the functional form of the underlying sampling distribution (also see Mittelhammer and Judge, 2011). Also note that profiling out $q$ and $\gamma$ is a way of handling the case in which one does not have an informed basis for choosing reference distribution values $q$ for the Bernoulli probabilities. Given such information as noted in Chapter 9, the approach outlined next could proceed conditionally on those values.

### 10.4.1 EML Estimation

An ML estimator of a BRM, based on the class of MPD distributions, may be defined by optimizing the following log-likelihood function for the observed sample observations:

$$\ell(\boldsymbol{\beta}, q, \gamma \mid \mathbf{y},\mathbf{x}) = \sum_{i=1}^{n} [y_i \ln(p(\mathbf{x}_{i.}\boldsymbol{\beta}; q, \gamma)) + (1 - y_i)\ln(1 - p(\mathbf{x}_{i.}\boldsymbol{\beta}; q, \gamma))] \tag{10.4.1}$$

This is the EML approach to using the functional form of the distributions defined in the MPD solution to the stochastic inverse problem, first discussed in Section 7.4. It is instructive to consider maximizing the likelihood in the following two steps:

i) first defining the profile likelihood function of $\boldsymbol{\beta}$ as

$$p\ell(\boldsymbol{\beta} \mid \mathbf{y},\mathbf{x}) \equiv \sup_{q,\gamma}\{\ell(\boldsymbol{\beta}, q, \gamma \mid \mathbf{y},\mathbf{x})\}, \tag{10.4.2}$$

and

ii) then deriving the ML estimator of $\boldsymbol{\beta}$ by maximizing the profile likelihood as

$$\hat{\boldsymbol{\beta}}_{eml} = \arg\sup_{\boldsymbol{\beta}}\{p\ell(\boldsymbol{\beta} \mid \mathbf{y},\mathbf{x})\} \equiv \arg\sup_{\boldsymbol{\beta}} \left\{ \left\{ \sup_{\gamma, q}\{\ell(\boldsymbol{\beta}, q, \gamma \mid \mathbf{y},\mathbf{x})\} \right\} \right\}. \tag{10.4.3}$$

One can interpret the likelihood profiling step (10.4.2) as determining the optimal MPD distribution associated with any choice of the $\boldsymbol{\beta}$ vector. The second ML step, (10.4.3), may be interpreted as determining the overall optimal estimate of the parameters of the linear index argument in the CDF that determines the binary response probabilities. The computational search for the maximum of the likelihood is facilitated by the concavity of the MPD CDFs for all distributions where $\gamma \leq 1$.

Patefield (1977, 1985) and Murphy and van der Vaart (2000) demonstrate that the profile likelihood, $p\ell(\boldsymbol{\beta} \mid \mathbf{y},\mathbf{x})$, can be used in effectively the same way as an ordinary likelihood for purposes of defining an appropriate score function, $\frac{\partial p\ell(\boldsymbol{\beta}\mid\mathbf{y},\mathbf{x})}{\partial\boldsymbol{\beta}}$, and an information matrix representation of the asymptotic covariance matrix with respect to the ML estimator $\hat{\boldsymbol{\beta}}_{ml}$, $[-E\frac{\partial^2 p\ell(\boldsymbol{\beta}\mid\mathbf{y},\mathbf{x})}{\partial\boldsymbol{\beta}\partial\boldsymbol{\beta}'}]^{-1}$. With regard to $\boldsymbol{\beta}$, the preceding score and information matrix definitions are equivalent to the appropriate submatrix of the information matrix calculated from the full likelihood as $\frac{\partial\ell(\boldsymbol{\theta}\mid\mathbf{y},\mathbf{x})}{\partial\boldsymbol{\beta}}$ and $[-E\frac{\ell(\boldsymbol{\theta}\mid\mathbf{y},\mathbf{x})}{\partial\boldsymbol{\theta}\partial\boldsymbol{\theta}'}]^{-1}$, respectively, where $\boldsymbol{\theta} \equiv [\boldsymbol{\beta}, q, \gamma]'$. The asymptotic covariance matrix for $\hat{\boldsymbol{\beta}}_{ml}$, together with the asymptotic normality of the ML estimator, $n^{1/2}(\hat{\boldsymbol{\beta}}_{ml} - \boldsymbol{\beta}) \xrightarrow{d} N(\mathbf{0}, [-E\frac{\partial^2 p\ell(\boldsymbol{\beta}\mid\mathbf{y},\mathbf{x})}{\partial\boldsymbol{\beta}\partial\boldsymbol{\beta}'}]^{-1})$, enabling asymptotic Chi-square distributions for the usual Wald, Lagrange multiplier, or likelihood ratio test statistics. This is analogous to traditional probit or logit contexts but rooted in a substantially more robust sampling distribution model.[1] In empirical applications, an estimate of the asymptotic covariance of $\hat{\boldsymbol{\beta}}$ is defined by $-[\frac{\partial^2 p\ell(\boldsymbol{\beta}\mid\mathbf{y},\mathbf{x})}{\partial\boldsymbol{\beta}\partial\boldsymbol{\beta}'}]^{-1}_{\boldsymbol{\beta}=\hat{\boldsymbol{\beta}}_{ml}}$.

[1] As in all applications of maximum likelihood, issues of regularity conditions arise for the asymptotics to apply. Under appropriate boundedness assumptions relating to X and given the boundedness and continuous differentiability of the MPD class of distributions, the extremum estimator asymptotics apply along the lines of Hansen (1982), Newey (1991), van der Vaart (1998), and Mittelhammer and Judge (2011). The most straightforward case is when global concavity holds, $\gamma \leq 1$, in which case the uniform probability convergence results of Pollard (1991) apply.

### 10.4.2 NLS-MPD Estimation

A NLS estimator of the BRM can be defined by minimizing the following sum of squared errors (SSE) function:

$$SSE(\boldsymbol{\beta}, q, \gamma \mid \mathbf{y},\mathbf{x}) = \sum_{i=1}^{n} [y_i - (p(\mathbf{x}_{i.}\boldsymbol{\beta}\,; q, \gamma))]^2. \qquad (10.4.4)$$

Given the heteroskedastic nature of the Bernoulli random variables, whereby the variance of the $i$th Bernoulli trial is given by $p_i(1 - p_i)$, one might seek gains in asymptotic efficiency by considering heteroskedasticity-adjusted SSE function, such as

$$SSE_w(\boldsymbol{\beta}, q, \gamma \mid \mathbf{y},\mathbf{x}) = \sum_{i=1}^{n} \frac{[y_i - (p(\mathbf{x}_{i.}\boldsymbol{\beta}; q, \gamma))]^2}{[p(\mathbf{x}_{i.}\boldsymbol{\beta}; q, \gamma)][1 - p(\mathbf{x}_{i.}\boldsymbol{\beta}; q, \gamma)]}. \qquad (10.4.5)$$

However, it is well known (e.g., Pagan and Ullah, 1999) that the first-order conditions for minimizing (10.4.5) are precisely the same as that of maximizing the likelihood in (10.4.1). Thus, one might proceed by focusing on the functionally and computationally simpler consistent estimator defined by minimizing (10.4.4).

Given that the uncorrected SSE is used as the estimation objective, the NLS estimator will have the asymptotic distribution

$$\hat{\boldsymbol{\beta}} \overset{a}{\sim} N(\boldsymbol{\beta}, [\nabla_{\boldsymbol{\beta}}\mathbf{p}'\nabla_{b}\mathbf{p}]^{-1}[\nabla_{\boldsymbol{\beta}}\mathbf{p}'\,\Psi\,\nabla_{\boldsymbol{\beta}}\mathbf{p}][\nabla_{\boldsymbol{\beta}}\mathbf{p}'\nabla_{\boldsymbol{\beta}}\mathbf{p}]^{-1}). \qquad (10.4.6)$$

In (10.4.6), $\nabla_{\boldsymbol{\beta}}\mathbf{p} \equiv [\frac{\partial \mathbf{p}(\mathbf{x}\boldsymbol{\beta}; q, \gamma)}{\partial \boldsymbol{\beta}'}]$ and $\Psi$ is a diagonal covariance matrix whose $i$th diagonal entry equals $[p(\mathbf{x}_{i.}\boldsymbol{\beta}; q, \gamma)][1 - p(\mathbf{x}_{i.}\boldsymbol{\beta}; q, \gamma)]$, which is the Bernoulli variance for the $i$th observation. In applications, the unknown parameters may be replaced by NLS estimates, and the resulting estimate of the covariance matrix can be used to define appropriate test and confidence region-generating statistics.

## 10.5 Sampling Performance

To investigate the finite sample estimation performance of the MPD, EML, and NLS-MPD estimators, and to indicate how they may be applied, the results of a range of sampling experiments are reported in this section. The sampling experiments are designed so that the sampling distribution underlying observed $p_i = P(y_i = 1)$ values achieve targeted mean and variability levels. They also map one-to-one with covariate values, which defines a covariate population data sampling process (DSP).

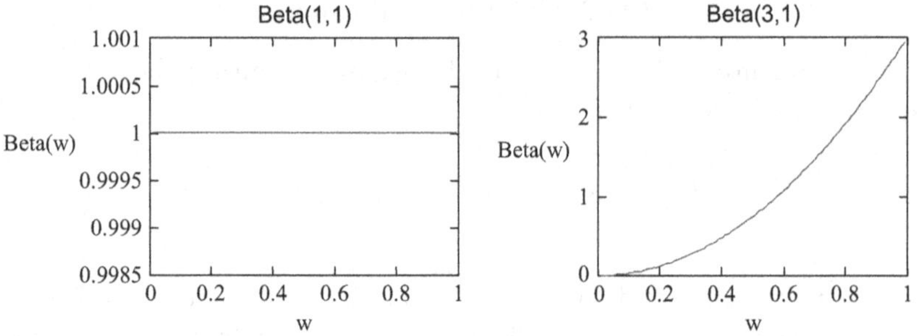


Figure 10.5.1. Population Distributions for $P(y = 1)$.

### 10.5.1 Sampling Design

Random samples of size $n = 100, 250$, and 500 of $P(y_i = 1)$ values were sampled from a Beta distribution, $B(a, b)$, with $b = 1$ and set to achieve targeted unconditional mean, $P(y_i = 1)$, levels of .5 or .75 (i.e., $a = \frac{b}{E(Y)(1-E(Y))}$ with $E(Y_i) = .5 \; or \; .75$). The resulting two distributions of $P(y_i = 1)$ values are uniform, centered at .5, or right-skewed and centered at .75, respectively. Graphs of the two population distributions are presented in Figure 10.5.1. The two distributions represent a situation in which all values of $P(y = 1)$ are either equally likely to be observed or else substantially more probable for $P(y = 1)$ values greater than .5 than less (note, $\int_{.5}^{1} Beta(w; 3, 1)dw = .875$).

A linear index representation of the Bernoulli probabilities is defined as

$$P(y_i = 1) = F(\beta_0 + \beta_1 x_i), \quad \text{for } i = 1, \ldots, n, \qquad (10.5.1)$$

where $F(\cdot)$ is the cumulative distribution or link function underlying the Bernoulli probabilities, and the $x_i'$s are chosen so that $x_i = (F^{-1}(P(y_i = 1)) - \beta_0)/\beta_1$. The values of the linear index parameters are $\beta_0 = 1$ and $\beta_1 = 2$. Explicit functional forms for $F(\cdot)$ include two MPD distributions, given by MPD($q = .5, \gamma = -1$) and MPD($q = .75, \gamma = 1.5$), as well as a N(0,1) distribution. The former MPD distribution is a symmetric distribution around zero associated with the "empirical likelihood" choice, $\gamma = -1$. This distribution has the real line for its support, and has substantially fatter tails then the N(0,1) distribution. The latter MPD distribution has finite support, is heavily skewed to the left, and has a density whose values increase at an increasing rate as the argument of the link function increases. The standard normal distribution is the link function that is optimal for the probit model of binary response. These three different link functions are illustrated in Figure 10.5.2.

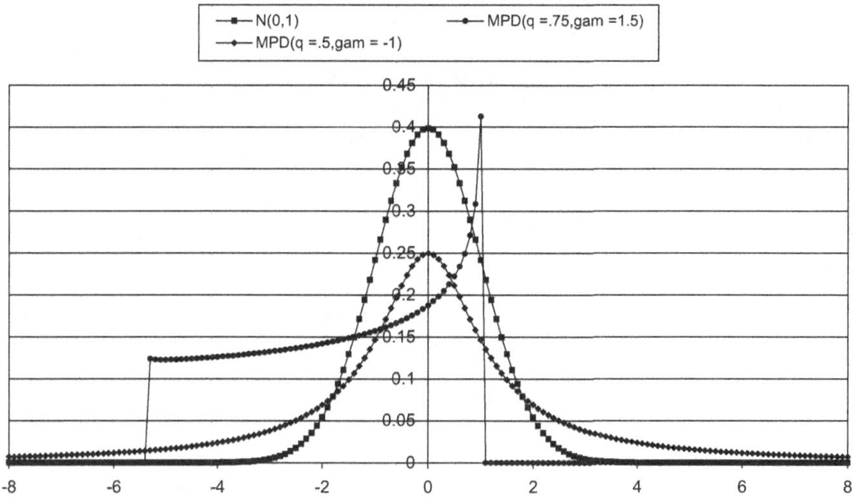


Figure 10.5.2. Link Functions: N(0,1), NPD (q = .5, gam = −1), MPD (q = .75, gam = 1.5).

The random outcomes of the binary responses are generated according to their respective Bernoulli probability distributions as

$$Y_i \sim Bernoulli(F(\beta_0 + \beta_1 x_i)), \quad i = 1, \ldots, n. \tag{10.5.2}$$

This implies a regression relationship of the form

$$Y_i = F(\beta_0 + \beta_1 x_i) + \varepsilon_i, \quad i = 1, \ldots, n \tag{10.5.3}$$

and acts as the definition of the residual outcome of $\varepsilon_i$.

The expected squared prediction error, defined by $\int_x (\hat{p}(x) - F(\beta_0 + \beta_1 x))^2 dF(\beta_0 + \beta_1 x)$, is used as the measure of estimation performance, where $\hat{p}(x)$ denotes the probability prediction from either an MPD estimator with reference probabilities q and parameter $\boldsymbol{\gamma}$. Henceforth, this will be denoted as an $\widehat{\text{MPD}}(q, \gamma)$, an EML, an NLS-MPD, or a probit-ML estimator. Empirically, the measure is calculated as the MSE, $n^{-1} \sum_{i=1}^{n} (\hat{p}(x_i) - F(\beta_0 + \beta_1 x_i))^2$.

All sampling results are based on 1,000 repetitions, and calculations were performed using Aptech Systems' GAUSS™ software. At this number of repetitions, all empirically calculated expectations of the performance measures are accurate, with standard errors of mean calculations typically .0001 or less in magnitude. We note that sampling results for the $\widehat{\text{MPD}}(.5, 0)$ estimator necessarily produce results identical to those of the standard ML logit estimator. This sampling design was also used in Mittelhammer and

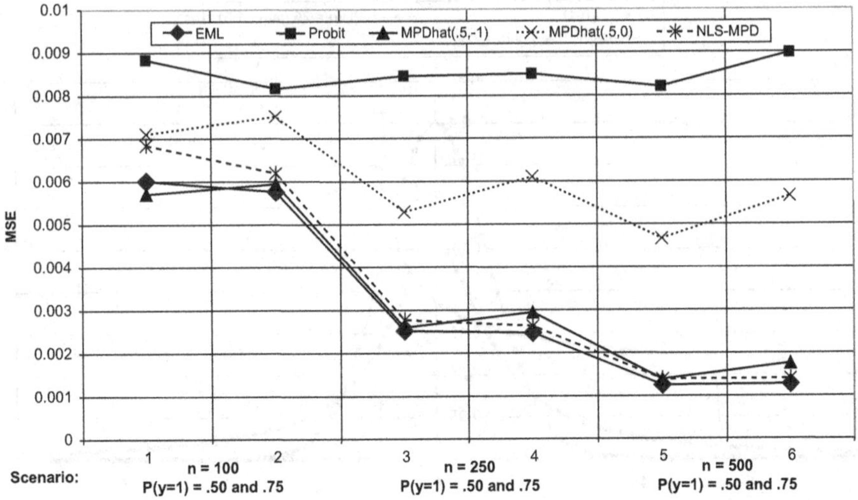


Figure 10.5.3. MSE for P(y = 1) Predictions, n = 100, 250, 500, DSP = MPD(.5, -1).

Judge (2011), where additional sampling results and estimator comparisons are reported.

## 10.5.2 Sampling Results

The expected squared prediction error results for the EML and NLS-MPD estimators, the probit estimator, and the two MPD estimators, $\widehat{\text{MPD}}(.5, -1)$ and $\widehat{\text{MPD}}(.5, 0)$, are displayed in Figure 10.5.3 for the MPD($q = .5$, $\gamma = -1$) DSP and in Figure 10.5.4 for the MPD($q = .75$, $\gamma = 1.5$) DSP. Given these DSP specifications for the link functions, the distribution underlying the $\widehat{\text{MPD}}(.5, -1)$ estimator is specified correctly for the former DSP, and neither $\widehat{\text{MPD}}(\text{q}, \gamma)$ estimator is specified correctly in the case of the latter DSP. In implementing the EML and NLS-MPD estimators, the feasible set of distributions examined was defined by $\gamma \in [-2, 2]$ and $q \in [.1, .9]$.

The probit estimator, which is a quasi-ML in these two data sampling applications, is strongly dominated by all of the alternative estimators, when the DSP is MPD($q = .5, \gamma = -1$). The correctly specified $\widehat{\text{MPD}}(.5, -1)$ estimator performs very well in MSE, but the EML estimator is effectively equal to or is superior to the $\widehat{\text{MPD}}(.5, -1)$ estimator across all scenarios. The NLS-MPD estimator also performs well and nearly equals the precision of the EML estimator except for the case of small sample size. When the DSP is MPD($q = .75, \gamma = 1.5$), the EML estimator continues to be the clear choice, with the NLS-MPD estimator again being almost as precise, especially for the larger sample sizes. The probit estimator is again

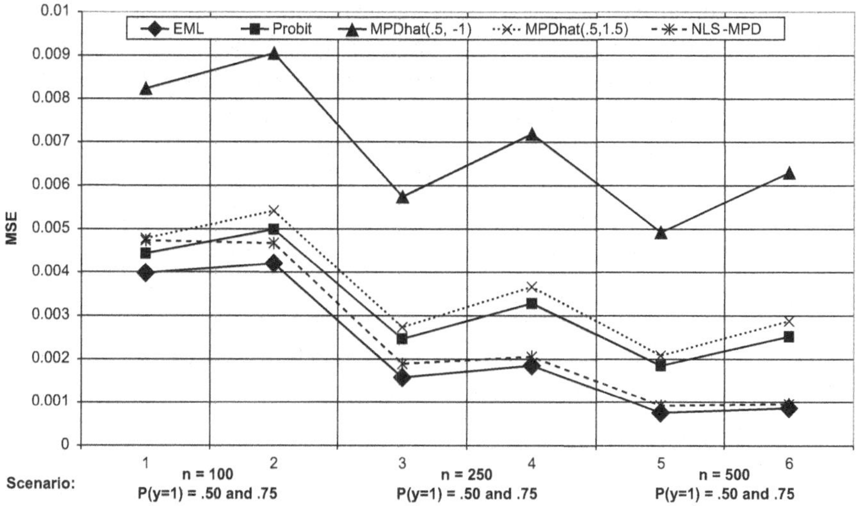


Figure 10.5.4. MSE for P(y = 1) Predictions, n = 100, 250, 500, DSP = MPD (.75, 1.5).

dominated as are the $\widehat{\text{MPD}}(.5, -1)$ and $\widehat{\text{MPD}}(.5, 0)$ estimators. The consistency of the EML and NLS-MPD estimators is reflected in both of the preceding figures as $n$ increases.

If one were omniscient and parametrically chose (the correct) N(0,1) probit model, the probit-ML estimator would, as indicated in Figure 10.5.5, be the superior choice in MSE performance. The superiority of the probit

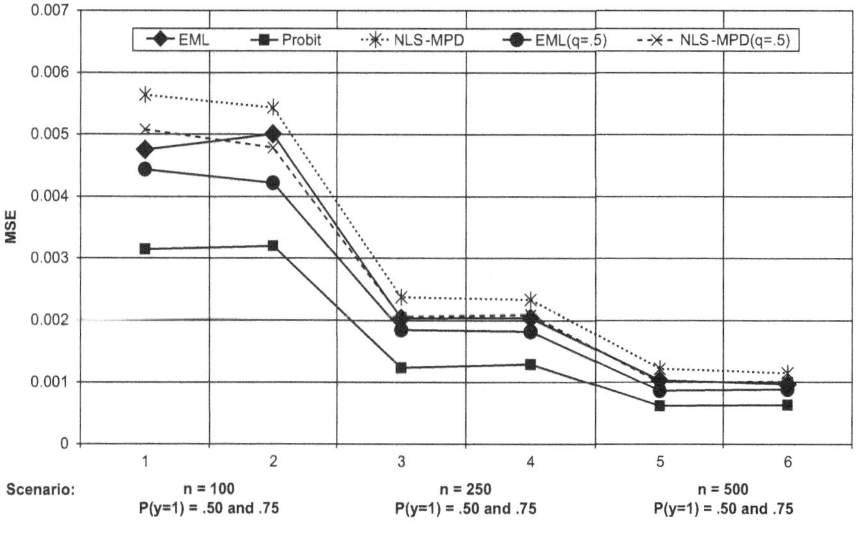


Figure 10.5.5. MSE for P(y = 1) Predictions, n = 100, 250, 500, DSP = N(0,1).

estimator diminishes relative to both the EML and NLS-MPD estimators as the sample size increases. If one chose to model the binary response probabilities by utilizing only symmetric distributions that are contained in the MPD-class (i.e., restricting $q = .5$), the relative superiority of the correctly specified probit estimator is diminished further. This is true for even the smallest sample size, as indicated by the EML ($q = .5$) results in Figure 10.5.5. Overall, the comparisons in Figure 10.5.5 indicate the precision gains that would occur by having correct prior information about distributional functional form and also indicate the unavoidable cost in practice when one does not correctly choose the underlying sampling model. The sampling results suggest that the EML, which is itself a Quasi-ML in this DSP application, contributes to mitigating this possible specification error cost to a notable degree.[2]

In general, the sampling results illustrate the robustness attainable from utilizing the large and flexible class of MPD distributions for modeling binary response when coupled with a EML or NLS approach for choosing optimally among the member distributions within the class. The method mitigates imprecision, due to lack of knowledge-misspecification of the true DSP underlying binary responses, and competes well with generally unknown and unattainable correct choices of the DSP.

## 10.6 Summary and Extensions

The Cressie-Read MPD family of probability distributions for the BRM was used to identify a new class of statistical models and associated estimators and inference procedures for modeling observations on binary response outcomes. The EML approach offers an operational basis for estimating the BRM via ML when there is uncertainty relative to distributional choice from among the members of the MPD class. The NLS-MPD approach provides an alternative method, based on an optimal probability prediction criterion, for estimating the BRM and resolving the uncertainty with respect to distributional choice. The MPD approach results in a highly flexible and distributionally robust approach to estimating BRMs that can be consistent, asymptotically normal, and efficient, even in the absence of knowledge of the true functional form of the underlying sampling distribution. Sampling experiments used to identify the small sample properties of estimators for a

[2] Note that the N(0,1) is not contained in the MPD class of distributions. However, there are a number of distributions in the class (e.g., the standard logistic) that emulate the N(0,1) rather closely, resulting in relatively effective quasi-ML behavior by estimators based on the MPD class.

range of members of the CR family suggest that the MPD-based estimators compared favorably to parametric methods that are based on true *but unknown* data sampling distributions.

## 10.7 Selected References


Cosslett, S. R. (1983), "Distribution-Free Maximum Likelihood Estimation of the Binary Choice Model," *Econometrica* **51**:765–782.

Cressie, N. and T. Read (1984), "Multinomial Goodness of Fit Tests," *Journal of the Royal Statistical Society, Series B* **46**:440–464.

Gabler, S., F. Laisney, and M. Lechner (1993), "Seminonparametric Estimation of Binary Choice Models with an Application to Labor Force Participation," *Journal of Business and Economic Statistics* **11**:61–80.

Gozalo, P. L. and O. Linton (1994), *Local Nonlinear Least Squares Estimation Using Parametric Information Nonparametrically.* Discussion Paper No. 1075, Cowles Foundation, Yale University.

Green, W. (2007), "Discrete Choice Modeling." *Handbook of Econometrics.* Vol. 2, Part 4.2, edited by T. Mills and K. Patterson, London: Palgrave.

Han, A. K. (1987), "Nonparametric Analysis of a Generalized Regression Model," *Journal of Econometrics* **35**:303–316.

Hansen, L. P. (1982), "Large Sample Properties of Generalized Method of Moments Estimators," *Econometrica* **50**:1029–1054.

Horowitz, J. L. (1992), "A Smoothed Maximum Score Estimator for the Binary Response Model," *Econometrica* **60**:505–531.

Ichimura, H. (1993), "Semiparametric Least Squares (SLS) and Weighted SLS Estimation of Single-Index Models," *Journal of Econometrics* **58**:71–120.

Klein, R. W. and R. H. Spady (1993), "An Efficient Semiparametric Estimator for Binary Response Models," *Econometrica* **61**(2):387–421.

Kuhn, H. W. and A. W. Tucker (1951), *Non-linear Programming.* In Proc. 2 Berkeley Symp. on Mathematical Statistics and Probability, pp. 481–492. University of California Press.

Manski, C. F. (1975), "The Maximum Score Estimation of the Stochastic Utility Model of Choice," *Journal of Econometrics* **3**:205–228.

McFadden, D. (1984), "Qualitative Response Models," in Z. Griliches and M. Intriligator (Eds.), *Handbook of Econometrics 2*, Amsterdam: North Holland, pp. 1395–1457.

———. (1974), "Conditional Logit Analysis of Qualitative Choice Behavior," in P. Zarembka (Ed.), *Frontiers of Econometrics*, New York: Academic Press, pp. 105–142.

Mittelhammer, R., G. Judge, and D. Miller (2000), *Econometric Foundations*, New York: Cambridge University Press.

Mittelhammer, R. and G. Judge (2011), "A Family of Empirical Likelihood Functions and Estimators for the Binary Response Model," *Journal of Econometrics*, doi:10.1016/j.jeconom.2011.04.002.

Murphy, S. A. and A. W. Van Der Vaart (2000). "On Profile Likelihood," *Journal of the American Statistical Association* **95**:449–465.

Newey, W. (1991), "Uniform Convergence in Probability and Stochastic Equicontinuity," *Econometrica* **59**:1161–1167.

Pagan, A. and A. Ullah (1999), *Nonparametric Econometrics*, New York: Cambridge University Press.

Pardo, L. (2006), *Statistical Inference Based on Divergence Measures*, Boca Raton, FL: Chapman and Hall.

Patefield, W. M. (1985), "Information from the Maximized Likelihood Function," *Biometrika* **72**:664–668.

______. (1977), "On the Maximized Likelihood Function," *Sankhya* **39**:92–96.

Pollard, D. (1991), "Asymptotics for Least Absolute Deviation Regression Estimators," *Econometric Theory* **7**:186–199.

Pratt, J. W. (1981), "Concavity of the Log Likelihood," *Journal of the American Statistical Association* **76**:103–106.

Read, T. R. and N. A. Cressie (1988), *Goodness of Fit Statistics for Discrete Multivariate Data*, New York: Springer Verlag.

Serfling, R. J. (1980), *Approximation Theorems of Mathematical Statistics*, New York: John Wiley & Sons.

Train, K. (2003), *Discrete Choice Methods with Simulation*, New York: Cambridge University Press.

Wang, W. and M. Zhou (1993), *Iterative Least Squares Estimator of Binary Choice Models: Semiparametric Approach.* Department of Statistics Technical Report No. 346, University of Kentucky.

Yuan, K. and R. I. Jennrich (1998), "Asymptotics of Estimating Equations Under Natural Conditions," *Journal of Multivariate Analysis* **65**:245–260.

Zellner, A. and P. Rossi (1984), "Bayesian Analysis for Dichotomous Response Models," *Journal of Econometrics* **25**:365–393.

## APPENDIX 10.A ASYMPTOTIC PROPERTIES OF $\widehat{\text{MPD}}(q, \gamma)$ – APPLICABILITY OF ASSUMPTIONS

If *iid* random sampling is in fact the sampling mechanism utilized for generating sample data, then in Section 10.3, assumption 1 is satisfied by definition. A sufficient condition for assumption 2 to be satisfied is that MPD(q, $\gamma$) be appropriately specified to represent the functional form of the true underlying CDF, $F(\mathbf{x}_{i.}\boldsymbol{\beta})$. This condition is analogous to correctly specifying the functional form of the probability distribution in a ML estimation problem (e.g., probit or logit). In this event,

$$E(\mathbf{G}_{ni}(\boldsymbol{\beta})) \equiv E(\mathbf{X}'_{i.}\varepsilon_i) = \mathbf{0}, \quad \text{and } \mathbf{G}_{ni}(\boldsymbol{\beta}),\ i = 1, \ldots, n, \text{ are } iid \qquad (10.A.1)$$

imply that

$$\mathbf{G}_n(\boldsymbol{\beta}) = n^{-1}\sum_{i=1}^{n}\mathbf{G}_{ni}(\boldsymbol{\beta}) \overset{wp1}{\rightarrow} \mathbf{0} \qquad (10.A.2)$$

by Kolmogorov's strong law of large numbers (Serfling, 1980, p. 27), resulting in the applicability of assumption 2.

Regarding assumption 3, note that the gradient of $\mathbf{G}_n(\boldsymbol{\lambda})$ is given by

$$\frac{\partial \mathbf{G}_n(\boldsymbol{\lambda})}{\partial \boldsymbol{\lambda}} \equiv -n^{-1} \sum_{i=1}^{n} \frac{\partial p(\mathbf{X}_{i.}\boldsymbol{\lambda})}{\partial \mathbf{X}_{i.}\boldsymbol{\lambda}} \mathbf{X}'_{i.}\mathbf{X}_{i.} = -n^{-1} \sum_{i=1}^{n} f(\mathbf{X}_{i.}\boldsymbol{\lambda})\mathbf{X}'_{i.}\mathbf{X}_{i.}, \quad (10.A.3)$$

where $f(\cdot)$ denotes a probability density function in the MPD class of distributions. It is apparent that the continuous differentiability of $\mathbf{G}_n(\boldsymbol{\lambda})$ depends on the continuity of $\frac{\partial p(z)}{\partial z} = f(z)$. This follows from the functional definition of $f(z)$ and the fact that, except on the boundaries of the supports of the distributions, $\frac{\partial p(z)}{\partial z}$ is continuous everywhere when $\gamma \leq 0$ and continuous except on an event having probability 0 when $\gamma > 0$. Moreover, because $F(w; q, \gamma) \in [0, 1]$, MPD densities are all bounded, as $f(z) < \xi < \infty$. Thus, $f(\mathbf{X}_{i.}\boldsymbol{\lambda})\mathbf{X}'_{i}\mathbf{X}_{i} < \xi \mathbf{X}'_{i.}\mathbf{X}_{i.}$, so $E(\sup_{\lambda}(f(\mathbf{X}_{i}\lambda)\mathbf{X}_{ij}\mathbf{X}_{ik})) < \xi E(\mathbf{X}_{ij}\mathbf{X}_{ik}) < \infty$, $\forall i, j$. Therefore, $\frac{\partial \mathbf{G}_n(\lambda)}{\partial \lambda}$ converges uniformly to $\frac{\partial \mathbf{G}(\lambda)}{\partial \lambda} \equiv E(f(\mathbf{X}_{1.}\boldsymbol{\lambda})\mathbf{X}'_{1.}\mathbf{X}_{1.})$, which will be nonsingular at $\boldsymbol{\lambda} = \boldsymbol{\beta}$ if $E(\mathbf{X}'_{1.}\mathbf{X}_{1.} \mid f(\mathbf{X}_{1.}\boldsymbol{\lambda}) > 0)$ is nonsingular.

Regarding the applicability of assumption 4 to the MPD-estimation problem, note that

$$n^{1/2}\mathbf{G}_n(\boldsymbol{\beta}) = n^{-1/2} \sum_{i=1}^{n} \mathbf{G}_{ni}(\boldsymbol{\beta}) = n^{-1/2} \sum_{i=1}^{n} \mathbf{X}_{i.}\varepsilon_{i.} \quad (10.A.4)$$

is a scaled sum of *iid* random vectors, each having a zero mean vector and a covariance matrix, $\mathbf{Cov}(\mathbf{X}'_{1.}\varepsilon_1) = E(F(\mathbf{X}_{1.}\boldsymbol{\beta})(1 - F(\mathbf{X}_{1.}\boldsymbol{\beta}))\mathbf{X}'_{1.}\mathbf{X}_{1.})$. Based on the multivariate version of the Lindberg-Levy Central Limit Theorem (Serfling, 1980, p. 28), $n^{-1/2} \sum_{i=1}^{n} \mathbf{X}'_{i.}\varepsilon_i \xrightarrow{d} N(\mathbf{0}, E(F(\mathbf{X}_{1.}\boldsymbol{\beta})(1 - F(\mathbf{X}_{1.}\boldsymbol{\beta})) \mathbf{X}'_{1.}\mathbf{X}_{1.}))$.

## APPENDIX 10.B CONSISTENCY

**Theorem 1:** *Under assumptions i)–iii), the* $\widehat{\text{MPD}}(q, \gamma)$ *estimator* $\hat{\boldsymbol{\lambda}} = \arg_{\lambda}[\mathbf{G}_n(\boldsymbol{\lambda}) = \mathbf{0}]$ *is a consistent estimator of* $\boldsymbol{\beta}$.

*Proof:* The assumptions imply the regularity conditions shown by Yuan and Jennrich (1998) to be sufficient for $\hat{\boldsymbol{\lambda}} = \arg_{\lambda}[\mathbf{G}_n(\boldsymbol{\lambda}) = \mathbf{0}] \xrightarrow{a.s.} \boldsymbol{\beta}$ and thus for $\hat{\boldsymbol{\lambda}}$ to be a (strongly) consistent estimator of, $\boldsymbol{\beta}$.

Consistency of $\mathbf{p}_{\text{MPD}} = \mathbf{p}(\mathbf{x}\boldsymbol{\lambda}_{\text{MPD}})$ follows immediately from the continuity of $\mathbf{p}(\mathbf{x}\boldsymbol{\lambda})$ in $\boldsymbol{\lambda}$.

## APPENDIX 10.C ASYMPTOTIC NORMALITY

**Theorem 2:** *Under assumptions i)–iv), the* $\widehat{\mathrm{MPD}}(q, \gamma)$ *estimator* $\hat{\boldsymbol{\lambda}} = \arg_{\boldsymbol{\lambda}}[\mathbf{G}_n(\boldsymbol{\lambda}) = \mathbf{0}]$ *is asymptotically normally distributed, with limiting distribution* $n^{1/2}(\hat{\boldsymbol{\lambda}} - \boldsymbol{\beta}) \xrightarrow{d} N(\mathbf{0}, \mathbf{A}^{-1}\mathbf{V}\mathbf{A}^{-1})$, *where* $\mathbf{A} = \frac{\partial \mathrm{G}(\boldsymbol{\lambda})}{\partial \boldsymbol{\lambda}} \equiv \mathrm{E}(\mathrm{f}(\mathbf{X}_{1}\boldsymbol{\beta})\mathbf{X}'_{1.}\mathbf{X}_{1.})$ *and* $\mathbf{V} = \mathrm{E}(\mathrm{F}(\mathbf{X}_{1.}\boldsymbol{\beta})(1 - \mathrm{F}(\mathbf{X}_{1.}\boldsymbol{\beta}))\mathbf{X}'_{1.}\mathbf{X}_{1.})$.

*Proof:* Upon establishing the appropriate definitions for **A** and **V** underlying the binary response model specification, the assumptions *i)-iv)* imply the regularity conditions shown by Yuan and Jennrich (1998) to be sufficient for the solution of the estimating equation to have the normal limiting distribution as defined.

# PART V

# OPTIMAL CONVEX DIVERGENCE

In the previous four chapters, we have introduced a flexible family of probability distributions, likelihood functions, estimators, and inference procedures based on information theoretic concepts. The usual case in econometrics is that the noisy indirect data are observed and known and the correct model underlying the genesis of that data is not. In this part of the book, to further address the unknown nature of the model, we propose taking a convex combination of two or more members of the estimators derived from members of the Cressie-Read family of divergence measures and optimize that combination relative to quadratic loss.

ELEVEN

# Choosing the Optimal Divergence under Quadratic Loss

## 11.1 Introduction

In econometric practice, the underlying data sampling process is seldom known. This lack of information has a potential impact on estimator performance and thus the precision of information recovery. A basic limitation of traditional likelihood-divergence approaches is that it is impossible to describe estimators-distributions of an arbitrary form. In this chapter, we recognize this estimation and inference problem and propose a loss function approach to choosing an optimum choice rule from a family of possible likelihood estimators. The resulting optimal likelihood function-estimator combination involves, given a loss function, a convex combination of likelihood functions from the Cressie-Read (CR) family of power divergence measures (PDM) that were introduced and analyzed in Chapters 7 through 10.

The basis for choosing a loss-based choice rule comes from questions asked by Gorban (1984), Gorban and Karlin (2003), and Judge and Mittelhammer (2004). Gorban and Karlin asked which density distributions will emerge if we take a convex combination of two entropy functionals, which, in our context, refers to two members of the CR family. Judge and Mittelhammer asked which combination of econometric models will emerge if we take a convex combination of two design matrices-models, using a quadratic loss choice rule. In this chapter, we change the question and ask which estimation rule will emerge from the CR family of likelihood functions if we take a convex combination of two or more members of the CR family (two or more $\gamma$s), subject to a squared error-quadratic loss measure. In the sections that follow, we develop a framework for seeking an answer to this question. A sampling experiment is used to illustrate the performance of the resulting estimation-choice rules.

In a concluding section, we return to Gorban and Karlin's suggestion of combining entropy functionals-CR likelihood functions and indicate how this leads to useful new distributions.

## 11.2 Econometric Model and the Cressie-Read (CR) Family

Let $\mathbf{Y}$ be an $n \times 1$ random vector and $\mathbf{X}$ be an $n \times k$ random matrix, and assume $\mathbf{Y}$ and $\mathbf{X}$ are linked-modeled, as $\mathbf{Y} = g(\mathbf{X}, \boldsymbol{\beta}) + \boldsymbol{\varepsilon}$. Given this general formulation, consider a simple semiparametric linear statistical model of the form $\mathbf{Y} = \mathbf{X}\boldsymbol{\beta} + \boldsymbol{\varepsilon}$. In this context, assume a random matrix of instrumental variables, $\mathbf{Z}$, whose elements are correlated with $\mathbf{X}$ but uncorrelated with $\boldsymbol{\varepsilon}$. This information is introduced into the statistical model by specifying the sample analog moment condition

$$\mathbf{h}(\mathbf{Y}, \mathbf{X}, \mathbf{Z}; \boldsymbol{\beta}) = n^{-1}[\mathbf{Z}'(\mathbf{Y} - \mathbf{X}\boldsymbol{\beta})] \xrightarrow{p} \mathbf{0}, \qquad (11.2.1)$$

relating to the underlying population moment condition, derived from the orthogonality of $\mathbf{Z}$, and the model noise defined by

$$E[\mathbf{Z}'(\mathbf{Y} - \mathbf{X}\boldsymbol{\beta})] = \mathbf{0}. \qquad (11.2.2)$$

As noted in Chapters 7 and 8, in contrast to traditional moment-based estimators, the information-theoretic approach permits the investigator to employ minimum divergence and maximum likelihood methods for model estimation and inference, without having to choose a specific parametric family of probability densities or likelihood functions based on them. In this context, we again focus on the general Cressie and Read (1984) and Read and Cressie (1988) power divergence family of statistics

$$I(\mathbf{p}, \mathbf{q}, \gamma) = \frac{1}{\gamma(\gamma+1)} \sum_{i=1}^{n} p_i \left[ \left( \frac{p_i}{q_i} \right)^{\gamma} - 1 \right], \qquad (11.2.3)$$

where $\gamma$ is a parameter that indexes members of the CR family and the $q_i$s are interpreted as reference probabilities that satisfy $q_i \in (0, 1), \forall i$ and $\sum_{i=1}^{n} q_i = 1$. This CR family embodies many of the required probability system characteristics, such as additivity and invariance with respect to a monotonic transformation of the divergence model. The minimum power divergence (MPD) estimation problem was formulated in Chapters 7 and 8 as the following extremum-type estimator for $\boldsymbol{\beta}$, for any particular choice of the $\gamma$ parameter:

$$\hat{\boldsymbol{\beta}}(\gamma) = \arg\max_{\boldsymbol{\beta}\in\mathbf{B}} \left[ \ell_E(\boldsymbol{\beta};\gamma) = \max_{\mathbf{p}} \left\{ -I(\mathbf{p},\mathbf{q},\gamma) \mid \sum_{i=1}^{n} p_i \mathbf{Z}'_{i.}(Y_i - \mathbf{X}_{i.}\boldsymbol{\beta}) = \mathbf{0}, \sum_{i=1}^{n} p_i = 1, p_i \geq 0\,\forall i \right\} \right], \tag{11.2.4}$$

where $\ell_{\mathrm{E}}(\boldsymbol{\beta};\gamma)$ can be interpreted as a profiled power divergence function of $\boldsymbol{\beta}$, parameterized by the parameter $\gamma$.[1]

As we noted in Chapter 7, three main integer variants of $I(\mathbf{p},\mathbf{q},\gamma)$ and the associated divergence measures $\ell_{\mathrm{E}}(\boldsymbol{\beta};\gamma)$ have emerged and received explicit attention in the econometrics literature. All are based on the reference distribution specification, $\mathbf{q} = n^{-1}\mathbf{1}_n$, where $\mathbf{1}_n$ denotes an $n \times 1$ vector of unit values. The specification, $\mathrm{CR}(\gamma = -1)$, leads to the traditional maximum empirical likelihood (MEL) objective function, $n^{-1}\sum_{i=1}^{n}\ln(p_i)$, $\mathrm{CR}(\gamma = 0)$ leads to the empirical exponential likelihood objective function, $-\sum_{i=1}^{n} p_i \ln(p_i)$, and $\mathrm{CR}(\gamma = 1)$ defines the log Euclidean or least squares likelihood function, $\frac{n}{2}(\sum_{i=1}^{n}(p_i^2 - \frac{1}{n})) \propto (\mathbf{p} - n^{-1}\mathbf{1}_n)'(\mathbf{p} - n^{-1}\mathbf{1}_n)$.

## 11.3 Choosing a Minimum Loss Estimation Rule

Although the MPD class of cumulative distribution functions (CDFs) provides a large and flexible family of distributions from which to choose a characterization of the inverse probabilities, knowledge of the underlying data sampling distribution remains a challenging impediment to effective empirical applications. In addition, the consistency and asymptotic normality of the MPD solutions rely on appropriate choices of $\mathbf{q}$ and $\gamma$ to specify the MPD distribution that coincides with the underlying data sampling distribution. In regard to $\gamma$, this is fully analogous to the specification issue involved when choosing, in a binary problem, either the normal or logistic distribution. In the case of the binary response model, discussed in Chapters 9 and 10, we were able to follow an empirical maximum likelihood approach for choosing $\mathbf{q}$ and $\gamma$, as well as for choosing the parameter vector

[1] Similar in concept to a profile likelihood function, the profile divergence measure (11.2.4) has the $\mathbf{p}$ variables "maximized out" of the divergence measure for any given values of $\boldsymbol{\beta}$ *and* $\gamma$. Some authors refer to this as "concentrating out" some of the variables in an objective function.

$\boldsymbol{\beta}$ in the linear index model. For more general stochastic inverse problems, in this chapter, we consider a generalization of the MPD approach for addressing the choice of the underlying probability distribution of the data observations.

Because information regarding the reference distribution is often sketchy, in developing a likelihood choice framework, we follow a least favorable choice rule and assume that $\mathbf{q}$ is uniformly distributed, so that $q_i = n^{-1}, \ \forall i$. Conditional on this reference distribution choice, in the context of a linear model specification and moment conditions based on the orthogonality of instruments and noise, in this section, we propose an operational basis for choosing $\gamma$ and moving toward mitigating the unknown sampling distribution problem. What we seek, given a sample of data, is a basis for choosing a loss-minimizing estimation rule.

### 11.3.1 Distance–Divergence Measures

In Section 11.2, we used the CR power divergence measure

$$\mathbf{CR} = I(\mathbf{p}, \mathbf{q}, \gamma) = \frac{1}{\gamma(1+\gamma)} \sum_{i=1}^{N} \left( p_i \left[ \left( \frac{p_i}{q_i} \right)^{\gamma} - 1 \right] \right) \tag{11.3.1}$$

to define a family of likelihood functions. Given this family of likelihood functions, one might emulate Gorban (1984) and Gorban and Karlin (2003) and consider a parametric family of concave entropy-likelihood functions, which satisfy additivity and trace conditions. Using the CR divergence measures, this parametric family is essentially the linear convex combination of the cases in which $\gamma = 0$ and $\gamma = -1$. This family is tractable analytically and provides a basis for joining (combining) statistically independent subsystems. When the base measure of the reference distribution $\mathbf{q}$ is taken to be a uniform probability density function (PDF), we arrive at a one-parameter family of additive convex Lyapunov functions (Weisstein [Math World] and Khalil 1996). In this context, one would be effectively considering the convex combination of the MEL and maximum empirical exponential likelihood (MEEL) measures discussed in Chapters 5 and 6. From the standpoint of extremum-minimization with respect to $\mathbf{p}$, the generalized divergence family reduces to

$$S_{\alpha}^{*}(q) = -\sum_{i=1}^{n} ((1-\alpha) p_i \ln(p_i/q_i) - \alpha q_i \ln p_i), \tag{11.3.2a}$$

which reduces further in the case of uniform $\mathbf{q}$ to

$$S_a^* = \sum_{i-1}^{n} (-(1-\alpha)p_i \ln(p_i) + \alpha \ln(p_i)), \quad 0 \le \alpha \le 1. \quad (11.3.2.b)$$

In the limit, as $\alpha \to 0$, the Kullback-Leibler or minimum I divergence $I(\mathbf{p} \parallel \mathbf{q})$ of the probability mass function $\mathbf{p}$, with respect to $\mathbf{q}$, is recovered. As $\alpha \to 1$, the MEL stochastic inverse problem solution results. *This generalized family of divergence measures permits a broadening of the canonical distribution functions and provides a framework for developing a loss-minimizing estimation rule.* In an extremum estimation context, when $\alpha = 1/2$, this results in what is known in the literature as Jeffrey's J-divergence (Grendar and Grendar, 2000). In this case, the full objective function, J-divergence $J(\mathbf{p} \parallel \mathbf{q}) = I(\mathbf{p} \parallel \mathbf{q}) + I(\mathbf{q} \parallel \mathbf{p})$, is just a convex combination of I-divergence $I(\mathbf{p} \parallel \mathbf{q})$ and the reverse I-divergence $I(\mathbf{q} \parallel \mathbf{p})$.

To give a simple overview of the convex combination minimizing estimation rule, a special-case optimum-loss minimizing combining rule is presented in Appendix 11.A. This special case provides a framework for dealing with the unknown nature of the underlying probability distribution function. In line with the complex nature of the problem, in the sections to follow, we demonstrate alternative convex estimation rules, which seek to choose among MPD-type estimators to minimize quadratic risk (QR).

### 11.3.2 A Minimum Quadratic Risk Estimation Rule

In this section, we use the well-known squared error loss criteria and associated QR function to make optimal use of a given set of discrete alternatives for the CR goodness-of-fit measures and associated estimators for $\boldsymbol{\beta}$. The method seeks to define the convex combination of a set of estimators for $\boldsymbol{\beta}$ that minimizes QR, where each estimator is defined by the solution to the extremum problem

$$\hat{\boldsymbol{\beta}}(\gamma) = \arg\max_{\boldsymbol{\beta} \in \mathbf{B}} \left[ \max_{\mathbf{p}} \left\{ -I(\mathbf{p}, \mathbf{q}, \gamma) | \sum_{i=1}^{n} p_i \mathbf{Z}_{i.}' (Y_i - \mathbf{X}_{i.} \boldsymbol{\beta}) = \mathbf{0}, \right.\right.$$
$$\left.\left. \sum_{i=1}^{n} p_i = 1, \quad p_i \ge 0 \, \forall i \right\} \right]. \quad (11.3.3)$$

The squared error loss function is defined by $\ell(\hat{\boldsymbol{\beta}}, \boldsymbol{\beta}) = (\hat{\boldsymbol{\beta}} - \boldsymbol{\beta})'(\hat{\boldsymbol{\beta}} - \boldsymbol{\beta})$ and has the corresponding QR function given by

$$\rho(\hat{\boldsymbol{\beta}}, \boldsymbol{\beta}) = E[\ell(\hat{\boldsymbol{\beta}}, \boldsymbol{\beta})] = E[(\hat{\boldsymbol{\beta}} - \boldsymbol{\beta})'(\hat{\boldsymbol{\beta}} - \boldsymbol{\beta})]. \qquad (11.3.4)$$

The convex combination of estimators is defined by

$$\bar{\boldsymbol{\beta}}(\alpha) = \sum_{j=1}^{J} \alpha_j \hat{\boldsymbol{\beta}}(\gamma_j), \textit{ where } \alpha_j \geq 0 \; \forall j, \textit{ and } \sum_{j=1}^{J} \alpha_j = 1. \qquad (11.3.5)$$

The optimum use of the discrete alternatives under QR is determined by choosing the particular convex combination of the estimators that minimizes QR, as

$$\bar{\boldsymbol{\beta}}(\hat{\alpha}) = \sum_{j=1}^{J} \hat{\alpha}_j \hat{\boldsymbol{\beta}}(\gamma_j), \text{ where } \hat{\alpha} = \underset{\alpha \in CH}{\arg\min}\{\rho(\bar{\boldsymbol{\beta}}(\alpha), \boldsymbol{\beta})\}, \qquad (11.3.6)$$

and $CH$ denotes the $J$-dimensional convex hull of possibilities for the $J \times 1$ $\boldsymbol{\alpha}$ vector, defined by the nonnegativity and adding-up conditions represented in (11.3.5).

This represents one possible method of addressing the combining issue, relative to an appropriate choice of the gamma parameter, in the definition of the CR power divergence criterion.

### 11.3.3 The Case of Two CR Alternatives

In this section, we consider the case in which there are two discrete alternative CR measures of interest. In this context, the analyst wishes to make optimal use of the information contained in the two associated estimators of $\boldsymbol{\beta}$, $\hat{\boldsymbol{\beta}}(\gamma_1)$ and $\hat{\boldsymbol{\beta}}(\gamma_2)$. The corresponding QR function may be written as

$$\begin{aligned}\rho(\bar{\boldsymbol{\beta}}(\alpha), \boldsymbol{\beta}) = E[[\alpha(\hat{\boldsymbol{\beta}}(\gamma_1) - \boldsymbol{\beta}) + (1-\alpha)(\hat{\boldsymbol{\beta}}(\gamma_2) - \boldsymbol{\beta})]'[\alpha(\hat{\boldsymbol{\beta}}(\gamma_1) - \boldsymbol{\beta}) \\ + (1-\alpha)(\hat{\boldsymbol{\beta}}(\gamma_2) - \boldsymbol{\beta})]] \qquad (11.3.7)\end{aligned}$$

and can be represented in terms of the QR functions of $\hat{\boldsymbol{\beta}}(\gamma_1)$ and $\hat{\boldsymbol{\beta}}(\gamma_2)$ as

$$\begin{aligned}\rho(\bar{\boldsymbol{\beta}}(\alpha), \boldsymbol{\beta}) = \alpha^2 \rho(\hat{\boldsymbol{\beta}}(\gamma_1), \boldsymbol{\beta}) + (1-\alpha)^2 \rho(\hat{\boldsymbol{\beta}}(\gamma_2), \boldsymbol{\beta}) \\ + 2\alpha(1-\alpha) E[(\hat{\boldsymbol{\beta}}(\gamma_1) - \boldsymbol{\beta})'(\hat{\boldsymbol{\beta}}(\gamma_2) - \boldsymbol{\beta})]. \qquad (11.3.8)\end{aligned}$$

To minimize $\rho(\bar{\boldsymbol{\beta}}(\alpha), \boldsymbol{\beta})$, the first-order condition, with respect to $\alpha$, is given by

$$\begin{aligned}\frac{d\rho(\bar{\boldsymbol{\beta}}(\alpha), \boldsymbol{\beta})}{d\alpha} &= 2\alpha\rho(\hat{\boldsymbol{\beta}}(\gamma_1), \boldsymbol{\beta}) - 2(1-\alpha)\rho(\hat{\boldsymbol{\beta}}(\gamma_2), \boldsymbol{\beta}) \\ &\quad + 2(1-2\alpha)E[(\hat{\boldsymbol{\beta}}(\gamma_1) - \boldsymbol{\beta})'(\hat{\boldsymbol{\beta}}(\gamma_2) - \boldsymbol{\beta})] = 0 \quad (11.3.9)\end{aligned}$$

Solving for the optimal value of $\alpha$ yields

$$\hat{\alpha} = \frac{\rho(\hat{\boldsymbol{\beta}}(\gamma_2), \boldsymbol{\beta}) - E[(\hat{\boldsymbol{\beta}}(\gamma_1) - \boldsymbol{\beta})'(\hat{\boldsymbol{\beta}}(\gamma_2) - \boldsymbol{\beta})]}{\rho(\hat{\boldsymbol{\beta}}(\gamma_1), \boldsymbol{\beta}) + \rho(\hat{\boldsymbol{\beta}}(\gamma_2), \boldsymbol{\beta}) - 2E[(\hat{\boldsymbol{\beta}}(\gamma_1) - \boldsymbol{\beta})'(\hat{\boldsymbol{\beta}}(\gamma_2) - \boldsymbol{\beta})]}, \quad (11.3.10)$$

and the optimal convex-combined estimator is defined as

$$\bar{\boldsymbol{\beta}}(\hat{\alpha}) = \hat{\alpha}\hat{\boldsymbol{\beta}}(\gamma_1) + (1-\hat{\alpha})\hat{\boldsymbol{\beta}}(\gamma_2). \quad (11.3.11)$$

By construction, $\bar{\boldsymbol{\beta}}(\hat{\alpha})$ is QR superior to either $\hat{\boldsymbol{\beta}}(\gamma_1)$ or $\hat{\boldsymbol{\beta}}(\gamma_2)$, unless the optimal convex combination resides at one of the boundaries for $\alpha$, or the two estimators have identical risks and $E[(\hat{\boldsymbol{\beta}}(\gamma_1) - \boldsymbol{\beta})'(\hat{\boldsymbol{\beta}}(\gamma_2) - \boldsymbol{\beta})] = 0$. In any case, the resulting estimator $\bar{\boldsymbol{\beta}}(\hat{\alpha})$ is certainly no worse, QR-wise, than either $\hat{\boldsymbol{\beta}}(\gamma_1)$ or $\hat{\boldsymbol{\beta}}(\gamma_2)$.

### 11.3.4 Empirical Calculation of $\alpha$

To implement the optimal convex combination of estimators empirically, a value for $\hat{\alpha}$ in (11.3.10) is needed. The calculation of the exact $\hat{\alpha}$ value in (11.3.10) requires unknown parameters as well as unknown probability distributions. Thus, one must seek an estimate of $\hat{\alpha}$ based on sample observations. Working toward a useful estimate for $\hat{\alpha}$, note that

$$\begin{aligned}&E[(\hat{\boldsymbol{\beta}}(\gamma_1) - \hat{\boldsymbol{\beta}}(\gamma_2))'(\hat{\boldsymbol{\beta}}(\gamma_1) - \hat{\boldsymbol{\beta}}(\gamma_2))] \\ &\quad = E[(\hat{\boldsymbol{\beta}}(\gamma_1) - \boldsymbol{\beta})'(\hat{\boldsymbol{\beta}}(\gamma_1) - \boldsymbol{\beta})] + E[(\hat{\boldsymbol{\beta}}(\gamma_2) - \boldsymbol{\beta})'(\hat{\boldsymbol{\beta}}(\gamma_2) - \boldsymbol{\beta})] \\ &\qquad - 2E[(\hat{\boldsymbol{\beta}}(\gamma_1) - \boldsymbol{\beta})'(\hat{\boldsymbol{\beta}}(\gamma_2) - \boldsymbol{\beta})] \\ &\quad = \rho(\hat{\boldsymbol{\beta}}(\gamma_1), \boldsymbol{\beta}) + \rho(\hat{\boldsymbol{\beta}}(\gamma_2), \boldsymbol{\beta}) \\ &\qquad - 2E[(\hat{\boldsymbol{\beta}}(\gamma_1) - \boldsymbol{\beta})'(\hat{\boldsymbol{\beta}}(\gamma_2) - \boldsymbol{\beta})]. \quad (11.3.12)\end{aligned}$$

Thus, an unbiased estimate of the denominator term in (11.3.10) is given directly by calculating $(\hat{\boldsymbol{\beta}}(\gamma_1) - \hat{\boldsymbol{\beta}}(\gamma_2))'(\hat{\boldsymbol{\beta}}(\gamma_1) - \hat{\boldsymbol{\beta}}(\gamma_2))$. Given the consistency of both estimators, this value would consistently estimate the denominator of (11.3.10) as well.

Deriving an estimate of the numerator in (11.3.10) is challenging. The complication stems from the fact that, in general, the estimators $\hat{\beta}(\gamma)$ are all biased. Thus, neither the risk term nor the subtracted expectation of the cross-product term in (11.3.10) can be simplified. This complication persists, even under independence of the two estimators such as when the estimators are calculated from independent samples. Even under independence, the risk function $\rho(\hat{\beta}(\gamma_2), \beta)$ does not merely simplify to a function of variances as in Judge and Mittelhammer (2004). The term $E[(\hat{\beta}(\gamma_1) - \beta)'(\hat{\beta}(\gamma_2) - \beta)]$ remains nonzero and, in fact, is equal to a cross-product of bias vectors, $bias(\hat{\beta}(\gamma_1))'\, bias(\hat{\beta}(\gamma_2))$. However, assuming that moment conditions are correctly specified, the $\hat{\beta}(\gamma)$ estimators are consistent under regularity conditions no more stringent than the usual conditions imposed to obtain consistency in the generalized methods of moments (GMM) or the classical linear models. Thus, as an approximation, one might ignore the bias terms because they converge to zero as $n$ increases.[2]

Ignoring the bias terms and assuming that the estimators $\hat{\beta}(\gamma_1)$ and $\hat{\beta}(\gamma_2)$ are based on two independent samples of data, the expression for the optimal $\alpha$ simplifies to the following:

$$\hat{\alpha} = \frac{tr(Cov(\hat{\beta}(\gamma_2)))}{tr(Cov(\hat{\beta}(\gamma_1))) + tr(Cov(\hat{\beta}(\gamma_2)))}. \tag{11.3.13}$$

In effect, the use of this $\hat{\alpha}$ in forming a convex combination of the two estimators can be viewed as pursuing an objective of minimizing the variation in the resultant estimator (11.3.11), under the assumption that the biases of the estimators are less important.

A question that remains is the sampling performance of the estimators based on the estimated value $\hat{\alpha}$. To provide some perspective on the answer to this question, in the next section, we present the results of a sampling experiment that implements (11.3.13) in choosing a convex combination of the estimators $\hat{\beta}(\gamma = -1)$ and $\hat{\beta}(\gamma = 0)$. The objective is to define a new estimator that is a combination of both estimators and that performs better then either in terms of QR.

## 11.4 Finite Sample Implication

To illustrate finite sample performance of a convex combination of $\hat{\beta}(\gamma = -1)$ and $\hat{\beta}(\gamma = 0)$, we consider a simple data sampling process

[2] It is an open research question as to how the numerator of (11.3.10) can be appropriately estimated to operationalize the minimum QR estimator in the current application.

involving an instrumental variable model similar to that used by Hahn and Hausman (2002). The sampling model is

$$\begin{aligned} y_i &= x_i\beta + \varepsilon_i \\ x_i &= z_{i}\,\delta + v_i, \quad i = 1, \ldots, n \end{aligned} \tag{11.4.1}$$

where $y_i$ denotes the variable of interest, $x_i$ denotes a scalar endogenous regressor, $z_{i.}$ denotes a $1 \times 2$ row vector of instrumental variables, and $n$ denotes sample size. In the sampling experiment, the value of $\beta$ is set equal to 1, and $z_i$ and $(\varepsilon_i, v_i)'$ are independent and *iid* with probability distributions, $N(\mathbf{0}, \mathbf{I}_2)$, and, $N([\begin{smallmatrix}0\\0\end{smallmatrix}], [\begin{smallmatrix}1 & \tau\\ \tau & 1\end{smallmatrix}])$, respectively. The theoretical first stage $R^2$ is given by $R^2 = \frac{\delta'\delta}{\delta'\delta+1}$ and we let $\delta = [\begin{smallmatrix}\xi\\ \xi\end{smallmatrix}]$ so that $R^2 = \frac{2\xi^2}{2\xi^2+1}$. In this sample design, the parameter, $\tau$, determines the degree of endogeneity and $R^2$ determines the strength of the instruments $z_{i.}$ for $x_i$, with $\xi = (\frac{R^2}{2(1-R^2)})^{1/2}$. We examine sample of sizes $n = 100$ *and* 250, with $\tau = 0.5$ and $R^2 = 0.5$.

The covariance matrices used to implement the optimal convex combination weight in (11.3.13) (which are variances in this case because the $\hat{\boldsymbol{\beta}}(\gamma)$s are scalars) are of the following form (see Mittelhammer, Judge, and Miller 2000, 483–484):

$$\begin{aligned} \hat{\mathrm{var}}(\hat{\boldsymbol{\beta}}(\gamma)) = {} & \left( \left[ \sum_{i=1}^{n} \hat{p}_i(\gamma)\, x_i z_{i.} \right] \left[ \sum_{i=1}^{n} \hat{p}_i(\gamma) \left(y_i - x_i\hat{\beta}(\gamma)\right)^2 z'_{i.} z_{i.} \right]^{-1} \right. \\ & \left. \times \left[ \sum_{i=1}^{n} \hat{p}_i(\gamma)\, x_i z'_{i.} \right] \right)^{-1}, \end{aligned} \tag{11.4.2}$$

where the $\hat{p}_i(\gamma)$s are the data or probability weights calculated in the solution to the estimation problem, when either $\gamma = -1$ *or* $\gamma = 0$. The calculated convex weight (11.4.11) simplifies to $\hat{\alpha} = \frac{\mathrm{var}(\hat{\boldsymbol{\beta}}(\gamma=0))}{\mathrm{var}(\hat{\boldsymbol{\beta}}(\gamma=-1))+\mathrm{var}(\hat{\boldsymbol{\beta}}(\gamma=0))}$, and the convex combination estimator is given by $\bar{\beta}(\hat{\alpha}) = \hat{\alpha}\hat{\beta}(\gamma = -1) + (1 - \hat{\alpha})\hat{\beta}(\gamma = 0)$.

The results for the sampling experiment are presented in Table 11.4.1. It is evident that across all scenarios, the convex combination of the $\hat{\beta}(\gamma = -1)$ and $\hat{\beta}(\gamma = 0)$ estimators was substantially superior under quadratic loss to either of the individual estimators taken in isolation. It is also evident that the risks of the individual estimators are quite close in magnitude to one another across all scenarios. The MEL $(\gamma = -1)$ estimator is generally slightly better than the estimator based on the Kullback–Leibler $(\gamma = 0)$ distance measure for the larger sample size of 250 but not uniformly for the smaller sample size of 100. Given the similarity in mean squared error

Table 11.4.1. *MSE Results for Convex Combinations of* $\hat{\beta}(\gamma = -1)$ *and* $\hat{\beta}(\gamma = 0)$

| Scenario $\{n, \tau, R^2\}$ | MSE $(\hat{\beta}(\gamma = -1))$ | MSE $(\hat{\beta}(\gamma = 0))$ | $\bar{\hat{\alpha}}(\gamma = -1)$ | std $(\hat{\alpha})$ | MSE $(\bar{\beta}(\hat{\alpha}))$ |
|---|---|---|---|---|---|
| 100, 0.25, 0.75 | 0.00343 | 0.00364 | 0.49712 | 0.29082 | 0.00180 |
| 100, 0.5, 0.5 | 0.01129 | 0.01113 | 0.49996 | 0.07340 | 0.00528 |
| 100, 0.75, 0.25 | 0.03801 | 0.03159 | 0.48670 | 0.30753 | 0.02105 |
| 250, 0.25, 0.75 | 0.00122 | 0.00136 | 0.49978 | 0.01591 | 0.00062 |
| 250, 0.5, 0.5 | 0.00437 | 0.00452 | 0.50158 | 0.02813 | 0.00219 |
| 250, 0.75, 0.25 | 0.01309 | 0.01323 | 0.50031 | 0.07018 | 0.00639 |

(MSE) performance, it is not surprising that the optimal $\alpha$s for forming the convex combination had an average value in the neighborhood of 0.5. As the degree of endogeneity increases (i.e., when $\tau$ increases) and the effectiveness of the instruments decreases (i.e., when $R^2$ decreases), the QR of all of the estimators increases, but the overall performance of the estimators, and especially the convex combination estimator, remains very good.

## 11.5 Estimator Choice, $\gamma = (1, 0, -1)$

In Section 11.4, we considered the one-parameter family of additive convex functions for the limiting form of the two special cases, $\gamma = (0, -1)$. In this section, we recognize that under the CR family (11.3.1), three integer variants of $I(\mathbf{p}, \mathbf{q}, \gamma)$ and the associated power divergence functions have received attention in the econometric literature. Under a uniform reference distribution, we use the information in the three members of the CR family in obtaining a solution to the stochastic inverse problem. In this context, consider generalizing the convex combination of estimators to include $\gamma = 1$, the log Euclidean-linear probability model. This means that we now use (11.3.11) with $J = 3$ and examine convex combinations of estimators derived from three members of the CR family corresponding to $\gamma = (1, 0, -1)$, as

$$\begin{aligned}\bar{\boldsymbol{\beta}}(\hat{\alpha}) &= \hat{\alpha}_1 \hat{\boldsymbol{\beta}}(\gamma = -1) + \hat{\alpha}_2 \hat{\boldsymbol{\beta}}(\gamma = 0) \\ &\quad + (1 - \hat{\alpha}_1 - \hat{\alpha}_2)\hat{\boldsymbol{\beta}}(\gamma = 1),\end{aligned} \tag{11.5.1}$$

where $\hat{\alpha}_i \geq 0$, $i = 1, 2$ and $\hat{\alpha}_1 + \hat{\alpha}_2 \in [0, 1]$. This formulation adds the possibility, when in the limit $\alpha_1, \alpha_2 \to 0$, that the linear probability CDF is recovered and enlarges the members of the CR family of probability distributions that may be accessed relative to (11.3.11).

In extending the formulation of (11.3.11), the conceptual objective is now to choose $\boldsymbol{\alpha} = [\alpha_1, \alpha_2, \alpha_3]'$ to minimize the quadratic form $\boldsymbol{\alpha}' \text{MSE}[\hat{\boldsymbol{\beta}}(\gamma), \gamma = -1, 0, 1]\boldsymbol{\alpha}$ in the mean square error matrix MSE $[\hat{\boldsymbol{\beta}}(\gamma), \gamma = -1, 0, 1]$, where $\mathbf{1}_3'\boldsymbol{\alpha} = 1$ and $\boldsymbol{\alpha} \geq [\mathbf{0}]$. Using the independence assumptions made in Section 11.4 and ignoring the bias effects, which dissipate in the limit as sample size $n$ increases, the optimal choices of the convex weights are given as follows:

$$\alpha_i = \frac{tr(\text{cov}(\hat{\boldsymbol{\beta}}(\gamma_j)))tr(\text{cov}(\hat{\boldsymbol{\beta}}(\gamma_k)))}{\sum_{j=1}^{3}\sum_{k>j} tr(\text{cov}(\hat{\boldsymbol{\beta}}(\gamma_j)))tr(\text{cov}(\hat{\boldsymbol{\beta}}(\gamma_k)))}, \quad \text{for } i \neq j \neq k. \tag{11.5.2}$$

## 11.6 Sampling Performance

In this section, we continue to use the data sampling process that was described in Section 11.4 and, in fact, we use precisely the same data that was generated for defining the convex combination of the two estimators. We use the values of the $\alpha_i$s that are defined in (11.5.1) based on the covariance matrices defined in (11.4.2). The results provided in Table 11.6.1 represent an expanded version of Table 11.4.1. The results for the $\hat{\beta}(\gamma = 1)$ estimator are added, and the results for the convex combination of the three estimators replace the results for the combination of the two estimators.

The qualitative nature of the results emulates the results that were observed for the convex combination of the two estimators in the previous section. In particular, it is clear that across all scenarios, the convex combination of the $\hat{\beta}(\gamma = -1)$, $\hat{\beta}(\gamma = 0)$, and $\hat{\beta}(\gamma = 1)$ estimators was substantially MSE superior to either of the individual estimators taken in isolation. It is also evident that the MSE of the individual estimators remains quite close to one another in magnitude across all of the scenarios, with the MSE of the $\hat{\beta}(\gamma = 1)$ estimator being similar to the MSEs of the other two estimators.

Given the similarity in MSE performance across all three estimator alternatives, it is not surprising that the optimal $\alpha$s for forming the convex combination had an average value in the neighborhood of 0.33. As the degree of endogeneity increases (i.e., when $\tau$ increases) and the effectiveness of the instruments decreases (i.e., when $R^2$ decreases), the MSEs of all of the estimators increase. However, the overall sampling performance of the estimators, including especially the convex combination estimator, remains very good.

Table 11.6.1. *MSE Results for Convex Combinations of* $\hat{\beta}(\gamma = -1)$, $\hat{\beta}(\gamma = 0)$, *and* $\hat{\beta}(\gamma = 1)$

| Scenario $\{n, \tau, R^2\}$ | MSE $(\hat{\beta}(\gamma = -1))$ | MSE $(\hat{\beta}(\gamma = 0))$ | MSE $(\hat{\beta}(\gamma = 1))$ | $\bar{\hat{\alpha}}(\gamma = -1)$ (std $(\hat{\alpha})$) | $\hat{\alpha}(\gamma = 0)$ (std $(\hat{\alpha})$) | MSE $(\bar{\beta}(\hat{\alpha}))$ |
|---|---|---|---|---|---|---|
| 100, 0.25, 0.75 | 0.00343 | 0.00364 | 0.00352 | 0.32208 (0.07723) | 0.32409 (0.04275) | 0.00119 |
| 100, 0.5, 0.5 | 0.01129 | 0.01113 | 0.01167 | 0.32544 (0.06211) | 0.32328 (0.04555) | 0.00365 |
| 100, 0.75, 0.25 | 0.03801 | 0.03159 | 0.03609 | 0.33751 (0.35344) | 0.32406 (0.25189) | 0.01055 |
| 250, 0.25, 0.75 | 0.00122 | 0.00136 | 0.00142 | 0.32947 (0.01166) | 0.32975 (0.01163) | 0.00045 |
| 250, 0.5, 0.5 | 0.00437 | 0.00452 | 0.00419 | 0.33067 (0.02032) | 0.32865 (0.02110) | 0.00142 |
| 250, 0.75, 0.25 | 0.01309 | 0.01323 | 0.01310 | 0.33295 (0.09051) | 0.32990 (0.06104) | 0.00491 |

## 11.7 Concluding Remarks

In this chapter, we suggested estimation possibilities not accessible by considering individual members of the CR family. This was achieved by taking a convex combination of estimators associated with multiple members of the CR family, under minimum quadratic loss. Sampling experiments are conducted to illustrate the finite sample performance of the resulting estimation rules. The positive sampling performance of these initial convex combining formulations suggests possibilities for achieving improved estimator performance for members of the CR family.

Finally, in this chapter, we recognize that relevant statistical distributions underlying data sampling processes that result from solving MPD-estimation problems may not always be well described by popular integer choices for the power parameter in the CR divergence measure family. Building on the work of Gorban (1984) noted in Section 11.3, we note that it is possible to derive a one-parameter family of appropriate goodness-of-fit functions for describing certain statistical systems distributions. In the Gorban formulation, the resulting one-parameter family is essentially a convex combination of the CR integer functionals, $\gamma \to 0$ and $\gamma \to 1$. This one-parameter family of additive-trace form CR divergence functions leads to an additional rich set of distributions that broadens the set of probability distributions that can be derived from the CR power divergence family. With this new family, one can address, for example, long, nonexponential tails of the probability distribution. This new family of goodness-of-fit functions appears in a natural way as a subset of the CR family and is a topic of future research.

In closing, we should acknowledge the tentative nature of the formulations and sampling results presented in this chapter. We debated whether to include this chapter and decided, even at this preliminary stage, that presenting the ideas and corresponding sampling results might provide the impetus for additional research along these lines.

## 11.8 Selected References

Cressie, N. and T. Read (1984), "Multinomial Goodness of Fit Tests," *Journal of the Royal Statistical Society, Series B* **46**:440–464.

Gorban, A., P. Gorban, and G. Judge (2010), "Entropy: The Markov Ordering Approach." *Entropy*, **12**:1145–1193.

Gorban, A. N. (1984), *Equilibrium Encircling: Equations of Chemical Kinetics and Their Thermodynamic Analysis*, Nauka: Novosibirsk.

Gorban, A. N. and Karlin, I. V. (2003), "Family of Additive Entropy Functions out of Thermodynamic Limit," *Physical Review E*, **67**:016104.

Grendar, M. and M. Grendar (2000), "On the Probabilistic Rationale of I-Divergence and J-Divergence Minimization," arXiv:math/08037.

Hahn, J. and J. Hausman (2002), "A New Specification Test for the Validity of Instrumental Variables," *Econometrica*, **70**:163–189.

Haubold, H., A. Mathai, and R. Saxena (2004), "Boltzmann-Gibbs Entropy versus Tsallis Entropy," *Astrophysics and Space Science*, **290**:241–245.

James, W. and C. Stein (1961), "Estimation with Quadratic Loss," *Proceedings of Fourth Berkeley Symposium on Statistics and Probability*, pp. 361–379, University of California Press, Berkeley.

Jeffrey, H. (1948), *Theory of Probability*, 2nd ed., Oxford: Oxford University Press.

Judge, G. and M. E. Bock (1978), *The Statistical Implication of Pre-Test and Stein-Rule Estimators*, Amsterdam: North Holland.

Judge, G. and R. Mittelhammer (2004), "A Semiparametric Basis for Combining Estimation Problems under Quadratic Loss," *Journal of the American Statistical Association*, **99**:479–487.

Khalil, K. (1996), *Nonlinear Systems*, Englewood Cliffs, NJ: Prentice Hall.

Mittelhammer, R., G. Judge, and D. Miller (2000), *Econometric Foundations*, New York: Cambridge University Press.

Pardo, L. (2006), *Statistical Inference Based on Divergence Measures*, Boca Raton, FL: Chapman and Hall.

Read, T. R. and N. A. Cressie (1988), *Goodness of Fit Statistics for Discrete Multivariate Data*, New York: Springer Verlag.

Renyi, A. (1961), "On Measures of Entropy and Information," *Proceedings of the Fourth Berkeley Symposium on Mathematical Statistics and Probability*, pp. 547–561, University of California Press, Berkeley–Los Angeles.

Renyi, A. (1970), *Probability Theory*. Amsterdam: North-Holland.

Tsallis, C. (1988), "Possible Generalizations of the Boltzmann-Gibbs Statistics," *Journal of Statistical Physics*, **52**:479–487.

## APPENDIX 11.A A $\gamma = (0, -1)$ SPECIAL CASE CONVEX ESTIMATION RULE

In the context of the CR family (11.3.1), consider for expository purposes a convex linear combination of the statistically independent systems

$$\bar{\beta}(\alpha) = \alpha\hat{\beta} + (1-\alpha)\tilde{\beta}, \tag{11.A.1}$$

and the estimators are unbiased with covariance, $\text{cov}[{}^{\hat{\beta}}_{\tilde{\beta}}] = [\Sigma_{\Phi}]$. If we consider the QR $E[(\bar{\beta}_\alpha - \beta)'(\bar{\beta}_\alpha - \beta)]$, the loss function of the estimator $\bar{\beta}(\alpha) = E\|\bar{\beta}_\alpha - \beta\|^2 = \rho(\bar{\beta}(\alpha))$ is given by

$$\begin{aligned}\rho(\bar{\beta}(\alpha)) &= E[[\alpha(\hat{\beta}-\beta)+(1-\alpha)(\tilde{\beta}-\beta)]'[\alpha(\hat{\beta}-\beta)+(1-\alpha)(\tilde{\beta}-\beta)]]\\ &= \alpha^2 tr(\boldsymbol{\Sigma}) + (1-\alpha)^2 tr(\boldsymbol{\Phi}).\end{aligned} \tag{11.A.2}$$

To minimize $\rho(\bar{\beta}(\alpha))$, the first-order condition for $\alpha$ is

$$\alpha^* = 1 - \frac{tr(\boldsymbol{\Sigma})}{tr(\boldsymbol{\Sigma}) + tr(\boldsymbol{\Phi})}. \tag{11.A.3}$$

If the second-order condition is fulfilled, the estimator

$$\bar{\beta}(\alpha^*) = \alpha^*\hat{\beta} + (1-\alpha^*)\tilde{\beta} \tag{11.A.4}$$

is mean squared error superior to $\hat{\beta}$ or $\tilde{\beta}$.

Given the theoretical optimum, $\alpha^*$, to be operational, we need a basis for estimating $\alpha^*$. One way to do this is to use an unbiased estimator of the denominator in (11.A.3) or, in other words, an unbiased estimator of

$$E[(\hat{\beta} - \tilde{\beta})'(\hat{\beta} - \tilde{\beta})]. \tag{11.A.5}$$

Given unbiased and consistent estimators for $\Sigma$ and $\Phi$, an estimator of the optimal $\alpha$ is in the form of

$$\hat{\alpha}^* = 1 - \frac{tr(\hat{\boldsymbol{\Sigma}})}{(\hat{\beta} - \tilde{\beta})'(\hat{\beta} - \tilde{\beta})}, \tag{11.A.6}$$

and the optimal estimator under squared error loss (SEL) is

$$\bar{\beta}(\alpha^*) = \hat{\beta} - \frac{tr(\hat{\boldsymbol{\Sigma}})}{\|\hat{\beta} - \tilde{\beta}\|^2}(\hat{\beta} - \tilde{\beta}). \tag{11.A.7}$$

Not surprisingly, this comes out in the form of a Stein-like estimator (James and Stein, 1961; Judge and Bock, 1978), where given a sample of data, shrinkage is from $\hat{\beta}$ toward $\tilde{\beta}$. Given the squared error loss function, the shrinkage is determined by the relative bias-variance trade-off.

TWELVE

# Epilogue

Building on the traditional conceptual econometric base, this book has been concerned with how one goes about learning from a sample of indirect noisy observations and the corresponding econometric model, defined in terms of an ill-posed inverse problem. To develop a plausible basis for reasoning that recognizes the generally limited knowledge characteristics of the econometric enterprise, we have demonstrated a range of nontraditional methods of information recovery. The nature of indirect noisy observational sample data, together with an evaluation of the often meager informational base that exists on which to specify an empirical econometric model, leads naturally to changes in the way econometric models should be defined and the method by which estimation and inference can be conducted. In addressing this state of affairs, we introduced families of divergence measures and associated new families of likelihood functions to provide alternative bases for estimation and inference in a range of econometric problems. These methods have evolved over the past two decades and are gradually being evaluated by the arrow of time.

As noted in Chapter 1, many traditional econometric methods are not designed to cope with the special characteristics of economic data and the implied corresponding ill-posed stochastic inverse problem. A case in point is current attempts in economics to identify causal effects from observed data–statistical evidence. From an econometric point of view, the causal effects problem (determining unknown causes) involves the solution to a stochastic inverse problem based on indirect noisy observations of their effects. This sounds a lot like the semiparametric stochastic estimation and inference problem we introduced and sought a solution to in Chapters 4 and 5 and developed in the remaining chapters of the book.

Starting with Chapter 4, we have, in an information theoretic context, developed a widely varying collection of likelihood functions whose members constitute a complete class of potential probability distributions satisfying standard regression error orthogonality conditions. The resulting likelihood functions are both consistent with parametric specifications of a range of econometric models and minimally power divergent from possible reference distributions for the unknown and unobservable probabilities. The corresponding class of statistical models and associated estimators represents a large set of alternatives to traditional parametric and conventional semiparametric methods of analysis. The Cressie-Read class of divergence measures and associated likelihood functionals-probability distributions is not only just relevant as a basis for selecting a sampling distribution. The family also provides the possibility of combining members of the likelihood family and selecting the optimum sampling distribution under, say, a squared error, Kullback-Leibler loss, or maximum likelihood basis.

We emphasize that this is foundational material dealing with distributions that arise in the context of independent sampling. However, there is nothing in our moment-based information theoretic formulations that require that the observational data be independently distributed. In the random $(\mathbf{Y}, \mathbf{X})$ case, we looked mostly at *iid* sampling from a joint probability distribution. Weakly dependent sampling and more general non-*iid* sampling processes are logical extensions of the information theoretic methods discussed in this book. Research is ongoing regarding the development of information theoretic methods that can be used to frame econometric models and solve stochastic inverse problems in an increasingly widening range of economic applications.

# Abbreviations

## CHAPTER 1

| | |
|---|---|
| GMM | generalized method of moments |
| MOM | method of moments |
| MPD | minimum power divergence |

## CHAPTER 2

| | |
|---|---|
| BLUE | best linear unbiased estimator |
| CLTs | central limit theorems |
| DSP | data sampling process |
| E | extremum |
| GLR | generalized likelihood ratio |
| LM | Lagrange multiplier |
| LS | least squares |
| MVUE | minimum variance unbiased estimators |
| ML | maximum likelihood |
| PDF | probability density function |
| PLR | pseudolikelihood ratio |
| RHS | right-hand-side |
| UMPI | uniformly most powerful invariant |
| UMPU | uniformly most powerful unbiased |
| W | Wald |

## CHAPTER 3

| | |
|---|---|
| CRLB | Cramer-Rao lower bound |
| EOGMM | estimated optimal generalized method of moments |

| | |
|---|---|
| EEs | estimating equations |
| EF | estimating function |
| OptEF | optimal estimating functions |

CHAPTER 4

| | |
|---|---|
| EL | empirical likelihood |
| MEL | maximum empirical likelihood |
| NPML | nonparametric maximum likelihood |
| NR | Newton-Raphson |
| SIP | stochastic inverse problem |
| SPML | semiparametric maximum likelihood |

CHAPTER 5

| | |
|---|---|
| EDF | empirical distribution function |
| ELR | empirical likelihood ratio |
| NCI | normal confidence interval |

CHAPTER 6

| | |
|---|---|
| CEEL | cross entropy empirical likelihood |
| EEL | empirical exponential likelihood |
| ELC | empirical likelihood combination |
| KL | Kullback-Leiber |
| KLIC | Kullback-Leibler information criterion |
| MEEL | maximum exponential empirical likelihood |

CHAPTER 7

| | |
|---|---|
| CR | Cressie-Read |
| CRDM | Cressie-Read divergence measure |
| EML | empirical maximum likelihood |
| GEL | generalized empirical likelihood |
| LR | likelihood ratio |
| MLEL | maximum log Euclidean likelihood |
| R | Renyi |
| T | Tsallis |

## CHAPTER 8

CI confidence interval
MC Monte Carlo
MSE mean squared error

## CHAPTER 9

BRMs binary response models
CDF cumulative distribution function
FOC first-order conditions
IT information-theoretic

## CHAPTER 10

NLS-MPD nonlinear least squares-minimum power divergence
SSE sum of squared errors

## CHAPTER 11

PDM power divergence measures
QR quadratic risk

# Index

Printed in the United States
by Baker & Taylor Publisher Services